D0534258

Bullying in American Schools

A Social-Ecological Perspective on Prevention and Intervention

T 82218

SISKIYOU CO. OFFICE OF ED
LIBRARY
609 S. GOLD ST., YREKA, CA 96097

BULLYING IN AMERICAN SCHOOLS

A Social-Ecological Perspective on Prevention and Intervention

Edited by

Dorothy L. Espelage
University of Illinois, Urbana-Champaign

Susan M. Swearer
University of Nebraska, Lincoln

LAWRENCE ERLBAUM ASSOCIATES, PUBLISHERS
2004   Mahwah, New Jersey   London

Editor: Bill Webber
Editorial Assistant: Kristin Duch
Cover Design: Kathryn Houghtaling Lacey
Textbook Production Manager: Paul Smolenski
Full-Service & Composition: UG / GGS Information Services, Inc.
Text and Cover Printer: Hamilton Printing Company

This book was typeset in 10/12 pt Times.
The heads were typeset in Americana.

Copyright © 2004 by Lawrence Erlbaum Associates, Inc.
All rights reserved. No part of the book may be reproduced in any form,
by photostat, microform, retrieval system, or any other means,
without the prior written permission of the publisher.

Lawrence Erlbaum Associates, Inc., Publishers
10 Industrial Avenue
Mahwah, New Jersey 07430
www.erlbaum.com

Library of Congress Cataloging-in-Publication Data
Bullying in American schools : a social-ecological perspective on prevention and
   intervention / edited by Dorothy L. Espelage & Susan M. Swearer.
      p. cm.
   Includes bibliographical references and index.
   ISBN 0-8058-4559-3 (casebound)—0-8058-4560-7 (pbk: alk. paper)
      1. Bullying in schools—United States—Prevention. 2. Bullying
   in schools—United States—Psychological aspects. I. Espelage,
   Dorothy L. (Dorothy Lynn) II. Swearer, Susan M.

LB3013.32.B85 2004
371.5′8—dc22   2003049418

Books published by Lawrence Erlbaum Associates are printed on acid-free
paper, and their bindings are chosen for strength and durability.

Printed in the United States of America
10 9 8 7 6 5 4 3 2 1

To Penny, my mom, who imbued me with a strong work ethic
To Deron for his patience and support during this project
To Mackenzie, my niece, for keeping me young
DLE

To Scott for his unwavering love and support
To my parents for teaching me that it's not quantity, but quality that matters
To Catherine and Alexandra for reminding me what's truly important
SMS

And most of all, to all the students, parents, and educators who help narrow the gap between research and practice.

Contents

Foreword

Researcher/clinician Susan Sgroi once said, "You can't diagnose something if you don't believe it exists." She was referring to the fact that five decades ago most professionals estimated the frequency of child sexual abuse on the order of one in a million, whereas now the figure commonly cited is on the order of one in ten. Did this phenomenon become fantastically more common over the last century? Most researchers/clinicians think not. Rather, the phenomenon in front of us was hidden from view because of our self-defensive incredulity. As the German poet Goethe articulated, "What is most difficult for you? That which you think is easiest, To see what is before your eyes." I think in the phenomenon of bullying we face a comparable situation. Only recently have we begun to see its prevalence and its seriousness. Indeed, bullying has emerged as one of the major central negative forces at work in the lives of children and youth.

No one can deny that American children and youth have faced a series of challenges to their sense of safety and security in recent years. The events of September 11, 2001, were one such challenge. In the space of one day kids around the country were confronted with cataclysmic images of disaster that threatened their confidence in the ability of their society to protect them. But the image of planes crashing into the World Trade Towers was not the first such assault.

Two years earlier, America was aroused to a fever pitch of concern by the school massacre committed in Littleton, Colorado, on April 20, 1999. Indeed, surveys showed that media coverage of this story virtually outshadowed all others, and adults put what happened at Columbine at the top of their list of important stories for the entire year of 1999. But what are the lessons of Eric Harris, Dylan Klebold, Columbine High School, and September 11th? How do these serious events speak to the importance of physical violence and emotional violence as an issue facing American teenagers? Columbine and other instances of serious school violence are part of the emotional life that adolescents now experience, sometimes on a daily basis.

Columbine changed how our society views school violence—or at least it should have. Columbine offered an opportunity to open our nation's eyes to the pain so many of our kids feel as they confront emotional violence at school. The fact is many eyes were closed until that day in April 1999. The principal of Columbine High School, Frank DeAngeles, was asked two years later what he learned from what happened in his school that day. His response? "If someone had asked me on April 19, if it was possible that there were boys in my school so angry and troubled they were planning to kill us all, I would have said it was impossible. And then the next day it happened."

The school shooters acted in a terrible way and with a sense of outrage and even justification that many kids around America felt—and feel. These students believe that they have to endure a school dominated by emotional violence and that no one, specifically no adult, will do anything about it. In that belief they represent an extreme form of a common, shared experience. What is that common experience? It is the experience of bullying—as a perpetrator, a victim, or a bystander. Like sexual abuse, bullying is a core issue in the development and behavior of American kids. It is linked to the quality of their emotional lives and has far-reaching implications for their academic development, their relationships with adults and peers, and their sense of peace and well-being.

Here is what some of the students interviewed by my colleague Ellen deLara said about the shared, common phenomenon of bullying (as reported in our book *And Words Can Hurt Forever: How to Protect Adolescents from Bullying, Harassment, and Emotional Violence* (NY: The Free Press, 2002)).

Molly, age 16, is from a small, rural high school in the Northeast: "If you're bullied, that can really add up. And high school is such an environment to fit in and when you're bullied, you know, that hurts! But nobody could really stop that. No officials could really."

Dean, age 15, is a sophomore from a suburban high school of over 1,500 students in New York: "If you get pushed and pushed, sometime you're going to fight back. The teachers see it, but they don't do anything about it. When there's a fight going on, they just walk by. If you're there, you don't know what to do."

Another high school sophomore, Robert, age 16, attends a suburban high school of approximately 1,000 students in Massachusetts: "Everybody in middle school and high school gets teased or whatever. You have to just learn to deal with it. Sure the teachers see it, but they don't do anything about it. For one thing, they can't always tell what is serious teasing, like a threat, and what is just fooling around, you know? Some kids get it worse than others; I don't know why. Sometimes it makes you feel bad inside to see it."

This compelling work is just an example of the pioneering work that American scholars (Bartini, deLara, Espelage, Garbarino, Hazler, Hoover, Nansel, Pellegrini, Swearer) are producing in the area of bullying. Since Columbine, American researchers have turned their attention to studying the impact of chronic emotional and physical violence (i.e., bullying) and the effect that these forms of violence have on our students.

The impact of societal events (e.g., September 11th) combined with students' voices about their experiences, have set the stage for *Bullying in American Schools: A Social-Ecological Perspective on Prevention and Intervention*. In it, Dorothy Espelage and Susan Swearer have assembled an excellent roster of

American scholars. They have provided some of the research infrastructure needed to transform our new open-eyed awareness of bullying into protective and rehabilitative action on behalf of kids. Additionally, they have set these chapters in an ecological context where they belong, because bullying is not simply a matter of a few "bad" kids attacking a few "weak" kids. Bullying grows out of and feeds into social environments—dyadic relationships, systems of peer relations, structures of adult authority, school systems, and a larger culture. Thus, it is not enough to declare a "war on bullying"; it requires making peace with all kids through all the various micro-, meso-, exo-, and macro-systems that affect their lives. This book will contribute greatly to that process.

—James Garbarino

Contributors

Ryan S. Adams, Arizona State University, Counseling Psychology, 1011 E. Lemon St., Tempe, AZ, 85281; Phone: (480) 921-3481; E-mail: Ryan.S.Adams@asu.edu

Christi L. Bartolomucci, Emory University School of Medicine, 1440 Clifton Road, Atlanta, GA 30322

Kathy Berenson, New York State Psychiatric Institute - Unit 47, 1051 Riverside Drive, New York, New York 10032.

Paulette Tam Cary, University of Nebraska, Lincoln, Department of Educational Psychology, 114 Teachers College Hall, Lincoln, NE 68588-0345; Phone: (402) 472-5743; fax: (402) 896-5927; E-mail: pjtamcary@yahoo.com

Patricia Cohen, New York State Psychiatric Institute - Unit 47, 1051 Riverside Drive, New York, New York 10032; fax: (212) 740-5394; E-mail: prc2@columbia.edu

Michelle Kilpatrick Demaray, Department of Psychology, Northern Illinois University, DeKalb, IL 60115; Phone: (815) 753-7077; fax: (815) 753-8088; E-mail: mkdemaray@niu.edu

Donna Denning, Arizona State University, Department of Family and Human Development PO Box 872502, Tempe, AZ 85287-2502; Phone: (480) 965-6978; fax: (480) 965-6779; E-mail: donna.denning@asu.edu

Beth Doll, Educational Psychology, University of Nebraska, Lincoln, 36 Teachers College Hall, Lincoln, NE 68588-0345; Phone: (402) 472-2238; fax: (402) 472-8319; E-mail: BDOLL2@unl.edu

Shannon Dowd, Department of Educational Psychology, University of Nebraska, Lincoln, 239 Teachers College Hall, Lincoln, NE 68588-0345; Phone: (402) 472-2223; fax: (402) 472-8319; E-mail: sdowd75@yahoo.com

Renae D. Duncan, Department of Psychology, Wells 212, Murray State University, Murray, KY 42071; Phone: (270) 762-2851; (270) 762-3539; fax: (270) 762-2991; E-mail: renae.duncan@murraystate.edu

Dorothy L. Espelage, University of Illinois, Urbana-Champaign, Department of Educational Psychology, 226 Education Bldg., 1310 S. 6th St., Champaign, IL, 61820-6990; Phone: (217) 333-9139; fax: (217) 244-7620; E-mail: espelage@uiuc.edu

Richard A. Fabes, Arizona State University, Department of Family and Human Development PO Box 872502, Tempe, AZ 85287-2502; Phone: (480) 965-6978; fax: (480) 965-6779; E-mail: rfabes@asu.edu

James Garbarino, Elizabeth Lee Vincent Professor of Human Development, Co-Director of the Family Life Development Center at Cornell University, 427 E. Seneca Street, Ithaca, NY 14850; Fax: (607) 255-8562; E-mail: jg38@cornell.edu

Amy B. Goldstein, The Children's Hospital of Philadelphia, Dept. of Pediatric Psychology, 3405 Civic Center Blvd., Philadelphia, PA 19104

Amie E. Grills, Virginia Polytechnic Institute and State University, Child Study Center, 3100 Prices Fork Road, Blacksburg, VA 24060; Phone: (540) 818-1895; fax: (540) 231-4250; E-mail: agrills@vt.edu

Laura D. Hanish, Arizona State University, Department of Family and Human Development, PO Box 872502, Tempe, AZ 85287-2502; Phone: (480) 965-6978; (480) 965-8133; fax: (480) 965-6779; E-mail: laura.hanish@asu.edu

Kisha M. Haye, University of Nebraska, Lincoln, Department of Educational Psychology, 114 Teachers College Hall, Lincoln, NE 68588-0345; Phone: (402) 472-1194; fax: (402) 472-8319; E-mail: kmhaye@hotmail.com

Melissa K. Holt, Family Research Laboratory, University of New Hampshire 126 Horton Social Science Center, Durham, NH 03824; E-mail: mkholt@cisunix.unh.edu

Arthur M. Horne, Department of Counseling and Human Development Services, 402 Aderhold Hall, University of Georgia, Athens, GA 30602; Phone: (706) 542-4107; fax (706) 542-4130; Email: ahorne@coe.uga.edu

Jeffrey G. Johnson, New York State Psychiatric Institute - Unit 47, 1051 Riverside Drive, New York, New York 10032

Stephanie Kasen, New York State Psychiatric Institute - Unit 47, 1051 Riverside Drive, New York, New York 10032; fax: (212) 740-5394; E-mail: kasenst@pi.cpmc.columbia.edu, sk57@columbia.edu

Melissa A. Keyes, K12 Associates, LLC, 6314 Odana Road, Madison, WI 53719; Phone: (608) 232-7099; fax: (608) 232-9064; Website: *www.k12associates.com*; E-mail: mkeyes@k12associates.com

Becky Kochenderfer-Ladd, Psychology in Education, Arizona State University, Tempe, AZ, 85287-0611; Phone: (480) 965-3329; E-mail: Becky.Ladd@asu.edu

Stephen S. Leff, The Children's Hospital of Philadelphia, Dept. of Pediatric Psychology, 3405 Civic Center Blvd., Philadelphia, PA 19104; E-mail: leff@email.chop.edu

Susan P. Limber, Institute on Family and Neighborhood Life, Clemson University, 158 Poole Agricultural Center, Clemson, SC 29634; Phone: (864) 656-6320; fax: (864) 656-6281; E-mail: slimber@clemson.edu

Jeffrey D. Long, Department of Educational Psychology, Burton Hall, University of Minnesota, Minneapolis, MN 55455; Fax: (612) 624-8241; E-mail: longj@umn.edu

Christine Kerres Malecki, Department of Psychology, Northern Illinois University, DeKalb, IL 60115; Phone: (815) 753-1836; fax: (815) 753-8088; E-mail: cmalecki@niu.edu

Carol Lynn Martin, Arizona State University, Department of Family and Human Development, PO Box 872502, Tempe, AZ 85287-2502; Phone: (480) 965-6978; fax: (480) 965-6779; E-mail: carol.martin@asu.edu

Sarah Mebane, University of Illinois, Urbana-Champaign, Department of Educational Psychology, 306 W. Griggs St. Apt. 209, Urbana, IL 61801; Phone: (630) 291-0635; fax: (217) 244-7620; E-mail: mebane@uiuc.edu

Dawn Newman-Carlson, Carlson Health Promotion, P.A., 100 SW 75th Street, Suite #103, Gainesville, FL 32607-5779; Phone: (352) 332-2990; E-mail: carlsonhealthpromotion@cox.net.

Pamela Orpinas, Department of Health Promotion and Behavior, 319 Ramsey Center, University of Georgia, Athens, GA 30602; Phone: (706) 542-4370; fax: (706) 542-4956; E-mail: porpinas@scribe.coe.uga.edu

Anthony D. Pellegrini, Dept. of Ed Psych, Burton Hall, Univ of Minnesota, Minneapolis, MN 55455; Phone: (612) 625-4353; fax: (612) 624-8241; E-mail: pelle013@umn.edu

Thomas J. Power, The Children's Hospital of Philadelphia, University of Pennsylvania School of Medicine, The Children's Hospital of Philadelphia - CSH-116, 3405 Civic Center Blvd., Philadelphia, PA 19104; Phone: (215) 590-7447; fax: (215) 590-5637; E-mail: power@email.chop.edu

Philip C. Rodkin, University of Illinois at Urbana-Champaign, Department of Educational Psychology, 226 Education Building, MC-708, 1310 S. 6th. St., Champaign, Illinois 61820-6990; Phone: (217) 333-0527; Lab: (217) 244-9319; fax: (217) 244-7620; E-mail: rodkin@uiuc.edu

Barri Rosenbluth, SafePlace: Domestic Violence & Sexual Assault Survival Center, P.O. Box 19454, Austin, TX 78760; Phone: (512) 356-1628; fax: (512) 385-0662; E-mail: brosenbluth@austin-safeplace.org

Ellen Sanchez, Safeplace, P.O. Box 19454, Austin, TX, 78760; Phone: (512) 356-1591; E-mail: esanchez@austin-safeplace.org

Susan M. Sheridan, University of Nebraska, Lincoln, Department of Educational Psychology, 239 Teachers College Hall, Lincoln, NE 68588-0345; Phone: (402) 472-6941; fax: (402) 472-8319 E-mail: ssheridan2@unl.edu

Erin Siemers, University of Nebraska, Lincoln, Department of Educational Psychology, 114 Teachers College Hall, Lincoln, NE 68588-0345; Phone: (402) 472-2207; fax: (402) 472-8319; E-mail: erinsiemers@hotmail.com

Samuel Song, University of Nebraska, Lincoln, Department of Educational Psychology, 114 Teachers College Hall, Lincoln, NE 68588-0345; Phone: (402) 472-5416; fax: (402) 472-8319; E-mail: ssong54@yahoo.com

Susan M. Swearer, University of Nebraska, Lincoln, Department of Educational Psychology, 40 Teachers College Hall, Lincoln, NE 68588-0345; Phone: (402) 472-1741; fax: (402) 472-8319; E-mail: sswearer@unlserve.unl.edu

Linda A. Valle, CDC, Division of Violence Prevention, 4770 Buford Highway Mailstop K-60, Atlanta, GA 30341; Phone: (770) 488-4297; fax: (770) 488-1011; E-mail: LValle@cdc.gov

Emily D. Warnes, University of Nebraska, Lincoln, Department of Educational Psychology, 239 Teachers College Hall, Lincoln, NE 68588-0345; Phone: (402) 472-2223; fax: (402) 472-8319; E-mail: emwarnes@yahoo.com

Daniel J. Whitaker, CDC, Division of Violence Prevention, 4770 Buford Highway, Mailstop K-60, Atlanta, GA 30341; Phone: (770) 488-4267; fax: (770) 488-1011; E-mail: DWhitaker@cdc.gov

About the Editors

Dorothy L. Espelage is Associate Professor of Counseling Psychology in the Department of Educational Psychology at the University of Illinois, Urbana-Champaign. She earned her Ph.D. in Counseling Psychology from Indiana University in 1997. She has conducted research on bullying for the last seven years. As a result, she presents regularly at national conferences and is author of over 30 professional publications. She is on the editorial board for *Journal of Counseling and Development*. She has presented hundreds of workshops and in-service training seminars for teachers, administrators, counselors, and social workers across the U.S. Her research focuses on translating empirical findings into prevention and intervention programming. Dr. Espelage has appeared on many television news and talk shows, including *The Today Show, CNN, CBS Evening News*, and *The Oprah Winfrey Show,* and has been quoted in the national print press, including *Time Magazine, USA Today*, and *People* magazine.

Susan M. Swearer is Assistant Professor of School Psychology in the Department of Educational Psychology at the University of Nebraska, Lincoln. She earned her Ph.D. in School Psychology from The University of Texas at Austin in 1997. She has conducted research on the relationship between depression and anxiety and externalizing problems (with a specific emphasis on bullying) in children and adolescents for the past decade. Dr. Swearer regularly presents at national conferences and conducts workshops on bullying and victimization in school-aged youth. She writes regularly on the topic of bullying and is on the editorial review boards for *Education and Treatment of Children, School Psychology Quarterly*, and *School Psychology Review*. Her research project on bullying, "Target bullying: Ecologically-based prevention and intervention for schools," teaches school personnel how to collect ecologically valid data on bullying and use those data to guide prevention and intervention efforts.

1

Introduction: A Social-Ecological Framework of Bullying Among Youth

Susan M. Swearer
University of Nebraska, Lincoln

Dorothy L. Espelage
University of Illinois, Urbana-Champaign

Much of our knowledge about bullying behaviors comes from research conducted over the past several decades in Europe, Australia, and Canada. For the past decade, research in the United States lagged behind our European, Australian, and Canadian counterparts. This book seeks to fill this void by forwarding research about bullying across contexts that has been conducted with participants in the United States. In this chapter, we will propose a social-ecological framework within which bullying occurs. We will argue that bullying has to be understood across individual, family, peer, school, and community contexts. Bullying and victimization are ecological phenomena that are established and perpetuated over time as the result of the complex interplay between inter- and intra-individual variables (Swearer & Doll, 2001). In order to develop and implement effective bullying prevention and intervention programs, we must understand the social ecology that establishes and maintains bullying and victimization behaviors.

While research conducted in other countries has been critical to our understanding of bullying and victimization among school-aged youth, we contend that the unique contexts which comprise U.S. schools, and in which research on bullying is conducted, argues for a U.S. examination of this ubiquitous phenomenon. For example, in most research samples in the United States, active parental consent must be obtained. This research protection will undoubtedly influence the demographics of the participants. Researchers in other countries do not necessarily need to conduct research under this constraint. Additionally, with the recent media attention given to school violence in the U.S., many state legislatures have mandated bullying policies at the local and state levels. How might these policies affect research conducted on bullying in our schools? For example, a Secret Service analysis of targeted school violence found that 71% of the school shooters in the U.S. (from 1974 to 2000) reported being chronically bullied (Vossekuil, Fein, Reddy, Borum, & Modzeleski, 2002). How might this connection between school violence and bullying affect research conducted on bullying in our schools? Research policies, legislative mandates, and school shootings appear to be unique contextual factors related to studying bullying in the United States.

Only one large-scale study on bullying in the United States has been conducted (Nansel, Overpeck, Pilla, Ruan, Simons-Morton, & Scheidt, 2001). In this study, 15,686 6th-through 10th-grade students completed surveys on bullying. 29.9% reported moderate to frequent involvement in bullying when they were assessed in 1998. Of those 29.9%, 13% self-identified as bullies, 10.6% self-identified as victims, and 6.3% self-identified as bully-victims. Bullying behaviors were found to occur more frequently in middle school than in high school, and boys were more likely than girls to be involved in the bullying dynamic. Additionally, bully-victims displayed the most pervasive negative psychosocial outcomes. There were no differences in bullying across urban, suburban, and rural areas. However, while this is an important study conducted in the United States, bullying was assessed using only a self-report questionnaire. Despite this methodological limitation, this study provides an important examination of bullying among U.S. youth and provides a basis for future directions for bullying research in U.S. schools.

A Social-Ecological Systems Perspective on Bullying and Victimization

The idea that multiple environments influence individuals is not a new concept. In fact, much has been written on the reciprocal interplay between the individual, family, peer group, school, community, and culture (Bronfenbrenner, 1979; Burstyn et al., 2001; Coie & Jacobs, 1993; Fraser, 1996; Garbarino, 2001; Henggeler, Schoenwald, Borduin, Rowland, & Cunningham, 1998; Jonson-Reid, 1998; Linney, 2000). This reciprocal interplay between individuals involved in the bully/victim continuum is depicted in Fig. 1.1. This social-ecological perspective has been applied to our conceptualization of bullying behaviors (Garbarino & deLara, 2002; Newman, Horne, & Bartolomucci, 2000; Olweus, 1993; Swearer & Doll,

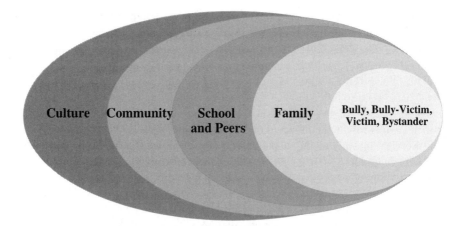

FIG. 1.1.   A social-ecological framework of bullying among youth.

2001). In a nutshell, bullying does not occur in isolation. This phenomenon is encouraged and/or inhibited as a result of the complex relationships between the individual, family, peer group, school, community, and culture.

As depicted in Fig. 1.1, the individual is at the center of his or her social ecology. The individual involved in bullying may be involved as a bully, bully-victim, victim, or bystander. Individual factors will influence participation in bullying. For example, how might gender mediate the engagement in bullying? The bully, bully-victim, victim, or bystander exists within a family. How might the family influence bullying behaviors? Modeling of bullying between siblings or caregivers can influence the development of bullying and/or victimization in the individual. The social ecology also includes the peer group and the school. How might school climate effect bullying and/or victimization? If the individual attends a school where a pro-bullying climate exists, then he or she may be more likely to be involved in bullying. If the individual's peer group supports bullying, then the individual may be more likely to engage in these behaviors. Extending outward, the community encompasses the school, peer group, family, and the individual. How might the community support or inhibit bullying? Finally, culture encompasses the aforementioned contexts in the social ecology. How might cultural norms and beliefs support or inhibit participation in the bully/victim continuum?

Ecological-systems theory purports that all individuals are part of interrelated systems that locate the individual at the center and move out from the center to include all systems that affect the individual (Bronfenbrenner, 1979). Figure 1.1 depicts the interrelatedness of these systems, which interact to influence human behavior. According to Bronfenbrenner's theory, the child is an inseparable part of a social network comprised of four interrelated systems: microsystem, mesosystem, exosystem, and macrosystem. The child is at the center of, and actively involved with, this interplay of systems. The microsystem includes the child's relationship with one system (e.g., home *or* classroom *or* playground). The microsystem depicts the child's immediate interaction with others, and includes others' reactions to bullying behaviors. This conceptualization of the microsystem also includes the status of the child along the bully/victim continuum. Thus, the bully, bully-victim, victim, or bystander interacts with others in his or her social environment, and this interaction either exacerbates or mitigates bullying and/or victimization behaviors. The mesosystem includes the interrelationship between systems in the child's life (e.g., home *and* school). The mesosystem depicts the congruence between two or more environments, such as the congruence between home and school regarding bullying behavior. The exosystem includes influences from other contexts, such as the effect of a school district's antibullying policy or parental involvement in the school system. Finally, the macrosystem is the influence of cultural mores, such as societal attitudes toward bullying behaviors. Bronfenbrenner's theory will provide the framework for both the research described in this book and the prevention and intervention suggestions that logically follow from the research.

The social ecology that encompasses the daily life of youth dictates engagement or nonengagement in bullying and/or victimization behaviors (Espelage, Bosworth, & Simon, 2000). Because individuals are affected by their surroundings, it logically follows that interventions also need to target the environments in which youth function. Interventions that do not target the multiple environments in which youth exist are likely to be less effective than interventions that address the social ecology (Kerns & Prinz, 2002). This assertion is related to consistent findings that youth who are involved in aggressive behaviors experience problems in multiple areas, including the family, peer group, school, and community (Dahlberg & Potter, 2001; Kellam, Rebok, Ialongo, & Mayer, 1994).

It is important to determine whether or not an intervention is effective in preventing and/or reducing bullying behaviors. Thus, assessment of the bullying phenomenon must utilize multiple methods of assessment, use multiple informants, and include assessments across contexts. While this can be a daunting task, best practices demands that we assess the social ecology if we are to accurately determine the effects of bullying prevention and intervention programming. An example of this type of best practice is reflected in a schema proposed and implemented by Capaldi and colleagues (1997). These researchers state that data should be collected across settings (e.g., home, school, community, laboratory) by multiple informants (e.g., observers, children, peers, parents, teachers) and using multiple methods (e.g., home observations, lab tasks, classroom, playground, questionnaires, interviews, phone interviews, standardized tests, records). This comprehensive approach has been successfully applied at the Oregon Social Learning Center and should be replicated in bullying prevention and intervention research.

There are over 300 published violence prevention school-based programs (Howard, Flora, & Griffin, 1999); however, less than a quarter of these programs are empirically validated. How are schools to choose which program may be best for their school ecology? It is our belief that schools must conduct a multi-method, multi-informant, and multicontextual assessment in order to understand their particular bullying dynamic. Based on this assessment, schools can identify programs that may be implemented successfully in their particular school and community. Kerns and Prinz (2002) review individual-focused programs, family-focused programs, and system-focused programs that address the prevention of violence-related behaviors in youth. Their review is an excellent guide for educators seeking guidance in choosing a violence-prevention program.

Every school is defined by its own unique ecology. As has been previously articulated, schools should conduct an individual needs assessment and then chose school-based interventions based on the results of their own data (Boxer & Dubow, 2001). This may seem to be a daunting task. Figure 1.2 provides a rubric of the steps school personnel can take to assess the bully/victim continuum in their own school. We hope that *Bullying in American Schools: A Social-Ecological Perspective on Prevention and Intervention* will aid educators and psychologists in making data-based decisions regarding bullying prevention and intervention programming.

This book is an exciting compilation of research conducted across the United States by a representative group of researchers, including developmental psychologists, social psychologists, counseling psychologists, school psychologists, and clinical psychologists who are examining bullying in school-aged youth. As such, we hope to present a picture of the complexity of bullying behaviors and offer suggestions for using data-based decision-making to intervene and reduce bullying behaviors in our nation's schools. Given the complexity of bullying and victimization, we hope that this book will provide guidance for schools as they develop prevention and intervention programming for bullying. In the sections that follow, we will outline the chapters contained in this book.

---

1. Consider partnering with university researchers to conduct an assessment of bullying behaviors.
2. Conduct a school-wide anonymous assessment of bullying behaviors.
3. Include multiple informants (students, teachers, school staff, parents).
4. Use self-report, other report (nomination inventories), observations.
5. Graph data to create a picture of the scope of bullying in a particular school.
6. Use the data to conduct classroom presentations on bullying.
7. Use the data to create interventions for bullying.
8. Use the data to establish preventative measures to create an antibullying climate.
9. Share data with parent groups (e.g., PTA).
10. Create a data-based decision-making climate though the use of individual school data to help guide prevention and intervention programming.

FIG. 1.2. Rubric for data-based decision making in bullying-prevention and intervention programming.

Individual Characteristics Associated With Bullying

Although the child is at the center of the social ecology that influences bullying behaviors, individual personality characteristics will help determine engagement in bullying and/or victimization. Part I illustrates the importance of individual characteristics across bully/victim subtypes. No discussion would be complete without recognition of the relationship between gender and bullying and victimization which is often cited in the literature. While many chapters discuss the interplay between gender and other individual characteristics (e.g., depression, empathy) and other environmental characteristics (e.g., peer influence, family factors), one chapter specifically addresses this issue in depth. In *Gender Differences in Bullying: Moving Beyond Mean Level Differences*, Espelage, Mebane, and Swearer summarize the complex literature associated with gender differences in aggression and victimization levels. This discussion first addresses the extant literature on gender differences in bullying, and then it addresses the plethora of recent research on relational aggression. These authors encourage scholars and practitioners to look beyond mean level differences in these types of aggression and to embark on a more comprehensive analysis of how boys and girls are socialized to use aggression. Theories are presented that link individual and environmental factors into an ecological examination of gender and aggression. Relational aggression and relational victimization are both examined in great detail.

In the next chapter, titled *Empathy, Caring, and Bullying: Toward an Understanding of a Complex Association,* Espelage, Mebane, and Ryan continue a discussion of gender differences in their review of the literature on the relations between empathy and bullying. The chapter begins with an attempt to define multiple aspects of empathy constructs such as empathic concern, multiple perspective-taking, caring, and consideration of others. Merging traditional research on empathy as an inhibitor of aggression with more recent investigations of empathy and bullying, the authors argue that much research is needed to understand the complex role of empathy and bullying among children and adolescents. This complexity is further supported with results of an empathy study of middle-school children. The chapter ends with descriptions of several bullying prevention and intervention programs, specifically focusing on how developers have incorporated empathy training.

The influence of internalizing disorders in bullies, victims, and bully-victims has received increased attention in the past five years. These disorders are the focus of the next chapter, entitled *Internalizing Problems in Students Involved in Bullying and Victimization: Implications for Intervention* and written by Swearer, Grills, Haye, and Tam. A literature review of depression, anxiety, hopelessness, and locus of control is followed by a review of sample intervention programs that address internalizing psychopathology in youth. The review of the literature suggests that addressing these serious symptoms through individual psychotherapeutic interventions is an important component of bullying-prevention and intervention programming.

Peer Characteristics Associated With Bullying

The theoretical framework used in this book to understand bullying and victimization includes the extension of individual characteristics to environmental systems such as peer groups as explored in Part II. Two chapters address how peer groups relate to bullying across the school years. In the first chapter, *Peer Ecologies of Aggression and Bullying*, Rodkin takes the reader on an intriguing journey through the last century of theoretical and empirical writings on peer groups and their influences on aggression and bullying. The chapter includes a review of the literature on how groups form and how groups influence their members through early elementary school and the middle school years. This section sets the stage for the discussion of the association between peer-group membership and aggression, including bullying. From a developmental perspective, Rodkin summarizes how the peer group emerges as a solid, major socializing agent of aggression by the middle school years. To evaluate peer-group influence, researchers and educators need to incorporate sociometric methodologies into their assessments directed at identifying the factors that maintain bullying within their schools. Therefore, Rodkin describes several approaches to sociometry that should be considered.

Complementing Rodkin's work is the next chapter, entitled *Part of the Solution and Part of the Problem: The Role of Peers in Bullying, Dominance, and Victimization During the Transition from Primary School Through Secondary School*. In this chapter, Pellegrini and Long draw upon dominance theory to illustrate how bullying increases across the transition from primary to secondary school. They argue through empirical data that bullying is used as a strategy to gain status as peers in an environment in which establishing new social groups is imperative. Pellegrini and Long provide additional support showing that that increases in bullying and physical aggression during this transition are moderated by gender; boys often hold more favorable views toward bullying and physical aggression than girls. A number of hypotheses are examined to explain the observed increase in bullying. These include changes in peer affiliation or number of friends, cross-gender bullying, and attraction to the opposite gender. While the major focus is on how dominance theory explains an increase in bullying and aggression, this work also highlights how peer influence and/or peer affiliation can buffer the impact of victimization for students.

Classroom Characteristics Associated With Bullying

Peers are embedded within classrooms. Therefore, Part III explores how teachers and classrooms influence bullying and aggression during the school years. Three chapters illustrate those teacher attributes and classroom factors that foster and maintain bullying. *Teachers' Attitudes Toward Bullying*, written by Holt and Keyes, explores how teachers define and view bullying, the extent to which they see bullying, and how their perceptions of school climate relate to their own views. These authors review the very limited literature base on these issues and call for more research in this area. They follow this review with survey results of an investigation that included 797 elementary, middle, and high-school teachers in which one of the key findings was the reluctance of high-school teachers to intervene in bully episodes in comparison to elementary- and middle-school teachers. With the goal of linking these findings to intervention strategies, Holt and Keyes highlight how teachers are included in three comprehensive prevention programs.

The next chapter in this section, *Bullying Among Young Children: The Influence of Peers and Teachers*, integrates the theoretical and empirical writings on peer influence with those on teacher aspects on aggression. Hanish, Kochenderfer-Ladd, Fabes, Martin, and Denning offer a unique perspective on the role of peers and teachers in bullying because they focus on preschool and kindergarten children—populations essentially ignored by aggression scholars. These authors infuse data obtained from 167 preschoolers and kindergartners into their discussion of prevalence and developmental trends of bullying, teachers' awareness of bullying, peer dynamics including interactions patterns, and quality of teacher-child relationships. Recommendations are provided for creating a school context that might minimize bullying among peers.

The interaction between individual characteristics, peers, teachers, and families within the classroom context is the focus on the next chapter, *Classroom Ecologies That Support or Discourage Bullying*, by Doll, Song, & Siemers. Through an empirical investigation of second through fifth graders, the authors examine the relative influence of two types of data on the level of classroom bullying, including social relationships found within the classroom and individual characteristics. Social relationships are those connections among peers, teachers, and families. Individual characteristics, conceptualized as human agency, include students' sense of self-efficacy, self-determination, and the ability to control behavioral conduct. Findings of this study are merged with the existing literature to identify the natural supports in the classroom that neutralize and minimize bullying.

Beyond the Individual, Peer Group, and Classroom: Considering School Climate, Family Relationships, Social Support, and Innovative School Partnerships

Students are affected not only by peers but also by other ecological systems, including the school environments beyond the classroom, family life, and the intersection between families and school systems. Part IV includes four chapters that implicate these systems in fostering and maintaining bullying in our schools.

These chapters also highlight the potential for these systems to work in our favor in combating bullying. Kasen, Berenson, Cohen, and Johnson, in their chapter *The Effects of School Climate on Changes in Aggressive and Other Behaviors Related to Bullying*, address a significant gap in the literature by examining how the social and emotional climate of the school facilitates or deters school bullying. These authors first review 40 years of empirical evidence on how schools influence child development, with the goal of identifying those school factors that make a difference. School policies, interaction patterns between teachers, students, and the overall school atmosphere are provided as examples. The discussion then turns to those school-level factors that influence bullying and how bullying reciprocally influences school climate. The authors present a unique data set in which 500 students and their families across 250 schools completed a $2\frac{1}{2}$ year longitudinal investigation; according to the data, parenting practices and school climate factors had a significant impact on changes in bullying. Specific suggestions for reducing bullying through school climate modifications are provided.

Much of the discussion of peers and teachers has centered on attitudes, interactional patterns, and frequency of behavior. What has been lacking in most discussions of ecological influences is the quality of these interactions and the potential for these relationships to buffer the stress associated with victimization.

In the next chapter, *The Role of Social Support in the Lives of Bullies, Victims, and Bully-Victims*, Malecki and Demaray review the theoretical and empirical literature on social support. They first offer several definitions of social support and its varied components, followed by a discussion of the Stress-Buffering and Main Effect theories associated with the mechanism of social support as well as several theories explicating the functions of social support. This strong conceptual introduction to social support is then followed by a brief discussion of several commonly used measures of social support. Next, the authors review the two studies that have focused exclusively on perceptions of social support from various sources (e.g., teachers, parents, peers) among bullies and victims. They finish with a discussion of their own work, in which social support has moderated the association between victimization and psychological outcomes.

Building on the notion of social support, the next chapter, entitled *The Impact of Family Relationships on School Bullying and Their Victims*, examines how attachment theory, social-learning theory, and family-systems theory explain how children's emotional and behavioral difficulties, including bullying, emerge. After this broad discussion, Duncan specifically addresses the characteristics of siblings and parents of bullies, victims, and bullies-victims. Examination of familial environment is an integral part of both individual psychotherapeutic approaches and school wide prevention approaches.

The chapter, *Home-School Collaboration and Bullying: An Ecological Approach to Increase Social Competence in Children and Youth*, represents the most comprehensive approach to bullying prevention. Sheridan, Warnes, and

Dowd discuss exactly what the title implies—that is, an intervention that considers the complex interaction between familial and school contexts. The Conjoint Behavioral Consultation model (CBC; Sheridan et al., 1996) is introduced as a means of bringing parents and teachers together to address the academic, social, and behavioral needs of a student. This model includes problem identification through the assessment of ecological and contextual variables as well as child characteristics; selection of a target behavior; problem analysis; implementation of child-focused strategies, parent training, and peer- and school-based interventions; and a discussion of treatment evaluation. Once the CBC model is discussed in great detail, a case study of an 8-year-old, 3rd-grade male who has been bullied and reacts with aggression (e.g., bully-victim) is then provided to illustrate each of the preceding tasks. This chapter demonstrates the power that collaborations between families and schools can have on bullying behaviors in school.

The chapter by Leff, Power, and Goldstein, entitled *Outcome Measures to Assess the Effectiveness of Bullying-Prevention Programs in the Schools*, is imperative for any teacher, administrator, researcher, graduate student, or agency worker who is evaluating the effectiveness of a bullying-prevention or intervention program. These authors review seven classes of outcome measures, including nurse logs of injuries, discipline referrals, self-report measures, teacher-report measures, peer sociometric measures, behavioral observations, and playground- and lunchroom-supervisor measures. These measures are described, psychometric properties are reviewed, strengths and weaknesses of each measure are summarized, and the authors indicate where future modifications or research endeavors need to be addressed for each measure. Users of these measures are encouraged to take multimethod and multi-informant approaches and tailor the selection of measures to the unique aspects of the prevention or intervention program.

Effective Prevention and Intervention Programs

Part V focuses on specific aspects of prevention and intervention planning. The final three chapters include the discussion of specific prevention programs. In their chapter entitled *Elementary School Bully Busters Program: Understanding Why Children Bully and What to Do About It,* Horne, Orpinas, Newman-Carlson, and Bartolomucci summarize the teacher-based prevention program *Bully Busters* (Horne et al., 2003). This chapter consists of four sections. First, a brief section on how to explain bullying to elementary-school children opens the chapter. Second, these comments lead to a discussion of the assumptions underlying the program. These assumptions are that changing the environment is easier than changing the individual, prevention is better than intervention, and—in order to change the environment—support and understanding among teachers must be established. Third, the authors detail specific skills for bullying prevention, such as understanding the ABCs, recognizing a teacher's sphere of influence, and teaching respectful, polite language. Finally, each of the eight modules of Bully Busters is discussed, from teacher instruction in increasing awareness of bullying among students to recognizing the bully and victim to interventions for the bully and victim. This program is a comprehensive, theory-based program designed to assist teachers in creating safe, bully-free classrooms.

In the next chapter, entitled *Expect Respect: A School-Based Intervention to Promote Awareness and Effective Responses to Bullying and Sex Harassment*, Whitaker, Rosenbluth, Valle, and Sanchez describe and evaluate a prevention program that addresses bullying as well as sexual harassment in elementary school. The Expect Respect program was based on the Olweus Bullying Prevention Program (see Limber in this volume), which takes a whole-school approach to preventing bullying and harassment by preparing all school staff and community members to recognize and respond to these behaviors. This program includes a 12-week curriculum adapted from *Bullyproof* (Stein & Sjostrom, 1996), which focuses on increasing the ability and willingness of bystanders to intervene in bullying episodes, thereby reducing the social acceptance of bullying and sexual harassment. It also includes staff training, policy development, parent education, and support services. This chapter details these components and provides evaluation data for six intervention schools and six control schools.

The concluding chapter of the book, written by Limber and entitled *Implementation of the Olweus Bullying-Prevention Program in American Schools: Lessons Learned from the Field*, is more than a description of Olweus's program as implemented in the United States. Certainly, Limber does describe this comprehensive community-wide program in detail, but what is unique about this chapter is the consideration of mistakes that have been made in bullying prevention and intervention efforts in the United States and what lessons have been gained from these mistakes. This provides an excellent ending to the book and clearly articulates the constraints to be mindful of as educators, mental health professionals, and researchers embark on the next wave of bullying-prevention and intervention research from an ecological perspective.

REFERENCES

Boxer, P. & Dubow, E. F. (2001). A social-cognitive information-processing model for school-based aggression reduction and prevention programs: Issues for research and practice. *Applied and Preventive Psychology, 10,* 177–192.

Bronfenbrenner, U. (1979). *The ecology of human development: Experiments by nature and design.* Cambridge, MA: Harvard University Press.

Burstyn, J. N., Bender, G., Casella, R., Gordon, H. W., Guerra, D. P., Luschen, K. V., Stevens, R., & Williams, K. M. (2001). *Preventing violence in schools: A challenge to American democracy.* Mahwah, NJ: Lawrence Erlbaum Associates.

Capaldi, D. M., Chamberlain, P., Fetrow, R. A., & Wilson, J. E. (1997). Conducting ecologically valid prevention research: Recruiting and retaining a "whole village" in multimethod, multiagent studies. *American Journal of Community Psychology, 25*, 471–492.

Coie, J. D. & Jacobs, M. R. (1993). The role of social context in the prevention of conduct disorder. *Development and Psychopathology, 5*, 263–275.

Dahlberg, L. L. & Potter, L. B. (2001). Youth violence: Developmental pathways and prevention challenges. *American Journal of Preventive Medicine, 20*, 3–14.

Espelage, D. L., Bosworth, K., & Simon, T. R. (2000). Examining the social context of bullying behaviors in early adolescence. *Journal of Counseling and Development, 78*, 326–333.

Fraser, M. W. (1996). Aggressive behavior in childhood and early adolescence: An ecological-developmental perspective on youth violence. *Social Work, 41*, 347–361.

Garbarino, J. (2001). An ecological perspective on the effects on violence on children. *Journal of Community Psychology, 29*, 361–378.

Garbarino, J. & deLara, E. (2002). *And Words Can Hurt Forever: How to Protect Adolescents From Bullying, Harassment, and Emotional Violence*. New York: The Free Press.

Henggeler, S. W., Schoenwald, S. K., Borduin, C. M., Rowland, M. D., & Cunningham, P. B. (1998). *Multisystemic treatment of antisocial behavior in children and adolescents*. New York: The Guilford Press.

Howard, K. A., Flora, J., & Griffin, M. (1999). Violence-prevention programs in schools: State of the science and implications for future research. *Applied & Preventive Psychology, 8*, 197–215.

Jonson-Reid, M. (1998). Youth violence and exposure to violence in childhood: An ecological review. *Aggression and Violent Behavior, 3*, 159–179.

Kellam, S. G., Rebok. G. W., Ialongo, N., & Mayer, L. S. (1994). The course and malleability of aggressive behavior from early first grade into middle school: Results of a developmental epidemiologically-based preventive trial. *Journal of Child Psychology and Psychiatry, 35*, 259–281.

Kerns, S. E. & Prinz, R. J. (2002). Critical issues in the prevention of violence-related behavior in youth. *Clinical Child and Family Psychology Review, 5*, 133–160.

Linney, J. A. (2000). Assessing ecological constructs and community context. In J. Rappaport & Seidman, E. (Eds.), *Handbook of Community Psychology* (pp. 647–668). New York: Kluwer Academic/ Plenum Publishers.

Nansel, T. R., Overpeck, M., Pilla, R. S., Ruan, W. J., Simon-Morton, B., & Scheidt, P. (2001). Bullying behaviors among U.S. youth: Prevalence and association with psychosocial adjustment. *Journal of the American Medical Association, 285*, 2094–2100.

Newman, D. A., Horne, A. M., & Bartolomucci, C. L. (2000). *Bully busters: A teacher's manual for helping bullies, victims, and bystanders*. Champaign, IL: Research Press.

Olweus, D. (1993). *Bullying at school*. Oxford, UK: Blackwell Publishing.

Swearer, S. M. & Doll, B. (2001). Bullying in schools: An ecological framework. *Journal of Emotional Abuse, 2*, 7–23.

Vossekuil, B., Fein, R. A., Reddy, M., Borum, R., & Modzeleski, W. (2002). *The Final Report and Findings of the Safe School Initiative: Implications for the Prevention of School Attacks in the United States*. U.S. Secret Service and U.S. Department of Education. Washington, D.C.

I

Individual Characteristics Associated With Bullying

2

Gender Differences in Bullying: Moving Beyond Mean Level Differences

Dorothy L. Espelage, Sarah E. Mebane
University of Illinois, Urbana-Champaign

Susan M. Swearer
University of Nebraska, Lincoln

Are boys more aggressive than girls? Although a tremendous amount of research over the last several decades supports an answer of "yes" (Block, 1983; Parke & Slaby, 1983), more recent research would also support an answer of "it depends" (Knight, Guthrie, Page, & Fabes, 2002). That is, it depends on important contextual factors that might vary across investigations such as the definition of aggression, the method of assessment employed, and the age of the child/adolescent.

Although these contextual and situational variables are important to consider when gender differences in aggression are evaluated, there exists a movement in the theoretical and empirical literature to extend our focus beyond simply describing aggressive boys in one way and aggressive girls in another way (Underwood, Galen, & Paquette, 2001). Thus, many scholars are developing and/or testing developmental theories that might explain *why* gender differences in aggression consistently emerge (Espelage, Holt, & Henkel, 2003; Pellegrini, 2002). These developmental theories often involve consideration of interactions among children and their social environments such as peers, schools, and families.

Despite these recent theoretical advances, Underwood and colleagues argue, among other things, that there continues to be great difficulty in understanding gender and aggression in children because scholars fail to use consistent definitions, measures, and methods to identify subtypes of aggression.

Certainly, we agree with this argument. However, we also contend that the challenges that the various disciplines (e.g., sociology, psychology, education) face in studying aggression are likely the consequence of two historical trends in the aggression literature. The first trend relates to the fact that sociologists and criminologists have been historically concerned with aggression and antisocial behavior among boys and men, and they have only recently emphasized female aggression and female offending in their research (Steffensmeier & Broidy, 1999). Despite the remarkable increase in the percentage of female offenders in this country (Snyder & Sickmund, 1999), the disparity in male and female offending is still very large; males offend at much higher rates than females do. This disparity leads some scholars to argue that male aggression and offending should have a higher priority in research endeavors than the study of female aggression. Therefore, boys and men continue to be over-represented in study samples, which is also true of studies of school-age children and adolescents (e.g., Rodkin, Farmer, Pearl, & Van Acker, 2000). A second trend in the empirical literature followed the seminal work by Crick and Grotpeter (1995). In this investigation, "relational aggression" emerged as a form of aggression thought to be more characteristic of girls in which the goal is to hurt others by damaging their reputation or their relationships. What quickly ensued was a flurry of research on this new form of "female aggression." These two trends have, at least in part, contributed to what we see as a dichotomous view of aggression—male versus female aggression—that has prevented us from understanding the complexity of these behaviors in all children and adolescents. Furthermore, the "gender paradox" provides further support for the need to study aggression and bullying among both males and females (Loeber & Kennan, 1994). The gender paradox postulates that although females have lower prevalence rates of aggression and antisocial behavior than males, they are in fact at greater risk for psychological maladjustment.

Therefore, we argue that in order to continue moving forward with prevention and intervention efforts to curb aggression and bullying in schools, researchers must attend to the social contexts that promote and maintain aggression among both genders. Thus, rather than rehash the statistics on gender differences in aggression in this chapter, the remaining sections will include discussions of the following: (a) the recent research on individual and environmental characteristics associated specifically with *bullying* that can be used to understand gender differences and (b) the empirical work on *relational aggression*, highlighting what questions remain in this area of scholarship. In these two sections, developmental theories for how aggression and bullying emerges among the genders will be integrated throughout. More specifically, theories focused on individual characteristics such as anger and psychological maladjustment, social information processing, and empathic responding are included. Theories that consider the interaction between the individual child/adolescent and the larger social context will also be reviewed (e.g. homophily, dominance, attraction).

Overt Aggression and Bullying

Frequency of Bullying and Victimization Among Boys and Girls

A brief discussion of the research on gender differences in the frequency of bullying and victimization is presented here with a word of caution. These are trends, and therefore, do not represent the experience of all children and adolescents. In general, boys are more likely to engage in physical bullying than girls (Espelage, Bosworth, & Simon, 2000; Hyde, 1986; McDermott, 1996); however, gender differences in verbal bullying are less consistent (Knight et al., 2002). Girls are often cited as using more relational aggression (e.g., threatening to withdraw from a relationship) than boys (Crick & Grotpeter, 1995), but some studies find no differences (Prinstein, Boergers, & Vernberg, 2001). Therefore, scholars caution against drawing any definitive conclusions about gender differences in bullying and how these differences relate to psychosocial adjustment until more large-scale longitudinal studies are conducted. Perhaps the most salient take-home message from these studies is that both boys and girls are aggressive, and individuals working with children should not make assumptions about the nature of their aggression but should conduct a clinical interview and assessment to ascertain this information. A thorough discussion of relational aggression is included in the last half of this chapter.

Normative Beliefs About Bullying Among Boys and Girls

When considering changes in bullying over the school years, it is also important to consider how children and adolescents view bullying. That is, do they develop a more positive attitude toward bullying as they get older? There is convincing evidence that, as children enter early adolescence, aggression is viewed as less negative by peers (Bukowski, Sippola, & Newcomb, 2000; Graham & Juvonen, 1998a) and that boys tend to have more positive views of bullying than girls (Crick & Werner, 1998). Differences appear to emerge during the transition from primary to secondary schools that are partially explained through dominance theory (Pellegrini & Long, 2002) and attraction theory (Bukowski et al., 2000), which are discussed later in this chapter. These recent investigations highlight the importance of examining beliefs within the larger social context of same-gender peer relations and opposite-gender interactions during early adolescence, when many developmental changes converge.

Affective Functioning in Bullying and Victimization

As prevention and intervention programs are selected for children and adolescents, individual characteristics need to be considered and closely examined as potential correlates of bullying and victimization. Instead of focusing on gender differences directly in each section of this chapter, the goal here is to discuss how research informs the way we think about how aggression and bullying might emerge for males and females.

Anger.   Although anger has been examined in only a handful of studies specifically on bullying, this construct has been discussed in the research on subtypes of aggression for some time (Dodge, 1991; Price & Dodge, 1989). Dodge and colleagues distinguished between reactive and proactive aggression. Generally, reactive aggression reflects an angry and volatile approach to others, whereas proactive aggression uses aggressive acts to meet a person's goals and might not involve an angry reaction to a specific precipitating event. Some researchers have conceptualized bullying as proactive aggression because students who bully do so to attain social position and maintain control over others. Even though Dodge and colleagues examined anger as a potential precursor to reactive aggression, their definition does not necessarily support a connection between anger and proactive aggression. However, in a more recent study of 558 middle school students, anger was found to be the strongest predictor of bullying (Bosworth, Espelage, & Simon, 1999). Anger was also a significant predictor of an increase in this behavior over a six-month period; students who were the most angry in the fall semester reported an increase in bullying over the school year (Espelage, Bosworth, & Simon, 2001). It is important to note that these results were significant for *both* males and females. These findings, combined with the consistent connection between aggression and anger, suggest that anger-management training will be beneficial for some students who bully their peers. However, more research needs to be conducted on bullying and anger so that it is clear what components of anger management need to be specifically targeted.

Depression/Anxiety.   Depression has been found to be a common symptom experienced by male and female victims of bullying (Callagan & Joseph, 1995; Neary & Joseph, 1994). Furthermore, Craig (1998) found higher depression levels for girls in comparison to boys who were victimized. Depression is not, however, unique to victims only. Clinically elevated depression levels have been found for both male and female students who bully their peers (Austin & Joseph, 1996; Slee, 1995). Bully-victims, those students who bully and have been bullied, have also been found to have higher rates of depression than bullies (Austin & Joseph, 1996), and in other studies, bully-victims report higher depression levels than victims (Swearer, Song, Cary, Eagle, & Mickelson, 2001).

Anxiety is also a salient mental-health concern that should be considered in intervention planning for bullies, victims, and bully-victims. There has been very little research conducted on anxiety and bullying specifically, and the research that is available has yielded inconsistent findings. Some studies find that victims of bullying have higher rates of anxiety than bullies (Craig, 1998; Olweus, 1994; Slee, 1994), while others find that bullies and victims report similar levels of anxiety (Duncan, 1999). To complicate the picture, bully-victims have also been found to have higher levels of anxiety when compared to bullies or victims (Duncan, 1999; Swearer et al., 1999).

What is often missing from these investigations is the consideration of whether gender moderates the association between bullying/victimization and these psychological outcomes. In addition, researchers increasingly recognize that there is great heterogeneity in how students react to victimization. As a result, recent research has focused on understanding how victimization leads to depression or anxiety (e.g., peer rejection, loneliness, hopelessness) and how victimization does not always lead to psychological maladjustment (e.g., locus of control, attributions) (Graham & Juvonen, 1998b; Kochenderfer-Ladd & Ladd, 2001). These potential moderators and mediators might be particularly more salient for males than females, or vice versa.

Social Skill Deficit vs. Theory of Mind. A current debate among aggression scholars also informs the discussion of the impact of gender on bullying and victimization. One of the most influential explanatory models of aggression is based on *social information processing* (Crick & Dodge, 1994; Dodge & Coie, 1987). This model posits that impairment in social problem-solving is implicated in the development of aggression. Specifically, research has found that aggressive individuals are more likely to show encoding problems such as hostile attribution error, and deficits at the level of representation, such as a poor understanding of others' mental states (Crick & Dodge, 1994). However, more recently, scholars have begun to question whether this model applies to all types of aggression, especially bullying. Given that bullying includes indirect forms of aggression, such as lying and spreading rumors that lead to the victim's exclusion from the group, and that the physical violence is in most of the cases carefully planned, it is plausible that at least some bullies have a social understanding of their behavior.

Following this logic, Sutton and colleagues (1999) challenged a social skills deficit model approach to bullying, and emphasized that some bullies understand other people very well and may use this understanding to their own advantage (Sutton, Smith, & Swettenham, 1999). These authors conceptualize their arguments using the framework of *Theory of Mind*, a concept that refers to one's ability to attribute mental states to others and oneself (Leslie, 1987). Using this framework, the authors contend that some bullies may possess a theory of mind because they target vulnerable children who will tolerate victimization and who are not likely to receive support from peers (Salmivalli, Lagerspetz, Bjorkqvist, Osterman, & Kaukiainen, 1996).

How does the debate between advocates of the social information processing theory and proponents of the theory of mind framework relate to gender differences in bullying? Sutton and colleagues argue that the ability to understand other mind states is especially relevant in the context of relational bullying, a type of aggression that hurts its victims by targeting their relationships. Developmental literature has consistently found that girls develop a superior theory of mind relative to boys during early adolescence (Baron-Cohen & Hammer, 1996). Furthermore, girls are often more likely to use indirect forms of aggression, such as relational aggression (Bjorkqvist, Lagerspetz, & Kaukiainen, 1992). For example, in a study that analyzed aggression themes for an early adolescent population, girls reported that their early adolescence was marked by an increase in social ostracism, involving "manipulation of groups acceptance through alienation, ostracism, or character defamation." The girl-girl conflicts were significantly more relational than either boy-boy or boy-girl conflicts (Cairns, Cairns, Neckerman, Ferguson, & Gariepy, 1989). The parallelism between the refinement of theory of mind in girls and the prevalence of relational aggression in this sex group suggests that girls may resort increasingly to this type of aggression because they possess a theory of mind that allows them to manipulate others' opinions to their own advantage better. What is less clear is whether an enhanced theory of mind leads to overt aggression in girls. More research is needed on theory of mind and bullying in order to substantiate the claims made by Sutton and colleagues. Until then, there is at least preliminary evidence that not all children and adolescents who bully their peers lack social skills (Sutton, Smith, & Swettenham, 1999).

Empathy.   This debate extends to the next individual characteristic-empathy. Many bullying-prevention programs include empathy training based on the extensive literature documenting the role of empathy in suppressing aggression (Miller & Eisenberg, 1988). Research suggests that self-declared bullies sometimes report feeling sorry after bullying their peers (Borg, 1998); however, many bullying-prevention and intervention programs assume that these students lack empathy. A closer examination of the association among gender, empathy, and bullying reveals a complicated picture; studies suggest that the interplay between aggression and empathy occurs differently in females than in males (Cohen & Strayer, 1996; Espelage, Mebane, & Adams, 2003; Feshbach, 1997). This also depends on the component of empathy being measured and the type of aggression under study. We encourage practitioners to conduct a thorough assessment of empathy (including cognitive and affective dimensions) rather than assume all students who bully their peers have similar levels of empathy. We do believe that the extant research does support prevention and intervention efforts that foster prosocial and respectful behaviors.

Peer-level Characteristics Associated With Bullying and Victimization

Peers have long been implicated in influencing children's and adolescents' social behavior (see Hartup, 1983 for a review). Given the social-ecological perspective that individual characteristics of adolescents interact with group-level factors, many scholars have turned their attention to how peers contribute to aggression and bullying (Espelage et al., 2003; Pellegrini & Long, 2002; Rodkin et al., 2000).

Homophily Hypothesis. Peer-group membership becomes extremely important during late childhood and early adolescence (Eccles, Wigfield, & Schiefele, 1998; Rubin, Bukowski, & Parker, 1998). It is during this developmental time period that peer groups form based on similarities in propinquity, gender, and race (Cairns & Cairns, 1994; Leung, 1994), and groups tend to be similar on behavioral dimensions such as smoking behavior (Ennett & Bauman, 1994) and academic achievement (Ryan, 2001). This within-group similarity is called *homophily* (Berndt, 1982; Cohen, 1977; Kandel, 1978). While the homophily hypothesis has been supported in studies of overt, physical aggression among elementary school students (Cairns, Leung, & Cairns, 1995), there is only one study in which the homophily hypothesis is evaluated specifically with bullying. In a study of middle school students, social network analysis (SNA) was used to identify peer networks and hierarchical linear modeling (HLM) was employed to determine the extent to which peers influenced each other in bullying their peers. Results supported the homophily hypothesis for bullying and fighting among sixth through eighth graders over a one-year period (Espelage et al., 2003). The effect was stronger for bullying than fighting, suggesting that peer influence plays a bigger role for low-level aggression than fighting. Put simply, students tended to hang out with students who bullied at similar frequencies, and students who hung out with kids who bullied others increased in the amount of self-reported bullying over the school year. Although males in this sample reported slightly more bullying than females, this study was a nice demonstration of how mean level differences can obscure mechanisms that influence males and females. That is, the homophily hypothesis for bullying was supported for both male and female peer groups. These findings suggest that prevention efforts should incorporate a discussion with students about the pressure from peers to engage in bullying and the real barriers to going against this powerful pressure.

Dominance Theory. Early adolescence is also a time in which there is an increase in the amount of bullying (Pellegrini, 2002; Pellegrini & Long, 2002; Smith, Madsen, & Moody, 1999). A potential explanation for this increase is dominance theory. Dominance is viewed as a relationship factor in which individuals are arranged in a hierarchy in terms of their access to resources (Dunbar,

1988). Pellegrini (2002) argues that the transition to middle school requires students to renegotiate their dominance relationships, and bullying is thought to be a deliberate strategy used to attain dominance in newly formed peer groups. In an empirical test of dominance theory of proactive aggression and bullying, Pellegrini and Long (2002) found, at least in one sample, that bullying was used more frequently by boys who targeted their aggression toward other boys during this transition. Certainly, this research supports the idea that males engage in more bullying than girls during the transition to middle school, but it also highlights the importance of studying this increase as a result of the complex interaction among the need for dominance, changes in social surroundings and peer-group structure, and the desire to interact with the opposite sex.

Attraction Theory.   Attraction theory posits that young adolescents, in their need to establish separation from their parents, become attracted to other youth who possess characteristics that reflect independence (e.g., delinquency, aggression, disobedience) and are less attracted to individuals who possess characteristics more descriptive of childhood (e.g., compliance, obedience) (Bukowski et al., 2000; Moffitt, 1993). These authors argue that early adolescents manage the transition from primary to secondary schools through their attractions to peers who are aggressive. In their study of 217 boys and girls during this transition, Bukowski and colleagues found that girls' and boys' attraction to aggressive peers increased upon the entry to middle school. This increase was greater for girls, which is consistent with Pellegrini and Bartini (2001)'s finding that at the end of middle school girls nominated "dominant boys" as dates to a hypothetical party. This theory, along with the homophily hypothesis and dominance theory, demonstrates the complex nature of bullying during early adolescence and underscores the need to move beyond descriptive studies of aggression among boys and girls.

Relational Aggression

Feminist Perspective on Aggression

For decades, males have been considered the more aggressive gender. In hundreds of studies, most of the research on aggression has found that, as a group, boys exhibit significantly higher levels of aggression than girls do (for review see Coie & Dodge, 1998). These studies indicate that boys engage in more conflict and more forceful aggressive acts. Gender differences begin to emerge by the time children reach preschool and continue to widen through adolescence. This trend has been found across socioeconomic groups and across cultures. These differences have often been interpreted as an overall lack of aggressiveness in girls' peer interactions (Crick & Grotpeter, 1995).

Recently, however, a number of researchers have begun to question whether males are the more aggressive gender. Historically, many studies on aggression have excluded girls from the sample (Crick & Rose, 2001). Furthermore, these studies have defined aggression as physically aggressive acts. The argument has been posited that if the definition of aggression was broadened to include different types of aggressive acts then the relationship between gender and aggression would become less clear (Crick & Grotpeter, 1995). That is, a more feminist perspective of aggression (in which the definition included nonphysical, covert, and social components) challenges the traditional conception that males are more aggressive. Thus, new theories about the documented gender differences in the expression of aggression have emerged. These reconceptualizations are largely based on the argument that, while boys may exhibit more physical aggression, there are other forms of aggression that might be more typical of girls.

Several different terms have been used to describe female-oriented types of aggression, including indirect aggression, relational aggression, and social aggression. Indirect aggression is defined as "social manipulation, attacking the target in circuitous ways" (Oesterman et al., 1998, p. 1). Relational aggression includes "behaviors that are intended to significantly damage another child's friendships or feelings of inclusion by the peer group" (Crick & Grotpeter, 1995, p. 711). Finally social aggression consists of behaviors that are directed toward causing harm to another person's self-esteem and/or social status (Underwood et al., 2001). Some behaviors that are considered indirect, relational, or social aggression include spreading rumors, excluding peers from one's social group, and withdrawing friendship or acceptance. Although these terms differ slightly in how they are defined, assessed, and used, they share many common characteristics. Each of these terms is used to describe behaviors that are *social* in nature; they involve damaging the victim's relationships and do not include the use of direct, overt aggression (e.g., fighting or verbal threats). For clarity purposes, the term *relational aggression* will be used throughout this chapter to refer to these behaviors.

The recognition that aggression can include more subtle, covert forms of behavior directed at social relationships has lead to a number of empirical questions. Do gender differences emerge if studies include measures of relational aggression? What do these gender differences look like? Do girls, in fact, engage in more relational aggression than boys do? Are there correlations between relational aggression and children's social-psychological adjustment, as there are with overt aggression? Are there gender differences in children who are victims of relational aggression? What is the impact of relational victimization on psychological adjustment? Do children view acts of relational aggression as aggressive? What developmental processes are related to relation aggression?

To date, research has yet to provide definitive answers to these questions. This is not surprising, given that scholars have turned their attention to this type of aggression only in the last eight years. Despite this slow start in studying relational aggression, a plethora of studies have followed this construct across the early school years into adolescence and even with college samples.

Social Goals

Before findings of research on relational aggression can be discussed, it is important to address a driving force behind the focus on relational aggression: the importance of *social goals*. The argument has been made that aggression is often embedded in the goals and values of the peer group (Crick & Grotpeter, 1995). A key component here is that the goals and values of the peer group often differ for males and females. That is, research has indicated that themes of instrumentality and physical dominance are important to male peer groups (Block, 1983; Pellegrini, 2002). Thus, following this argument, boys would tend to aggress with different forms of physical and verbal aggression, such as hitting, pushing, or threatening others, which could be potentially damaging to others' sense of dominance. These physical forms of aggression are the primary focus of the majority of the extant literature on aggression in males. On the other hand, studies show that female peer groups focus less on dominance and instrumentality, instead placing greater emphasis on relational issues. For example, girls strive toward the goal of achieving close, intimate connections with others (Block, 1983). Therefore, a logical extension is that girls would express aggression in ways that are intended to damage relationships or feelings of inclusion of other children.

Exploring Relational Aggression

The last decade of research on relational aggression has made a tremendous contribution to our knowledge about this subtype of aggression. The next sections summarize much of the current research on relational aggression and relational victimization. First, the literature on the controversial notion that relational aggression is unique to females is reviewed. Second, the impact of relational aggression on the perpetrator and victim is presented. Third, attributional theory is presented as a way to think about potential interventions. Finally, developmental changes in relational aggression are explored.

Gender Differences in Relational Aggressors.   In numerous studies, relational aggression has been shown to be more prevalent among girls than boys because boys typically engage in more overt forms of aggression (e.g., Crick, 1996; Crick, Casas, & Mosher, 1997; Crick & Grotpeter, 1995; Rys & Bear, 1997). Different measurement techniques have been used, including peer reports, teacher reports, self reports, and naturalistic observations. Although a description of each study supporting these gender differences is beyond the scope of this chapter, the results will be presented in an integrated fashion with a particular focus on highlighting the questions that remain in this area.

Crick and Grotpeter (1995) conducted one of the first studies examining relational aggression and in many ways opened the door for future research on this type of aggression. The study included 491 3rd-through 6th-graders from four public schools in a Midwestern town. A 19-item peer nomination instrument was used to assess relational aggression, overt aggression, prosocial behavior, and isolation. Students were given a list of their fellow classmates, and were then asked to nominate up to three classmates for each item. The 5-item relational aggression subscale included items such as "when mad, gets even by keeping the person from being in their group any more" and "tells friends that they will stop liking them unless friends do what they say." The 3-item overt aggression scale included the following items: "hits, pushes others," "yells, calls others mean names," and "starts fights." The peer nomination scores were then summed, and the participants were classified into four distinct groups: relationally aggressive, overtly aggressive, both overtly and relationally aggressive, and nonaggressive. There was no gender difference in the number of students who were classified in the nonaggressive group; 73.0% of the boys and 78.3% of the girls fell into this group. However, statistically significant gender differences were found for the overtly aggressive group; 15.6% of the boys and 0.4% of the girls were in this group. Furthermore, the relationally aggressive group consisted of 2.0% of the boys and 17.4% of the girls. The remaining children (9.4% of the boys, 3.8% of the girls), were placed in the relationally and overtly aggressive group. Thus, this study is often cited as support for the theory that girls are more relationally aggressive than boys.

A second study, conducted by Rys and Bear (1997) attempted to replicate the findings of Crick and Grotpeter (1995). Rys and Bear assessed relational aggression among other forms of aggression in 131 third graders and 135 sixth graders, from nine elementary schools and five middle schools in the mid-Atlantic public school system. Given their goal of replicating the Crick and Grotpeter study, they used the same peer nomination measure to assess children's aggressive and prosocial behaviors. Multivariate analyses of gender and grade effects on the peer nomination measures of relational aggression, overt aggression, and prosocial behaviors yielded a main effect for gender but no main effect for grade; the interaction between gender and grade was not significant. Follow-up univariate tests indicated that there were no gender differences in relational aggression. However, boys were more overtly aggressive than girls and girls were more prosocial than boys. Based on the peer nominations, students were placed into one of four groups (overtly aggressive, relationally aggressive, both overtly and relationally aggressive, and nonaggressive). Statistical analyses on the different groups yielded significant gender differences. In the overtly aggressive group, 83% were boys, and in the relationally aggressive group, 95% were girls.

There are a number of studies that indicate similar results, supporting the idea that boys are more overtly aggressive, whereas girls are more relationally aggressive. However, some researchers have found contradictory information. For example, one study of 904 elementary school children found boys to be more overtly *and* relationally aggressive (Henington, Hughes, Cavell, & Thompson, 1997). Similarly, findings in a study of 268 middle school students indicated that there were no significant gender differences on relational aggression when implementing the Crick and Grotpeter (1995) relational aggression scale (Espelage et al., 2003). These contradictory findings indicate that although the introduction of more covert forms of aggression has been informative, there is need for further research to explore the construct of relational aggression.

Although there are contradictory findings in whether or not gender differences relate to the frequency of relational aggression, it does appear that boys and girls hold variant views about how the sexes differ in aggression (Crick, Bigbee, & Howes, 1996). That is, in responses to two open-ended questions ("What do boys do when they are mad at someone?", "What do girls do when they are mad at someone?"), both boys and girls cited relational aggression more when describing girls' interactions and physical aggression more frequently in describing boys' interactions. In the same study, Crick and colleagues also found that children viewed relationally aggressive acts as angry and harmful behaviors when they asked students what boys and girls do to each other when they want to be mean to another child.

Correlates of Relational Aggression.   Much of the past research on aggression has been devoted to the study of correlates between aggressive behaviors and their negative effects. Longitudinal investigations have shown that childhood aggression is one of the best-known social predictors of future maladjustment (Parker & Asher, 1987). Individuals who are involved in aggressive acts are at risk of developing social, emotional, behavioral, and academic problems. These can include displaying disruptive and delinquent behaviors, inattention in the classroom, symptoms of anxiety and depression, disrupted peer relationships, and diminished academic achievement (for review see Hanish & Guerra, 2000).

Recently, investigations have been conducted to assess the degree to which being a perpetrator of relational aggression is related to social-psychological maladjustment. Many of these studies indicate that being relationally aggressive is, in fact, significantly and uniquely related to social-psychological maladjustment. More specifically, relational aggression is related to peer rejection, loneliness, isolation, depression, and negative self-perceptions, independent of overt aggression (Crick, Casas, & Mosher, 1996; Crick & Grotpeter, 1995; Crick & Grotpeter, 1996; Rys & Bear, 1997). Also, longitudinal studies indicate that individual differences in relational aggression are relatively stable over time and that relational aggression is predictive of future social maladjustment beyond that predicted by overt aggression (Crick, 1995; Crick, 1996).

Although being relationally aggressive in general is related to social-psychological adjustment, it is important to note that some findings suggest that there may be gender differences in these relations. For example, Crick and Grotpeter (1995) found that relationally aggressive children were lonelier than their relationally nonaggressive peers, but this difference was apparent for girls only. Similarly, they found that the perceived acceptance reported by relationally aggressive boys did not significantly differ from that of nonaggressive children, but for relationally aggressive girls there was a significant difference. In a study by Rys and Bear (1997), findings indicate that relational aggression explained variance in peer rejection beyond that of overt aggression only for girls. Similarly, Crick (1996) reported that relational aggression added significantly to overt aggression in the prediction of future social adjustment for girls, but relational aggression did not add explanatory power for boys. These findings indicate that the correlates of relational aggression may be different for boys and girls. One possible explanation for these differences might be that acts of relational aggression target and harm social goals that are more salient for girl peer groups. Further research is needed to explore these possible gender differences.

Relational Victimization

The majority of studies on relational aggression have focused on the aggressor, or the person engaging in relationally aggressive acts. Yet, it is important to also explore the role of relational aggression on victims. Essentially, relational victims are individuals who are the frequent targets of others' relationally aggressive acts, behaviors in which relationships are used as a means of harm (Crick & Grotpeter, 1996). The few studies that have focused on relational victimization have yielded important findings, including evidence of the validity and significance of a relational form of peer victimization.

Early research on relational aggression provided evidence that relationally aggressive acts are more distressing for girls than they are for boys (Crick, 1995). This result, coupled with the findings on the correlates of relational aggression for the aggressor, suggested that studying relational victimization may provide unique information about aversive peer experiences that is not explained by physical, overt aggression (Crick & Grotpeter, 1996). Thus, it was important to develop a reliable measure to assess relational victimization. Crick & Grotpeter (1996) have created the Social Experiences Questionnaire (SEQ). The SEQ is a self-report measure that includes three subscales (five items each) designed to assess overt victimization (e.g., getting pushed, kicked, or shoved), relational victimization (e.g., having lies told about them, being left out on purpose when it's time to play or do an activity), and recipients of prosocial acts (e.g., getting help from another kid when they need it, getting cheered up by another kid when they feel upset). In the next sections of this chapter studies of relational victimization that employ the SEQ will be discussed.

Gender Differences in Relational Victimization.   In initial explorations of relational victimization, some important gender differences emerge. For example, Crick & Bigbee (1998) conducted a study on 383 fourth and fifth graders, in which they used scores from the SEQ to identify four different groups of students: those who are not victimized, those who are relationally victimized, those who are overtly victimized, and those who are relationally and overtly victimized. Results indicated that the relationally victimized group consisted mostly of girls. In contrast, the overtly victimized group and the overtly/relationally victimized group consisted mostly of boys. Thus, this study supports the theory that boys are more overtly victimized and girls are more relationally victimized. However, these findings are not consistent across studies. Some studies on relational aggression find no significant differences in girls' reports and boys' reports of relational victimization, suggesting that both genders may experience similar levels of relational aggression (e.g., Crick & Grotpeter, 1996; Paquette & Underwood, 1999; Phelps, 2001). Certainly, more research is needed to explore the gender differences in children who are relationally victimized, yet there is some evidence that relational victimization is more typical for girls than overt victimization (e.g., Crick & Bigbee, 1998; Crick & Grotpeter, 1996; Phelps, 2001). In other words, when girls are victimized, it is more likely that they are being relationally victimized than overtly victimized.

Correlates of Relational Victimization.   Victimization research indicates that there is an association between relational victimization and social/psychological adjustment. Relational victimization has been linked to poor peer relationships and rejection by peers, internalizing problems, and a lack of prosocial skills during the preschool years (Crick, Casas, & Ku, 1999). In adolescence, similar trends have been identified, wherein relational victimization was significantly associated with internalizing problems (e.g., emotional distress and loneliness) and problems with self-restraint (Crick & Bigbee, 1998). Additionally, there is support for the idea that relational victimization is significantly related to social psychological adjustment difficulties, including depression (Crick & Grotpeter, 1996). In many instances, these correlations provide information beyond what is provided with an examination of overt aggression.

It is important to note that the impact of relational aggression on victims may vary. Relational aggression can be experienced in differing degrees, and there is evidence to suggest that children can experience occasional relational victimization without significant harm, but when negative treatment becomes more frequent, victims are more likely to experience adjustment difficulties (Crick et al., 2001).

The Role of Attributions in Relational Aggression

As mentioned earlier in this chapter, there has been a tremendous amount of empirical research supporting the *social information processing (SIP) model* of children's social development. Much research has been done on social information processing models of children's social behavior, and this model has advanced our understanding of many aspects of children's social adjustment, including aspects related to aggression. Given the social nature of relational aggression, this model may be particularly salient in furthering our understanding of relational aggression. Involvement in relationally aggressive acts, as the aggressor or the victim, may place children at risk for social and psychological difficulties. Thus, it is important to explore some of the cognitive processes occurring for children who engage in and are victims of relational aggression. In this section *attributions of intent*, a component of the SIP model, will be explored.

Making *attributions of intent* is a social cognitive task that involves interpreting social cues and using those to infer the motives of others. In terms of aggression, children assess whether a peer is acting with benign or hostile intent. Extant research on aggression and intent attributions found that some aggressive children are more likely to attribute malicious intent to provocations, even when the provocations are ambiguous in nature (Crick, 1995; Crick & Dodge, 1994). This tendency is called a *hostile attributional bias*. This bias combined with other deficits in SIP has been found to increase the likelihood that the child will behave aggressively (for review, see Crick & Dodge, 1994).

Many of the studies on aggression and intent attributions, like much of the research on aggression, have yet to examine relationally aggressive behaviors. Given the role that hostile attribution biases play in overt aggression, the question emerged as to the association between intent attributions and relational aggression. As research on relational aggression has expanded, initial explorations on this question have been conducted. The most frequently cited study on relational aggression and intent attributions was conducted by Crick (1995) on 252 students, in grades three through six. In addition to using the previously described peer nomination scale to assess relational and overt aggression, the author adapted a hypothetical-situation instrument from previous studies to measure intent attributions. This instrument consists of 10 stories, 5 of which depict provocation and 5 of which depict relational aggression. In each of the stories the provocateur's intent is ambiguous. For each story students were asked to answer 2 questions. The first question asked the child to choose among four possible reasons for the provocation; two reflected hostile intent, and two reflected benign intent. The second question asked children whether the provocation was intended to be mean (hostile) or not mean (benign). Results revealed that compared to nonaggressive children, those who were more relationally aggressive held significantly more hostile attributions for relational provocative situations. Thus, findings support the idea that relationally aggressive children exhibit a social information-processing pattern that is similar to overtly aggressive children. While we have begun to explore the association between relational aggression and attributions of intent, an important direction for future study would be to explore possible gender differences in the likelihood of exhibiting a hostile attribution bias. The development of possible interventions would benefit from gaining a better understanding of these cognitive processes. It will also be important to explore how anger relates to both attributions and bullying, especially for relational aggression.

Developmental Perspectives on Relational Aggression

Because the study of relational aggression is still relatively new, we know very little about the developmental course of these behaviors across the school years (Crick & Rose, 2001). Most of the studies examining relational aggression have focused on school age children, primarily in Grades 3 through 6. However, preliminary data suggest that relationally aggressive behaviors can be reliably distinguished from overtly aggressive behaviors as earlier as three to five years of age (e.g., Crick et al., 1997). These behaviors remain distinct from overt forms of aggression through middle childhood (e.g., Crick & Grotpeter, 1996) and adolescence (Morales & Crick, 1999). Furthermore, studies on college students indicate that relational aggression continues to be a distinct construct, playing an important role in psychosocial adjustment (Werner & Crick, 1999), and that relational aggression can have harmful effects in romantic relationships (Linder, Crick, & Collins, 2002).

Based on theoretical and empirical research on children's social development, an increase in relational aggression after early childhood can be understood from several different perspectives. First, relational aggression requires enhanced cognitive abilities in order to manipulate the social environment (for review, see Crick & Rose, 2001). That is, relationally aggressive behaviors require an understanding of the dynamics of interpersonal relationships, perspective-taking abilities, and appropriate timing of aggression. In addition, recently scholars have argued that the development of a "theory of mind," or the ability to gauge very accurately one's surroundings and use this understanding to one's advantage, might be implicated as a partial explanation for the increase in relational aggression (Sutton et al., 1999). This heightened theory of mind is not present in younger children, which might explain the lower prevalence of relational aggression. Further support for the role of cognitive ability is the finding that when young children do engage in relational aggression, these behaviors tend to be simple, immediate, and direct confrontative behaviors. For example, young children might cover their ears when a peer is talking to signal ignoring (Crick et al., 1999).

In addition to an increase in cognitive abilities during the middle school years, there are additional changes in the nature and complexity of children's social interactions. During early adolescence, there are dramatic changes in the importance and functions of peer groups. These changes include an increase in intimacy in friendships (Crick & Rose, 2001), increased importance placed on cliques (Rubin et al., 1998), and increasing gender integration within the peer group (Pellegrini, 2002). These changes common in adolescence may lead to an increase in relational aggression. For example, as the level of intimacy and self-disclosure increase, it is possible that relationally aggressive children use self-disclosures of others in relationally aggressive acts (e.g., spreading rumors). Given the dearth of literature on the developmental trajectory of relational aggression, future research should focus on examining how relational aggression changes in content and form and how it functions across different age groups.

Lessons From Relational Aggression Research

When researchers challenged the traditional view that boys are more overtly aggressive than girls by broadening the definition of aggression to include less overt forms of aggression, the result was an explosion of important research exploring the gender differences that traditionally emerged in the study of aggression. In the short time that has followed, studies on relational aggression have made invaluable contributions to the body of knowledge on aggression in youngsters. Findings from these studies support the idea that relational aggression is a form of aggression that is distinct from overt aggression and plays a unique role in youth psychological and social adjustment. However, from a review of the literature it is clear that there is still much that we do not know about relational aggression, as evidenced by the often-conflicting findings in different studies on relational aggression. In addition to contradictory findings, there are also a number of new directions in which to take the study of relational aggression. Thus, exploring relational aggression has played, and should continue to play, an important role in advancing our understanding of gender differences in aggression.

Translating Research Into Practice: Implications for Bullying-Prevention and Intervention Programs

What does this research mean for bullying-prevention and intervention efforts? First, and foremost, we must engage in reasoned analysis and discussion about assessment, etiology, and interventions for aggression and bullying among males and females. Throughout this book the importance of assessment will be emphasized as an important tool for prevention planning. School staff and administrators will be encouraged to survey children and adolescents, teachers, parents, and other staff members in their *own* school or school district so that they can tailor interventions to their unique ecology. Based on the research, however, it is important to make certain that bullying is assessed in a multidimensional manner, including scales that tap physical forms of aggression, nonphysical and verbal aspects, and relational or social components. As the etiology of bullying is addressed through prevention efforts, it is important to consider the powerful influence of peer culture on bullying for both males and females. It is particularly important to talk with young adolescents about the pressure to engage in bullying in order to fit in and obtain status. We need to also resist the urge to view bullying in terms of the "gender dichotomy." Not all aggressive girls are relationally aggressive, and not all aggressive boys are physically aggressive. Finally, readers are encouraged to keep in mind the arguments set forth in this chapter as they engage in prevention and intervention planning. Gender interacts with all levels of the social ecology of schools, including peers, families, schools, and communities.

REFERENCES

Austin, S., & Joseph, S. (1996). Assessment of bully/victim problems in 8 to 11 year olds. *British Journal of Educational Psychology, 66*, 447–456.

Baron-Cohen, S., & Hammer, J. (1997). Is autism and extreme form of the "male brain"? *Advances in Infancy Research, 11*, 193–217.

Berndt, T. J. (1982). The features and effects of friendship in early adolescence. *Child Development, 53*, 1447–1460.

Bjorkqvist, K., Lagerspetz, K., & Kaukiainen, A. (1992). Do girls manipulate and boys fight?: Developmental trends in regard to direct and indirect aggression. *Aggressive Behavior, 18*, 815–823.

Block, J. H. (1983). Differential premises arising from differential socialization of the sexes: Some conjectures. *Child Development, 54*, 1335–1354.

Borg, M. G. (1998). The emotional reactions of school bullies and their victims. *Educational Psychology, 18*, 433–443.

Bosworth, K., Espelage, D. L., & Simon, T. R. (1999). Factors associated with bullying behaviors in middle school students. *Journal of Early Adolescence, 19*, 341–362.

Bukowski, W. M., Sippola, L. A., & Newcomb, A. F. (2000). Variations in patterns of attraction to same- and other-sex peers during early adolescence. *Developmental Psychology, 36*, 147–154.

Cairns, R. B., & Cairns, B. D. (1994). *Lifelines and risks: Pathways of youth in our time*. Cambridge, England: Cambridge University Press.

Cairns, R. B., Cairns, B. D., Neckerman, H. J., Ferguson, L. L., & Gariepy, J. L.(1989). Growth and aggression: I. Childhood to early adolescence. *Developmental Psychology, 25*, 320–330.

Cairns, R. B., Leung, M. C., & Cairns, B. D. (1995). Social networks over time and space in adolescence. In L. J. Crockett & A. C. Crouter (Eds.), *Pathways through adolescence: Individual development in relation to social contexts*. The Penn State series on child and adolescent development. (pp. 35–56). Hillsdale, NJ: Lawrence Erlbaum.

Callagan, S., & Joseph, S. (1995). Self-concept and peer victimization among school-children. *Personality and Individual Differences, 18*, 161–163.

Cohen, J. M. (1977). Sources of peer group homogeneity. *Sociology of Education, 50*, 227–241.

Cohen, D., & Strayer, J. (1996). Empathy in conduct disordered and comparison youth. *Developmental Psychology, 32*, 988–998.

Coie, J. D., & Dodge, K. A. (1998). Aggression and antisocial behavior. In N. Eisenberg (Ed.), *Handbook of Child Psychology, Vol. 3* (pp. 779–862). New York: Wiley.

Craig, W. M. (1998). The relationship among bullying, victimization, depression, anxiety, and aggression in elementary school children. *Personality and Individual Differences, 24*, 123–130.

Crick, N. R. (1995). Relational aggression: The role of intent attributions, feelings of distress, and provocation type. *Development and Psychopathology, 7*, 313–322.

Crick, N. R. (1996). The role of relational aggression, overt aggression, and prosocial behavior in the prediction of children's future social adjustment. *Child Development, 67*, 2317–2327.

Crick, N. R., & Bigbee, M. A. (1998). Relational and overt forms of peer victimization: A multi-informant approach. *Journal of Consulting and Clinical Psychology, 66*, 337–347.

Crick, N. R., Bigbee, M. A., & Howes, C. (1996). Gender differences in children's normative beliefs about aggression: How do I hurt thee? Let me count the ways. *Child Development, 67*, 1003–1014.

Crick, N. R., Casas, J. F., & Ku, H. C. (1999). Relational and physical forms of peer victimization in preschool. *Developmental Psychology, 35*, 376–385.

Crick, N. R., Casas, J. F., & Mosher, M. (1997). Relational and overt aggression in preschool. *Developmental Psychology, 33,* 579–588.

Crick, N. R., & Dodge, K. A. (1994). A review and reformulation of social information-processing mechanisms in children'' social adjustment. *Psychological Bulletin, 115,* 74–101.

Crick, N. R., & Grotpeter, J. K. (1995). Relational aggression, gender, and social-psychological adjustment. *Child Development, 66,* 710–722.

Crick, N. R., & Grotpeter, J. K. (1996). Children's treatment by peers: Victims of relational and overt aggression. *Development and Psychopathology, 8,* 367–380.

Crick, N. R., Nelson, D. R., Morales, J. R., Cullerton-Sen, C., Casas, J. F., & Hickman, S. E. (2001). Relational victimization in childhood and adolescence. In J. Juvonen & S. Graham (Eds.), *Peer harassment in school: The plight of the vulnerable and victimized* (pp. 196–214). New York, NY: Guilford.

Crick, N. R., & Rose, A. J. (2001). Toward a gender-balanced approach to the study of social-emotional development: A look at relational aggression. In P. H. Miller & E. K. Scholnick (Eds.), *Toward a feminist developmental psychology* (pp. 153–168). New York: Routledge.

Crick, N. R., & Werner, N. E. (1998). Response decision processes in relational and overt aggression. *Child Development, 69,* 1630–1639.

Dodge, K. A. (1991). The structure and function of reactive and proactive aggression. In D. J. Pepler & K. H. Rubin (Eds.), *The development and treatment of childhood aggression* (pp. 201–216). Hillsdale, NJ: Erlbaum.

Dodge, K. A., & Coie, J. D. (1987). Social information processing factors in reactive and proactive aggression in children's peer groups. *Journal of Personality and Social Psychology, 53,* 1146–1158.

Dunbar, R. I. M. (1988). *Primate social systems.* Ithaca: Cornell University Press.

Duncan, R. D. (1999). Maltreatment by parents and peers: The relationship between child abuse, bully victimization, and psychological distress. *Child Maltreatment, 4,* 45–55.

Eccles, J. S., Wigfield, A., & Schiefele, U. (1998), Motivation to succeed. In N. Eisenberg (Ed.). *Handbook of child psychology, Vol. 3* (pp. 1017–1096). New York :Wiley.

Ennett, S. T., & Bauman, K. E. (1994). The contribution of influence and selection to adolescent peer group homogeneity: The case of adolescent cigarette smoking. *Journal of Personality and Social Psychology, 67,* 653–663.

Espelage, D. L., Bosworth, K., & Simon, T. R. (2000). Examining the social context of bullying behaviors in early adolescence. *Journal of Counseling and Development, 78,* 326–333.

Espelage, D. L., Bosworth, K., & Simon, T. R. (2001). Short-term stability and prospective correlates of bullying in middle-school students: An examination of potential demographic, psychosocial, and environmental influences. *Violence & Victims, 16,* 411–426.

Espelage, D. L., Holt, M. K., & Henkel, R. R. (2003). Examination of peer group contextual effects on aggression during early adolescence. *Child Development, 74,* 205–220.

Espelage, D. L., Mebane, S. E., & Adams, R. S. (2003). Empathy, Caring, & Bullying: Understanding of a complex association. In D. L. Espelage & S. Swearer (Eds.), *Bullying in American schools: A social-ecological perspective of prevention and intervention* (pp. 37–61). Hillsdale, NJ: Lawrence Erlbaum.

Feshbach, N. D. (1997). Empathy: The formative years. Implications for clinical practice. In A. C. Bohart & L. S. Greenberg (Eds.), *Empathy reconsidered: Directions for psychotherapy* (pp. 33–59). Washington, DC: American Psychological Association.

Graham, S., & Juvonen, J. (1998). Self-blame and peer victimization in middle school: An attributional analysis. *Developmental Psychology, 34,* 587–599.

Graham, S., & Juvonen, J. (1998). A social cognitive perspective on peer aggression and victimization. In R. Vasta (Ed.), *Annals of child development* (pp. 23–70). London: Jessica Kingsley Publishers.

Hanish, L. D., & Guerra, N. G. (2000). Children Who Get Victimized at School: What is known? What can be done? *Professional School Counseling, 4(2),* 113–119.

Hartup, W. W. (1983). Peer groups. In P. H. Mussen (ed.), *Handbook of child psychology* (4th ed.), Vol. 4: Socialization, personality, and social development (E. M. Hetherington, ed.). New York: Wiley.

Henington, C., Hughes, J. N., Cavell, T. A., & Thompson, B. (1997). The role of relational aggression in identifying aggressive boys and girls. *Journal of School Psychology, 36*, 457–477.

Hyde, J. S. (1986). Gender differences in aggression. In J. S. Hyde & M. C. Linn (Eds.), *The psychology of gender: Advances through meta-analysis* (pp. 51–66). Baltimore, MD: Johns Hopkins University Press.

Kandel, D. B. (1978). Homophily, selection, and socialization in adolescent friendships. *American Journal of Sociology, 84*, 427–436.

Knight, G. P., Guthrie, I. K., Page, M. C., & Fabes, R. A. (2002). Emotional arousal and gender differences in aggression: A meta-analysis. *Aggressive Behavior, 28*, 266–393.

Kochenderfer-Ladd, B., & Ladd, G. W. (2001). Variations in peer victimization: Relations to children's maladjustment. In J. Juvonen & S. Graham (Eds.), *Peer harassment in school: The plight of the vulnerable and victimized* (pp. 25–72). New York, NY: Guilford.

Leslie, A. M.(1987). Pretense and representation: The origins of "theory of mind." *Psychological Review, 94*, 412–426

Leung, M. C. (1994). Social cognition and social networks of Chinese schoolchildren in Hong Kong. *Dissertation Abstracts International, 54* (12-B).

Linder, J. R., Crick, N. R., & Collins, W. A. (2002). Relational aggression and victimization in young adults' romantic relationships: Associations with perceptions of parent, peer, and romantic relationship quality. *Social Development, 11*, 69–86.

Loeber, R., & Kennan, K. (1994). Interaction between conduct disorder and its comorbid conditions: Effects of age and gender. *Clinical Psychology Review, 14*, 497–523.

McDermott, P. A. (1996). A nationwide study of developmental and gender prevalence for psychopathology in childhood and adolescence. *Journal of Abnormal Child Psychology, 24*, 53–66.

Miller, P. A., & Eisenberg, N. (1988). The relationship of empathy to aggressive and externalizing/antisocial behavior. *Psychological Bulletin, 103*, 324–344.

Moffitt, T. E. (1993). Adolescent-limited and life-course-persistent anti-social behavior: A developmental taxonomy. *Psychological Review, 100*, 674–701.

Morales, J. R., & Crick, N. R. (1999, April). *Hostile attribution and aggression in adolescent peer and romantic relationships*. Poster presented at the Biennial Meetings of the Society for Research in Child Development, Albuquerque, NM.

Neary, A., & Joseph, S. (1994). Peer victimization and its relationship to self-concept and depression among schoolgirls. *Personality and Individual Differences, 16*, 183–186.

Oesterman, K., Bjoerkqvist, K., Lagerspetz, K. M. J, Kaukiainen, A., Landau, S. F., Fraczek, A., Caprara, G. V. (1998). Cross-cultural evidence of female indirect aggression. *Aggressive Behavior, 24*, 1–8.

Olweus, D. (1994). Bullying at school: Long-term outcomes for the victims and an effective school-based intervention program. In L. R. Huesmann, *Aggressive behavior: Current perspectives* (pp. 97–130). New York: Plenum.

Paquette, J. A., & Underwood, M. K. (1999). Gender differences in young adolescents' experiences of peer victimization: Social and physical aggression. *Merrill-Palmer Quarterly, 45*, 242–266.

Parke, R. D., & Slaby, R. G. (1983). The development of aggression. In P. Musen (Series Ed.) & E. M. Hetherington (Ed.), *Handbook of child psychology: Vol. 4. Socialization, personality, and social development* (pp. 547–641). New York: Wiley.

Parker, J. G., & Asher, S. R. (1987). Peer relations and later personal adjustment: Are low-accepted children at risk? *Psychological Bulletin, 102*, 357–389.

Pellegrini, A. D. (2002). Bullying and victimization in middle school: A dominance relations perspective. *Educational Psychologist, 37*, 151–163.

Pellegrini, A. D., & Bartini, M. (2001). Dominance in Early Adolescent Boys: Affiliative and Aggressive Dimensions and Possible Functions. *Merrill-Palmer Quarterly, 47*, 142–163.

Pellegrini, A. D. & Long, J. (2002). A longitudinal study of bullying, dominance, and victimization during the transition from primary to secondary school. *British Journal of Developmental Psychology, 20*, 259–280.

Phelps, C. E. R. (2001). Children's responses to overt and relational aggression. *Journal of Clinical Child Psychology, 30*, 240–252.

Price, J. M., & Dodge, K. A. (1989). Reactive and proactive aggression in childhood: Relations to peer status and social context dimensions. *Journal of Abnormal Child Psychology, 17*, 455–471.

Prinstein, M. J., Boergers, J., & Vernberg, E. M. (2001). Overt and relational aggression in adolescents: Social-psychological adjustment of aggressors and victims. *Journal of Clinical Child Psychology, 30*, 479–491.

Rodkin, P. C., Farmer, T. W., Pearl, R., & Van Acker, R. (2000). Heterogeneity of popular boys: Antisocial and prosocial configurations. *Developmental Psychology, 36*, 14–24.

Rubin, K. H., Bukowski, W., & Parker, J. G. (1998). Peer interactions, relationships, and groups. In W. Damon (Series Ed.) & N. Eisenberg (Vol. Ed.), *Handbook of child psychology: Vol 3. Social, emotional, and personality development* (5th ed.). New York: Wiley.

Ryan, A. M. (2001). The peer group as a context for the development of young adolescent motivation and achievement. *Child Development, 72*, 1135–1150.

Rys, G. S., & Bear, G. G. (1997). Relational aggression and peer relations: Gender and developmental issues. *Merrill-Palmer Quarterly, 43*, 87–106.

Salmivalli, C., Lagerspetz, K., Bjorkqvist, K., Osterman, K., & Kaukiainen, A. (1996). Bullying as a group process: Participant roles and their relations to social status within the group. *Aggressive Behavior, 22*, 1–15.

Slee, P. T. (1994). Situational and interpersonal correlates of anxiety associated with peer victimization. *Child Psychiatry and Human Development, 25*, 97–107.

Slee, P. T. (1995). Peer victimization and its relationship to depression among Australian primary school students. *Personality & Individual Differences, 18*, 57–62.

Smith, P. K., Madsen, K. C., & Moody, J. C. (1999). What causes the age decline in reports of being bullied at school? Toward a developmental analysis of risks of being bullied. *Educational Research, 41*, 267–285.

Snyder, H., & Sickmund, M. (1999). *Juvenile offenders and victims: 1999 national report.* Washington, DC: Office of Juvenile Justice and Delinquency Prevention.

Steffensmeier, D., & Broidy, L. (1999). Explaining female offending. In Lynne Goodstein (Ed.), *Women, Crime, and Criminal Justice: Contemporary Issues.* Los Angeles: Roxbury Press.

Sutton, J., Smith, P. K., & Sutton, J., Smith, P. K., & Swettenham, J. (1999). Bullying and "theory of mind": A critique of the "social skills deficit" view of anti-social behaviour. *Social Development, 8(1)*, 117–127.

Swearer, S. M., Song, S. Y., Cary, P. T., Eagle, J. W., & Mickelson, W. T. (2001). Psychosocial correlates in bullying and victimization: The relationship between depression, anxiety, and bully/victim status. *Journal of Emotional Abuse, 2*, 95–121.

Underwood, M. K., Galen, B. R., &, Paquette, J. A. (2001). Top ten challenges for understanding gender and aggression in children: Why can't we all just get along? *Social Development, 10*, 248–266.

Werner, N. E., & Crick, N. R. (1999). Relational aggression and social-psychological adjustment in a college sample. *Journal of Abnormal Psychology, 108*, 615–623.

3

Empathy, Caring, and Bullying: Toward an Understanding of Complex Associations

Dorothy L. Espelage, Sarah E. Mebane
University of Illinois, Urbana-Champaign

Ryan S. Adams
Arizona State University

I was talking about someone just to fit in with the group and then later on they were crying and I would be like, 'Why did I do that?'

—8th-grade female bully

Students bully so they can be a part of a group and they do it so the group will respect them more. I used to do it with my friends, but now I don't because it hurts people. . . .

—7th-grade male bully

These responses from students delineate the complex nature of bullying during early adolescence. Students struggle between the desire to "fit in" and the desire to not hurt others. Through an interview study about bullying, these quotes provide some support for the importance of understanding how kids think about the feelings of others (Espelage & Asidao, 2001). However, the association between empathy and bullying is not always straightforward. For many years, research has documented that empathy does promote prosocial behavior, yet the link between empathy and aggression has been explored less, and findings have been less conclusive (for review see Eisenberg, 1988). The operationalization and measurement of empathy, as well as gender differences in the expression of empathy and aggression across the early developmental years, are complex. This complexity often complicates the interpretation of study findings. Despite the inconsistent findings in the extant literature, there is general consensus that attending, fostering, and promoting empathy in children and adolescents could relate to the development of prosocial behavior and to the prevention of aggressive behavior.

Many character education, anger management, and social problem-solving prevention/intervention programs include some component of empathy training (e.g., Goldstein, Glick, & Gibbs, 1998; Newman, Horne, & Bartolomucci, 2000; Pecukonis, 1990). Several of these programs are described in more detail at the end of this chapter. However, this chapter will begin with a brief literature review of the definitions of empathy, potential age and gender differences in empathic responding, and the associations among empathy, prosocial, and antisocial behavior. This will be followed by a brief review of one paper published on the relation between empathy and bullying. Next, an investigation of a sample of middle school students will be included to examine gender and grade differences in aggression and empathy, and to investigate how these links differ depending on how empathy is measured and what type of aggression is assessed.

Defining Empathy

Historical Perspective.   Empathy is generally defined as

> an emotional response that emanates from the emotional state of another individual, and although empathy is defined as a shared emotional response, it is contingent on cognitive as well as emotional factors. (Feshbach, 1997, p. 35)

Although it is currently well accepted that empathy involves both cognitive and emotional facets, this has not always been the case. In the early years of empathy research, definitions of this construct were either cognitive in nature (e.g., Mead, 1934) or affective (e.g., Berger, 1962; Sullivan, 1953) but never both. Later cognitive work in this area defined empathy as role-taking and perspective-taking, and scholars who viewed it as affective were concerned with the emotional experiences of an empathic response. These theoretical camps eventually joined in their thinking during the 1970s and cognitive-affective models emerged. The Integrative Cognitive-Affective model (Feshbach, 1975, 1978) is an excellent example of this type of model and views empathy as a function of three components: (1) cognitive ability to discriminate affective cues in others; (2) mature cognitive skills involved in assuming the perspective and role of another person; and (3) emotional responsiveness or the affective ability to experience emotions.

These components clearly reflect the multiple dimensions from which empathy may be defined.

Multidimensional Approach of Empathy Assessment. The trend toward integration of the cognitive and affective dimensions of empathy continued during the 1980s and is reflected in the Interpersonal Reactivity Index (IRI; Davis, 1980). This measure was developed within a theoretical perspective in which empathy is viewed as a multidimensional set of constructs that are related but distinct. This model of empathy is highlighted because it has strong theoretical and empirical support (Davis, 1996). The IRI includes scales related to four components of empathy: perspective taking (the ability to adopt the psychological point of view of others), empathic concern (the feelings of concern for unfortunate others), personal distress (feelings of personal anxiety in tense interpersonal settings), and fantasy (the tendency to transpose self imaginatively into the feelings and actions of fictitious characters). Findings from empirical investigations of this measure support the association between empathy and better interpersonal functioning, higher self-esteem, and greater social competence across adolescent and adult samples (Davis, 1983, 1996). Later in this chapter we will illustrate how these scales relate to aggression subtypes for a sample of middle school students.

Empathy and Prosocial Behavior

While research generally supports the assumption that empathy tends to be positively associated with prosocial behaviors or concern for others, there are also studies that do not sustain this link (for a review see Eisenberg & Miller, 1987). These discrepancies are usually attributed to study characteristics such as different measures to assess empathy, different age groups, and variant contextual factors. However, the ability to experience the affect of others is associated with altruism or helping behaviors in even very young children (Zahn-Waxler & Radke-Yarrow, 1990) and has been shown to increase in children following empathy training (Feshbach, 1983). Furthermore, the connection between these factors is complex. For example, Coke, Batson, and McDavis (1978) proposed a two-stage model of empathetic mediation of helping behavior. They found that perspective taking did not directly affect helping; it affected helping only through its effect on empathetic emotion. Thus, the link between empathy and prosocial behaviors remains an important area of study.

The linkages between empathy and prosocial behavior appear to become more evident during early adolescence. Adolescents' ability to place information into a broader social context has been examined by researchers in response to Selman's theory of social perspective-taking (1980) and Kohlberg's theory of moral development (1976). Each is derived from Piaget's cognitive-developmental model, and posits a series of stages in social cognitive development from childhood to adulthood. According to these models, the advances in social cognition that occur during early and late adolescence enable individuals to take into account the perspectives of those around them. Given the link between empathy and prosocial behavior, one would thus expect empathy, especially perspective-taking, to reduce the likelihood of an adolescent's involvement in aggressive behaviors. This literature will be reviewed next.

Empathy Relationships With Aggressive Behaviors

Deficits in the capacity to respond to others with empathic emotions or behaviors appear to be linked to various antisocial behaviors and externalizing psychopathologies, including aggression and conduct disorder (Cohen & Strayer, 1996; Miller & Eisenberg, 1988). Further, differences in expressions of empathy across males and females, and the importance of empathy and the inhibition of delinquent behaviors are both well established in the psychological literature (Davis, 1996; Miller & Eisenberg, 1988). Gender differences in psychopathology during early adolescence have been consistently linked to gender differences in affective components of empathy (i.e., empathic concern for the feelings of others) but not always cognitive components of empathy (i.e., perspective-taking) (Cohen & Strayer, 1996). However, there has been no attempt to investigate whether these differences relate to all subtypes of aggression (e.g., bullying, fighting, relational aggression). This oversight is notable, especially because many prevention and intervention efforts designed to curtail anger, bullying, and aggression in children and adolescents have included empathy training in some capacity, including emphasizing respect, caring, and social problem-solving. Thus, further investigation is needed to delineate whether empathy training should be tailored differently for males and females.

Empathy Relationships With Bullying Behaviors

One of the only studies to *specifically* address empathic responding and bullying behavior was conducted by Endresen and Olweus (2001). Four large representative samples of Norwegian adolescents, ranging in age from 13 to 16 years, completed the *Empathic Responsiveness Questionnaire* (Olweus & Endresen, 1998) and two subscales taken from the *Olweus Bully/Victim Questionnaire* (Olweus, 1989, 1996), including the *Positive Attitude to Bullying* (five items) and the *Bullying Others* (four items) scales. The empathy measure consists of 12 items comprising three subscales, including an empathy distress subscale (e.g., "It often makes me distressed when I see something sad on TV"), a sympathetic reaction toward girls subscale (e.g., "When I see a girl who is hurt, I wish to help her") and a sympathetic reaction toward boys subscale (e.g., "Seeing a boy who is sad makes me want to comfort him"). Students indicate on a six-point scale whether the item applies to them, from "not at all" through "applies exactly".

Results indicated that girls reported higher total levels of empathic responsiveness, including greater levels of emotional distress and more empathic concern (for boys and girls as stimuli) than boys in the sample. Effectsize data suggested that these gender differences were strong. With respect to the association of empathic responsiveness and bullying others, the correlations for males were relatively weak between the *Bully Others* scale and the *Empathy* scale ($rs = -.06$ to $-.17$) for girls and slightly lower for boys ($rs = -.02$ to $-.19$). They did find, however, that a positive attitude toward bullying mediated the association between empathic concern and the frequency of bullying others. In other words, kids with high levels of empathic concern tended to view bullying as negative and therefore bullied others less. This mediation was found for both boys and girls. This study highlights the importance of considering attitudes toward bullying in understanding how empathy relates to this type of aggression.

Need for Continued Research on Empathy and Bullying

Although there has been a plethora of research on the role of empathy in promoting prosocial behavior and inhibiting antisocial behavior, few studies have specifically addressed empathy and bullying behavior. The one direct empirical investigation of bullying and empathy (Endresen & Olweus, 2001) was limited by using a measure that assessed a narrow definition of empathy and a narrow assessment of bullying which might have contributed to their finding of a weak association between empathy and bullying others. Thus, there is need for further study in this area for several reasons. First, very few studies have assessed empathy from a multidimensional nature, including both cognitive and affective facets, within the context of American schools. Second, differences in empathy across subtypes of aggression, such as bullying, fighting, and relational aggression, have not been addressed either. Finally, there has been no consideration of how empathy might vary across the bully-victim continuum. This continuum argues for the categorization of students into one of several groups that have unique bullying and victimization experiences (Espelage & Holt, 2001; Olweus, 2001; Swearer, Song, Cary, Eagle, & Mickelson, 2001). That is, students often fall within one of several groups including the following: (1) *no status or controls* are students with no significant history of victimization and report not bullying others; (2) *bullies* are those students that bully others regularly but are not victimized themselves; (3) *bully-victims* are those students who have bullied their peers and have been victimized; (4) *aggressive-bullies* are those students who bully their peers through verbal and physical attacks; and (5) *victims* report being teased and harassed by their peers on a regular basis but do not tease others.

Current Study

Although the study here addresses some of the gaps in the extant literature, it does not represent the gold standard, but demonstrates the types of research questions that remain and the complexity of the connection between empathy and bullying and other forms of aggression. Here, empathy is conceptualized as multidimensional and analyses are conducted on bullying as well as fighting and relational aggression. We examine the associations among gender, empathy, and bullying across the bully-victim continuum. In addition, positive attitude toward bullying is tested as a mediator between empathic concern/perspective-taking and bullying in order to attempt to replicate the findings of Endresen and Olweus (2001).

Study Participants

These data represent Wave 1 of an ongoing longitudinal investigation of bullying during early adolescence. In the early fall of 2002, parental permission forms were sent to all 289 students registered at a Midwestern school and parents were asked to sign and return the consent form only if they did not want their child to participate in the study. Of the 289 students, 268 (93%) were granted permission from their parents to participate and were present on the day of data collection. Twenty students returned permission forms from their parents denying permission, and one student elected not to participate. Of these 268 students, 47.8% were males ($n = 128$) and 50.4% were females ($n = 135$), with 1.9% ($n = 5$) not responding. Of the participants, 33.6% were 6th graders ($n = 90$), 34.0% were 7th graders ($n = 91$), and 32.5% were 8th graders ($n = 87$). Approximately 91.4% were White, 3.7% were African American, 2.6% were Native American, 1.1% were Hispanic, and .4% were Asian American, and the remaining .7% did not choose a response.

Procedure

Participants completed the study survey during a 45-minute free period. Surveys were administered to groups ranging in size from seven to twenty-five students. Students sat such that they were not close to one another. Once students were arranged the project was introduced to them. Students were informed that we would be asking them questions about aggression, their feelings, and their friends, and were given a pencil and a highlighter for their participation. Students were asked to give their written consent by signing their name on the front colored coversheet. Names were collected to allow for matching students' data in a later phase of this study; students were informed that their name would be converted to a number once we had collected their data and assured them of confidentiality and anonymity. In each classroom, one of two trained examiners read each item and response option aloud while a second team member monitored students' progress. The reader's speed varied based on the grade level of the classroom. Students were allowed to ask questions if they had difficulty understanding any words.

Measures

The study survey consisted of three sections: (1) demographic questions, (2) bullying/aggression and victimization scales, and (3) empathy scales and an attitude toward bullying scale.

Demographic Variables

Self-reports of gender, grade, and race were included as demographic characteristics.

Bullying, Fighting, Victimization, and Relational Aggression

The survey included self-reported measures of bullying, fighting, and victimization experiences and a measure of relational aggression.

Self-reported Bullying. The 9-item University of Illinois Bully Scale (UIBS; Espelage & Holt, 2001) was used to assess bullying behavior including teasing, social exclusion, name-calling, and rumor spreading. Researchers developed this scale based on interviews with middle school students and a review of the research literature on existing bullying measures. The nine items were submitted to principal axis factoring with a sample of 422 middle school students and factor loadings for these items ranged from .52 to .75 and accounted for 31% of the variance in the factor analysis. Students are asked to indicate how often in the past 30 days they have engaged in each behavior (e.g., "I teased other students" and "I upset other students for the fun of it"). Response options include "never," "1 or 2 times," "3 or 4 times," "5 or 6 times," and "7 or more times." Higher scores indicate more self-reported bullying behaviors. Espelage and Holt (2001) found a Cronbach alpha coefficient of .87 indicating that the items were internally consistent. The Bullying Scale was found to be moderately correlated ($r = .65$) with the Youth Self-Report Aggression Scale (Achenbach, 1991), suggesting convergent validity. This scale was also found to converge with peer nomination data (Espelage, Holt, & Henkel, 2003). This scale was not significantly correlated with the University of Illinois Victimization Scale ($r = .12$), providing evidence of discriminant validity. A Cronbach alpha coefficient of .91 was found for the current sample.

Self-reported Fighting. The occurrence of physical fighting was assessed using the five-item University of Illinois Fight Scale (UIFS; Espelage & Holt,

2001). Students are asked to answer such items as "I got in a physical fight" and "I fought students I could easily beat," in terms of how often such behaviors have occurred in the past 30 days. Response options include *Never, 1 or 2 times, 3 or 4 times, 5 or 6 times,* and *7 or more times.* Higher scores are indicative of higher self-reported fighting. Factor loadings ranged from .50 to .82 for these five items and accounted for 12% of the variance and this scale emerged as a distinct factor from the University of Illinois Bullying Scale in a confirmatory factor analysis (Espelage & Holt, 2001). These authors reported a Cronbach alpha coefficient of .83 for this scale. This Fighting Scale had a low correlation with the Illinois Victimization Scale ($r = .21$), indicating discriminant validity, and was moderately correlated with the Bullying Scale ($r = .58$), evidence of convergent validity. A Cronbach alpha coefficient of .86 was found for the current study.

Self-reported Victimization.   Victimization from peers was assessed using the four-item University of Illinois Victimization scale (UIVS; Espelage & Holt, 2001). Students are asked how often the following things have happened to them in the past 30 days: "Other students called me names," "Other students made fun of me," "Other students picked on me," and "I got hit and pushed by other students." Response options include *Never, 1 or 2 times, 3 or 4 times, 5 or 6 times,* and *7 or more times.* Higher scores indicate more self-reported victimization. Factor loadings ranged from .55 to .92 for these four items, which accounted for 6 % of the variance. A Cronbach alpha coefficient of .93 was found for the current study.

Relational Aggression.   Relational aggression was assessed with a scale developed by Crick (1996) that consists of five items that measure exclusion, rumor spreading, and other activities meant to damage another child's reputation or social relationships. Students are asked to indicate how often they engage in each particular behavior (e.g., "When I am mad at someone I get back at the person by not letting the person be in my group anymore"). Response options are *Never, Almost never, Sometimes, Almost all the time,* and *All the time.* This scale emerged as a distinct scale in a confirmatory factor analysis (Crick, 1996). A Cronbach alpha coefficient of .89 was reported (Crick, 1996). For this study a Cronbach alpha of .76 was found.

Empathy

Given the multidimensional nature of empathy, several measures were used to assess components that have been identified consistently in the literature. First, the *Consideration of Others* scale from the Weinberger Adjustment Inventory (WAI; Weinberger & Schwartz, 1990) was used to measure cognitive and behavioral empathy. Second, two scales (*Perspective-taking* and *Empathic Concern*) from the Interpersonal Reactivity Index (IRI; Davis, 1980) were included to assess cognitive and emotional aspects of empathy. Finally, the *Engagement in Caring Acts* scale from the Children's Peer Relationship Scale (Crick & Grotpeter, 1996) was added to the survey to measure behaviors.

WAI Consideration of Others Scale.   The *Consideration of Others* sub-scale from the WAI (Weinberger & Schwartz, 1990) is a 7-item scale designed to assess the degree to which individuals are attentive to the emotions and general well-being of others. Students are asked how true or false each statement is for them. Items tap cognitive aspects of empathy (e.g., "Before I do something, I think about how it will affect the people around me") and behavioral aspects of empathy (e.g., "I enjoy doing things for other people, even when I don't receive anything in return"). Response options include *False, Somewhat false, Not sure, Somewhat true*, and *True*. A Cronbach alpha coefficient of .87 was found for the current study sample.

Interpersonal Reactivity Index (IRI) Scales.   The IRI (Davis, 1980; 1983) was developed as a multidimensional assessment of empathy. Empathy is conceptualized as a set of constructs that are all related to a general concern for others. However, it is also viewed as consisting of distinct components of empathy, including perspective-taking, empathic concern, personal distress, and fantasy. Two of the four IRI scales were used in this study. First, the *Perspective-taking* scale consists of seven items that assesses the "tendency to spontaneously adopt the psychological point of view other others" (Davis, 1983, p. 114). This is the cognitive component of empathy. An example item is "I try to look at everybody's side of a disagreement before I make a decision." The second scale that was used is a seven-item *Empathic Concern* scale designed to assess empathy and concern through "other-oriented feelings of sympathy and concern for unfortunate others" (Davis, 1983, p. 114). An example item is "When I see someone being taken advantage of, I feel kind of protective towards them." Respondents are asked to indicate the extent to which each statement describes him/her. Response options include a 5-point scale with the anchors of "Does not describe me well" through "Describes me very well." Internal consistency coefficients have ranged from .71 to .77 for the scales and test-retest reliabilities of .62 to .71 have been reported for high school and college populations (Davis, 1980; Davis & Franzoi, 1991). Cronbach alpha coefficients of .70 was found in this study for the *Perspective-taking* scale and .85 for the *Empathic Concern* scale. Furthermore, Davis and his colleagues have demonstrated the differences between these two components of empathy (Davis, 1983; Davis, Hull, Young, & Warren, 1987; Davis & Oathout, 1987).

Engagement in Caring Acts Scale.   Crick and Grotpeter's (1996) scale includes four items assessing how often students demonstrate concern and care for other students (e.g., "Try to cheer up other kids who feel upset or sad"; "Say or do nice things for other kids"). Response options include *Never, Almost never, Sometimes, Almost all the time*, and *All the time*. A Cronbach alpha coefficient of .76 was found for the current study.

Positive Attitude Toward Bullying

A four-item scale was developed specifically for this investigation but was based on responses from an interview study with middle school children and bullying (Espelage & Asidao, 2001) and a review of the bullying literature. Students are asked how much they agree or disagree with statements related to their attitude toward bullying (e.g., "A little teasing doesn't hurt anyone"). Response options are *Strongly disagree, Disagree, Agree,* and *Strongly agree.* Higher scores on this scale are interpreted as having a favorable or positive view of bullying. A Cronbach alpha coefficient of .81 was found for the current study.

Results

Gender and Grade Differences

Bullying, Fighting, Relational Aggression, and Victimization. One multivariate analysis of variance (MANOVA) was conducted to evaluate sex and grade differences across the *Bullying, Fighting, Relational Aggression,* and *Victimization* scales. Overall significant main effects were found for gender ($\Lambda = .96$; $F = 2.99$, $p < .05$) and grade ($\Lambda = .92$; $F = 2.57$, $p < .01$). Follow-up univariate analyses of variance (ANOVAs) indicated that males reported more bullying and fighting than females ($ps < .01$; Table 3.1), but no gender differences were found for relational aggression or victimization. Follow-up ANOVAs for grade indicated that grade differences were found only for the Bullying scale. Significant grade differences were followed up with Tukey post-hoc comparisons; seventh and eighth graders indicated significantly more bullying than sixth graders ($ps < .05$; Table 3.1). Despite these significant statistical differences, effect size data suggest that these differences were small (gender $\eta^2 = .05$; grade $\eta^2 = .04$). An interesting finding was an overall significant MANOVA effect for the interaction between gender and grade ($\Lambda = .94$; $F = 1.99$, $p < .05$); follow-up ANOVAs indicated that this interaction was significant for the *Relational Aggression* scale. It appears that males reported more relational aggression than females in sixth and seventh graders; however, this pattern was reversed for eighth graders (Table 3.1). These results should be interpreted with caution given the small sample size in each group.

To compare our results to previous studies, students who scored 1 standard deviation above the mean on the Bullying Scale were categorized as Bullies, and the remaining individuals were considered Nonbullies. Based on this categorization, 47 students (17.5%) of the sample were in the Bully group, which is consistent with previous investigations (Espelage, Bosworth, & Simon, 2000; Olweus, 1993). A significant gender difference was found between the Bully and Nonbully group with 23% ($n = 30$) of the males and 11% ($n = 15$) of the females being placed in the Bully group ($\chi^2 = 7.14$, $p < .001$). A significant grade effect was found with the percentage of students classified as Bullies increasing across

TABLE 3.1

Gender and Grade Differences on Bullying, Fighting, Relational Aggression, and Victimization Self-Report Scales & Empathy Scales.

Scale	Male Students			Female Students			ANOVA F		
	6th	7th	8th	6th	7th	8th	Gender	Grade	Gender by Grade
Bullying	1.50 (.76)	1.77 (.66)	1.73 (.67)	1.28 (.33)	1.42 (.41)	1.74 (.71)	6.21*	7.16**	1.89
Fighting	1.52 (.99)	1.76 (.83)	1.63 (.79)	1.28 (.41)	1.25 (.37)	1.61 (.63)	8.89**	1.99	2.45
Relational Aggression	1.75 (.68)	1.74 (.66)	1.58 (.61)	1.47 (.39)	1.54 (.62)	1.80 (.71)	1.22	.33	3.78*
Victimization	1.99 (1.09)	1.78 (.86)	1.65 (.67)	1.78 (.84)	2.09 (1.03)	2.02 (.99)	1.84	.24	2.60
WAI COO	3.60 (.81)	3.19 (.82)	2.73 (.96)	3.78 (.97)	3.81 (.76)	3.26 (.94)	16.31**	13.96**	1.53
Caring Acts	3.39 (.86)	2.92 (.78)	2.74 (.72)	3.63 (.85)	3.64 (.69)	3.31 (.89)	26.34**	7.66**	2.14
IRI Empathic Concern	3.50 (.73)	3.03 (.82)	3.00 (.75)	3.59 (.78)	3.74 (.72)	3.36 (.92)	15.47**	4.41**	3.29*
IRI Perspective-taking	3.28 (.78)	3.10 (.79)	2.78 (.79)	3.37 (.77)	3.62 (.80)	3.06 (.87)	9.01*	7.83**	1.59

$*p < .05.$ $**p < .01.$

the three grades. Approximately 10% ($n = 9$) of sixth graders, 19% ($n = 17$) of seventh graders, and 24% ($n = 21$) of eighth graders were categorized as Bullies ($\chi^2 = 6.54, p < .05$).

Overall, these results indicate that males at a mean level report more fighting and bullying than females, but these effects were small when effect size data were evaluated. Findings indicate that there were no significant gender differences on relational aggression or victimization. The finding that boys and girls do not differ on relational aggression is consistent with previous research (Crick & Grotpeter, 1996) but inconsistent with studies finding gender differences (Crick & Bigbee, 1998).

Empathy Scales

Next, we evaluated the extent to which males and females and students across sixth through eighth grade differed in their level of empathy across the four study measures. As outlined in the Introduction of this chapter, gender differences in empathy depends largely on how the construct is measured, with larger differences found when affective empathy is the variable of interest (Miller & Eisenberg, 1988). Empathy also tends to increase as children mature (Eisenberg & Lennon, 1983). Therefore, gender and grade differences across our multidimensional assessment of empathy were tested using a MANOVA where gender was the independent variable and where there were four dependent variables (*WAI-COO, Caring Acts, IRI Empathic Concern, IRI Perspective-taking*).

Significant MANOVA results emerged for gender ($\Lambda = .89$; $F = 7.56$, $p < .01$) and for grade ($\Lambda = .87$; $F = 4.32, p < .01$); the overall MANOVA was not significant for the interaction between gender and grade. Follow-up ANOVAs for gender indicated that females scored significantly higher than males on caring, consideration of others, empathic concern, and perspective-taking ($ps < .01$; Table 3.1). Examination of the effectsize data suggests that gender differences were strongest for caring behaviors ($\eta^2 = .10$) and weakest for perspective-taking ($\eta^2 = .04$), which is somewhat consistent with our expectations. With respect to grade, follow-up ANOVAs revealed that there was a significant grade effect for all four measures ($ps < .05$; Table 3.1). Tukey post-hoc comparisons were not consistent with our hypotheses; sixth and seventh graders reported more caring behaviors, empathic concern, consideration of others, and perspective-taking than eighth graders (Table 3.1).

Interscale Correlations Among Empathy Variables

In order to gain some understanding of how the four empathy scales in this study relate, a series of correlation coefficients were calculated first for the entire sample and then separately for males and females (Table 3.2).

For the entire sample, the four scales that tap empathy attitudes and behaviors were moderately correlated and significant at the $p < .001$ level. The

TABLE 3.2
Interscale Correlations Between Empathy Measures for Males and Females.

	Scale			
Scale	WAI COO	Caring Acts	IRI Empathic Concern	IRI Perspective-taking
WAI COO	—	.64	.57	.61
Caring Acts	.65	—		.42
IRI Empathic Concern	.55	.43	—	.59
IRI Perspective-taking	.51	.45	.51	—

Note. Correlation coefficients for male participants in left bottom section of table and coefficients for female participants in right top section of table. All correlations coefficients significant at $p < .01$.

Consideration of Others scale was positively associated with the *Empathic Concern* and *Perspective-taking* scales ($rs = .59$), but had a higher correlation with the *Caring Acts* scale ($r = .67$). The *Caring Acts* scale was also positively related to *Empathic Concern* and *Perspective-taking* ($rs = .48$), which were themselves moderately related ($r = .57$). Given that these scales have 16–38% shared variance, they are not redundant; rather, they are distinct components.

A similar pattern of correlation coefficients was found for males and females with two exceptions (see Table 3.2). The *Consideration of Others* scale correlated slightly more with the *Perspective-taking* scale for females ($r = .61$) than for males ($r = .51$). Similarly, *Empathic Concern* and *Perspective-taking* were more highly correlated for females ($r = .59$) than for males ($r = .51$). These differences reached statistical significance and suggest that the interrelations between empathic concern or consideration of others' feelings and the ability to understand another person's point of view might differ as a function of gender.

Correlations Among Empathy Variables and Aggression

Next, we examined the extent to which these four empathy scales were associated with bullying, fighting, and relational aggression. Correlation coefficients were calculated among the empathy variables and each type of aggression for the entire sample followed by separate sets of correlation coefficients for males and females (see Table 3.3).

Empathy and Bullying. For the entire sample, the associations between the four empathy scales and self-reported bullying were slightly negative with correlation coefficients ranging form −.21 (*Caring Acts*) through −.33 (*Consideration of Others*). These correlations indicated that more caring, empathy, and perspective-taking were associated with less bullying. All correlation coefficients were significant at the $p < .001$ level. Similar results emerged for males and females for the association between *Perspective-taking* and *Bullying*

TABLE 3.3
Interscale Correlations Between Empathy and Aggression
Measures for Males and Females.

| | Aggression Scales | | | | | |
| | Males | | | Females | | |
Empathy Scale	Bullying	Fighting	Relational Aggression	Bullying	Fighting	Relational Aggression
WAI COO	−.29**	−.19	−.20*	−.35**	−.28**	−.44**
Caring Acts	−.21*	−.16	−.09	−.11	−.11	−.21*
IRI Empathic Concern	−.31**	−.18	−.23**	−.15	−.20	−.40**
IRI Perspective-taking	−.28**	−.16	−.09	−.25**	−.28**	−.35**

$*p < .05. **p < .01.$

($rs = −.28, −.25$ respectively) and *Consideration of Others* and *Bullying* ($rs = −.29, −.35$ respectively).

However, differences emerged between males and females in the relation between *Bullying* and *Empathic Concern*, where the association was stronger for males ($r = −.30$) than for females ($r = −.15$) (see Table 3.3). This pattern was also found for the association between *Caring Acts* and *Bullying* for males ($r = −.21$) and females ($r = −.11$). Although conclusions should be tentative given that this is just one sample, these data do suggest that the link between empathy and bullying might differ as a result of the component of empathy understudy and the gender of the respondent.

Empathy and Fighting. These same analyses were conducted with the *Fighting* scale. Overall, the associations between the empathy scales and fighting were low and negative ranging from −.18 (*Empathic Concern*) through −.24 (*Consideration of Others*). None of these correlations reached significance of $p < .01$. However, examination of these relations for males and females yielded some noteworthy differences. For males, none of the correlations between empathy scales and fighting were significant ($rs = −.16$ through −.19; see Table 3.3), suggesting that empathy does little to inhibit physical aggression. In contrast, two correlations were significant for females; fighting was significantly related to *Consideration of Others* and *Perspective-taking* ($rs = −.28$, $ps < .001$). Comparing these results to those reported above for the association between empathy and bullying, empathy tends to inhibit both bullying and fighting for females, but looks to be less important in understanding male physical aggression.

Empathy and Relational Aggression. Given the recent research on a common form of aggression that is directed at a friendship through rumor spreading and threats of withdrawing a friendship, we correlated our empathy scales with Crick's *Relational Aggression* scale. For the entire sample, relational aggression scale scores were negatively correlated with the *Caring Acts* scale ($r = -.17$, *Consideration of Others* scale ($r = -.32$), *Empathic Concern* scale ($r = -.31$), and *Perspective-taking* scale ($r = -.23$; $ps < .01$). These associations for the entire sample were found to be driven by the correlations for females (See Table 3.3). That is, only two of these associations were significant for males, including low correlations between relational aggression and the *Empathic Concern* ($r = -.23$) and *Consideration of Others* scales ($r = -.20$). In stark contrast, all of the empathy scales were related to relational aggression for females; the strongest correlations were found with the *Consideration of Others* scale ($r = -.44$) and *Empathic Concern* scale ($r = -.40$). Lower correlations were found between relational aggression and the *Perspective-taking* scale ($r = -.35$) and the *Caring Acts* scale ($r = -.21$). This is particularly important to investigate in future investigations considering that males reported engaging in similar or even slightly higher rates of relational aggression than females. Although mean levels of relational aggression were negligible, empathy appears to be particularly salient in buffering the frequency of relational aggression that females engage in.

Testing Attitude as a Mediator Between Empathy and Bullying

According to Baron and Kenny (1986), ". . . a given variable may be said to function as a mediator to the extent that it accounts for the relation between the predictor and criterion" (p. 1176). In order for a variable to be considered a mediator, the following conditions must be met between the independent variable (IV), dependent variable (DV), and the mediator (MED): (1) IV must be associated with DV; (2) IV must be associated with MED; (3) MED must be associated with DV; and (4) the association between the IV and DV is significantly reduced after controlling for MED. To evaluate whether the relation between empathy (IV) and bullying (DV) is partially explained by a positive attitude toward bullying (MED), a series of regression analyses were conducted separately for males and females. These analyses were conducted only with the IRI *Empathic Concern* scale and the *Perspective-taking* scale to limit the number of tests. A test of mediation of empathic concern was not conducted for females because the relation between the IRI Empathic Concern scale and the Bullying scale was not significant ($r = -.15$). However, it was tested for males and it was found that the conditions were met for mediation; empathic concern and bullying was partially mediated by a positive attitude toward bullying. Similarly, a positive attitude toward bullying was also found to mediate the association between perspective-taking and bullying behaviors for both males and females. These findings suggest that, with the exception of empathic concern for females, the direct effect of empathy on bullying is better understood in a model that considers how students view bullying.

Using Cluster Analysis to Identify Bully/Victim Subtypes

The heterogeneity of bully and victim groups has been well-established (Espelage & Holt, 2001; Olweus, 2001; Swearer et al., 2001). In order to capture the variety of bullying experiences reported by students, cluster analysis was used to identify the types of bully/victim groups in the study sample. Mean scores on the self-report Bullying, Fighting, and Victimization scales were first analyzed using Ward's algorithm (Borgen & Barnett, 1987; Ward, 1963) to derive cluster solutions. Results of cluster analyses utilizing both of these methods suggested that a 4-cluster solution was appropriate for the data.

Following calculation of the cluster solution via these hierarchical methods, we re-analyzed the data utilizing a nonhierarchical clustering method, k-means iterative partitioning. This method requires that the number of clusters be specified in advance. Milligan (1980) has suggested that k-means clustering is an appropriate follow-up analysis to hierarchical clustering techniques.

Means and standard deviations of scores on the Bullying, Fighting, and Victimization scales for each cluster are presented in Table 3.4. The first group ($n = 140$) consisted of those students with scores on the scales below the scale means, indicating low mean levels of bullying, fighting, or victimization in the last 30 days (*No Status*). The second group ($n = 50$) had the highest value on the Victimization Scale with no elevations on the Bullying or Fighting Scale (*Victims*). A third group ($n = 62$) had the highest value—above the scale mean—on the Bullying Scale with small mean scores on the Fighting and Victimization Scales (*Bullies*). The last group consisted of a few students ($n = 14$) but was retained as a group because it is often cited in the literature as an important subtype of bullying. These students reported being victimized and bullying others (*Bully-victims*). Significant gender differences were found among the clusters

TABLE 3.4
Means (Standard Deviations) Among Bully/Victim Cluster
Groups on Bullying, Fighting, and Victimization Scales.

	Bully/Victim Subtype			
Scale	No Status ($n = 140$)	Victims ($n = 50$)	Bully-victims ($n = 14$)	Bullies ($n = 62$)
Bullying	1.24 (.24)	1.47 (.52)	3.13 (.88)	2.04 (.44)
Fighting	1.18 (.25)	1.39 (.52)	3.91 (.76)	1.77 (.47)
Victimization	1.37 (.36)	3.57 (.70)	1.61 (.64)	1.28 (.44)

($\chi^2 = 12.72$, $p < .01$); 9.4% of males compared to 1.5% of females were classified as Bully-victims and 27.6% of males compared to 19.4% of females were classified as Bullies.

Empathy Across the Bully/Victim Continuum

In a final set of analyses, we tested whether empathy levels on our four scales differed across the bully/victim subtypes identified through the cluster analysis. Given the gender differences in bullying and fighting as well as empathy levels, gender was considered as an independent variable along with cluster membership (e.g., bully, bully-victim) and the four empathy scales were treated as dependent variables. An overall MANOVA effect was found for cluster membership ($\Lambda = .84$; $F = 3.84$, $p < .001$; $\eta^2 = .06$) and for gender ($\Lambda = .95$; $F = 3.46$, $p < .01$; $\eta^2 = .05$). The MANOVA effect for cluster by gender was not significant. Follow-up ANOVAs indicated that the four bully-victim subtypes differed significantly on two of the scales, *Caring Acts* and *Consideration of Others* scales (see Table 3.5). Tukey post-hoc comparisons revealed that Victims reported significantly more caring behaviors than No Status, Bullies, or Bully-victims ($ps < .001$), and that Bully-victims indicated less caring behavior than No Status students ($p < .05$). With respect to consideration of others, Victims had higher scores than Bullies and Bully-victims ($ps < .01$), but did not differ from No Status students. Bully-victims reported less consideration of others than Victims and No Status students ($ps < .001$), but did not differ from Bullies. It is no surprise that Victims have the highest levels of caring behaviors, but it is a little disturbing that bullies and no status students have equivalent levels of these behaviors. Furthermore, the fact that Bully-victims have the lowest amount of concern for others and are less likely to engage in caring acts puts them at particularly high risk for future adjustment problems.

Summary of Empathy Study

This study has illustrated the complexity of understanding the role of empathy on bullying and other forms of aggression. While males and females differed only slightly in their level of bullying and fighting, females reported more caring acts, empathy, and greater perspective-taking ability than males. However, it is important to note that the strongest gender differences emerged for the affective dimensions and lowest for the cognitive dimension of perspective-taking.

Important differences also emerged for the concept of relational aggression, which is often considered to be "female aggression." Although males and females did not differ in their self-reports of relational aggression, empathy was found to be highly associated with relational aggression for females only. That is, high amounts of empathy is associated with less relational aggression in

TABLE 3.5

Means (Standard Deviations) Among Bully/Victim Cluster Groups on Empathy Scales.

Scale	No Status (n = 140)		Victims (n = 50)		Bully-Victims (n = 14)		Bullies (n = 62)		ANOVA F (Cluster)
	Males	Females	Males	Females	Males	Females	Males	Females	
WAI COO	3.28 (.91)	3.76 (.85)	3.59 (.98)	3.77 (.81)	2.83 (.59)	3.14 (2.1)	2.85 (.88)	3.13 (.98)	6.88*
Caring Acts	3.02 (.84)	3.42 (.80)	3.37 (.76)	3.98 (.76)	2.63 (.95)	3.50 (.99)	2.95 (.77)	3.42 (.70)	4.48*
IRI Empathic Concern	3.22 (.75)	3.62 (.74)	3.39 (.84)	3.76 (.97)	2.65 (.58)	3.35 (2.0)	3.18 (.84)	3.24 (.66)	2.52
IRI Perspective-taking	3.09 (.79)	3.47 (.81)	2.99 (.84)	3.39 (.91)	2.52 (.94)	2.64 (1.2)	3.19 (.72)	3.07 (.69)	1.91

$*p < .01$.

females, but there is no association for males. In addition to this, empathy was found to be an inhibitor of bullying and fighting for females, but only negatively correlated with bullying for males. Fighting appears to be explained by different characteristics for males. Our findings that the impact of each empathy component appears to differ for males and females is consistent with the view that the structure and function of empathy differ between genders (Feshbach, 1997). Future research should identify potential mediators and moderators that might better explain the association between these constructs. Finally, it is important to consider how bully/victim subtypes differ in their level of empathy before implementing an empathy training module.

Translating Research Into Practice: Implications for Bullying-Prevention and Intervention Programs

Although the majority of bullying-prevention programs to do not emphasize empathy, some of them include an element of empathy training. Four of these types of programs are described in the following sections. The first of which, the Cognitive/Affective Empathy Training Program (Pecukonis, 1990), is a program that focuses solely on teaching and enhancing empathy of children and adolescents. Bully Busters (Newman et al., 2000), The No-Bullying Program (Britney & Title, 1996), and Aggression Replacement Training (Goldstein et al., 1998) all focus broadly on aggression prevention but include modules on empathy training.

The Cognitive/Affective Empathy Training Program

Cognitive/Affective Empathy Training (Pecukonis, 1990) is a program that concurrently seeks to improve levels of empathetic response in aggressive adolescents and to decrease levels of aggression by addressing cognitive and affective deficits. The program focuses on four different topics: interpreting the affect of others, role-taking, choosing and utilizing an appropriate level of affect, and event analysis. These topics are presented sequentially in four different sessions, once reasonable gains have been made on one topic, participants continue to the next topic. Sessions include a variety of teaching methods, including visual, audio, and kinesthetic modalities. Empirical validation of the effectiveness of this program is relatively limited, but some evidence suggests that this program is effective in raising levels of affective empathy (Pecukonis, 1990). Pecukonis (1990) conducted a study investigating the effects of the program on 24 aggressive adolescent females (ages 14–17 years) in a residential treatment center, and found that participants in the training program experienced an increase in both affective empathy and their understanding of the positive and emotional experiences of others.

The No-Bullying Program: Preventing
Bully/Victim Violence at School

The No-Bully Program (Britney & Title, 1996) is designed to guide middle school students through six sessions, which are from 40 to 60 minutes long, on bully violence prevention. The program objectives are to help students define bullying, gain a better understanding of both the effects and characteristics of bullying, develop empathy for the victims of bullying, and learn how to get help in a bullying situation. The program is designed to be implemented by teachers in the schools in the classroom setting, and employs a number of different teaching strategies. The strategies include kinesthetic learning tactics, brainstorming, role-playing, group discussion, and handouts. In the session that focuses on empathy, students are taught to recognize the difference between bullying and peer conflict, gain a better understanding of how it feels to be bullied, realize that victims need their help, and to generally increase their level of empathy for victims. Although this program is designed to be effective in preventing bullying in middle school, the effectiveness of the program has not been empirically tested.

Bully Busters

Bully Busters (Newman et al., 2000) is an educational program in which students go through a series of seven training modules, each of which has the objective of controlling and preventing bullying behavior. More specifically, the goal of the Bully Busters program is to both reduce the occurrences of bullying and to induce conditions less conducive to bullying, such as creating a positive classroom climate, where bullying behavior is not tolerated, rules and consequences are consistent, and the teacher has high self-efficacy and positive expectations of the students. The more people involved in program implementation increase effectiveness, but the program can be implemented by an individual teacher, a team of teachers and other support staff, or as part of the school curriculum with school-wide support. The seven modules include the following topics: increasing awareness of bullying, recognizing the bully, recognizing the victim, interventions for bullying behavior, interventions and recommendations to assist victims, the role of prevention, and relaxation and coping skills. Each of these modules includes three or four classroom activities as well as discussion questions to aid in the processing of each idea. Bully Busters has a strong empathy component. The program defines empathy as the ability to understand "how it feels to walk in someone else's shoes" and the ability "to be a good listener," and to express those abilities.

The implementation of the empathy-training portion of the program involves three phases. First, instructors engage students in an initial discussion of the term empathy, ultimately giving the students the definitions of empathy, a description of the empathic response, and the key components of empathy. Second, students work through an empathy exercise in dyads. In this exercise, entitled "Please Let Me Understand," students are presented with two scenarios in which a student is the victim of a bullying episode. Students are asked to write down how the victim may feel as well as examples of non-empathic and empathic responses. Third, once the exercise is completed, the teacher convenes the class into a large group and leads an in-depth discussion of empathy. A recent study to test the effectiveness of the Bully Busters program found that it was effective in increasing teachers' knowledge of and use of bullying-intervention skills, as well as reducing the amount of bullying in the classroom (Newman & Horne, in press).

Aggression Replacement Training (ART)

Aggression Replacement Training (ART; Goldstein et al., 1998) is a program designed to combat aggression in early adolescence. The program duration can vary, but it typically includes a 10-week curriculum, where group members attend a 45–50 minute ART session three times a week. ART uses a multichannel approach, in that it begins with the idea that aggression is a complex process, involving behavioral, cognitive, and emotional components. Thus, ART addresses each of these in three coordinated components: Skillstreaming (the behavioral component), Anger Control Training (the emotional component), and Moral Reasoning Training (the cognitive component).

Skillstreaming, the first of the three components, is a set of procedures designed to enhance prosocial skills. In this phase of ART, 50 prosocial skills are identified, and small groups of aggressive adolescents are guided through instruction on each of the skills. In Skillstreaming, the program employs techniques of modeling, role-playing, performance feedback, and transfer training. These skills comprise 7 types: beginning social skills (e.g., listening, having a conversation, saying thank you), advanced social skills (e.g., asking for help, apologizing), skills for dealing with feelings (e.g., knowing your feelings, understanding the feelings of others, expressing emotion), skill alternatives to aggression (e.g., helping others, negotiating, responding to teasing), skills for dealing with stress (e.g., making a complaint, responding to failure, dealing with group pressure), and planning skills (e.g., setting a goal, making a decision, concentrating on a task).

Anger Control Training is the emotional component of ART. Where Skillstreaming teaches participants what to do in problematic situations, Anger Control Training emphasizes what not to do. This component of ART aims to enhance the self-control, reduction, or management of anger and aggression. This objective is achieved by training youth to respond to provocations using a chain of responses that focus on triggers, cues, reducers, reminders, alternatives to anger, and self-evaluation.

Finally, the Moral Reasoning Training, the cognitive component, works to compliment and reinforce the other two training components by engaging participants in thinking and talking about moral reasoning. Participants are given a series of realistic problem situations, in which the characters involved are faced with difficult moral decisions. The participants read the situation, answer a number of questions about the situation, and then engage in a group discussion.

While empathy is not specifically addressed in these initial three components, the developers of the ART program found that embedding ART in a broader curriculum enhances the long-term effectiveness of the program (Goldstein, McGinnis, Sprafkin, Gershaw, & Klein, 1997). The broader curriculum is called the Prepare curriculum (Goldstein et al., 1997; Goldstein et al., 1998), and includes ten courses, of which the first three are the components of the original ART. The remaining seven courses of this broader program are stress management, cooperation training, problem-solving training, situational perception training, understanding and using group processes, empathy training, and recruiting supportive models. This more comprehensive curriculum has the potential to maximize both transfer and maintenance of the skills acquired in ART.

The empathy portion of this larger curriculum defines empathy as a multistage process of perception of emotional cues, affective reverberation of the emotions perceived, their cognitive labeling, and communication (Goldstein et al., 1998). Each of these four components is taught in the training program. In combination with the other portions of the training program, empathy training is effective in promoting skill acquisition, improving anger control, decreasing the frequency of acting-out behaviors, and increasing the frequency of pro-social behaviors (Goldstein et al., 1998).

Summary

The association between empathy and bullying is not clear. Despite inconsistent findings in the existing literature there has been a general consensus that attending, fostering, and promoting empathy in children and adolescents could relate to the development of prosocial behaviors while serving to decrease aggressive behaviors. This chapter reviewed the historical approaches that have been taken in defining empathy as either emotionally based (e.g., empathetic concern) or cognitively based (e.g., perspective taking), and presented the need for research to reflect the more modern multidimensional definition of empathy, as suggested by Davis (1980). Few studies have considered the specific relationship between empathy and bullying, instead focusing generally on aggressive behavior. The current study evaluated gender and grade differences in bullying, other forms of aggression, and empathy. Although the current study is not the gold standard for exploring these complex relationships it serves as a catalyst for deeper examination. Despite the difficulty in sorting through the true relationship between empathy and bullying, it is clear that empathy-training programs, such as those presented in this chapter, are continuing to be implemented in our schools. The need for research to support these programs' effectiveness and to guide future developments in this area is essential to understand the relations between empathy and bullying.

REFERENCES

Achenbach, T. M. (1991). *Manual for the Youth Self-Report and 1991 Profile*. Burlington, VT: University of Vermont Department of Psychiatry.

Baron, R. M., & Kenny, D. A. (1986). The moderator-mediator variable distinction in social psychological research: Conceptual, strategic, and statistical considerations. *Journal of Personality and Social Psychology, 51*, 1173–1182.

Berger, S. M. (1962). Conditioning through vicarious instigation? *Psychological Review, 69*, 450–456.

Borgen, F. H., & Barnett, D. C. (1987). Applying cluster analysis in counseling psychology research. *Journal of Counseling Psychology, 34*, 456–468.

Britney, J., & Title, B. B. (1996). The no-bully program: Preventing bully/victim violence at school. Minneapolis, MN: Johnson Institute-QVS, Inc.

Cohen, D., & Strayer, J. (1996). Empathy in conduct disordered and comparison youth. *Developmental Psychology, 32*, 988–998.

Coke, J., Batson, C., & McDavis, K. (1978). Empathic mediation of helping: A two-stage model. *Journal of Personality and Social Psychology*, 36, 752–766.

Crick, N. R. (1996). The role of relational aggression, overt aggression, and prosocial behavior in the prediction of children's future social adjustment. *Child Development, 67*, 2317–2327.

Crick, N. R., & Bigbee, M. A. (1998). Relational and overt forms of peer victimization: A multi-informant approach. *Journal of Consulting and Clinical Psychology, 66*, 337–347.

Crick, N. R., & Grotpeter, J. K. (1996). Children's treatment by peers: Victims of relational and overt aggression. *Development and Psychopathology, 8*, 367–380.

Davis, M. H. (1980). A multidimensional approach to individual differences in empathy. *JSAS Catalog of Selected Documents in Psychology, 10*, 85.

Davis, M. H. (1983). Measuring individual differences in empathy: Evidence for a multidimensional approach. *Journal of Personality and Social Psychology, 44*, 113–126.

Davis, M. H. (1996). Empathy: A social psychological approach. Dubugue, IA: Williams C. Brown.

Davis, M. H., & Franzoi, S. L. (1991). Stability and change in adolescent self-consciousness and empathy. *Journal of Research in Personality, 25*, 70–87.

Davis, M. H., Hull, J. C., Young, R. D., & Warren, G. G. (1987). Emotional reactions to dramatic film stimuli: The influence of cognitive and emotional empathy. *Journal of Personality and Social Psychology*, 52, 126–133.

Davis, M. H., & Oathout, H. A. (1987). Maintenance of satisfaction in romantic relationships: Empathy and relational competence. *Journal of Personality and Social Psychology*, 53, 397–410.

Eisenberg, N. (1988). The development of prosocial and aggressive behavior. In M. H. Bornstein & M. E. Lamb (Eds.), *Developmental Psychology: An Advanced Textbook* (pp. 461–495). Hillsdale, New Jersey: Lawrence Erlbaum.

Eisenberg, N., & Lennon, R. (1983). Sex differences in empathy and related capacities. *Psychological Bulletin, 94*, 100–131.

Eisenberg, N., & Miller, P. A., (1987). The relation of empathy to prosocial and related behaviors. *Psychological Bulletin, 101*, 91–119.

Endresen, I. M., & Olweus, D. (2001). Self-reported empathy in Norwegian adolescents: Sex differences, age trends, and relationship to bullying. In A. C. Bohart and C. Arthur, & Stipek, D. J. (Eds.), (2001), *Constructive & destructive behavior: Implications for family, school, & society* (pp. 147–165). Washington, DC: American Psychological Association.

Espelage, D., & Asidao, C. (2001). Interviews with middle school students: Bullying, victimization, and contextual factors. *Journal of Emotional Abuse, 2*, 49–62.

Espelage, D. L., Bosworth, K., & Simon, T. R. (2000). Examining the social context of bullying behaviors in early adolescence. *Journal of Counseling and Development, 78*, 326–333.

Espelage, D. L., & Holt, M. L. (2001). Bullying and victimization during early adolescence: peer influences and psychosocial correlates. *Journal of Emotional Abuse, 2*(3), 123–142.

Espelage, D. L., Holt, M. K., & Henkel, R. R. (2003). Examination of peer group contextual effects on aggression during early adolescence. *Child Development, 74*, 205–220.

Feshbach, N. D. (1975). Empathy in children: Some theoretical and empirical considerations. *The Counseling Psychologist, 5*, 25–30.

Feshbach, N. D. (1978). Studies of empathic behavior in children. In B. A. Maher (Ed.), *Progress in Experimental Personality Research* (Vol. 8, pp. 1–47). New York: Academic Press.

Feshbach, N. D. (1983). Learning to care: A positive approach to child training and discipline. *Journal of Clinical Child Psychology, 12*, 266–271.

Feshbach, N. D. (1997). Empathy: The formative years. Implications for clinical practice. In A. C. Bohart & L. S. Greenberg (Eds.), *Empathy reconsidered: Directions for psychotherapy* (pp. 33–59). Washington, DC: American Psychological Association.

Goldstein, A. P., Glick, B., & Gibbs, J. C. (1998). Aggression Replacement Training: A comprehensive intervention for aggressive youth (Revised Edition). Champaign, IL: Research Press.

Goldstein, A. P., McGinnis, E., Sprafkin, R. P, Gershaw, N. J., & Klein, P. (1997). Skillstreaming the Adolescent: New strategies and perspectives for teaching prosocial skills. Champaign, IL: Research Press.

Kohlberg, L. (1976). Moral stages and moralization: The cognitive-developmental approach. In *Moral development and behavior: Theory, research, and social issues*, Lickona, T. (Ed.). New York: Holt, Rinehart and Winston.

Mead, G. H. (1934). *Mind, self, and society*. Chicago: University of Chicago Press.

Miller, P. A., & Eisenberg, N. (1988). The relationship of empathy to aggressive and externalizing/antisocial behavior. *Psychological Bulletin, 103*, 324–344.

Milligan, G. W. (1980). An examination of the effects of six types of error perturbation on fifteen clustering algorithms. *Psychometrika, 50*, 159–179.

Newman, D. A., Horne, A. M., & Bartolomucci, C. L. (2000). *Bully Busters: A teacher's manual for helping bullies, victims, and bystanders*. Champaign, Illinois: Research Press.

Newman, D. A., & Horne, A. M. (in press). Bully Busters: A psychoeducational intervention for reducing bullying behavior in middle school students. Journal of Child Development.

Olweus, D. (1989). *The Olweus Bully/Victim Questionnaire* [Mimeo]. HEMIL-senteret, Univesitetet I Bergen, Norway.

Olweus, D. (1996). *The Revised Olweus Bully/Victim Questionnaire* [Mimeo]. HEMIL-senteret, Univesitetet I Bergen, Norway.

Olweus, D. (1993). Bully/victim problems among schoolchildren: Long-term consequences and an effective intervention program. In S. Hodgins, *Mental Disorder and Crime* (pp. 317–349). Thousand Oaks, CA: Sage Publications.

Olweus, D. (2001). Peer harassment: A critical analysis and some important issues. In J. Juveonen & S. Graham (Eds.), *Peer harassment in school: The plight of the vulnerable and victimized* (pp. 3–23). New York, NY: Guilford.

Olweus, D., & Endresen, I. M. (1998). The importance of sex-of-stimulus object: Age trends and sex differences in empathic responsiveness. *Social Development, 7*, 370–388.

Pecukonis, E. V. (1990). A cognitive/affective empathy training program as a function of ego development in aggressive adolescent females. *Adolescence, 25*, 59–76.

Selman, R. (1980). *The growth of interpersonal understanding: Developmental and clinical analyses*. New York: Academic Press.

Sullivan, H. S. (1953). *The interpersonal theory of psychiatry*. New York: Norton.

Swearer, S. M., Song, S. Y., Cary, P. T., Eagle, J. W., & Mickelson, W. T. (2001). Psychosocial correlates in bullying and victimization: The relationship between depression, anxiety, and bully/
victim status. *Journal of Emotional Abuse, 2*, 95–121.

Ward, J. H. (1963). Hierarchical grouping to optimize an objective function. *Journal of the American
Statistical Association, 58*, 236–244.

Weinberger, D. A. & Schwartz, G. E. (1990). Distress and restraint as superordinate dimensions of
self-reported adjustment: A typological perspective. *Journal of Personality, 58*, 381–417.

Zahn-Waxler, C., & Radke-Yarrow, M. (1990). The origins of empathic concern. *Motivation and
emotion, 14*, 107–130.

4

Internalizing Problems in Students Involved in Bullying and Victimization: Implications for Intervention

Susan M. Swearer
University of Nebraska, Lincoln

Amie E. Grills
Western New England College

Kisha M. Haye, Paulette Tam Cary
University of Nebraska, Lincoln

Misery is . . .
Misery is when you go to school and bullies pick on you.
Misery is when you share with someone, but they don't share with you.
Misery is when bullies become friends, and friends become bullies.
Misery is when you go to school and people threaten you by telling you that they will get you after school.
Misery is when you are at breakfast recess and people push you around for no reason.
Misery is when people invite everyone but you to play tag and football.
                    —Written by a 10-year-old depressed and anxious male bully-victim

This chapter reviews the literature on internalizing difficulties among youth who are involved in bullying (bullies, victims, and bully-victims). Specifically, it examines the literature on depression, hopelessness, locus of control, and anxiety. It is the goal of this chapter to examine the relationship between internalizing problems in bullying and victimization with the hope of providing guidance for professionals and parents who work with youth experiencing this ubiquitous phenomenon.

Depression, Hopelessness, Locus of Control, and the Bully/Victim Continuum

Depression and the Bully/Victim Continuum

Students who experience problems with depression often report feelings of sadness, anger, worthlessness, and hopelessness. How might these feelings be related to bullying and victimization? As the opening poem, "Misery is . . ." illustrates, students who are bullied often feel hopeless about themselves and their situation.

The prevalence of depressive disorders among school-aged youth vary depending upon age and sex and appear to be increasing. Generally, prevalence rates for major depressive disorder range from 2% to 8%, and prevalence rates for dysthymic disorder range from 1% to 9% (Kazdin & Marciano, 1998). The following symptoms occur most often in childhood depression: (a) dysphoric mood, irritability, and weepiness, (b) low self-esteem, hopelessness, decline in school performance, and poor concentration, (c) slower psychomotor behavior, social withdrawal, and increased aggressive behaviors, and (d) fatigue, difficulty sleeping, weight loss or weight gain, and somatic complaints (Kovacs & Beck, 1977). Thus, symptoms of depression in youth are related to both inter- and intrapersonal functioning.

Researchers have found that depressed individuals hold negative views of themselves, the world, and the future (Kovacs & Beck, 1977). The negative cognitive triad of depression includes negative thoughts and attitudes towards oneself, the world, and the future. The negative expectations that characterize hopelessness can stem from stressful events that have occurred throughout the lifespan (Kazdin, Rodgers, & Colbus, 1986). As the poem "Misery is . . ." illustrates, bullying can be a stressful event that can have pervasive negative psychological effects.

Researchers and clinicians have identified a significant association between depression and low self-esteem, or self-worth. Self-esteem is the construct that represents negative thoughts about oneself (Marciano & Kazdin, 1994) and victims of bullying tend to have lower self-esteem, display more signs of loneliness, and depression, than students who do not participate in bullying (Callaghan & Joseph, 1995; Swearer, Song, Cary, Eagle, & Mickelson, 2001). For instance,

O'Moore and Kirkham (2001) investigated the relation between self-esteem and bullying among children ages 8 to 18 using the Piers-Harris Self-Concept Scale. The authors found that both bullies and victims reported lower levels of self-esteem compared to individuals who did not experience bullying. Furthermore, bully-victims of all ages reported significantly lower levels of self-esteem than either bullies or victims. O'Moore and Kirkham also found that individuals involved in bullying more frequently, regardless of status, reported lower global self-esteem scores.

There are several reasons why low self-esteem might be a factor leading to victimization. Egan and Perry (1998) conducted a study examining the extent to which self-concept and self-esteem contributed to victimization among children in third through seventh grades. The authors found that low self-esteem was related to victimization by peers in several different ways. For example, by not actively defending themselves, children may be increasingly targeted as victims. Also, behaviors such as social withdrawal and crying are visible to peers and might create the perception of an easy target for bullying. Egan and Perry reported that repeated victimization led to decreased self-esteem over time. Several researchers have documented a relation between peer victimization and low self-worth (Austin & Joseph, 1996; Callaghan & Joseph, 1995; Graham & Juvonen, 1998; Grills & Ollendick, 2002; Neary & Joseph, 1994; Ross, 1996; Slee & Rigby, 1993). Similarly, children who are classified as victims have been found to report lower self-worth than their bullying and uninvolved peers, who tend not to differ from one another (Andreou, 2000; Boulton & Underwood, 1992).

Victims are a complex group. Carney and Merrell (2001) described two types of victims that exist in the bully/victim continuum. The first of these is the submissive victim; in previous literature, this type of victim has also been described as passive/submissive (Olweus, 1994). These types of victims are characterized as anxious, insecure, and not likely to retaliate when attacked. Submissive victims often withdraw and/or cry when bullied by others and are the most common type of victim. The provocative victim is the second type. This type of victim tends to provoke bullying through his or her behavior towards peers. Provocative victims are also likely to retaliate towards their aggressor (Olweus, 1994). These individuals are often not liked by their peer group and tend to be at risk for adjustment difficulties (Batsche, 1997). Low self-esteem and increased levels of depression are problems for both types of victims (Carney & Merrell, 2001).

Similarly, depression has been consistently associated with bullying in youth (Biggam & Power, 1999; Craig, 1998; Hanish & Guerra, 2000; Kaltiala-Heino, Rimpela, Rantanen, & Rimpela, 2000; Kumpulainen, Rasanen, & Puura, 2001). Previous research suggests that all participants in the bully/victim cycle, regardless of status (i.e., victim, bully-victim, or bully), are likely to display symptoms of depression (Austin & Joseph, 1996; Kumpulainen, Räsänen, & Hentonnen, 1999), with bully-victims displaying the highest levels of depression (Haynie et al., 2001; Kaltiala-Heino, Rimpela, Marttunen, Rimpela, & Rantanen, 1999;

Kumpulainen et al., 2001; Swearer et al., 2001). Kumpulainen and colleagues (2001) conducted a study examining the prevalence of psychiatric disorders among individuals involved in bullying. They found higher rate of depression among the bully-victims in comparison to victims, bullies, and controls. The results revealed that approximately 18% of the bully-victims, 13% of the bullies, and 10% of the victims were diagnosed with a depressive disorder.

There are potentially grave consequences associated with depression and bullying. Kaltiala-Heino et al. (1999) assessed the relationship between bully/victim status and depression and suicidal ideation among adolescents ages 14 to 16. The authors reported that after controlling for age and gender, bully-victims exhibited the highest risk for depression, followed by victims and then bullies. Bully-victims were also the most at-risk group for suicidal ideation, followed by bullies and then victims. The high occurrence of suicidal ideation among participants along the bully/victim continuum is not surprising considering that bullying is not a static event; rather, it occurs as repeated events over time (Hazler & Carney, 2000). Additionally, findings from a recent analysis of school shootings from 1974 to 2000 indicate that 78% of the attackers had a history of suicide attempts or suicidal thoughts and 61% had a history of serious depression (Vossekuil, Fein, Reddy, Borum, & Modzeleski, 2002).

Hopelessness and the Bully/Victim Continuum

The hopelessness theory of depression, which considers *hopelessness depression* a subtype of depression (Abramson, Metalsky, & Alloy, 1989), recognizes symptoms of depression that relate more specifically to hopelessness as an identifiable form of depression. Hopelessness is defined as negative expectations towards oneself and the future (Kazdin, Rodgers, & Colbus, 1986) and is related to Beck's concept of the negative cognitive triad.

According to previous research, hopelessness is likely to precede depression and suicidal ideation (Abramson et al., 1989; Kazdin, French, Unis, Esveldt Dawson, & Sherick, 1983). Marciano and Kazdin (1994) conducted a study of 123 children aged 6 to 13 years that examined the role of self-esteem in discerning between suicidal ideators, attempters, and nonsuicidal inpatient children. Participants completed the Children's Depression Inventory, the Hopelessness Scale for Children, and the Self-Esteem Inventory. The researchers found that suicidal children reported significantly higher levels of depression, hopelessness, and lower self-esteem than their non-suicidal peers. Most importantly, the research identified depression as the best predictor of suicidal ideation and suicide attempts.

Individuals may experience depression and hopelessness when they perceive environmental events as uncontrollable; thus, they "give up" because they believe that their behavior cannot influence their environment (Kaslow, Brown, & Mee, 1994). Abramson, Seligman, & Teasdale (1978) proposed a reformulated learned helplessness model of depression that postulated when faced with negative events, individuals who attribute the negative events to internal, global, and stable causes are more likely to become depressed than individuals without this attributional style. Such an attributional style leads individuals to expect that no action will control the outcome of similar events, resulting in helplessness, hopelessness, passivity, and depression (Abramson, Metalsky, & Alloy, 1989).

Several studies have found that depressive symptoms are positively correlated with the tendency to make internal, stable, and global attributions for negative events and external, specific, and unstable attributions for positive events (see reviews in Dodge, 1993 and Quiggle, Garber, Panak, & Dodge, 1992). This attributional style has been shown to predict future depressive symptoms and diagnosis in children (Kaslow, Rehm, & Siegel, 1984; Nolen-Hoeksema, Girus, & Seligmen, 1992). Depressed children demonstrate a bias toward viewing their future as hopeless and their own abilities as lacking (Kazdin, Rodgers, & Colbus, 1986; Weisz, Sweeney, Profitt, & Carr, 1993). Due to errors in information processing, depressed children demonstrate a propensity to focus on the negative events occurring in their lives to the exclusion of the positive (Stark, Napolitano, Swearer, Schmidt, Jaramillo, & Hoyle, 1996). These errors in information processing are related to the individual's locus of control.

Locus of Control and the Bully/Victim Continuum

Locus of control refers to individuals' beliefs about the causes of events in their lives (Rotter, 1966). Individuals who believe they have control over their environment possess an internal locus of control orientation; whereas, individuals who believe their environment is under the control of forces external to themselves possess an external locus of control. The influence of locus of control is important because it may guide a child's first reaction in a particular situation (Jackson, Frick, & Dravage-Bush, 2000). In addition, researchers have suggested that locus of control may be one cognitive process that contributes to the etiology and maintenance of aggressive behavior (Halloran, Doumas, John, & Margolin, 1999; Romi & Itskowitz, 1990).

Slee (1993) has conducted the only study to date that attempted to investigate the connection between children's locus of control orientation and their bully/ victim status (i.e., bully, victim, or no status). Participants included 76 Australian primary school children, (aged 5 to 7) who were categorized as bullies, victims, or no status based on self- and teacher reports. A pretend story about an imaginary child who began to pick on another child by calling him or her names, pushing, and making fun of the child was read to each participant. The story also stated that the provocation occurred for no apparent reason and occurred repeatedly over a week. After being read the pretend story, the participants were asked why they thought the imaginary child picked on the other child. Responses to this question determined the participants' locus of control orientation. Responses were coded as internal if they referred to factors within the imaginary child and external if they referred to factors external to the imaginary child. The responses of bullies demonstrated a strong association with an external locus of control. No status students' responses were associated with an internal locus of control, while victims' responses failed to demonstrate a preference for internal or external locus of control.

Although only one study to date has looked specifically at locus of control beliefs in relation to bully/victim status, several studies have investigated locus of control beliefs and aggression. Findings support the existence of a positive relationship between external locus of control and aggression (Halloran et al., 1999; Österman, Björkqvist, Lagerspetz, Charpentier, Caprara & Pastorelli). Since bullying is generally considered a form of aggression (Moeller, 2001), participation in bullying behavior may also be related to an external locus of control orientation.

As discussed in this chapter, it appears that students involved in bullying experience depressive symptomatology, including a sense of hopelessness and an external locus of control. It is likely that bullying causes undue stress for those who are victimized (Craig, 1998; Rigby, 1996) which can lead to feelings of depression. Craig (1998) suggests that the depression might be a reflection of the individual's coping style. It is also possible that individuals who display symptoms of depression are probable targets for bullying (Kaltiala-Heino et al., 1999). The victim's behaviors and emotional state may contribute to repeated incidents of bullying. The continued victimization likely perpetuates the internalizing difficulties that the victim experiences (Swearer et al., 2001).

Anxiety and Bullying

Anxiety-related symptoms have also been implicated for youngsters involved in the bully/victim continuum. Anxiety disorders are of the most commonly diagnosed conditions in childhood, with prevalence estimates of approximately 8–17% reported (Costello et al., 1988; Kashani et al., 1987; Kearney, Eisen, & Schaefer, 1995). The experience of anxiety is often marked by an array of emotional, behavioral, and cognitive responses. The overall anxious response typically consists of motoric (e.g., avoidance), physiological (e.g., increased heart rate), and subjective (e.g., fearful thoughts) reactions that interact in complex and diverse ways both within and across individuals (Wicks-Nelson & Israel, 1991).

Children have been found to exhibit a number of negative behavioral and psychological problems in conjunction with symptoms of anxiety. Researchers have frequently reported the connection between anxiety and social incompetence (Grills & Ollendick, 2002; La Greca, Dandes, Wick, Shaw, & Stone, 1988; Strauss, Last, Hersen, & Kazdin, 1988), loneliness (Crick & Ladd, 1993), low self-worth (Bernstein & Garfinkel, 1986; Grills & Ollendick, 2002;

La Greca & Fetter, 1995), and school refusal behaviors (Bernstein & Garfinkel, 1986). Interpersonal difficulties, such as establishing and maintaining social and peer relationships, have also been documented for anxious children. For instance, researchers have noted that anxious children are often viewed as shy or withdrawn and tend to be socially neglected or ignored by their peers (Boulton & Smith, 1994; Strauss, Frame, & Forehand, 1987; Strauss, Lahey, Frick, Frame, & Hynd, 1988).

In recent years, researchers have shown increasing interest in discerning how anxiety might also be involved in peer victimization experiences, with the majority of studies investigating the relation being anxiety and victim status. Anxious behaviors have been described as both preexisting characteristics of victims, as well as consequences of being victimized. Several researchers have observed that victims display internalizing behavior patterns (e.g., withdrawal, isolation; Besag, 1989; Hodges & Perry, 1999; Olweus, 1993; Ross, 1996). Thus, these anxious behaviors may provoke victimization, as bullying peers may view these behaviors as an indication that the victim is weaker or less likely to receive support from others.

More often, anxiety has been proposed to result from or maintain victimization by peers. A child may develop anxious symptoms directly from the victimization experiences or these symptoms may be influenced (e.g., mediated/moderated) by additional factors. Anxious symptoms may develop directly if children respond to victimization with hypervigilance to their surroundings and the opinions of others (Roth, Coles, & Heimberg, 2002). Since a child who has been labeled as a victim tends to continue being bullied years later (Kumpulainen et al., 1999; Olweus, 1997; Perry, Kusel, & Perry 1988), repeated hypervigilance paired with exposure to potentially harmful situations may lead to a generalized anxiety state.

Furthermore, anxiety regarding social situations may be especially likely to develop as bullying typically occurs within social or group settings (Craig & Pepler, 1995). In response to these feelings of anxiety, the child may increasingly attempt to escape or avoid social activities altogether. However, with limited exposure to social activities, children are denied the normative socialization experiences necessary for learning appropriate social skills as well as discovering they can experience positive peer interactions. Relatedly, researchers have found that victims show increased rates of school refusal (Salmon, James, Cassidy, & Javaloyes, 2000), school absenteeism (Slee, 1994), somatic anxiety symptoms (Rigby, 1996), and physical health complaints (Williams, Chambers, Logan, & Robinson, 1996); which may more accurately reflect children's desire to avoid school and thus, victimization. Thus, victimization may lead to anxious behaviors, which perpetuate victimization experiences and subsequently lead to greater anxiety (Roth et al., 2002).

Although it remains unclear whether anxiety primarily serves an initiating or maintaining role, a link between victim status and anxiety symptoms has been clearly demonstrated. Concurrently, higher rates of bullying experiences have been significantly associated with greater anxiety (Craig, 1998; Grills & Ollendick, 2002; Hodges & Perry, 1996; Lagerspetz, Bjoerkqvist, Berts, & King, 1982; Olweus, 1995; Salmon et al., 1998; Swearer et al., 2001) and social anxiety (Boulton & Smith, 1994; Crick & Grotpeter, 1995; Graham & Juvonen, 1998; Grills & Ollendick, 2002; Slee, 1994; Walters & Inderbitzen, 1998), in general. More explicitly, victims have been found to report greater anxiety than bullies or no status (i.e., comparison) children (Bernstein & Watson, 1997; Craig, 1998; Olweus, 1994; Perry et al., 1988; Swearer et al., 2001). Further, Hawker and Boulton's (2000) meta-analysis revealed mean effect sizes significantly greater than zero for both social and generalized anxiety, demonstrating greater levels of these psychosocial adjustment problems in victims than in non-victims. Furthermore, Salmon et al. (2000) found victims to be more anxious than bullies who were equally or less anxious than their peers. Although Lagerspetz et al. (1982) did not find significant differences between bullies and victims based on children's own reports of anxiety, when teachers were asked to freely describe the victims they were depicted by anxious and withdrawn characteristics (e.g., shy and afraid).

Another recent investigation examined relations between a history of being verbally teased and internalizing symptoms in a large sample of college students (Roth et al., 2002). Retrospective reports of victimization from childhood were significantly correlated with adult levels of trait anxiety, social anxiety, worry, and anxiety sensitivity (as well as depression). Comparison of the correlation coefficients obtained for the various measures of anxiety revealed stronger associations for victimization with social anxiety, trait anxiety, and anxiety sensitivity (which did not differ from one another) than for worry. Thus, although bullying behaviors have been reported to decrease with age (Byrne, 1994; Salmivalli, Lappalainen, & Lagerspetz, 1998), the negative effects of experiencing peer victimization in childhood have been found to persist into the adolescent and early adult years (Kumpulainen et al., 1999; Olweus, 1993; Roth et al., 2002).

An alternative pathway to anxiety involves the possible mediating or moderating role of other pertinent variables such as self-blame or self-worth. For example, Graham and Juvonen (1998) found the victim-maladjustment (i.e., social anxiety, loneliness) relation to be partially mediated by characterological self-blame. Similarly, internalizing problems may result in children who incorporate the negative feedback inherent in being bullied into their self-views (Crick & Bigbee, 1998; Olweus, 1993, 1997). Thus, damage to one's perceptions of self-worth may be an additional mechanism through which peer victimization experiences can result in increased anxiety.

A recent study illustrated the self-worth-anxiety connection for children who experience frequent bullying as a stressor. Grills and Ollendick (2002) examined the possible mediating and moderating role of self-worth in 280 middle school children. Analyses revealed a mediating role of self-worth for girls, suggesting that victimization experiences negatively influenced girls' views of themselves and helped explain the elevated levels of anxiety also reported by them. For boys, self-worth moderated the peer victimization-anxiety relation, such that fewer anxiety symptoms were reported by victimized boys who reported having high self-worth as compared with victimized boys who indicated lower self-worth.

As previously noted, there is a paucity of literature specifically directed toward explaining the possible role of anxiety for bullies. Therefore, existing proposals tend to be drawn from studies of aggression in children. Two main hypotheses regarding anxiety and aggression have been put forth. The first of these suggests that the presence of comorbid anxiety may increase aggressive responses in children. For example, Kashani, Dueser, and Reid's (1991) study revealed significant associations between anxiety and physical as well as verbal aggression. That is, for some children anxiety may be seen as a weakness that they try to compensate for by acting aggressively with peers. Alternatively, anxious feelings may put the child on alert for signs of danger within interpersonal situations. In line with this notion, Barrett, Rapee, Dadds, and Ryan (1996) reported that anxious children tended to misinterpret ambiguous situations as threatening. Thus in some instances, an anxious child may misinterpret the intentions of others (e.g., being brushed past by another child is interpreted as starting a fight) and react in an aggressive or "retaliatory" manner towards the perceived threat.

The second theory proposes that anxiety may mitigate aggressive responses in children; perhaps due to increased caution or inhibition of feelings. Support for this theory comes from studies demonstrating less aggressive reactions in children with comorbid symptoms of anxiety. To illustrate, Walker et al. (1991) found fewer peer-reported descriptions of aggression for children who had conduct disorder with comorbid anxiety as compared with children who had conduct disorder only (without comorbid anxiety).

Overall, research findings for bullying and anxiety have been inconsistent. For instance, Craig (1998) found involvement in relational and verbal bullying each predicted anxiety in middle school children. Similarly, studies by Kaltiala-Heino et al. (2000) as well as by Duncan (1999) revealed similarly elevated rates of anxiety in bullies and victims as compared with not involved children. However, in contrast to these studies, others have reported no evidence of increased anxiety in bullies (Lagerspetz et al., 1982; Olweus, 1994; Salmon et al., 2000). Therefore, it is difficult to draw any firm conclusions regarding the role of anxiety in bullies.

In summary, anxiety has been implicated as a correlate of all aspects of victimization (i.e., victim, bully-victim, bully), with the overall greatest evidence of impairment reported for victims and bully-victims. However, the exact role of anxiety (e.g., precipitates, provokes, maintains, follows) in these relations remains unclear. Thus, the next step for research on the relationship between internalizing problems and bullying should be to conduct longitudinal studies with the goal of more clearly determining the nature of this relation. Future studies should also further investigate possible differences in the expression of anxious and depressive symptomatology for the various subtypes along the bully/victim continuum. Furthermore, researchers should continue to explore potential mediators and moderators of internalizing symptoms in order to best understand this relation as well as develop the most effective intervention and prevention strategies.

Bully-Victims: Vulnerability for Internalizing Problems

The notion of bully/victims appears to closely resemble Olweus' (1993, 1997) description of provocative victims. According to Olweus, provocative victims tend to evidence a combination of anxious and aggressive behaviors as well as frequently display hyperactive behavior problems and retaliate when victimized. A recent study of personality characteristics found this group to share components of victims (high neuroticism) and bullies (high psychoticism) as compared with not involved children (Mynard & Joseph, 2000). Thus, it appears that being both a bully and a victim is related to greater internalizing difficulties.

Although some have suggested that bully-victims are the most significantly impaired in terms of overall adjustment difficulties (Craig, 1998; Rigby, 1996; Swearer et al., 2001), few studies have specifically examined the possible role of anxiety in mediating bullying and victimization. The investigations that have been conducted have generally found increased levels of anxiety in children classified as bully-victims. To illustrate, the previously described studies by Kaltiala-Heino et al. (2000) and Duncan (1999) found anxiety symptoms (as well as depression) to be highest for bully-victims, followed by bullies and victims (all of whom reported greater anxiety than not participating and rarely involved children). Although not quite as high as the victim-only group, bully-victims in Craig's (1998) study were also found to have higher anxiety scores than bullies and comparison children.

Translating Research Into Practice: Implications for Bullying-Prevention and Intervention Programs

Given the findings that students who do not participate in bullying report the lowest levels of psychopathology when compared to students involved in bullying (Austin & Joseph, 1996; Kumpulainen et al., 2001; Swearer et al., 2001), it is imperative that researchers and educators find effective mechanisms to reduce involvement in bullying. Effective bullying intervention or prevention programs should be designed to simultaneously target all aspects of children's lives including peers, family, schools, and the larger community (Colvin, Tobin, Beard, Hagan, & Sprague, 1998; Hanish & Guerra, 2000). Hanish and Guerra (2000) noted that this type of approach attempts to prevent the efforts of change at one level (e.g., school) from being overshadowed by tendencies at another (e.g., home). Similarly, several authors have warned against only targeting individual children (e.g., victims) for interventions (Colvin et al., 1998; Hanish & Guerra, 2000). Rather, including all children has been suggested to be more effective (Salmivalli, 1999), such that it allows for modification of the entire peer group.

This review suggests that students who are involved in the bully/victim continuum are at increased risk for depression, anxiety, and related difficulties (i.e., external locus of control, increased sense of hopelessness, and low self-esteem). These difficulties can range from adjustment problems to more serious consequences, including suicide. Hazler and Carney (2000) conceptualize bullying as part of the lower end of a violence continuum, with murder and suicide being at the opposite end. This continuum demonstrates how bullying behaviors can lead to extreme responses. Given the relationship between suicidal ideation and bullying, effective interventions must address internalizing symptoms in addition to externalizing symptoms (Swearer et al., 2001).

Suggested Interventions for Depression

Individuals along the bully/victim continuum experiencing hopelessness would likely benefit from a therapeutic component that includes increasing positive views of the future. Abramson et al. (1989) suggested two therapeutic approaches to treating hopelessness: (1) a direct approach to treating hopelessness including reattribution training, and (2) an indirect treatment approach including a modification of the environment that induces hopefulness through pleasant-events scheduling. Both problem-solving training and cognitive restructuring have been suggested as intervention strategies for hopelessness (Stark, Sander, Yancy, Bronik, & Hoke, 2000); thus, targeting the individual's attributions or behaviors that contribute to the hopelessness are therapeutic approaches that can be utilized as a component of bullying-intervention programs.

Group treatments for depression have also been found to be effective. Lewinsohn, Clarke, Hops, and Andrews (1990) conducted a study that examined the effectiveness of a cognitive-behavioral group intervention for adolescents with depression in comparison to a wait-list group. The study consisted of two treatment groups that both utilized the same adolescent group, while one also included a parent component. Both group treatment interventions were found to be effective in reducing the adolescents' level of depression. The group intervention for the adolescents included teaching specific skills to increase pleasurable activities, techniques to control depressive thoughts, relaxation, and skills to improve social interaction. Group treatment may be useful for victims and bully-victims who are depressed. However, previous research suggests that group interventions are *not* useful for aggressive youth (Dishion, McCord, & Poulin, 1999); therefore, group approaches should be used cautiously with bullies.

In order to identify and implement appropriate and efficacious interventions for bullying and victimization, the status a student endorses along the bully/victim continuum must be considered. Students who both are bullied and who bully others (bully-victims) have been reported to be the most at-risk for depression (Kaltiala-Heino et al., 1999; Kumpulainen et al., 2001; Swearer et al., 2001). Interventions for bully-victims need to address the internalizing symptomatology, as well as the aggressive (i.e., bullying) behaviors (Kaltiala-Heino et al., 1999). A treatment manual such as *ACTION: A Workbook for Overcoming Depression* (Stark et al., 1996) in combination with the *Keeping Your Cool: The Anger Management Workbook* (Nelson & Finch, 1996) can be a useful strategy for working with bully-victims who are experiencing depressive symptomatology.

Suggested Interventions for Anxiety

Interventions targeted for individuals experiencing victimization should be appropriate to the characteristics the victim displays. A passive victim is likely to express symptoms of depression and would benefit from a therapeutic intervention addressing the development of increased self-esteem (Carney & Merrell, 2001) and alternative coping skills (Batsche, 1997). Depression might be a reflection of the victim's coping style (Craig, 1998). Therefore, utilizing bullying interventions that teach alternative coping methods, such as assertiveness training, could help in reducing continued victimization (Smith, Shu, & Madsen, 2001). A provocative victim is more likely to benefit from an intervention aimed at reducing his or her level of aggression (Batsche, 1997). This approach should teach students skills that can be used in place of the aggressive behaviors (i.e., aggression replacement training).

It is also important to distinguish between depressive and anxious symptoms when intervening with students along the bully/victim continuum. Lonigan, Carey, and Finch (1994) conducted a study that examined self-reported depression and anxiety among 233 inpatient children aged 6 to 17, who were diagnosed with either an anxiety disorder or a depressive disorder. The authors reported that although there was some overlap between self-reports of depression and anxiety, there were characteristics that distinguished between children diagnosed with depression and those diagnosed with anxiety. Children who were diagnosed with a depressive disorder reported less satisfaction with themselves and more difficulties with loss of interest and motivation than anxious children. Anxious children endorsed more distress about the future, their happiness, and how others respond to them. It is important that interventions address the different needs of individuals possessing depressive or anxious symptomatology.

Although interventions have not been designed to specifically target children who are both involved in victimization and display symptoms of anxiety, several more general strategies from the literature on anxiety can be applied to this population. It is also often important to include peers in the treatment of socially anxious children in order to provide practice as well as naturalistic exposure opportunities. Peer relations research showing greater improvement for treatments including non-problematic peers versus those that have not (Bierman & Furman, 1984) provide further support for these proposals.

Specific treatments for generalized as well as social anxiety have been developed and empirically supported for children and may be applicable to victims of bullying who display these characteristics. For example, the *Coping Cat* (cf. Kendall, Kane, Howard, & Siqueland, 1990) is an empirically supported treatment that has been developed for children with generalized anxiety. Similarly, treatment manuals are available for working with children who have social anxiety, such as *Cognitive Behavioral Group Treatment for Adolescents* (cf. Albano, Marten, Holt, Heimberg, & Barlow, 1995) or *Social Effectiveness Therapy for Children* (cf. Beidel, Turner, & Morris, 1996; 1999). These approaches are generally designed for individual or small group treatment, but could also be utilized by school counselors. Likewise, components of these interventions could be incorporated into larger school-based efforts to provide children with anxiety reduction skills.

Similarly, it seems that most children can benefit from learning strategies used in the treatment of anxiety. Relaxation training teaches children a skill that could be applied at any point when they might feel tense or anxious. For example, children can be taught to relax muscle groups in order to release tension from their body (i.e., progressive muscle relaxation). In addition, breathing retraining exercises can be taught to reduce anxiety and calm the child during times of stress. Scripts for these procedures are available and can be employed to teach progressive muscle relaxation and breathing retraining skills that help the child feel more relaxed in anxiety-producing situations. Younger children may benefit from scripts that include imagery (e.g., pretend you are squeezing a lemon to illustrate muscle relaxation) or facilitate appropriate practice of the skill (e.g., placing a plastic cup on the stomach to demonstrate diaphragmatic breathing). Anxiety management strategies can be taught individually or in small groups to maximize cooperation and minimize disruption.

Social skills training may be important for children involved in bullying such that it provides useful strategies for interacting with peers in a positive manner. The main goal of social skills training is introducing and reviewing techniques that will assist children in the initiation and maintenance of peer relationships. Social skills training programs generally include the following components: modeling, coaching, rehearsal, feedback, and reinforcement (Gresham, 2002). To begin, a specific social skill should be targeted (e.g., positive conflict resolution) and thoroughly described and discussed within the classroom. The instructor should also model the skill to demonstrate the appropriate enactment of it. Following this, children should be directed to role-play the skill and practice should continue until all children are comfortable with it. Next, peers should be encouraged to describe both positive and negative aspects of the role play. The final step involves the application of the social skill to an actual situation with reinforcement for completion of this step.

LaGreca and Fetter (1995) have identified several skills important for positive peer interactions (i.e., showing enjoyment of interactions, greeting, joining, inviting, conversation, sharing/cooperation, complimenting/giving positive feedback, and conflict resolution) as well as the key components for each of these. Social skills training programs have been successfully utilized with children who are rejected or low in acceptance (Bierman & Furman, 1984). Likewise, Hanish and Guerra (2000) found children identified as high risk for victimization by peers to respond favorably to social skills training. Social skills training programs have also been successfully used with aggressive and antisocial youths in individual, group, and classroom settings (Kazdin, Esveldt-Dawson, French, & Unis, 1987; Ollendick & Hersen, 1979; Ollendick & Winett, 1984), suggesting the appropriateness of this strategy for bullies as well. Furthermore, a number of social skills training programs are available for clinicians to select among to best suit the population targeted (cf. Colvin et al., 1998).

Assertiveness training and social problem solving have also been recommended for children involved in peer victimization (Salmivalli, 1999). That is, victims of bullying who withdraw or show other signs of anxiety as well as counteraggression (i.e., bully-victims) may benefit from alternative responses to peer attacks. For example, Salmivalli, Karhunen, and Lagerspetz (1996) found bullying was more likely to reoccur in children who reacted to bullying with withdrawn/helpless behaviors (e.g., crying) or reciprocal aggressiveness, whereas bullying was found to decrease for children who responded calmly or in a way that portrayed them as unaffected. Thus, in addition to the previously described anxiety management strategies, children may benefit from learning alternative ways to cope with bullying (e.g., walking away, asserting their rights). Similarly, assertiveness training may benefit uninvolved children (i.e., neither victims nor bullies) by teaching various techniques such as how to stand up for a child who is being bullied or to alert a teacher instead of watching and/or encouraging the bully (Salmivalli, 1999). However, it seems likely that successful incorporation of assertiveness training should also include training of school staff and administrators. That is, school personnel should provide support to the victimized child who asserts his/her rights as well as be trained to appropriately address and deal with victimization.

An additional approach that appears to merge the anxiety and victimization intervention literatures is that of peer involvement strategies. Peers are often involved in the previously described strategies; however for anxious children, particularly those with social anxiety concerns, peer involvement plays a crucial role. For example, Beidel and Turner (1998) have included "peer generalization" in their treatment of socially phobic adolescents such that practice of skills with nonanxious peers is incorporated into the treatment procedures. Further exposing anxious children to peers through structured extracurricular and after-school activities may also be beneficial to provide positive peer experiences which may reduce anxiety regarding these interactions. In addition, involvement in these activities would likely foster friendships, which in turn, could reduce bullying behaviors.

Peer-pairing or intergroup intervention techniques have also been suggested for children with peer relationship (LaGreca & Fetter, 1995) or victimization problems (Kenrick, Neuberg, & Cialdini, 1999). Support for the use of these strategies can be ascertained from research findings regarding peer cliques or groups. For example, children within their respective groups are more likely to victimize an out-group member before another in-group member (Kenrick et al., 1999). Thus, pairing peers from diverse groups or with different skill levels during cooperative peer activities may assist rejected or victimized peers in terms of gaining access into different cliques or networks. Specifically, interpersonal contact among different groups has been found to reduce intergroup hostility when utilized within certain conditions. For example, when paired with certain educational programs, especially those that teach perspective-taking and problem-solving skills, intergroup contact has been shown to increase tolerance of out-group members (Landis & Brislin, 1983; Schaller, Asp, Rosell, & Heim, 1996). Furthermore, research has found that intergroup conflict is most successfully reduced when: the groups interact on an individual level (Pettigrew, 1997); the groups work together toward common goals (Cook, 1985); and the out-group members possess abilities that challenge the negative stereotypes of their groups (Blanchard, Weigel, & Cook, 1975).

Several researchers and educators (Aronson, Blaney, Stephan, Sikes, & Snapp, 1978; DeVries & Slavin, 1978; Johnson, Johnson, & Maruyama, 1984; Johnson & Johnson, 1994; Stevens & Slavin, 1995) have proposed ways to restructure the classroom environment to foster intergroup cooperation. For example, the *Jigsaw Classroom*, designed by Aronson and colleagues (1978) could be modified and applied to reduce victimization and associated feelings of anxiety. To illustrate, children could be separated into small mixed victimization and anxiety status groups, with related assignments given to each student for independent research. Following the Jigsaw Classroom approach, these students would then regroup and convey their knowledge and findings to one another. Since each student's assignment is only one piece of the puzzle, he or she depends on the five classmates to learn the whole lesson (Aronson et al., 1978). Each child has equal responsibilities and one-on-one involvement with the other team members. Research has shown that students in these types of cooperative classrooms are not only likely to improve their grades (Johnson & Johnson, 1994; Stevens & Slavin, 1995), but are also more likely to reduce hostility toward previously identified outgroup members (Johnson et al., 1984; Miller & Brewer, 1984).

Summary

Anxiety-disorder treatment manuals (or components thereof) and depressive disorder treatment manuals (or components thereof) may be most beneficial for children who show clinically significant levels of anxious and depressive behaviors and need individualized treatment. Furthermore, several skill-building approaches (i.e., anxiety management, social-skills training, coping-skills training, pleasant-events scheduling, assertiveness training, problem solving, and peer cooperativeness/mediation) that may be applied on a more universal level, may be beneficial in helping students cope with bullying. It seems likely that a combination of several of these approaches may be most beneficial for reducing peer conflicts as well as any associated symptoms of depression and anxiety among children involved in bullying. However, research that examines the effectiveness of the aforementioned various techniques and their effect on bullying and victimization is greatly needed. Future research should attempt to determine which of these strategies (either alone or in combination) are most successful at helping students respond effectively to the psychological consequences of bullying.

REFERENCES

Abramson, L. Y., Metalsky, G. I., & Alloy, L. B. (1989). Hopelessness depression: A theory-based subtype of depression. *Psychological Review, 96,* 358–372.

Abramson, L. Y., Seligman, M. E. P., & Teasdale, J. (1978). Learned helplessness in humans: Critique and reformulation. *Journal of Abnormal Psychology, 87,* 49–74.

Albano, A. M., Marten, P. A., Holt, C. S., Heimberg, R. G., & Barlow, D. H. (1995). Cognitive-behavioral group treatment for social phobia in adolescents: A preliminary study. *The Journal of Nervous and Mental Disease, 183,* 649–656.

Andreou, E. (2000). Bully/victim problems and their association with psychological constructs in 8 to 12-year-old-greek schoolchildren. *Aggressive Behavior, 26,* 49–56.

Aronson, E., Blaney, N., Stephan, C., Sikes, J., & Snapp, M. (1978). *The jigsaw classroom.* Beverly Hills, CA: Sage.

Austin, S., & Joseph, S. (1996). Assessment of bully/victim problems in 8- to 11-year-olds. *British Journal of Educational Psychology, 66,* 447–456.

Barrett, P. M., Rapee, R. M., Dadds, M. M., & Ryan, S. M. (1996). Family enhancement of cognitive style in anxious and aggressive children. *Journal of Abnormal Child Psychology, 24,* 187–203.

Batsche, G. M. (1997). Bullying. In G. G. Bear, K. M. Minke, & A. Thomas (Eds.), *Children's needs II: Development, problems and alternatives* (pp. 171–179). Bethesda, IN: National Association of School Psychologists.

Beidel, D. C., & Turner. S. M. (1998). *Shy children, phobic adults: Nature and treatment of social phobia.* Washington, DC: American Psychiatric Association.

Beidel, D. C., Turner, S. M., & Morris, T. L. (1996). *Social effectiveness therapy for children: A treatment manual.* Unpublished manuscript, Medical University of South Carolina.

Beidel, D. C., Turner, S. M., & Morris, T. L. (1999). Psychopathology of childhood social phobia. *Journal of the American Academy of Child and Adolescent Psychiatry, 38,* 643–650.

Bernstein, G. A., & Garfinkel, B. D. (1986). School phobia: The overlap of affective and anxiety disorders. *Journal of the American Academy of Child Psychiatry, 25,* 235–241.

Bernstein, J. Y., & Watson, M. W. (1997). Children who are targets of bullying: A victim pattern. *Journal of Interpersonal Violence, 12*, 483–498.

Besag, V. E. (1989). *Bullies and victims in schools.* Milton Keynes: Open University Press.

Bierman, K. L., & Furman, W. (1984). The effects of social-skills training and peer involvement on the social adjustment of preadolescents. *Child Development, 55*, 151–162.

Biggam, F. H., & Power, K. G. (1999). Social problem-solving skills and psychological distress among incarcerated young offenders: The issue of bullying and victimization. *Cognitive Therapy and Research, 23*, 307–326.

Blanchard, F. A., Weigel, R. H., & Cook, S. W. (1975). The effect of relative competence of group members upon interpersonal attraction in cooperating interracial groups. *Journal of Personality and Social Psychology, 32*, 519–530.

Boulton, M. J., & Smith, P. K. (1994). Bully/victim problems in middle school children: Stability, self perceived competence, peer perceptions and peer acceptance. *British Journal of Developmental Psychology, 12*, 315–329.

Boulton, M. J., & Underwood, K. (1992). Bully/victim problems among middle school children. *British Journal of Educational Psychology, 62*, 73–87.

Byrne, B. (1994). *Coping with bullying in schools.* New York: Cassell Villiers House.

Callaghan, S., & Joseph, S. (1995). Self-concept and peer victimization among schoolchildren. *Personality and Individual Differences, 18*, 161–163.

Carney, A. G., & Merrell, K. W. (2001). Bullying in schools: Perspectives on understanding and preventing an international problem. *School Psychology International, 22*, 364–382.

Colvin, G., Tobin, T., Beard, K., Hagan, S., & Sprague, J. (1998). The school bully: Assessing the problem, developing interventions, and future research directions. *Journal of Behavioral Education, 8*, 293–319.

Cook, S. W. (1985). Experimenting on social issues: The case of school desegregation. *American Psychologist, 40*, 452–460.

Costello, E. J., Costello, A. J., Edelbrock, C., Burns, B. J., Dulcan, M. K., Brent, D., & Janiszewski, S. (1988). Psychiatric disorders in pediatric primary care: Prevalence and risk factors, *Archives of General Psychiatry, 45*, 1107–1116.

Craig, W. M. (1998). The relationship among bullying, victimization, depression, anxiety, and aggression in elementary school children. *Personality and Individual Differences, 24*, 123–130.

Craig, W. M., & Pepler, D. J. (1995). Peer processes in bullying and victimization: A naturalistic study. *Exceptionality Education in Canada, 4*, 81–95.

Crick, N. R., & Bigbee, M. A. (1998). Relational and overt forms of peer victimization: A multi-informant approach. *Journal of Consulting and Clinical Psychology, 66*, 337–347.

Crick, N. R., & Grotpeter, J. K. (1995). Relational aggression, gender, and social-psychological adjustment. *Child Development, 66*, 710–722.

Crick, N. R., & Ladd, G. W. (1993). Children's perceptions of their peer experiences: Attributions, loneliness, social anxiety, and social avoidance. *Developmental Psychology, 29*, 244–254.

DeVries, D. L., & Slavin, R. E. (1978). Teams-games-tournament (TGT): Review of 10 classroom experiments. *Journal of Research and Development in Education, 12*, 28–38.

Dishion, T. J., McCord, J., & Poulin, F. (1999). When interventions harm: Peer groups and problem behavior. *American Psychologist, 54*, 755–764.

Dodge, K. A. (1993). Social-cognitive mechanisms in the development of conduct disorder and depression. *Annual Reviews of Psychology, 44*, 559–584.

Duncan, R. D. (1999). Peer and sibling aggression: An investigation of intra- and extrafamilial bullying. *Journal of Interpersonal Violence, 14*, 871–886.

Egan, S. K., & Perry, D. G. (1998). Does low self-regard invite victimization? *Developmental Psychology, 34*, 299–309.

Graham, S., & Juvonen, J. (1998). Self-blame and peer victimization in middle school: An attributional analysis. *Developmental Psychology, 34*, 587–599.

Gresham, F. M. (2002). Best practices in social-skills training. In A. Thomas & J. Grimes, *Best Practices in School Psychology – IV* (pp. 1029–1040). Bethesda, MD: NASP.

Grills, A. E., & Ollendick, T. H. (2002). Peer victimization, global self-worth, and anxiety in middle school children. *Journal of Clinical Child and Adolescent Psychology, 31*, 59–68.

Halloran, E. C., Doumas, D. M., John, R. S., & Margolin, G. (1999). The relationship between aggression in children and locus of control beliefs. *Journal of Genetic Psychology, 160*, 5–21.

Hanish, L. D., & Guerra, N. G. (2000). Children who get victimized at school: What is known? What can be done? *Professional School Counseling, 4*, 113–119.

Hanish, L. D., & Guerra, N. G. (2002). A longitudinal analysis of patterns of adjustment following peer victimization. *Development and Psychopathology, 14*, 69–89.

Haynie, D. L., Nansel, T., Eitel, P., Crump, A. D., Saylor, K., Yu, K., et al. (2001). Bullies, victims, and bully/victims: Distinct groups of at-risk youth. *Journal of Early Adolescence, 21*, 29–49.

Hazler, R. J., & Carney, J. V. (2000). When victims turn aggressors: Factors in the development of deadly school violence. *Professional School Counseling, 4*, 105–112.

Hodges, E., & Perry, D. (1996). Victims of peer abuse: An overview. *Journal of Emotional and Behavioral Problems, 5*, 23–28.

Hodges, E., & Perry, D. (1999). Personal and interpersonal antecedents and consequences of victimization by peers. *Journal of Personality and Social Psychology, 76*, 677–685.

Jackson, Y., Frick, P., & Dravage-Bush, J. (2000). Perceptions of control in children with externalizing and mixed behavior disorders. *Child Psychiatry and Human Development, 31*, 43–58.

Johnson, D. W., & Johnson, R. T. (1994). Cooperative learning in the culturally diverse classroom. In R. DeVillar, C. Fultis, & J. Cummings (Eds.), *Cultural diversity in schools*. New York: SUNY Press.

Johnson, D. W., Johnson, R., & Maruyama, G. (1984). Goal interdependence and interpersonal attraction in heterogeneous classrooms: A meta-analysis. In N. Miller & M. B. Brewer (Eds.), *Groups in Contact* (pp. 187–213). New York: Academic Press.

Kaltiala-Heino, R., Rimpela, M., Marttunen, M., Rimpela, A., & Rantanen, P. (1999). Bullying, depression, and suicidal ideation in Finnish adolescents: School survey. *British Medical Journal, 319*, 348–351.

Kaltiala-Heino, R., Rimpela, M., Rantanen, P., & Rimpela, A. (2000). Bullying at school: An indicator of adolescents at risk for mental disorders. *Journal of Adolescence, 23*, 661–674.

Kashani, J. H., Beck, N. C., Hoeper, E. W., Fallahi, C., Corcoran, C. M., McAllister, J. A., Rosenberg, T. K., & Reid, J. C. (1987). Psychiatric disorders in a community sample of adolescents. *American Journal of Psychiatry, 144*, 584–589.

Kashani, J. H., Deuser, W., & Reid, J. C. (1991). Aggression and anxiety: A new look at an old notion. *Journal of the American Academy of Child and Adolescent Psychiatry, 30*, 218–223.

Kaslow, N. J., Brown, R. T., & Mee, L. L. (1994). Cognitive and behavioral correlates of childhood depression: A developmental perspective. In W. M. Reynolds & H. F. Johnston (Eds.), *Handbook of depression in children and adolescents* (pp. 97–121). New York: Plenum.

Kaslow, N. J., Rehm, L. P., & Siegel, A. W. (1984). Social-cognitive and cognitive correlates of depression in children. *Journal of Abnormal Child Psychology, 12*, 605–620.

Kazdin, A. E., Esveldt-Dawson, K., French, N. H., & Unis, A. S. (1987). Problem-solving skills training and relationship therapy in the treatment of antisocial child behavior. *Journal of Consulting and Clinical Psychology, 55*, 76–85.

Kazdin, A. E., French, N. H., Unis, A. S., Esveldt-Dawson, K., & Sherick, R. B. (1983). Hopelessness, depression, and suicidal intent among psychiatrically disturbed inpatient children. *Journal of Consulting and Clinical Psychology, 51*, 504–510.

Kazdin, A. E., Rodgers, A., & Colbus, D. (1986). The hopelessness scale for children: Psychometric characteristics and concurrent validity. *Journal of Consulting and Clinical Psychology, 54*, 241–245.

Kearney, C. A., Eisen, A. R., & Schaefer, C. E. (1995). General issues underlying the diagnosis and treatment of child and adolescent anxiety disorders. In A. R. Eisen, C. A. Kearney,

& C. E. Schaefer (Eds.), *Clinical handbook of anxiety disorders in children and adolescents.* New Jersey: Jason Aronson, Inc.

Kendall, P. C., Kane, M., Howard, B., & Siqueland, L. (1990). *Cognitive-Behavioral Treatment of Anxious Children: Treatment Manual.* Available from the author, Department of Psychology, Temple University, Philadelphia, PA.

Kenrick, D. T., Neuberg, S. L., & Cialdini, R. B. (1999). *Social psychology: Unraveling the mystery.* Boston: Allyn and Bacon.

Kovacs, M., & Beck, A. T. (1977). An empirical-clinical approach toward a definition of childhood depression. In J. G. Schulterbrandt & A. Raskin (Eds.), *Depression in childhood: Diagnosis, treatment, and conceptual models* (pp. 1–25). New York: Raven.

Kumpulainen, K., Räsänen, E., & Henttonen, I. (1999). Children involved in bullying: Psychological disturbance and the persistence of the involvement. *Child Abuse and Neglect, 23,* 1253–1262.

Kumpulainen, K., Räsänen, E., & Puura, K. (2001). Psychiatric disorders and the use of mental health services among children involved in bullying. *Aggressive Behavior, 27,* 102–110.

Lagerspetz, K. M., Bjoerkqvist, K., Berts, M., & King, E. (1982). Group aggression among school children in three schools. *Scandinavian Journal of Psychology, 23,* 45–52.

LaGreca, A. M., Dandes, S. K., Wick, P., Shaw, K., & Stone, W. L. (1988). Development of the social anxiety scale for children: Reliability and concurrent validity. *Journal of Clinical Child Psychology, 17,* 84–91.

LaGreca, A. M., & Fetter, M. D. (1995). Peer relations. In A. R. Eisen, C. A. Kearney, & C. E. Schaefer (Eds.), *Clinical handbook of anxiety disorders in children and adolescents.* New Jersey: Jason Aronson Inc.

Landis, D., & Brislin, R. W. (1983). *Handbook of intercultural training.* New York: Pergamon.

Lewinsohn, P. M., Clarke, G. N., Hops, H., & Andrews, J. (1990). Cognitive-behavioral treatment for depressed adolescents. *Behavior Therapy, 21,* 385–401.

Lonigan, C. J., Carey, M. P., & Finch, A. J., Jr. (1994). Anxiety and depression in children and adolescents: Negative affectivity and the utility of self-reports. *Journal of Consulting and Clinical Psychology, 62,* 1000–1008.

Marciano, P. L., & Kazdin, A. E. (1994). Self-esteem, depression, hopelessness, and suicidal intent among psychiatrically disturbed inpatient children. *Journal of Clinical Child Psychology, 23,* 151–160.

Miller, N., & Brewer, M. B. (1984). *Groups in contact.* New York: Academic Press.

Moeller, T. G. (2001). *Youth aggression and violence: A psychological approach.* Mahwah, NJ: Lawrence Erlbaum Associates, Publishers.

Mynard, H., & Joseph, S. (2000). Development of the multidimensional peer-victimization scale. *Aggressive Behavior, 26,* 169–178.

Neary, A., & Joseph, S. (1994). Peer victimization and its relationship to self-concept and depression among school children. *Personality and Individual Differences, 16,* 183–186.

Nelson, W. M., III, & Finch, A. J., Jr. (1996). *Keeping your cool: The anger management workbook* (Parts 1 and 2). Ardmore, PA: Workbook Publishing.

Nolen-Hoksema, S., Girus, J., & Seligman, M. (1992). Predictors and consequences of childhood depressive symptoms: A 5-year longitudinal study. *Journal of Abnormal Psychology, 101,* 405–422.

Ollendick, T. H., & Hersen, M. (1979). Social skills training for juvenile delinquents. *Behaviour Research and Therapy, 17,* 547–554.

Ollendick, T. H., & Winett, R. A. (1984). Primary prevention of child behavior problems. In P. H. Bornstein & A. E. Kazdin (Eds.), *Handbook of clinical behavior therapy with children* (pp. 805–832). Homewood, IL: Dorsey Press.

Olweus, D. (1993). Bully/victim problems among schoolchildren: Long-term consequences and an effective intervention program. In S. Hodgins (Ed.), *Mental disorders and crime.* Newbury Park, CA: Sage.

Olweus, D. (1994). Annotation: Bullying at school: Basic facts and effects of a school-based intervention program. *Journal of Child Psychology and Psychiatry, 35*, 1171–1190.

Olweus, D. (1995). Bullying or peer abuse at school: Facts and intervention. *Current Directions in Psychological Science, 4*, 196–200.

Olweus, D. (1997). Bully/victim problems in school: Knowledge base and an effective intervention program. *The Irish Journal of Psychology, 18*, 170–190.

O'Moore, M., & Kirkham, C. (2001). Self-esteem and its relationship to bullying behaviour. *Aggressive Behavior, 27*, 269–283.

Österman, K., Björkqvist, K., Lagerspetz, K., Charpentier, S., Caprara, G., & Pastorelli, C. (1999). Locus of control and three types of aggression. *Aggressive Behavior, 25* 61–65.

Perry, D. G., Kusel, S., & Perry, L. (1988). Victims of peer aggression. *Developmental Psychology, 24*, 807–814.

Pettigrew, T. F. (1997). Generalized intergroup contact effects on prejudice. *Personality and Social Psychology Bulletin, 23*, 173–185.

Quiggle, N. L., Garber, J., Panak, W. F., & Dodge, K. A. (1992). Social information processing in aggressive and depressed children. *Child Development, 63*, 1305–1320.

Rigby, K. (1996). *Bullying in schools: And what to do about it*. The Australian Council for Educational Research.

Romi, S., & Itskowitz, R. (1990). The relationship between locus of control and type of aggression in middle-class and culturally deprived children. *Personality and Individual Differences, 11*, 327–333.

Ross, D. M. (1996). *Childhood bullying and teasing: What school personnel, other professionals, and parents can do*. Alexandria, VA: American Counseling Association.

Roth, D. A., Coles, M. E., & Heimberg, R. G. (2002). The relationship between memories for childhood teasing and anxiety and depression in adulthood. *Journal of Anxiety Disorders, 16*, 149–164.

Rotter, J. B. (1966). Generalized expectancies for internal versus external control of reinforcement. *Psychological Monographs: General and Applied, 80*, 1–28.

Salmivalli, C. (1999). Participant role approach to school bullying: Implications for intervention. *Journal of Adolescence, 22*, 453–459.

Salmivalli, C., Karhunen, J., & Lagerspetz, K. M. J. (1996). How do the victims respond to bullying? *Aggressive Behavior, 22*, 99–109.

Salmivalli, C., Lappalainen, M., & Lagerspetz, K. M. J. (1998). Stability and change of behavior in connection with bullying in schools: A two-year follow-up. *Aggressive Behavior, 24*, 205–218.

Salmon, G., James, A., Cassidy, E. L., & Javaloyes, M. A. (2000). Bullying a review: Presentations to an adolescent psychiatric service and within a school for emotionally and behaviourally disturbed children. *Clinical Child Psychology and Psychiatry, 5*, 563–579.

Schaller, M., Asp, C. H., Rosell, M. C., & Heim, S. J. (1996). Training in statistical reasoning inhibits the formation of erroneous group stereotypes. *Personality and Social Psychology Bulletin, 22*, 829–844.

Slee, P. T. (1993). Bullying: A preliminary investigation of its nature and the effects of social cognition. *Early Child Development and Care, 87*, 47–57.

Slee, P. T. (1994). Situational and interpersonal correlates of anxiety associated with peer victimization. *Child Psychiatry and Human Development, 25*, 97–107.

Slee, P. T., & Rigby, K. (1993). Australian school children's self-appraisal of interpersonal relations: The bullying experience. *Child Psychiatry and Human Development, 23*, 272–282.

Smith, P. K., Shu, S., & Madsen, K. (2001). Characteristics of victims of school bullying: Developmental changes in coping strategies and skills. In J. Juvonen & S. Graham (Eds.), *Peer harassment in school: The plight of the vulnerable and victimized* (pp. 332–352). New York, NY: Guilford Press.

Stark, K. D., Kendall, P. C., McCarthy, M., Stafford, M., Barron, R., & Thomeer, M. (1996). ACTION: A workbook for overcoming depression. Ardmore, PA: Workbook Publishing.

Stark, K. D., Napolitano, S., Swearer, S., Schmidt, K., Jaramillo, D., & Hoyle, J. (1996). Issues in the treatment of depression. *Applied & Preventive Psychology, 5,* 59–83.

Stark, K. D., Sander, J. B., Yancy, M. G., Bronik, M. D., & Hoke, J. A. (2000). Treatment of depression in childhood and adolescence: Cognitive-behavioral procedures for the individual and family. In P. C. Kendall (Ed.), *Child and adolescent therapy: Cognitive-behavioral procedures* (pp. 173–234). NY: The Guilford Press.

Stevens, R., & Slavin, R. (1995). The cooperative elementary school: Effects on student's achievement, attitudes, and social relations. *American Educational Research Journal, 32,* 321–351.

Strauss, C. C., Frame, C. L., & Forehand, R. (1987). Psychosocial impairment associated with anxiety in children. *Journal of Clinical Child Psychology, 16,* 433–443.

Strauss, C. C., Lahey, B. B., Frick, P., Frame, C. L., & Hynd, G. W. (1988). Peer social status of children with anxiety disorders. *Journal of Consulting and Clinical Psychology, 56,* 137–141.

Strauss, C. C., Last, C. G., Hersen, M., & Kazdin, A. E. (1988). Association between anxiety and depression in children and adolescents with anxiety disorders. *Journal of Abnormal Child Psychology, 16,* 57–68.

Swearer, S. M., Song, S. Y., Cary, P. T., Eagle, J. W., & Mickelson, W. T. (2001). Psychosocial correlates in bullying and victimization: The relationship between depression, anxiety, and bully/victim status. *Journal of Emotional Abuse, 2,* 95–121.

Vossekuil, B., Fein, R. A., Reddy, M., Borum, R., & Modzeleski, W. (2002). *The final report and findings of the Safe School Initiative: Implications for the prevention of school attacks in the United States.* U.S. Secret Service and U.S. Department of Education. Washington, DC.

Walker, J. L., Lahey, B. B., Russo, M. F., Frick, P. J., Christ, M. A. G., McBurnett, K., Loeber, R., Stouthamer-Loeber, M., & Green, S. (1991). Anxiety, inhibition, and conduct disorder in children: I. Relations to social impairment. *Journal of the American Academy of Child and Adolescent Psychiatry, 30,* 187–191.

Walters, K. S., & Inderbitzen, H. M. (1998). Social anxiety and peer relations among adolescents: Testing a psychobiological model. *Journal of Anxiety Disorders, 12,* 183–198.

Weisz, J. R., Sweeney, L., Proffitt, V., & Carr, T. (1993). Control-related beliefs and self-reported depressive symptoms in late childhood. *Journal of Abnormal Psychology, 102,* 411–418.

Wicks-Nelson, R., & Israel, A. C. (1991). *Behavior disorders of childhood (Eds).* New Jersey: Simon and Schuster.

Williams, K., Chambers, M., Logan, S., & Robinson, D. (1996). Association of common health symptoms with bullying in primary school children. *British Medical Journal, 313,* 17–19.

II

Peer Characteristics
Associated With Bullying

5

Peer Ecologies of Aggression and Bullying

Philip C. Rodkin
University of Illinois, Urbana-Champaign

The peer ecology is a proximal ecology that the child interacts with directly, what Bronfenbrenner (1979) calls a microsystem, embedded within larger ecological systems (e.g., neighborhood climate, school institutional culture, ethnic/racial subculture, national culture). Lewin (1943) wrote that the proximal ecology (or immediate situation) was the most important environmental influence on child behavior. As applied to bullies, the peer ecology can take on a variety of forms. Classic research portrays a hostile and rejecting peer ecology for many aggressive children, who reactively lash out as they sense provocation from others (e.g., Asher & Coie, 1990). For bullies who are also victims of harassment (Juvonen & Graham, 2001), this kind of peer ecology comes very close to reality. Some bullies are friendless and lonely; others gain acceptance but only in small, peripheral social networks consisting mainly of unpopular, aggressive children like the bully him- or herself (Coie & Dodge, 1998; McDougall, Hymel, Vaillancourt, & Mercer, 2001; Rubin, Bukowski, & Parker, 1998). Whether taking shape as isolation or acceptance by deviant peers, the peer ecology of unpopular bullies is fertile soil for aggressive behaviors to thrive.

Researchers have recently focused their efforts on bullies who experience another kind of peer ecology. Some aggressive children are popular (LaFontana & Cillessen, 2002; Luthar & McMahon, 1996; Parkhurst & Hopmeyer, 1998; Prinstein & Cillessen, in press; Rodkin, Farmer, Pearl, & Van Acker, 2000), and some bullies are leaders in their peer culture, expert manipulators of their social environment (Sutton, Smith, & Swettenham, 1999; but see Arsenio & Lemerise, 2001; Crick & Dodge, 1999) who rely on a network of supporters and subordinates to help achieve their subversive goals (Salmivalli, Huttunen, & Lagerspetz, 1997). Popular bullies implicate the values of mainstream childhood culture as possibly encouraging aggression and victimization against others (Rodkin et al., 2000). Bullies who actively engage peer culture experience a very different, more complicated environment than bullies whom peers generally reject or marginalize. As such, they present a distinct set of challenges to educators and researchers interested in bullying and in children's peer ecologies.

The goal of this chapter is to describe the peer ecology of bullies who enjoy social status and social affiliations. The chapter proceeds in four parts. First comes an historical overview of groups in social-ecological theory. For almost a century, group process has been a cardinal tenet of social-ecological perspectives. Social-ecological researchers have taken group influence seriously, examining the mechanisms that lead children to acquire and maintain influence over others. The second section provides an overview of contemporary research on children's peer groups and aggressive behavior, including bullying. Groups organize children's behavior in the peer ecology and help shape the values and sentiments of peer culture—and ultimately children's socialization of one another (Maccoby, 1998). Group influence may seem like an adolescent phenomenon, but relevant points of origin lie as early as the toddler years, and are squarely in place by middle childhood. Aggression is particularly dependent on the operation of social networks: interpersonally contagious, easy to spark in group situations, and connected to social identities like gender and ethnicity. This review is directed towards the broader issue of childhood aggression, but investigations that deal specifically with bullying are noted.

The final two sections of this chapter focus on implications for practice and intervention. The third section highlights sociometric methodologies. Researchers and school service personnel should broaden their use of sociometric assessment techniques to identify children's groups and the power dynamics involved in bullying. Prevention and intervention programs without a sketch of bullies' (and victims') social network affiliations are operating without a map of the social ecology. Ideally, educators could take lessons from the days of Gronlund (1959) when simple sociometric techniques were applied in classrooms on a regular, preventative basis. The chapter concludes with some thoughts about what a uniquely American approach to bullying might entail.

Groups in Social-ecological Perspective

> The themes of individual submission to group pressure, the conflict of conscience and authority, and the constructive role that groups have on the individual seem to be central to an individual's experience with the social world.
>
> Milgram (1977/1992, p. 198)

The power of groups can be extraordinary. Groups enlarge the human potential for learning and kindness. Mental health professionals use groups as a tool in therapeutic applications, organizational consultants use groups to promote creativity and morale, and educators use groups to foster achievement and interracial harmony (e.g., Aronson, Blaney, Stephan, Sikes, & Snapp, 1978; Webb & Palinscar, 1996). Groups also bring out the worst in people, providing cover for those who participate in or ignore manipulation, violence, and terror (Latané & Darley, 1970). Groups influence what people believe about others, the world at large, and even themselves. Whether the group consists of progressive college women (Crandall, 1988; Newcomb, 1966) or the acolytes of a cult (Galanter, 1999), guiding group ideologies can become internalized into individuals' value systems where they can be maintained long after the group itself has disintegrated (Bar-Tal, 1990). Some groups, most notably ethnic or racial groups, fashion personal identity and sense of self (Tajfel, 1978). Other groups wipe out personal identity, making individual autonomy, personality, and will suddenly irrelevant (Milgram, 1973). The potential of groups to influence for good or for ill nearly every aspect of social cognition, emotion, and behavior is what led Stanley Milgram to write in the preceding epigraph that the group is foundational to the human experience.

Some of the most important investigations of human groups have included children and young adolescents as participants (e.g., Lewin, Lippitt, & White, 1939; Lippitt, Polansky, Redl, & Rosen, 1952; Sherif, 1956; Tajfel, 1978). Group influence has even been demonstrated among toddlers. Merei (1949), in a fascinating and forgotten study, worked with Czech nursery children to show that playgroups with a history of interaction resist efforts at change. Merei watched playgroups of toddlers over a period of time and picked out children who most acted like leaders (on the basis of an elaborate observational coding scheme). He then removed the "leaders" from their original playgroup and put them in a new, pre-existing playgroup. Despite their best efforts, the nursery-school leaders were usually unable to change the habits, traditions, and customs of their new playmates. Leaders barked out demands and bullied around group members, but they were only successful in obtaining compliance when they ordered group members "to do exactly what they would have done anyway (p. 28)." Merei (1949, p. 34) saw group phenomena as *emergent*—more than just a complicated extension of dyadic (i.e., two-person) relationships. He interpreted his findings as indicating a " 'plus' arising from 'groupness' which raises the power of the group above the aggregate strength of its members [through] habits, customs, rules, and relationships" (p. 43). Habits, customs, and other aspects of culture were group-level properties that could not be captured effectively simply through the analysis of the group leader, or other group members, or their friendships.

Despite the strong, historical connection between group psychology and children's social development, interest in children's groups has waned in the last generation of scholarship. At least two events contributed to what Cairns, Xie, and Leung (1998) noted was a "neglect of social networks" (i.e., groups and other affiliations beyond the dyad) in work on children's social relationships, and to Bukowski and Sippola's (2001, p. 356) call to "put the 'group' back into peer group research." First, small group and social development researchers lost interest in each others' work. Contemporary small-group research is filtered through the concerns of organizational psychology and experimental social cognition and rarely includes child participants or longitudinal designs (e.g., Hare, Blumberg, Davies, & Kent, 1996). This has practical consequences that inhibit collaboration. In social development, the hardest part about studying groups in natural ecologies is identifying the right groups in the first place (see Espelage, Holt, & Henkel, 2003). Social psychological studies deal with formally-defined groups (e.g., teams in organizations) or groups created on the spot by experimental design. The problems of group identification that bedevil developmental researchers rarely come up in social psychology.

Second, researchers have tended to view groups as extensions of two-person dyads, the "peer group" as simply the collective sum or average of children within a particular ecology (Allen, 1981; Cairns et al., 1998). The broader questions involved are the following: Do groups emerge from the interactions among individuals within a group, or should group phenomena be reduced to processes operating at individual and dyadic levels? Can group phenomena be captured by statistically summing or averaging responses among children within an ecology, or are more refined analytic strategies needed? Is there indeed, in Merei's (1949) words, a "plus" arising from groupness?

These questions go to the heart of what a social-ecological perspective is all about: the idea that social environments are multileveled and characterized by hierarchical micro- to macrosocial structures (e.g., peer social network, classroom, school, community, national culture) that Bronfenbrenner (1979, p. 3) "conceived as a set of nested structures, each inside the next, like a set of Russian dolls." When groups are reduced to individual- or dyadic-level processes, the reality of groups as a true social structure is questioned (Warriner, 1956). If groups are not real, or treated as such in theory and method, Bronfenbrenner's (1979) ecological system becomes more like a house of cards than a set of Russian dolls. Indeed, from his earliest writings Bronfenbrenner (1944) insisted that groups were a fundamental element of the child's social environment and attempted to measure group characteristics.

Many of the most profound social psychologists, including Asch (1959), Milgram (1977, 1992), and Sherif (1951), consistently argued that groups were emergent social structures. Cairns et al. (1998) tell of a similar debate about individuals and groups lying at the core of social development scholarship since the late 19th century. Kurt Lewin (1943, p. 334), who Bronfenbrenner (1979, p. xi) referred to as a "giant" in social-ecological theory, laid out the issue 60 years ago:

> [E]ducation is group work. Education of children and adults, education in families and schools never deals with the individual on the one hand and the subject to be taught on the other. It is common knowledge that the success of a teacher of French depends as much on the social atmosphere he creates as on his mastering the French language or the laws of learning. . . . The psychologist who has spent an immense amount of his time studying learning curves has left the problems of social management in education almost entirely to the practitioner, who is forced to base his procedure on the primitive method of trial and error, or upon a peculiar mix of philosophy and instinct.

Consider that the "individual" is a bully (or an ally of a bully) and antibullying messages are the "subject to be taught." Replace the "teacher of French" with a "teacher of nonviolence." The "social atmosphere" to which Lewin refers is like Merei's (1949) "'plus' arising from 'groupness.'" The "laws of learning" are an allusion to the individual-level focus of mid-20th century American behaviorist paradigms, which evolved into contemporary social learning frameworks. Today, few educational psychologists spend much time poring over learning curves but the reductionist epistemology that lies behind behavioristic approaches is alive and well. This may be why psychologists have made only limited progress towards Lewin's agenda of mapping and manipulating the social atmosphere of a classroom, or towards Allen's (1981) call for investigating groups in peer relations research. From a contextualist standpoint, the atmosphere—or culture—of a peer ecology emerges from interactions between children in which group processes are key. This is particularly true when the peer ecology comes to value aggressive and bullying behavior.

Children's Peer Groups

It is hardly a coincidence that Lewin's research dealt with groups (e.g., Lewin, 1943) and aggression (e.g., Lewin, Lippitt, & White, 1939). Bob Cairns also made theoretical contributions to the study of social behavior (e.g., Cairns, 1986) and empirical contributions to research on aggression and groups (Cairns & Cairns, 1994). Groups and aggression have long been connected in the minds of ecological theorists and in the reality of human behavior, even though most groups are not aggressive and aggressive behavior need not always occur in groups. In this section some basic features of children's groups are described, with emphasis on aggression and bullying.

Organizational Features of Children's Groups

Groups are a natural feature of peer ecologies at school. Children consistently report (at rates approaching 95%) that their classroom contains multiple groups (Farmer, Van Acker, Pearl, & Rodkin, 1999; Pearl et al., 1998). Children's identification of peer groups, even when they are not members of the group, tends to be highly accurate (Cairns & Cairns, 1994; Cairns et al., 1998). Studies using social cognitive mapping procedures to identify groups indicate that 85–90% of elementary children belong to a group. Gest, Farmer, Cairns, and Xie (in press) report observational evidence on the reality of group structures. They showed that fourth and seventh grade children interacted with members of their group at a rate four times higher than with other same-sex classmates. Lansford and Parker (1999) reported that third to fifth grade children grouped experimentally into triads (for purposes of intimate discussion, or cooperative or competitive play) interacted with one another in ways that could not be easily decomposed into a series of dyadic relationships. These studies suggest that groups are a fundamental, emergent microsocial structure in the child's ecological system.

Children sort themselves and are sorted by adults into distinct groups in which children selectively affiliate with one another. Children within a group can be or become similar upon an unlimited array of attributes, but three classes of similarity (or *homophily*) are most common. First, children who behave similarly and/or share key goals and beliefs are more likely to be in the same group. Friendships and groups become established along concordances in aggression, shyness, depressive symptomology, academic motivation, and prosocial behavior among other characteristics (Haselager, Hartup, van Lieshout, & Riksen-Walraven, 1998; McPherson, Smith-Lovin, & Cook, 2001). Second, groups form along demographic lines, including gender, race and ethnicity, age, and social class. Virtually all middle childhood groups are segregated by gender (Benenson, Maiese, Dolenszky, Dolensky, Sinclair, & Simpson, 2002; Maccoby, 1998) and segregation along ethnicity is also very common (Hallinan & Smith, 1989). Third, groups form because of shared interests and pastimes, including participation in the same extracurricular activities and common enjoyment of particular places, parks, and establishments. More distal contexts can also influence determinants of similarity. Community characteristics and school policies such as tracking, degree of racial integration, and special education practices can have a top-down effect on peer ecologies (Kubitschek & Hallinan, 1998). Children in the same friendships or groups also become more similar over time, presumably due to shared socialization to group norms and standards (Espelage et al., 2003).

The other side of the homophily coin is complementarity: for every attribute on which group members are similar there may be more on which they are dissimilar. It is true that strongly cohesive groups demand unanimity in acceptance of basic group goals and norms that can encompass very substantial aspects of individuals' lives (Bar-Tal, 1990; Galanter, 1999). Some children's groups reach high levels of cohesiveness; most do not. Kiesner, Cadinu, Poulin, and Bucci (2002) showed that sixth and seventh graders were more similar to their group on problem behavior when they were mutually recognized as group members, and they grew more similar to group members over a 1-year interval when they strongly identified with their group. Under less cohesive conditions individual-group similarity was less pronounced. Groups value individuals with unique strengths that can benefit the group as a whole—an aggressive group gains by including a member with high academic competence; an academically-oriented group of children may thrive by including an affiliate skilled in aggression. Sherif (1956) reported that children's groups at summer camp were finely differentiated by role, with individual members having niches, such as cook, leader, and watchman that emerged in the early stages of group formation.

Groups differ in how they are internally organized. Some groups are hierarchical, with one leader, a small number of lieutenants, and many followers with lower levels of social status. Other groups are more egalitarian and less differentiated by status. Sherif (1956) found that egalitarian groups of boys were more successful in intergroup competitions than highly stratified groups. Lewin et al. (1939) reported that democratic groups of boys performed better and had healthier morales than fascistic groups. Contemporary studies of group organization have focused more on differences between boys and girls, a definite ommission of early work. Eleanor Maccoby (1998) wrote that male peer groups are more cohesive, exclusionary, and separate from adult culture than female peer groups. These differences are not merely incidental; Maccoby's main thesis is that boys and girls *become* different as they interact with one another in school-based peer group contexts (see also Adler & Adler, 1998). Benenson et al. (2002) used an experimental design to study 9- to 10-year-olds who played a competitive game involving stress and disappointment within a 6-person group (more characteristic of boys' natural peer relations) and a two-person dyad (more characteristic of girls' natural peer relations). Children in groups were self-assertive: externalizing, boastful, and conflictual. Children in dyads were self-deprecating, displayed internalizing characteristics, and sometimes even sacrificed their own chances of winning to benefit their competitor. Benenson et al. (2002) concluded that the differing structural organization of male and female peer affiliations may play a critical role in boys' propensity for assertiveness.

Aggression and Bullying

Groups provide children with multiple routes for integrating into their peer ecology. Some groups echo dominant societal values, but others give social shelter to children who resist adult-endorsed messages (e.g., Ferguson, 2000; Fordham & Ogbu, 1986; McFarland, 2001). The function of peer groups as vehicles of defiance and nonconformity is perhaps mostly clearly seen in adolescence but has roots in middle childhood.

Farmer, Leung, Pearl, Rodkin, Cadwallader, and Van Acker (2002) directly questioned the deviant peer group hypothesis (e.g., Reid & Eddy, 1997), which suggests that aggressive youth are members of small, peripheral groups situated on the perimeter of conventional social networks. In a study of fourth to sixth graders, they found that aggressive boys (but less so aggressive girls) were well-connected in their peer ecology. Far from being relegated to a low-status, deviant group, aggressive boys affiliated with a wide range of aggressive and nonaggressive peers. Two-thirds of aggressive boys and one-half of aggressive girls affiliated in groups whose members were mostly (over 50%) nonaggressive. Farmer et al. (2002) recommended that the focus of violence prevention programs should extend beyond aggressive youth and deviant groups and also address nonaggressive peers who may support antisocial behavior. Interestingly, aggressive girls were more likely than aggressive boys to fit the deviant peer group framework, possibly because aggression is less normative or valued among girls and hence is more likely to be segregated away from the mainstream peer ecology.

Using the same sample as Farmer et al. (2002), Rodkin (2002) examined children who nominated aggressive peers as among the three "coolest" kids in their school. According to a strict similarity view, children nominating aggressive children as cool should be aggressive themselves. However, if bullying and aggression work via group processes then children in aggressive groups should perceive aggressive children as cool, even if the nominators are themselves nonaggressive. Results indicated that aggressive children nominated other aggressive children as cool, but children's nominations of who's cool were as-sociated with their group membership even after nominators' individual levels of aggression (and popularity) and ethnic group affiliation were controlled. Children in aggressive groups nominated aggressive children as cool, even if nominators were nonaggressive themselves. Aggressive children nominated nonaggressive children as cool, but only if they were in nonaggressive groups. These findings held for boy and girl same-gender cool nominations. Rodkin (2002) also found that some aggressive boys were disproportionately nominated as cool by girls (see also Bukowski, Sippola, & Newcomb, 2000). This suggests that at least some aggressive boys have a wide base of support in elementary classrooms. Other findings indicated that, consistent with Farmer et al. (2002), aggressive girls had a narrower base of support that drew more strongly from girls like themselves.

Adolescent friends engage one another in "deviancy training," where norms favoring aggression are established and nourished over time, contributing to the development of substance use (e.g., tobacco, alcohol, marijuana) in young adulthood (Dishion & Owen, 2002). Haynie (2001) found that the nature of the groups in which friendships are embedded (e.g., their cohesiveness, adolescents' status within the group) conditioned friendship-delinquency associations. Peer influence on delinquency was most pronounced when groups were cohesive (see also Kiesner et al., 2002) and target adolescents had high social status. McFarland (2001) stressed the role of social networks in everyday forms of student defiance of authority, downplaying the importance of individual traits, or distal macroso-cial features such as race or class. According to McFarland (2001), many students with advantaged positions in the peer ecology undermine classroom affairs whenever they get the chance. Children on the periphery of the peer ecology may also attempt to disrupt class activity, but they usually fail and are rejected by teachers and peers alike.

Groups and aggressive behavior create complex opportunities for one another. Xie, Swift, Cairns, and Cairns (2002) examined how seventh graders from the Carolina Longitudinal Study spoke about their interpersonal conflicts. Most con-flicts involved group and not just dyadic processes. Some forms of aggression, termed "social aggression" by Xie et al. (2002), is non-confrontational, more characteristic of girls, and uses the peer ecology as an active vehicle of attack. In cases of social aggression, which includes behaviors like gossip, rumor, and so-cial ostracism, the identity of the perpetrator is not obvious. Unlike other forms of aggression that are reciprocated in kind, social aggression tends to be followed with direct relational aggression (that could also involve the social network).

Bullies rely upon interpersonal similarity and difference and the internal orga-nization of their groups to achieve goals that are important to them. Bullies tend to be friends with other bullies (Pellegrini, Bartini, & Brooks, 1999). In addition, research showing that aggressive children interact with nonaggressive children has been growing. Aggressive children engage their peer ecology (using both ag-gressive and prosocial behaviors) at higher rates than nonaggressive children, and interact with aggressive and nonaggressive children alike (Pepler, Craig, & Roberts, 1998). During middle childhood, the relationship between bullies and victims involves much of the elementary classroom (O'Connell, Peplar, & Craig, 1999; Pierce & Cohen, 1995). Many children who are not themselves aggressive validate bullies with applause, or play supporting roles in bully-led peer groups (O'Connell et al., 1999; Salmivalli et al., 1997). Bullies who use proactive or instrumental aggression are often popular within their groups (Pellegrini et al., 1999) and their groups tend to be larger than those of non-bullies (Boulton, 1999). Salmivalli et al. (1997) reported that bullying was a group activity in which group members had different, distinct roles (e.g., leading the attack, as-sisting, reinforcing) and where bullies relied on their network of supporters, sub-ordinates, and scapegoats to establish and exercise influence. Hawkins, Pepler, and Craig (2001) suggest that just as peers can enable bullies, they can also be successful at intervening in a bullying episode. These studies show that although bullies preferentially affiliate with one another, they are not generally segregated from their nonaggressive peers.

In sum, the peer ecologies of bullying take on multiple forms. Bullies who are also victims, or who predominately aggress in reaction to provocation, face re-jection and stigmatization. Their segregation from the mainstream peer ecology makes them easy to detect. Other bullies use peers as allies, and as such may be difficult to isolate or earmark for adjustment difficulties. In particular, peer groups are a primary vehicle through which aggression is propagated and valued. The next section turns to sociometric methodologies as a way to objectify and measure the social affiliations of bullies who are well-integrated in their peer ecologies.

Translating Research Into Practice: Implications for Bullying-Prevention and Intervention Programs

Sociometry in Social Development and Education

Ecological approaches to bullying require that appropriate ecologies be identified and measured. Fortunately, social developmentalists are rediscovering the contributions of J. L. Moreno (1934) that so influenced Urie Bronfenbrenner's (1944) early work. New monographs on sociometric methodology have appeared (Bukowski & Cillessen, 1998; Cillessen & Bukowski, 2000) and there have been first attempts to synthesize the diversity of methods available for uncovering group structure (Bagwell, Coie, Terry, & Lochman, 2000; Espelage et al., 2003; Gest et al., in press; Terry, 2000). Further advances in the identification of social networks and the assessment of social status are key for future progress. Sociometric methods also have an overlooked place in educational practices for bullying prevention and intervention, but also may carry some ethical concerns.

Sociometry and Social Development.   Sociograms, first used by Moreno (1934), are a map of children's peer ecologies, including their ties to one another and their social status. The information in sociograms about children's social networks can be extremely valuable. Muzafer Sherif (1951), who had a discerning interest in children's conflict, built sociograms to track the evolving group structures of teams of boys who competed and collaborated with one another at Robbers Cave and other camp settings. Sherif closely followed children who occupied (sometimes temporarily) high-status roles. High-status children, after all, have the greatest influence in shaping peer-culture values and beliefs. Sociograms and related social-network assessments fell out of fashion as scholarship turned away from children's attitudes, norms, and group and intergroup conflicts (Renshaw, 1981). More than twenty years ago, Vernon Allen (1981) urged social development researchers to give serious consideration to group phenomena such as coalition-forming, social identity, intergroup relations, and majority pressure. Around the same time, Bob Cairns (1983, 1986) warned that omitting social network information from sociometric methodologies would restrict our understanding of childhood aggression, particularly when aggressors were well-integrated into their peer ecology.

The literature review that came previously speaks to the continuing relevance of Allen and Cairns' concerns (see also Bukowski & Sippola, 2001; Rubin et al., 1998). Ecologically-minded researchers should ask whether group structures and status hierarchies can be adequately extracted from the next generation of sociometric procedures. Cairns (1983, p. 436) expressed excitement mixed with caution when reviewing the then-new sociometric status classification system of Coie, Dodge, & Coppotelli (1982) that became the gold standard of the field:

> The resurgence of interest in sociometric procedures reflects one of the most important recent trends in contemporary social development research. It goes hand-in-hand with the rediscovery of the interactional orientations of J. M. Baldwin, G. H. Mead, and L. S. Cottrell, and the social-ecological arguments of K. Lewin, R. Barker, and U. Bronfenbrenner . . . [further progress] requires careful attention to the steps taken in the assessment and organization of information about social structures. In particular, assumptions borrowed directly from the psychometrics of individual-difference assessment cannot be generalized without ado to the description of social networks . . . the current generation has a chance to succeed where the last one faded away.

Soon after making these comments, Cairns developed social cognitive mapping (SCM) procedures—the only sociometric procedure specifically tailored to interactional, social-ecological concerns (Cairns et al., 1998). The traditional SCM probe asks children: "Are there kids in your classroom [school] who hang around together a lot? Who are they?" Children list all the groups they can think of, including but not limited to their own peer group(s). Although SCM probes are sometimes given with the help of a class roster, Cairns preferred that children list groups strictly from memory. SCM probes have been administered in one-on-one interviews and written group-administered surveys. The hallmarks of the Cairns system: distrust of self-reports of group affiliation, direct group-level assessment, reliance on children's subjective representations of their ecology, have strong conceptual rationales and demonstrated empirical utility (Cairns & Cairns, 1994; Cairns et al., 1998; Gest et al., in press; Kindermann, 1998). They should be carefully scrutinized and put to the test in future work, particularly in relation to social-network analytic methods that derive from other intellectual traditions.

Assessments of social status are increasingly multidimensional (Gest, Graham-Bermann, & Hartup, 2001; Lease et al., 2002), broadening out from social preference (i.e., likeability minus dislikeability) to include dominance (Hawker & Boulton, 2001; Hawley, 1999), peer-perceived popularity (Gorman, Kim, & Schimmelbusch, 2002; LaFontana & Cillessen, 2002; Parkhurst & Hopmeyer, 1998; Prinstein & Cillessen, in press), teacher ratings of popularity (Farmer et al., 2002; Rodkin, et al., 2000), and peer perceptions of coolness (Graham & Juvonen, 2002; Rodkin, 2002), likeability, friendliness, humor, appearance, power, and being listened to (Luthar & McMahon, 1996; Vaillancourt, Hymel, & McDougall, in press). These are important breakthroughs because they suggest that the richness and variety of children's peer ecologies—a horizontal peer group structure and a vertical social status hierarchy—can be measured with greater sensitivity and accuracy. Taken together, methods that uncover children's social affiliations and social position situate bullies and victims to one another and to the larger peer ecology.

Sociometry and Education.   The relevance of sociometric methodologies to educators lies in how school service providers think about the peer ecology of bullying—the questions they ask, the curricula and prevention programs they purchase, the classroom and school practices they adopt. As Swearer and Doll (2001) note, examining bullying in schools from an ecological framework is directly linked to intervention and practice (see also Pepler, Craig, & O'Connell, 2001). On this note, Farmer's (2000) implications for intervention are particularly instructive. Farmer (2000) deals with aggression among students with disabilities, not on bullying *per se,* but the message generalizes: researchers and educators have historically overlooked the variety of ways that children who aggress integrate into, manipulate, and rely on their social networks. Faced with concrete instances of bullying, school service providers can usefully ask the kinds of ecologically-minded questions that Farmer (2000) examines in depth, such as: Is the bully a member of a group? Has the bully's group formed a coalition with other groups? Is the bully a group leader, a wannabe? School service providers should keep in mind these questions when evaluating the sensitivity of potential antibullying curricula to peer ecological contexts.

In an era of constant testing, educators should revisit the use of sociometric testing for regular, preventative use. Apart from intense ethnography, there is no better way than through sociometric technology to assess the underlying structure of peer ecologies, and from there to situate bullies and victims and their relationships to one another. Sociometric procedures can be easy to use (and misuse), but once upon a time professional educators were encouraged and trained in understanding their students' social environment objectively, and not by the subjective, "trial and error" procedures derided by Lewin (1943; see also Gronlund, 1959). In one of the premier educational psychology texts of its day, University of Illinois researchers Glenn Myers Blair, Stewart Jones, and Ray Simpson suggested that sociometric techniques were "one of the most practical and useful types of evidence about children in appraising their interpersonal relationships (1968, p. 520)." Variants of the basic sociometric liked most and liked least questions are still asked by researchers, but hardly ever by teachers.

A word on the ethics of studying children's perceptions of one another is appropriate. Anyone who has collected sociometric data cannot help but feel some awkwardness and regret when asking school-aged children who they like least, or for that matter, who is a bully or who is mean to others. These concerns loom larger still when sociometric tests are administered, as they often are, in a group format. Many parents strive to have their children avoid taking a negative approach to others as part of a larger ideology of caregiving. Can the study of children's enemies and conflicts, bullying and victimization, sustain serious moral inquiry and today's institutional review board standards? At the end of the day, this is a question for parents and schools to answer. Sensitive researchers of children's social development will always respect the concerns and authority of parents and school administrators to define what is and is not right for their children, making the best of whatever decision arrived at by children's legal guardians. But sensitive researchers also need to state forthrightly, and without defensiveness, the larger importance of delving into children's conflicts and problems with the best available tools.

Parents and schools come to child development researchers looking for expertise when frustrated by children's conflicts, or when trying to implement programs geared towards making a positive psychology of childhood socialization a reality as well as an ideal. There is no way around the proposition that dealing with sensitive issues requires sensitive (and confidential) research. No political scientist could understand national or international relations without keeping close track of conflicts and how they develop. No diplomat who only reluctantly recognizes animosities could formulate realistic strategies that promote peace and harmony. By the same token, a science of children's social relations is incomplete without concepts for understanding dislike, bullying, and an array of methodologies for sensitively assessing interpersonal negativity. Hopefully, the new directions opened by this volume will encourage fresh research on peer sexual harassment, bully-victim relationships, intergroup and interethnic relations, and other critical elements of child and adult societies alike. Real progress and satisfying answers to these areas of continued societal concern should justify our examination of the "dark side" of children's relationships.

An American Approach to Bullying?

How might we fashion an American approach to bullying? The very question reminds us that bullying is a social problem of international significance. The seminal work on bullying comes from overseas. The Scandinavian countries have been particularly influential in framing how child psychologists think about bully-ing. Smith, Cowie, Olafsson, and Liefooghe (2002) note that a Norwegian scholar, Heinemann, was one of the first to write on bullying. The world's foremost bullying expert, Dan Olweus, is from Bergen and has directed interventions across Norway and Sweden. Today, collaborative laboratories and field investigations focused on bullying are placed in at least fourteen countries outside the United States (Smith et al., 2002). There is a wealth of information out there in the world that reflects upon humankind's fundamental concern with aggression among children. Many of the specific findings and strategies employed by international researchers will likely generalize to the American case and provide a solid framework for interventions here.

An American approach to bullying should enrich theoretical perspectives on childhood aggression. This volume features ecological approaches that have a strong European lineage reaching back to early 20th century gestalt theory (e.g., Magnusson, 1998). American work on aggression and peer relationships has been more influenced by homegrown social learning and social skills paradigms, and also by H. S. Sullivan's (1948/1953) seminal work on childhood friendships as a *sine qua non* of mental heath. These are different traditions that lead naturally to different ways of framing child development and behavior. Olweus (2001), in his introduction to Juvonen and Graham's *Peer Harassment in School* volume, explicitly contrasts what he calls North American and Scandinavian traditions on peer research. The North American tradition centers on popular prosocial children, with mental health and lots of friends, and unpopular aggressive children, who are socially marginalized and at-risk for later adjustment difficulties. This description fits many children, but Olweus (2001) argued that the American spotlight on rejection made it difficult to hone in on powerful bullies who aggress against weaker peers with the assistance of friends and allies. As researchers focus on the problem of bullying from ecological and social learning perspectives (e.g., Crick & Dodge, 1999; Sutton et al., 1999), conflicts and collaborations, antithesis and synthesis will emerge. This can only be good for the field's ability to understand bullying in more sophisticated, societally useful ways.

American culture may pose some unique hurdles to bullying prevention programs, at least in comparison to the Scandinavian countries where the most impressive, best-known interventions have been implemented. American society values aggression when it is expressed through normatively legitimate channels (Jackman, 2002). Many American subcultures, including (at least) the white South and poor, inner-city neighborhoods, seem to uphold a culture of honor where aggression as a defense of reputation and social status is the right thing for males to do (Nisbett & Cohen, 1996). More generally, economic competition and military power are rooted in the American macrosystem; rebelliousness and individualism are ennobled in American cultural icons. American children receive multiple messages, some favorable, about aggressive behavior. In this light, it is even more surprising that the high social status of some aggressive children has been a consistent theme of the Scandinavian but not North American tradition, although this picture may change with future research. North American educators may want to consider that many children may express private if not public resistance to seemingly innocuous anti-aggression messages (cf. Ferguson, 2000). Peer culture can align with the bully. Hymel, Bonanno, Henderson, and McCreith (2002) found that some 8th to 10th grade students in British Columbia engaged in a process of moral disengagement—blaming the victim, providing rationales—when confronted with bullying in their school (see also Latané & Darley, 1970). Resistance and opposition are common words used to describe American youth, even before adolescence, and the problem may be even more pronounced within diverse, ethnically heterogeneous school environments (e.g., Ferguson, 2000; Fordham & Ogbu, 1986; McFarland, 2001). Interventionists should not take children's endorsement of an anti-bullying agenda for granted, even when heads are nodding in the desired direction.

American researchers and educators should evaluate whether or not they enjoy a level of commitment among adults that is necessary for any given anti-bullying program to be effective. Part of the American ethos is that those of us with a history of wrongdoing or problem behavior should be carefully monitored, but the rest of us are best left alone. In Scandinavian countries, where this ideology is less pronounced, researchers have been granted considerable control over students' social environments that American educators may not be able to match. For example, Olweus (1993, p. 71) notes that his emphasis on close supervision of and intervention in children's lunch and recess activities led some teachers to complain of acting "like a policeman." Scandinavian researchers had great caché to recruit schools and impact students' school lives as part of a national political and legislative agenda in Norway and Sweden to decrease bullying. Olweus (2001) writes about bullying in the elevated language of international human rights (see also Bukowski & Sippola, 2001) but many Americans see bullying as just part of growing up, or a notice to victims that they need to toughen up (Angier, 2001).

As with their children, the public assent of some adults to anti-bullying programs may belie indifference or opposition. For example, adult school officials have fostered norms among boys that legitimated sexually harassing, criminally liable actions towards girls (Rodkin & Fischer, in press). The natural social dynamics of peer ecologies can overpower messages from adults, sometimes even drawing in the adults themselves. The sociometric and social network techniques advocated in this chapter encourages researchers and educators to examine the peer ecology directly and objectively from children's own perspectives, without assuming how peer culture is structured or what it most values.

This important volume arrives at a moment in time, in the aftermath of the Columbine shootings, some celebrity attention, and a more general increase in safety and security concerns, when more North Americans are taking bullying seriously. Will it be maintained? A community theater group in Vancouver recently featured local secondary school students producing "Don't Say a Word," an interactive, engaging creative production about bullying and its moral implications. This kind of untraditional intervention, designed to impact the attitudes and behaviors of mainstream North American culture—adults and children—may be just as critical as attempts to directly change the attitudes and behaviors of bullies themselves. The values that all children hold, or come to believe in interaction with each other, ultimately set the stage for how bullying and victimization will be framed in North American schools.

ACKNOWLEDGMENT

This work was supported by a Faculty Fellows grant from the Bureau of Educational Research, College of Education, University of Illinois at Urbana-Champaign. Correspondence may be addressed to Philip C. Rodkin, 220B Education Building, Mail Code 708, Department of Educational Psychology, University of Illinois at Urbana-Champaign, 1310 S. 6th St., Champaign, IL 61820. Electronic mail may be sent to: <rodkin@uiuc.edu>.

REFERENCES

Adler, P. A., & Adler, P. (1998). *Peer power: Preadolescent culture and identity.* New Brunswick, NJ: Rutgers University Press.

Allen, V. L. (1981). Self, social group, and social structure: Surmises about the study of children's friendships. In S. R. Asher & J. M. Gottman (Eds.), *The development of children's friendships* (pp. 182–203). New York: Cambridge University Press.

Angier, N. (2001, May 20). Bully for you: When push comes to shove. *New York Times,* Sec. 4, pp. 1, 4.

Aronson, E., Blaney, N. T., Stephan, C., Sikes, J., & Snapp, M. (1978). *The jigsaw classroom.* Beverly Hills, CA: Sage.

Arsenio, W. F., & Lemerise, E. A. (2001). Varieties of childhood bullying: Values, emotion process, and social competence. *Social Development, 10,* 59–73.

Asch, S. E. (1959). A perspective on social psychology. In S. Koch (Ed.), *Psychology: A study of a science. Study I: Conceptual and systematic; Volume 3: Formulations of the person and the social context* (pp. 363–383). New York: McGraw-Hill.

Asher, S. R., & Coie, J. D. (Eds.) (1990). *Peer rejection in childhood.* New York: Cambridge University Press.

Bagwell, C. L., Coie, J. D., Terry, R. A., & Lochman, J. E. (2000) Peer clique participation and social status in preadolescence. *Merrill-Palmer Quarterly, 46,* 280–305.

Bar-Tal, D. (1990). *Group beliefs: A conception for analyzing group structure, processes, and behavior.* New York: Springer-Verlag.

Benenson, J. F., Maiese, R., Dolenszky, E., Dolensky, N., Sinclair, N., & Simpson, A. (2002). Group size regulates self-assertive versus self-deprecating responses to internal competition. *Child Development, 73,* 1818–1829.

Blair, G. M., Jones, R. S., & Simpson, R. H. (1968). *Educational psychology* (3rd ed.) New York: Macmillan.

Boulton, M. J. (1999). Concurrent and longitudinal relations between children's playground behavior and social preference, victimization, and bullying. *Child Development, 70,* 944–954.

Bronfenbrenner, U. (1944). A constant frame of reference for sociometric research: II. Experiment and inference. *Sociometry, 7,* 40–75.

Bronfenbrenner, U. (1979). *The ecology of human development: Experiments by nature and design.* Cambridge, MA: Harvard University Press.

Bukowski, W. M., & Cillessen, A. H. N. (Eds.) (1998). *Sociometry then and now: Building on six decades of measuring children's experiences in the peer group.* San Francisco: Jossey-Bass.

Bukowski, W. M., & Sippola, L. K. (2001). Groups, individuals, and victimization: A view of the peer system. In J. Juvonen & S. Graham (Eds.), *Peer harassment in school: The plight of the vulnerable and victimized* (pp. 355–377). New York: Guilford.

Bukowski, W. M., Sippola, L. K., & Newcomb, A. F. (2000). Variations in patterns of attraction to same- and other-sex peers during early adolescence. *Developmental Psychology, 36,* 147–154.

Cairns, R. B. (1986). Phenomena lost: Issues in the study of development. In J. Valsiner (Ed.), *The individual subject and scientific psychology* (pp. 97–111). New York: Plenum Press.

Cairns, R. B. (1983). Sociometry, psychometry, and social structure: A commentary on six recent studies of popular, rejected, and neglected children. *Merrill-Palmer Quarterly, 29,* 429–438.

Cairns, R. B., & Cairns, B. D. (1994). *Lifelines and risks: Pathways of youth in our time.* Cambridge, UK: Cambridge University Press.

Cairns, R. B., Xie, H., & Leung, M-C. (1998). The popularity of friendship and the neglect of social networks: Toward a new balance. In W. M. Bukowski & A. H. Cillessen (Eds.), *Sociometry then and now: Building on six decades of measuring children's experiences with the peer group* (pp. 25–53). San Francisco: Jossey-Bass.

Cillessen, A. H. N., & Bukowski, W. M. (Eds.) (2000). *Recent advances in the measurement of acceptance and rejection in the peer system.* San Francisco: Jossey-Bass.

Coie, J. D., & Dodge, K. A. (1998). Aggression and antisocial behavior. In W. Damon (Series Ed.) & N. Eisenberg (Vol. Ed.), *Handbook of child psychology: Social, emotional, and personality development* (5th ed., vol. 3, pp. 779–862). New York: Wiley.

Coie, J. D., Dodge, K. A., & Coppotelli, H. (1982). Dimensions and types of social status: A cross-age perspective. *Developmental Psychology, 18*, 557–570.

Crandall, C. S. (1988). Social contagion of binge eating. *Journal of Personality and Social Psychology, 55*, 588–598.

Crick, N. R., & Dodge, K. A. (1999). 'Superiority' is in the eye of the beholder: A comment on Sutton, Smith, and Swettenham. *Social Development, 8*, 128–131.

Dishion, T. J., & Owen, L. D. (2002). A longitudinal analysis of friendships and substance use: Bidirectional influence from adolescence to adulthood. *Developmental Psychology, 38*, 480–491.

Espelage, D. L., Holt, M. K., & Henkel, R. R. (2003). Examination of peer-group contextual effects on aggression during early adolescence. *Child Development, 74*, 205–220.

Farmer, T. W. (2000). Misconceptions of peer rejection and problem behavior: Understanding aggression in students with mild disabilities. *Remedial and Special Education, 21*, 194–208.

Farmer, T. W., Leung, M-C., Pearl, R., Rodkin, P. C., Cadwallader, T. W., & Van Acker, R. (2002). Deviant or diverse peer groups? The peer affiliations of aggressive elementary students. *Journal of Educational Psychology, 94*, 611–620.

Farmer, T. W., Van Acker, R. M., Pearl, R., & Rodkin, P. C. (1999). Social networks and peer-assessed problem behavior in elementary classrooms: Students with and without disabilities. *Remedial and Special Education, 20*, 244–256.

Ferguson, A. A. (2000). *Bad boys: Public schools in the making of black masculinity.* Ann Arbor, MI: University of Michigan Press.

Fordham, S., & Ogbu, J. (1986). Black students' school success: Coping with the burden of acting White. *Urban Review, 18*, 176–206.

Galanter, M. (1999). *Cults: Faith, healing, and coercion* (2nd. ed.). New York: Oxford University Press.

Gest, S. D., Farmer, T. W., Cairns, B. D., & Xie, H. (in press). Identifying children's peer social networks in school classrooms: Links between peer reports and observed interactions. *Social Development.*

Gest, S. D., Graham-Bermann, S. A., & Hartup, W. W. (2001). Peer experience: Common and unique features of number of friendships, social network centrality, and sociometric status. *Social Development, 10*, 23–40.

Gorman, A. H., Kim, J., & Schimmelbusch, A. (2002). The attributes adolescents associate with peer popularity and teacher preference. *Journal of School Psychology, 40*, 143–165.

Graham, S., & Juvonen, J. (2002). Ethnicity, peer harassment, and adjustment in middle school: An exploratory study. *Journal of Early Adolescence, 22*, 173–199.

Gronlund, N. E. (1959). *Sociometry in the classroom.* New York: Harper & Brothers.

Hallinan, M. T., & Smith, S. S. (1989). Classroom characteristics and student friendship cliques. *Social Forces, 67*, 898–919.

Hare, A. P., Blumberg, H. H., Davies, M. F., & Kent, M. V. (1996). *Small groups: An introduction.* Westport, CT: Praeger.

Haselager, G. J. T., Hartup, W. W., van Lieshout, C. F. M., & Riksen-Walraven, J. M. A. (1998). Similarities between friends and nonfriends in middle childhood. *Child Development, 69*, 1198–1208.

Hawker, D. S. J., & Boulton, M. J. (2001). Subtypes of peer harassment and their correlates: A social dominance perspective. In J. Juvonen & S. Graham (Eds.), *Peer harassment in school: The plight of the vulnerable and victimized* (pp. 378–397). New York: Guilford.

Hawkins, D. L., Pepler, D. J., & Craig, W. M. (2001). Naturalistic observations of peer interventions in bullying. *Social Development, 10*, 512–527.

Hawley, P. H. (1999). The ontogenesis of social dominance: A strategy-based evolutionary perspective. *Developmental Review, 19*, 97–132.

Haynie, D. L. (2001). Delinquent peers revisited: Does network structure matter? *American Journal of Sociology, 106*, 1013–1057.

Hymel, S., Bonanno, R. A., Henderson, N. R., & McCreith, T. (2002). Moral disengagement and school bullying: An investigation of student attitudes and beliefs. In J. LeBlanc (Chair), *Aggression in the school setting.* Paper presented at the 15th World Meeting of the International Society for Research on Aggression, Montreal, PQ.

Jackman, M. R., (2002). Violence in social life. *Annual Review of Sociology, 28*, 387–415.

Juvonen, J., & Graham, S. (Eds.). (2001). *Peer harassment in school: The plight of the vulnerable and victimized.* New York: Guilford Press.

Kiesner, J., Cadinu, M., Poulin, F., & Bucci, M. (2002). Group identification in early adolescence: Its relation with peer adjustment and its moderator effect on peer influence. *Child Development, 73*, 196–208.

Kindermann, T. (1998). Children's development within peer groups: Using composite social maps to identify peer networks and to study their influences. In W. M. Bukowski & A. H. Cillessen (Eds.), *Sociometry then and now: Building on six decades of measuring children's experiences with the peer group* (pp. 55–82). San Francisco: Jossey-Bass.

Kubitschek, W. N., & Hallinan, M. T. (1998). Tracking and students' friendships. *Social Psychology Quarterly, 61*, 1–15.

LaFontana, K. M., & Cillessen, A. H. N. (2002). Children's perceptions of popular and unpopular peers: A multi-method assessment. *Developmental Psychology, 38*, 635–647.

Lansford, J. E., & Parker, J. G. (1999). Children's interactions in triads: Behavioral profiles and effects of gender and patterns of friendships among members. *Developmental Psychology, 35*, 80–93.

Latané, B. & Darley, J. M. (1970). *The unresponsive bystander: Why doesn't he help?* New York: Appleton-Century-Crofts.

Lease, A. M., Musgrove, K. T., & Axelrod, J. L. (2002). Dimensions of social status in preadolescent peer groups: Likeability, perceived popularity, and social dominance. *Social Development, 11*, 508–533.

Lewin, K. (1943). Psychology and the process of group living. *Journal of Social Psychology, 17*, 113–131.

Lewin, K., Lippitt, R., & White, R. (1939). Patterns of aggressive behavior in experimentally created "social climates." *Journal of Social Psychology, 10*, 271–299.

Lippitt, R., Polansky, N., Redl, F., & Rosen, S. (1952). The dynamics of power: A field study of social influence in groups of children. In G. E. Swanson, T. M. Newcomb, & E. L. Hartley (Eds.), *Readings in social psychology* (rev. ed., pp. 623–636). New York: Holt.

Luthar, S. S., & McMahon, T. J. (1996). Peer reputation among inner-city adolescents: Structure and correlates. *Journal of Research on Adolescence, 6*, 581–603.

Maccoby, E. E. (1998). *The two sexes: Growing up apart, coming together.* Cambridge, MA: Harvard University Press.

Magnusson, D. (1998). The logic and implications of a person-oriented approach. In R. B. Cairns, L. R. Bergman, & J. Kagan (Eds.), *Methods and models for studying the individual* (pp. 33–64). Thousand Oaks, CA: Sage.

McDougall, P., Hymel, S., Vaillancourt, T., & Mercer, L. (2001). The consequences of childhood peer rejection. In M. Leary (Ed.), *Interpersonal rejection.* (pp. 213–247). Washington DC: American Psychological Association Press.

McFarland, D. A. (2001). Student resistance: How the formal and informal organization of classrooms facilitate everyday forms of student defiance. *American Journal of Sociology, 107*, 612–678.

McPherson, M., Smith-Lovin, L., & Cook, J. M. (2001). Birds of a feather: Homophily in social networks. *Annual Review of Sociology, 27*, 415–444.

Merei, F. (1949). Group leadership and institutionalization. *Human Development, 2*, 23–39.

Milgram, S. (1973). *Obedience to authority.* New York: Harper.

Milgram, S. (1977/1992). *The individual in a social world: Essays and experiments* (Eds. J. Sabini & M. Silver; rev. ed.). New York: McGraw-Hill.

Moreno, J. L. (1934). *Who shall survive? A new approach to the problem of human interrelations.* Washington, DC: Nervous and Mental Disease Publishing.

Newcomb, T. M. (1966). The general nature of peer group influence. In T. M. Newcomb & E. K. Wilson (Eds.), *College peer groups* (pp. 2–16). Chicago: Aldine.

Nisbett, R. E., & Cohen, D. (1996). *Culture of honor: The psychology of violence in the South.* Bolder, CO: Westview Press.

O'Connell, P., Pepler, D., & Craig, W. (1999). Peer involvement in bullying: Insights and challenges for intervention. *Journal of Adolescence, 22,* 437–452.

Olweus, D. (1993). *Bullying at school: What we know and what we can do.* Oxford, UK: Blackwell.

Olweus, D. (2001). Peer harassment: A critical analysis and some important issues. In J. Juvonen & S. Graham (Eds.), *Peer harassment in school: The plight of the vulnerable and victimized* (pp. 1–20). New York: Guilford.

Parkhurst, J. T., & Hopmeyer, A. (1998). Sociometric popularity and peer-perceived popularity: Two distinct dimensions of peer status. *Journal of Early Adolescence, 18,* 125–144.

Pearl, R., Farmer, T. W., Van Acker, R., Rodkin, P. C., Bost, K. K., Coe, M., & Henley, W. (1998). The social integration of students with mild disabilities in general education classrooms: Peer group membership and peer-assessed social behavior. *Elementary School Journal, 99,* 167–185.

Pellegrini, A. D., Bartini, M., & Brooks, F. (1999). School bullies, victims, and aggressive victims: Factors relating to group affiliation and victimization in early adolescence. *Journal of Educational Psychology, 91,* 216–224.

Pepler, D. J., Craig, W. M., & O'Connell, P. (2001). Understanding bullying from a dynamic systems perspective. In P. K. Smith (Ed.), *Blackwell handbook of social development* (pp. 440–452). Cambridge, UK: Blackwell.

Pepler, D. J., Craig, W. M., & Roberts, W. L. (1998). Observations of aggressive and nonaggressive children on the school playground. *Merrill-Palmer Quarterly, 44,* 55–76.

Pierce, K. A., & Cohen, R. (1995). Aggressors and their victims: Toward a contextual framework for understanding children's aggressor-victim relationships. *Developmental Review, 15,* 292–310.

Prinstein, M. J., & Cillessen, A. H. N. (in press). Forms and functions of adolescent peer aggression associated with high levels of peer status. *Merrill Palmer Quarterly.*

Reid, J. B., & Eddy, J. M. (1997). The prevention of antisocial behavior: Some considerations in the search for effective interventions. In D. M. Stoff, J. D. Maser, & J. Breiling (Eds.), *Handbook of antisocial behavior* (pp. 343–356). New York: Wiley.

Renshaw, P. D. (1981). The roots of peer interaction research: A historical analysis of the 1930s. In S. R. Asher & J. M. Gottman (Eds.), *The development of children's friendships* (pp. 1–25). New York: Cambridge University Press.

Rodkin, P. C. (2002). *I think you're cool: Social status and group support for aggressive boys and girls.* Invited address to the 8th Triannual Meeting of the Northeast Social Development Consortium, New York, NY.

Rodkin, P. C., Farmer, T. W., Pearl, R., & Van Acker, R. (2000). Heterogeneity of popular boys: Antisocial and prosocial configurations. *Developmental Psychology, 36,* 14–24.

Rodkin, P. C., & Fischer, K. (in press). Sexual harassment and the cultures of childhood: Developmental, domestic violence, and legal perspectives. *Journal of Applied School Psychology.*

Rubin, K. H., Bukowski, W. M., & Parker, J. G. (1998). Peer interactions, relationships, and groups. In W. Damon (Series Ed.) & N. Eisenberg (Vol. Ed.), *Handbook of child psychology: Social, emotional, and personality development* (5th ed., vol. 3, pp. 619–700). New York: Wiley.

Salmivalli, C., Huttunen, A., & Lagerspetz, K. M. J. (1997). Peer networks and bullying in schools. *Scandinavian Journal of Psychology, 38,* 305–312.

Sherif, M. (1951). A preliminary experimental study of intergroup relations. In J. H. Rohrer & M. Sherif (Eds.), *Social psychology at the crossroads* (pp. 388–424). Harper & Brothers.

Sherif, M. (1956). Experiments in group conflict. *Scientific American, 195*, 54–58.

Smith, P. K., Cowie, H., Olafsson, R. F., & Liefooghe, A. P. D. (2002). Definitions of bullying: A comparison of terms used, and age and gender differences, in a fourteen-country international comparison. *Child Development, 73*, 1119–1133.

Sutton, J., Smith, P. K., & Swettenham, J. (1999). Bullying and 'theory of mind': A critique of the 'social skills deficit' view of anti-social behaviour. *Social Development, 8*, 117–127.

Sullivan, H. S. (1948/1953). *The interpersonal theory of psychiatry* (Eds., H. S. Perry & M. L. Gawel). New York: W. W. Norton.

Swearer, S. M., & Doll, B. (2001). Bullying in schools: An ecological framework. *Journal of Emotional Abuse, 2*, 7–24.

Tajfel, H. (Ed.). (1978). *Differentiation between social groups*. New York: Academic Press.

Terry, R. (2000). Recent advances in measurement theory and the use of sociometric techniques. In A. H. N. Cillessen & W. M. Bukowski (Eds.), *Recent advances in the measurement of acceptance and rejection in the peer system* (pp. 27–53). San Francisco: Jossey-Bass.

Vaillancourt, T., Hymel, S., & McDougall, P. (in press). Bullying is power: Implications for school-based intervention strategies. *Journal of Applied School Psychology*.

Warriner, C. K. (1956). Groups are real: A reaffirmation. *American Sociological Review, 21*, 549–554.

Webb, N. M., & Palinscar, A. S. (1996). Group processes in the classroom. In D. C. Berliner & R. C. Calfee (Eds.), *Handbook of educational psychology* (pp. 841–873). New York: Macmillan.

Xie, H., Swift, D. J., Cairns, B. D., & Cairns, R. B. (2002). Aggressive behaviors in social interaction and developmental adaptation: A narrative analysis of interpersonal conflicts during early adolescence. *Social Development, 11*, 205–224.

6

Part of the Solution and Part of the Problem: The Role of Peers in Bullying, Dominance, and Victimization During the Transition From Primary School Through Secondary School

Anthony D. Pellegrini and Jeffrey D. Long
University of Minnesota

Aggression and antisocial behavior in American schools are persistent and very visible problems, particularly as youngsters make the transition from childhood and primary school to adolescence and secondary school (National Center for Educational Statistics, 1995). Much of the aggression in schools during this period involves individuals "bullying" their peers (Bosworth, Espelage, & Simon, 1999; Coie & Dodge, 1998; Espelage, Bosworth, & Simon, 2000; Perry, Willard, & Perry, 1990). Bullying, which is more frequent among boys than girls, is characterized by youngsters purposefully "victimizing" their peers by repeatedly using negative actions, such as physical, verbal, or indirect aggression (e.g., Boulton & Smith, 1994; Espelage et al., 2000; Smith & Sharp, 1994). Bullying is also typified by a power differential where aggressors are more dominant than the targets (Olweus, 1993a, 1993b).

Bullying, for us, is a specific form of aggression and one that is used deliberately to secure resources (Pellegrini, 2002; Pellegrini & Long, 2002). In this regard it is a dimension of proactive aggression and distinct from aggression which is used reactively, or aggression which is used in response to social provocation (Dodge & Coie, 1987). More specifically, most bullies use aggression in a calculating way. They direct it at a specific target, for example someone they know has few allies, and they use it to achieve some end, for example, to show how strong they are or to get ahead of a peer in the lunch line.

Reactive aggression, on the other hand, is typically an emotional response to a provocation. For instance, in response to having milk accidentally spilt on him at lunch Johnny lashes out and punches the child who spilt the milk. Similarly, peers may provoke these reactive children on purpose so as to get a response, or a "rise." In either case these reactive youngsters are not effective in their uses of aggression. Indeed, their behavior has the opposite effect. They are disliked by their peers and often victimized as well as being aggressive. Appropriately, Olweus has labeled these youngsters as "provocative" victims.

The period of early adolescence is important for the study of bullying and victimization because youngsters' lives and peers have been negatively and positively implicated by bullying and victimization experiences. However, the influence of peers during this time period is complex and involves a number of developmental issues. First, bullying seems to be used as a way in which boys gain and maintain dominance status with peers. Second, this period represents an increased interest in heterosexual relationships which raises concerns that aggressive boys will victimize girls, therefore, it is important to examine cross-sex bullying. Third, it is also imperative that we examine the positive aspects of peer interactions. It is during this period of increased concern with peer status that friends and being popular can also buffer an individual from being bullied.

Bullying as a Strategy to Gain Status with Peers

Relative to earlier periods in development, aggression is viewed less negatively by peers during early adolescence (Bukowski, Sippola, & Newcomb, 2000; Graham & Juvonen, 1998; Moffitt, 1993; Pellegrini, Bartini, & Brooks, 1999). This view may reflect young adolescents' casual associations with bullies because they represent challenges to adult roles and values (Moffitt, 1993). After all, adolescence is a time when youngsters challenge adult roles and values as they search for and construct their own identities.

Correspondingly and probably exacerbating the problem, this period also witnesses a series of abrupt changes in youngsters' social lives. Firstly, adolescence is characterized by rapid body changes. The hormonal changes associated with increased body size also relate to the onset of sexual maturity, resulting in youngsters' increased interests in heterosexual relationships (e.g., Connolly, Goldberg, Pepler, & Craig, 1999). Such rapid change in body size leads to the re-organization of youngsters', but especially boys', social dominance hierarchies (Pellegrini & Bartini, 2001). Bigger and stronger boys become more dominant than their smaller peers. Boys' dominance status, in turn, is related to their attractiveness to girls (Pellegrini & Bartini, 2001).

Secondly, youngsters also move from typically small, personal primary schools with well-established social groups into larger, less supportive secondary schools. This transition requires the re-establishment of social relationships during a time when peer relations are particularly important (Eccles, Wigfield, & Schiefele, 1998). During such transitions, aggression is often used in the service of establishing status with peers, in the form of dominance relationships (Strayer, 1980). From this view, bullying is viewed as a deliberate strategy used to attain dominance as youngsters enter a new social group.

Dominance is defined as a relationship variable which orders individuals in terms of their access to resources (Dunbar, 1988). Dominance status is achieved as a result of a series of agonistic and reconciliation interchanges between individuals (deWaal, 1986; Pellegrini & Bartini, 2001; Strayer, 1980). Individuals who are able to use agonistic, among other, strategies effectively should be dominant and have greater access to resources. As we will discuss later, one such resource during early adolescence is access to heterosexual relationships.

Dominance theory also suggests that status is renegotiated as individuals experience rapid changes in body size and as they make the transition from one social group to another. At the end of primary school youngsters are the biggest and strongest in their schools, but when they move into secondary school, they are suddenly the smallest and the weakest. Thus, their dominance status drops with the initial transition to secondary school but then rises again as they progress through middle school.

Dominant individuals use both aggression and prosocial behavior to establish and maintain status with their peers. From this view, aggressive strategies are often used in the initial phases of the formation of dominance relationships, such as when individuals enter a new school. After the initial transition, more prosocial and cooperative strategies are used to consolidate status and allies and reconcile with former foes (Ljungberg, Westlund, & Forsberg, 1999; Pellegrini & Bartini, 2001).

This description is consistent with our data as youngsters made the transition from one school to another school (Pellegrini & Long, 2002). In this multi-method, multi-informant, longitudinal study we followed youngsters from the last year of primary school (fifth grade) across the first two years of middle school (sixth and seventh grades). Children were extensively observed across the entire school day and we asked about their own as well as their peers' bullying, victimization, dominance, and heterosexual relationships. These assessments were also collected from their teachers.

In this study, bullying increased from fifth to sixth grade, then decreased from sixth to seventh grade. Correspondingly, dominance dropped from fifth to sixth grade and increased in seventh grade. This result is consistent with dominance theory to the extent that we found increases in aggression as youngsters moved into a new school and thus tried to establish dominance. A decrease in dominance at the transition and a subsequent increase following the transition again is consistent with dominance theory. Once dominance was established, however, aggression in the form of bullying decreased and was no longer used to maintain dominance.

Dominance was directly and formally tested in this study by examining the degree to which bullying mediated the association between dominance during primary school and dominance during middle school. Our data supported the mediation hypothesis. That is, we found that in early phases of group formation in middle school dominance is expressed through bullying and other agonistic strategies. After groups are stabilized and the dominance hierarchy is stabilized, dominance is expressed through more prosocial and cooperative means. In short, bullying is a form of aggression used by individuals to achieve some end, in this case dominance status (Pellegrini & Bartini, 2001; Sutton, Smith, & Swettenham, 1999).

That the transition to middle school witnesses an initial increase in bullying, in the more general context of age related decline of bullying (Smith, Madsen, & Moody, 1999) provides further support for the dominance hypothesis. Specifically, a large body of research suggests that there is a monotonic decrease in bullying, victimization, and aggression with age (see Pellegrini, 2002 for a review). By this we mean that rates of bullying and victimization generally decrease as youngsters get older. These decreases have been reported in a series of large scale investigations, often with nationally representative samples, and include countries in western Europe and North America (see Pellegrini, 2002 for a review).

These monotonic decreases during early adolescence, however, are evident only when youngsters do not change schools. When same age youngsters do change schools, there is an initial increase at this transition point, followed by a decrease. More specifically, in the case where youngsters 10–14 years of age change schools there is an initial increase in reported bullying and victimization. Within a year, the down trend resumes. This decrease reflects re-established dominance relationships. Dominance hierarchies, when they are stabilized, serve the important function of reducing in-group aggression (Dunbar, 1988; Vaughn, 1999).

These trends, however, are moderated by sex differences. In keeping with extant work with younger children (e.g., Boulton & Smith, 1994), proactive aggression and bullying are more frequent among boys than girls. Indeed, boys use and endorse aggression, especially physical aggression, with other boys to establish and maintain dominance (Maccoby, 1998). Correspondingly, girls' attitudes toward bullying are more negative than those of boys (Crick & Werner, 1998; Maccoby, 1998; Pellegrini, 2002).

Gender differences reflect the fact that boys' aggression increases as they progress through middle school. It seems to be the case that boys, more than girls, view physical aggression and bullying more positively as they progress through the early phases of adolescence. This interpretation is consistent with our analyses of attitudes toward bullying. Bullying and proactive aggression are also viewed positively by peers during the period of early adolescence (e.g., Graham & Juvonen, 1998; Pellegrini et al., 1999), possibly, because they represent one way in which individuals can assert their individuality and independence by exhibiting behavior which is antithetical to adult norms (Moffitt, 1993).

While girls are less likely than boys to endorse bullying, and especially physical aggression, they do engage in bullying and aggression of a different sort. Specially, girls often engage in relational (Crick & Grotpeter, 1995) or indirect aggression (Bjorkqvist, 1994). Relational, or indirect aggression is characterized by indirect attacks on opponents. That is, rather than confronting an opponent directly, as in a physical fight, one child (a) may say something nasty about another (b) to a third party (c). Further, relational aggression is meant to damage a persons' reputation and/or social relationships. While these strategies seem to be proactive in the sense that they aim to get something done and they require some deliberation, they do not seem to be dominance strategies *per se*. Specifically, female groups do not tend to be organized according to dominance hierarchies in the same sense as boys' groups (Maccoby, 1998). However, Campbell (1999) has recently suggested that indirect aggression fits particularly well into sexual selection. Sexual selection theory, as originally proposed by Darwin (1871) and extended by Trivers (1972), suggests that males and females use different strategies to attract mates. Males—being physically bigger, stronger, and more physically active—compete with each other, often using physical aggression to gain status, as expressed in dominance hierarchies. High status relates to access to females. Females, on the other hand, are smaller and are most concerned with protecting themselves and their future offspring. Thus, they choose dominant mates and, when they are aggressive against their peers, do so indirectly. This indirectness minimizes direct confrontation and possible harm. It has been further proposed, though not empirically validated, that girls may use relational aggression to form coalitions and alliances against rival girls so as to gain access to their goals.

The fact that youngsters', but especially boys', views of bullying became less negative with time is both interesting and troubling. This trend may be related to the fact that boys target other boys for victimization and that their empathy for boys in distress decreases during this period while boys' and girls' empathy for girls increases at this time (Olweus & Endresen, 1998).

The Question of Cross-sex Bullying

Early adolescence witnesses the beginning of heterosexual relationships, thus study of bullying and victimization in adolescence should include examination of cross-sex victimization. Correspondingly, there has been concern voiced (Craig,

Pepler, Connolly, & Henderson, 2001) that boys who are bullies as children will continue to be bullies in adolescence and target girls. This issue is exacerbated by the finding that adolescent girls find aggressive boys attractive (Bukowski et al., 2000; Pellegrini & Bartini, 2001). In this section we discuss the problem of cross-sex aggression, focusing especially on male-on-female aggression.

Previous research suggests that youngsters who are victimized in childhood by their same sex peers are also victimized in heterosexual relationships in adolescence (Craig et al., 2001). Our research (Pellegrini & Long, 2002), as well as the results of a recent meta-analysis of same- and cross-sex aggression (Archer, 2001), suggests that this is not always the case. Boys were most frequently the targets of aggression initiated by other boys. Boys least frequently aimed their aggression at girls. Indeed, girls were most frequently targeted by other girls.

This finding that males' aggression is predominately intrasexual, rather than intersexual, is consistent within a dominance theory framework whereby males use aggression against other males, not females, to establish and maintain status in male groups (e.g., Chance, 1978; Pellegrini & Bartini, 2001). Dominance status, in turn, is attractive to female adolescents (Bukowski et al., 2000; Pellegrini & Bartini, 2001). Future research should examine more closely the ecology surrounding boys' uses of bullying strategies. For example, is it done in the presence of girls so that they can exhibit their physical prowess?

By extension, and as alluded to above, research is needed on the specific uses of relational aggression. We know that girls target other girls, but we do not know, for example, if they are using these strategies to isolate a specific peer, to form alliances, or to reconcile with former foes. Further, we need to know the function of these alliances, if they exist. What is it that they get from these girls? Is it access to dates or a place on the student counsel?

The Positive Role of Peers: Changes in Peer Affiliation in Primary and Secondary School and Victimization

Another hallmark of early adolescence is the rapid and qualitative change in social affiliations. These changes are precipitated by processes associated with the onset of puberty as well as corresponding changes in social institutions, with the change from primary to secondary school being especially relevant. These changes come at a time when the peer group is taking on increased importance for youngsters (Eccles et al., 1998; Simmons & Blyth, 1987). A long-standing critique of middle schools and junior high schools, especially in the United States, is that they do not support youngsters' formation of new cooperative, social groupings but instead exacerbate fractured social groups by having youngsters attend large schools which simultaneously stress individual competition over cooperation (Eccles et al., 1998).

Changes in Peer Affiliation.   Our research examined changes in peer affiliation as youngsters made the transition from primary through the first two years
of middle school (Pellegrini & Long, 2002). Affiliation can be defined in terms
of the number of friends youngsters have as well as individuals' popularity. We
find that the number of affiliations for youngsters decreased, at least initially
with the transition from primary to middle school but it began to recover by the
second year of middle school (in the seventh grade). It is probably the case that
students' affiliations decreased because they were entering a new and much
larger social institution, even though the schools made some effort to foster
informal interaction among peers.

The middle schools we studied provided some opportunities for youngsters to
affiliate with peers but they were seemingly slow to take effect. For example, the
weekly free time (called "Coke Breaks") typically occurred during the final hour
of classes on Friday afternoons. Youngsters went to a central gathering place,
purchased a soda, and then went back to their homerooms and interacted with
their peers. More concentrated mechanisms may be needed during the first year
of middle school to foster more varied and closer relationships within these
larger social networks during the school day. Social and interest-specific events,
such as clubs, limited to sixth graders could be organized. If the events are of adequate duration and frequency, peer relationships may be formed and increase in
number. These peer affiliations, in turn, may be important buffers of subsequent
victimization.

Peers as Buffers Against Victimization.   Peer affiliation is relevant to the
study of victimization because, like bullying, victimization takes place in the
context of the peer group. Recent research suggests that dimensions of peer affiliation, such as having friends and being liked by peers, buffers victimization
(Hodges & Perry, 1999; Pellegrini et al., 1999; Pellegrini & Long, 2002). Generally, the number and quality of friends protect individuals from victimization.
Youngsters who have friends, especially friends who are strong and popular,
seem to inhibit bullies from picking on them. Friends may act as individual
"guardians" for their more vulnerable peers.

Additionally, being popular with peers also seems to buffer victimization.
Specifically, we (Pellegrini et al., 1999; Pellegrini & Long, 2002) found that
popularity is a more robust buffer than the number of reciprocal friend nominations. Specifically, we found, using hierarchical linear modeling, that the number
of "liked most" nominations, relative to the number of reciprocal friends, was a robust negative predictor of victimization across the middle school years (Pellegrini &
Long, 2002). We argue that having a number of affiliates, relative to close
friends, seems to protect against bullying because being liked by a number of
peers represents the number of possible social sanctions or retaliation against
bullies. If a child victimizes an individual who is liked by a large number
of peers, he/she runs the very real risk of retaliation, public sanction, and peer

disapproval. That bullies are concerned with social status among their peers would suggest that they would not target peers with allies or other social affiliations.

Translating Theory Into Practice: Implications for Bullying-Prevention and Intervention Programs

In this chapter we examined bullying and victimization during a period when it had seldom been studied. Extant studies, for the most part, have studied primary school children. The early adolescent period merits attention because it is a period where disruptions in peer affiliations afford opportunities for peer victimization and increased use of aggression, possibly to establish peer status. Consistent with this proposition, we found that bullying is used as a strategy to achieve dominance status during the transition from primary to middle school. Dominance theory seems to explain the fact that boys target each other, not females, in aggressive bouts.

Although not directly addressed in this chapter, it is important to note that much of the research cited in support of the dominance theory utilized multiple measures from a variety of agents to assess the constructs. By using a more broad-band approach the validity of constructs such as bullying and victimization is maximized. Construct validity requires multimethod and multisource data (Cronbach, 1971; Cronbach & Meehl, 1955). We have used direct observational measures, self-reports, peer nominations, as well as teacher checklists. By contrast, much of the extant research has relied almost exclusively on the use of single agents and of single measures (e.g., peers' and teachers' ratings and nominations). This is problematic especially when the research involves assessment of group-level constructs that require input from multiple informants.

Using direct observations may, however, be too expensive to use in most school settings as they require a large number of observations on individuals across time to yield valid data. However, educators and clinicians could make use of relative inexpensive peer nomination, self-report, and teacher checklist methods. From both policy and research perspectives, each of these methods provides a different perspective on bullying and victimization (Pellegrini & Bartini, 2000) and, when aggregated, results in a clear, valid indicator of the constructs. It is important to use a variety of methods as this approach minimizes the risk of missing a problem.

Continuing in the policy vein, many of the findings in our research are troubling, especially the finding that attitudes towards bullying become more positive with time. As peer groups, schools, and families are major socialization agents of young adolescents, they should be made aware of these views. The negative consequences of these views for both victims and others should be presented to youngsters. Future research should also begin to search for possible origins of these views. Are there models for these sorts of behaviors in middle schools? We know from Olweus' (1993a) seminal work that school personnel sometimes model bullying behavior, by belittling or threatening students.

Further, the role of school-level variables in bullying, victimization, and peer affiliation is important to consider in future research and policy. It would be important to compile descriptions of school-level variables, such as school policies toward bullying, access to counselors, adult supervision of peer interactions, and opportunities to affiliate with peers, from different perspectives, such as students, teachers, and neutral observers. This level of description could be useful in designing schools for young adolescents that support positive peer relationships and reduce victimization.

Lastly, the fact that aggression in early adolescence increases when youngsters change schools and decreases when they do not also merits consideration by educational policy makers. If such changes are necessary, consideration should be given to practices that maximize opportunities for positive peer affilations and continuity of peer cohorts. For example, it may be possible for youngsters to stay in an intact group during the initial transition to middle school. As the transition unfolds, opportunities for positive peer interaction should be increased. Simultaneously, the modeling and reinforcing of coercive strategies by school personnel should not be tolerated.

ACKNOWLEDGMENT

This research was supported by a grant from the W. T. Grant Foundation. We acknowledge the support and cooperation of A. Byers, R. Covi, the Jackson County School Board, teachers and principals at participating schools, and the members of the Jackson County Schools Project. Correspondence should be addressed to A. D. Pellegrini, Department of Educational Psychology, Burton Hall, Pillsbury Dr. SE, University of Minnesota, Minneapolis, MN 55455, pelle013@umn.edu.

REFERENCES

Archer, J. A. (2001, October). *Are women or men more aggressive?* Paper presented at the G. Stanley Hall Lecture on Gender and Aggression, Williamstown, MA.

Bjorkqvist, K. (1994). Sex differences in physical, verbal, and indirect aggression: A review of recent research. *Sex Roles, 30,* 177–188.

Bosworth, K., Espelage, D. L., & Simon, T. R. (1999). Factors associated with bullying behaviors in middle school students. *Journal of Early Adolescence, 19,* 341–362.

Boulton, M. J., & Smith, P. K. (1994). Bully/victim problems in middle school children: Stability, self-perceived competence, peer perceptions, and peer acceptance. *British Journal of Developmental Psychology, 12,* 315–329.

Bukowski, W. M., Sippola, L. A., & Newcomb, A. F. (2000). Variations in patterns of attraction to same- and other-sex peers during early adolescence. *Developmental Psychology, 36,* 147–154.

Campbell, A. (1999). Staying alive: Evolution, culture, and women's intrasexual aggression. *Behavioral and Brain Sciences, 22,* 203–252.

Chance, M. R. A. (1978). Sex differences in attention structures. In L. Tiger, & H. T. Fowler, (Eds.), *Female hierarchies* (pp. 135–162). Chicago: Beresford Book Service.

Coie, J. D., & Dodge, K. A. (1998). Aggression and antisocial behavior. In N. Eisenberg (Ed.). *Handbook of child psychology, Vol. 3* (pp. 779–862). New York: Wiley.

Connolly, J., Goldberg, A., Pepler, D., & Craig, W. M. (1999). Development and significance of cross-sex activities in early adolescence. *Journal of Youth and Adolescence, 24*, 123–130.

Craig, W. M., Pepler, D., Connolly, J., & Henderson, K. (2001). Developmental context of peer harassment in early adolescence: The role of puberty and the peer group. In J. Juvonen and S. Graham (Eds.), *Peer harassment in school: The plight of the vulnerable and victimized* (pp. 242–262). New York: Guilford.

Crick, N. R., & Grotpeter, J. (1995). Relational aggression, gender, and social psychological adjustment. *Child Development, 66*, 710–727.

Crick, N. R., & Werner, N. E. (1998). Response decision processes in relational and overt aggression. *Child Development, 69*, 1630–1639.

Cronbach, L . J. (1971). Validity. In R. L. Thorndike (Ed.), *Educational measurement* (pp. 443–507). Washington, D.C.: American Council on Education.

Cronbach, L. J., & Meehl, P. E. (1955). Construct validity in psychological tests. *Psychological Bulletin, 52*, 281–302.

Darwin, C. (1871). *The descent of man, and selection in relation to sex*. London: John Murray.

deWaal, F. B. M. (1986). The integration of dominance and social bonding in primates. *Journal of Theoretical Biology, 61*, 459–479.

Dodge, K. A., & Coie, J. D. (1987). Social information processing factors in reactive and proactive aggression in children's peer groups. *Journal of Personality and Social Psychology, 53*, 1146–1158.

Dunbar, R. I. M. (1988). *Primate social systems*. Ithaca: Cornell University Press.

Eccles, J. S., Wigfield, A., & Schiefele, U. (1998), Motivation to succeed. In N. Eisenberg (Ed.), *Handbook of child psychology, Vol. 3* (pp. 1017–1096). New York: Wiley.

Espelage, D. L., Bosworth, K., & Simon, T. R. (2000). Examining the social context of bullying behaviors in early adolescence. *Journal of Counseling & Development, 78*, 326–333.

Graham, S., & Juvonen, J. (1998). A social cognitive perspective on peer aggression and victimization. In R. Vasta (Ed.), *Annals of child development* (pp. 23–70). London: Jessica Kingsley Publishers.

Hodges, E. V., & Perry, D. G. (1999). Personal and interpersonal antecedents and consequences of victimization by peers. *Journal of Personality and Social Psychology, 76*, 677–685.

Ljungberg, T., Westlund, K., & Forsberg, A. J. L. (1999). Conflict resolution in 5-year-old boys. *Animal Behaviour, 58*, 1007 1016.

Maccoby, E. E. (1998). *The two sexes: Growing up apart, coming together*. Cambridge, MA: Harvard University Press.

Moffitt, T. E. (1993). Adolescent-limited and life-course-persistent anti-social behavior: A developmental taxonomy. *Psychological Review, 100*, 674–701.

National Center for Educational Statistics (1995, October). *Student victimization in schools*. Washington, D.D.: U.S. Department of Education.

Olweus, D. (1993a). *Bullying at school*. Cambridge, MA: Blackwell.

Olweus, D. (1993b). Victimization by peers. In K. H. Rubin & J. Asendorf (Eds.), *Social withdrawal, inhibition, and shyness in childhood* (pp. 315–341). Hillsdale, NJ: Erlbaum.

Olweus, D., & Endresen, I. M. (1998). The importance of sex-of-stimulus object: Age trends and sex differences in empathetic responses. *Social Development, 7*, 370–388.

Pellegrini, A. D. (2002). Bullying and victimization in middle school: A dominance relations perspective. *Educational Psychologist, 37*, 151–163.

Pellegrini, A. D., & Bartini, M. (2001). Dominance in early adolescent boys: Affiliative and aggressive dimensions and possible functions. *Merrill-Palmer Quarterly, 47*, 142–163.

Pellegrini, A. D., Bartini, M., & Brooks, F. (1999). School bullies, victims, and aggressive victims: Factors relating top group affiliation and victimization in early adolescence. *Journal of Educational Psychology, 91*, 216–224.

Pellegrini, A. D., & Long, J. (2002). A longitudinal study of bullying, dominance, and victimization during the transition from primary to secondary school. *British Journal of Developmental Psychology, 20*, 259–280.

Perry, D. G., Willard, J., & Perry, L. (1990). Peers' perceptions of consequences that victimized children provide aggressors. *Child Development, 61*, 1289–1309.

Simmons, R. G., & Blyth, D. A. (1987). *Moving into adolescence: The impact of pubertal change and school context.* Hawthorn, NY: Aldine de Gruyter.

Slee, P.T., & Rigby, K. (1993). Australian school children's self-appraisal of interpersonal relations: The bullying experience. *Child Psychiatry and Human Development, 23*, 273–287.

Smith, P. K., Madsen, K. C., & Moody, J. C. (1999). What causes the age decline in reports of being bullied at school? Toward a developmental analysis of risks of being bullied. *Educational Research, 41*, 267–285.

Smith, P. K., & Sharp, S. (1994). The problem of school bullying. In P. K. Smith & S. Sharp (Eds.), *School bullying* (pp. 1–19). London: Routledge.

Strayer, F. (1980). Social ecology of the preschool peer group. In W. A. Collins (Ed.), *The Minnesota symposia on child psychology: Development of cognition, affect, and social relations, Vol. 13* (pp. 165–196). Hillsdale, NJ: Erlbaum.

Sutton, J., Smith, P. K., & Swettenham, J. (1999). Socially undesirable need not be incompetent: A response to Crick and Dodge. *Social Development, 8*, 132–134.

Trivers, R. (1972). Parental investment and sexual selection. In B. Campbell (Ed.), *Sexual selection and the descent of man* (pp. 136–179). Chicago: Aldine.

Vaughn, B. E. (1999). Power is knowledge (and vice versa): A commentary on Winning some and losing some: A social relations approach to social dominance in toddler. *Merrill-Palmer Quarterly, 45*, 215–225.

III

Classroom Characteristics Associated With Bullying

7

Teachers' Attitudes Toward Bullying

Melissa K. Holt
University of New Hampshire

Melissa A. Keyes
K12 Associates, LLC

Bullying is recognized as one of the major problems facing United States' schools today. It occurs along a continuum, with students assuming roles including bully, victim, and bully/victim (Espelage, Bosworth, & Simon, 2000). Current estimates suggest that nearly 30% of American students are involved in bullying in one of these capacities (Nansel, Overpeck, Pilla, Ruan, Simons-Morton, & Scheidt, 2001). Initial research endeavors focused on bullying emerged in Scandinavia where, spurred by findings from investigators such as Olweus (e.g., Olweus, 1978), a nationwide campaign against bullying was implemented (Smith & Brain, 2000). This initiative, which began in the 1970's, set forth the following definition of bullying which remains current today: "A student is being bullied or victimized when he or she is exposed, repeatedly and over time, to negative actions on the part of one or more students" (Olweus, 2001). The preceding definition highlights the aggressive component of bullying as well as the associated inherent power imbalance and repetitive nature (Olweus, 2001). Although more recently researchers from the United States have begun to address bullying within primary and secondary schools, the comprehensive understanding necessary to inform effective interventions is still lacking. While it is possible to derive potentially helpful information from studies conducted outside of the United States, as Stein (2001) noted conclusions from such investigations should be interpreted cautiously given the ways in which the United States differs from the countries in which the majority of bullying research has taken place (e.g., the U.S. is less homogenous than most other countries surveyed).

Extant investigations of bullying in the United States have provided valuable insight into the problem, but have relied heavily on student questionnaires or student behavior observations (e.g., Leff, Kupersmidt, Patterson, & Power, 1999; Stockdale, Hangaduambo, Duys, Larson, & Sarvela, 2002). Although assessing students offers a crucial lens through which to understand bullying dynamics, it is also important to delineate school staff members' perspectives. School personnel have frequent interactions with students and are also often involved in bullying interventions (e.g., Newman, Horne, & Bartulomucci, 2000). Accordingly, it is critical that staff attitudes and behaviors are evaluated given their contribution to the pervasive school culture (Olweus, 1992), which, in turn serves to promote or to discourage bullying. Unfortunately, few studies have addressed attitudes maintained by adult members of the school community. As such, after reviewing background information on (1) the extent to which school staff recognize the occurrence of bullying within their schools, and (2) relevant school climate issues, we turn to a study of school personnel's attitudes affecting bullying that resulted in a targeted intervention program based on its findings. We conclude with a broader discussion of prevention and intervention programs involving school staff.

Do Teachers Recognize the Extent of Bullying?

Some studies have documented that teachers and students report similar levels of bullying. For example, an investigation of 344 youth and their teachers from a Swiss kindergarten revealed that there was relative consistency between rates of bullying and victimization delineated by teachers and students (Alsaker & Valkanover, 2001). A greater proportion of studies, however, have found that teachers report lower prevalence rates of bullying than students do. For instance, in a study focused on seven rural elementary schools in the United States, 739 students completed self-report measures of bullying and 37 teachers responded to parallel measures assessing bullying behaviors among children at their schools. Results indicated that teachers reported lower prevalence rates of bullying than students did (e.g., Stockdale et al., 2002). Similarly, a British investigation found that staff ($N = 13$) at an inner city secondary school underestimated the frequency with which bullying occurred; whereas 26% of students noted on a self-report measure that they had been bullied, staff believed that only 5% to 10% had been bullied (Pervin & Turner, 1994).

There are a number of factors that potentially contribute to these divergent bullying rates. For instance, teachers in the United States might not have historically reported bullying because it was not brought into the media spotlight as a salient issue until the 1999 school shooting at Columbine High School in Colorado. Until that point teachers might have dismissed bullying behaviors as non-hurtful interactions. In addition, school personnel are at a disadvantage for finding out about bullying that occurs when they are not around. For example, students might not be willing to inform staff about their victimization experiences out of fear that the bully will find out they told someone and retaliate (Espelage & Asidao, 2001), or because they do not believe that reporting incidents will lead to effective resolutions. Furthermore, even when teachers recognize the extent of bullying, they might not always be willing to report it. For instance, teachers at the preschool level who emphasize socialization as part of the educational experience might be hesitant to report problems with bullying and victimization for fear that it will reflect negatively upon their classroom management skills (e.g., Alsaker & Valkanover, 2001).

Literature also supports that teachers often maintain restricted working definitions of bullying, providing an addition reason why divergent rates might emerge from teachers' and students' responses to questionnaires. For example, findings from a study of 138 British teachers (preschool/infant, junior, and secondary schools) suggested that although teachers were aware of physical and verbal manifestations of bullying, they were not as likely to include social exclusion in their bullying definitions (Boulton, 1997). Similarly, 116 Canadian teacher trainees surveyed were more likely to identify physical attacks as bullying than verbal encounters, and typically rated social exclusion as less consistent with bullying than physical and verbal forms (Craig, Henderson, & Murphy, 2000). Furthermore, although researchers (e.g., Olweus, 2001; Smith & Brain, 2000) have set forth characteristics inherent in bullying (i.e., aggressive behavior, repetition, power imbalance) teachers do not always consider these factors. For instance, one group of 71 secondary school British teachers recognized that multiple types of bullying existed (e.g., physical, emotional) and understood the salience of power in bullying dynamics, but they did not mention repetition as a critical feature (Siann, Callaghan, & Lockhart, 1993). In sum, even if teachers observe bullying episodes of a particular nature (e.g., social exclusion), if the behaviors are not consistent with their definition of bullying they might not include these instances in their estimation of bullying frequency.

Finally, limited research supports the notion that individual characteristics of staff and students might influence staff perceptions of bullying. For instance, teacher sex has been posited to influence perceptions of bullying, although findings in this area have been inconclusive. Whereas Borg and Falzon's investigation (1989) indicated that male teachers were more likely to rate bullying as serious, Boulton (1997) found that pre-school through secondary school female teachers maintained more negative attitudes towards bullying behaviors. In addition, in one study teacher empathy was linked to views on bullying (Craig et al., 2000). Specifically, among the 116 Canadian teachers in training, greater teacher empathy was associated with an increased likelihood of identifying scenarios as bullying, an increased likelihood of intervention, and greater perceived seriousness of scenarios. Finally, bullies with particular demographic characteristics appear to be more easily recognized, suggesting that situations involving such youth might be more likely to be rated as bullying episodes. For example, in a study of elementary and middle school teachers, elementary school bullies were more likely to be identified than middle school bullies (Leff et al., 1999). In this same study, African-American bullies were more likely to be identified than bullies of other ethnicities, although as the authors noted this might have been due to an increased base rate in bullying among the African-American youth in the sample (Leff et al., 1999).

School Climate

As Swearer and Doll (2001) argue, bullying needs to be viewed from an ecological framework, and accordingly is best understood as an "interaction between the individual and his or her peer group, school, family, and community" (p. 19). With respect to the school's role, it is necessary to understand not only physical characteristics of school that influence bullying (e.g., physical layout of playgrounds), but also teachers' contributions to the school environment. One way in which to evaluate this area is through an exploration of school climate. As described by Tagiuri (1968), school climate is the "total environmental quality within an organization" (cited in Anderson, 1982). One element of Tagiuri's taxonomy is the school's "culture," which consists of factors such as beliefs and values. Those beliefs/values are manifested in the frequency and quality of interactions between adults and students, students and students, and adults and adults.

Beliefs/values also become evident through attitudes school staff convey. Attitudes directly and indirectly related to bullying are both important to consider. For instance, Hoover and Hazler (1994) note that when school personnel tolerate, ignore, or dismiss bullying behaviors they are conveying implicit messages about values that victimized students internalize. Conversely, if school staff hold attitudes not supportive of bullying behavior, and these are translated into voicing their opinions and/or actively intervening in bullying episodes, the school culture as a whole becomes less tolerant of bullying. In addition, it is important to evaluate the extent to which school cultures tolerate students who differ from the norm. Research has documented that students who do not "fit in" (Hoover, Oliver, & Thomson, 1993), are obese (Lagerspetz, 1982), are in remedial education (Byrne, 1994), and have developmental disabilities (Marini, Fairbairn, & Zuber, 2001) are more likely to be victimized by their peers. The attitudes school staff maintain toward students with such physical or academic challenges likely influence how youth treat such individuals. In sum, through developing a better sense of school personnel's attitudes directly and indirectly influencing bullying, more successful prevention and intervention programs can be developed.

An Evaluation of Teachers' Attitudes Toward Bullying

In an effort to enhance our understanding of ways in which American teachers' attitudes shape school climate and in turn potentially influence the occurrence of bullying, this investigation examined results gleaned from a survey administered to teachers and other staff (e.g., aides) in 18 Wisconsin schools. The central aim of this study was to explore school climate factors such as attitudes toward bullying, degree of overt hostility, attitudes toward diversity, and rule-setting policies. Moreover, the survey was designed to inform an intervention for pilot schools in Wisconsin; although understanding staff attitudes does not necessarily translate into understanding staff behaviors, evaluating attitudes is a necessary first component in designing effective interventions.

With respect to definitions framing this investigation, attitudes toward bullying were conceptualized as staff members' feelings toward teasing and their observations and value judgments of student behavior. Respect for diversity was viewed as teachers' feelings toward specific groups of students at their schools. Specifically, diversity in this context included differences in sex, race/ethnicity, sexual orientation, ability, socioeconomic status, and religion. Overt hostility was defined as observable actions or words that intimidate, humiliate, or otherwise hurt someone. Finally, the definition of equity was "fairness and justice or impartiality"; as noted by Bitters (1997) equity goes beyond equal educational opportunity.

Method

Participants.   Participants were 797 teachers and paraprofessionals/aides from 18 Wisconsin schools. Schools ranged from elementary to high school and included both rural and suburban communities. The number of respondents per school ranged from 11 to 133 ($M = 44.28$, $SD = 36.78$). There were 605 females (76%), 181 males (23%), and 11 (<1%) individuals not indicating their gender. Most participants were White (95.4%), followed by Asian (1%), Hispanic (0.6%), Mixed (0.3%), and Black (0.1%); 21 respondents did not denote their race (2.6%). With respect to academic background, teachers and paraprofessionals/aides reported the following educational experiences: HS GED (4%), some schooling beyond high school but no college degree (8%), technical or community college (4%), four-year college or university degree (11%), grade credits but no advanced degree (36%), master's degree (34%), doctorate degree (<1%). Seventeen participants (2%) did not reveal their educational history. Data on staff ages or years of experience were not collected. Among teachers participants taught a wide range of disciplines with the majority indicating that they were responsible for all subject areas.

Survey.   Surveys were distributed to teachers and other staff as a part of a larger state-wide investigation on school climate and diversity.[1] Instructions indicated that respondents would be asked about "how people work and learn together" in the school. Staff voluntarily filled out surveys and were assured confidentiality.

In addition to responding to demographic questions staff answered 50 questions, developed by a panel of experts in the field, assessing school climate constructs including attitudes toward bullying (e.g., "Teasing doesn't hurt"), degree of respect ("I often hear students saying disrespectful things"), attitudes toward diversity (e.g., "School makes all kinds of students feel welcome"), overt hostility (e.g., "Adults make jokes about race") and rule-setting (e.g., "Students help set rules") within their respective institutions. Some statements referred to the school in general (e.g., "In this school, staff are trained to intervene appropriately in student-to-student harassment") whereas other items inquired about individual teachers' beliefs and behaviors (e.g., "I tell people to stop if they're making a joke or stereotypic remark based on race"). Response options were: Strongly Disagree, Disagree, Agree, and Strongly Agree. To determine whether the questions represented distinct attitudinal constructs, these items were factor analyzed as part of the current study and findings from this analysis are presented in the Results section.

Results

Descriptive Analyses.   First, percentages of staff selecting each response value for items were computed to provide a general understanding of staff attitudes toward school climate factors. Representative items from the survey were selected and their corresponding ratings are displayed in Table 7.1.

With respect to bullying, 27% of school staff either agreed or strongly agreed that "a little teasing doesn't hurt." In addition, the majority of respondents (57%) believed that students would *not* intervene if they saw another student being teased or bothered. Conversely, most staff (93%) reported that adults *would* stop students from making hurtful comments to one another and stated that they would personally tell individuals making jokes based on race to stop (74%). In terms of training, two-thirds (65%) of the participants noted that staff received training on how to intervene in student-to-student harassment.

---

[1]Surveys for students (grades 2 through senior high school) and adults (parents, teachers/aides, administrators) are available from K12 Associates, LLC, 6314 Odana Road, Madison, WI 53719.
www.k12associates.com
Tel: (608) 232-7099
Fax: (608) 232-9064
e-mail: info@k12associates.com

TABLE 7.1

Percentages of Teachers Endorsing Each Response Category
for Selected Survey Items

	Strongly Agree	Agree	Disagree	Strongly Disagree
Teasing doesn't hurt.	2%	25%	51%	22%
If a student is being teased or bothered other students would stop it.	3%	40%	53%	4%
Students in my school are asked to help set rules and solve problems.	17%	59%	22%	2%
Adults here usually stop hurtful comments from students toward other students.	40%	53%	6%	1%
In this school, staff are trained to intervene appropriately in student-to-student harassment.	13%	52%	33%	2%
I tell people to stop if they're making a joke or stereotypic remark based on race.	21%	53%	25%	1%
We have taken systematic steps to provide a multicultural education.	13%	61%	23%	3%
I would be accepting of gay, lesbian, and bisexual students at this school.	40%	55%	4%	1%
The administrators in this school support staff in creating a harassment-free environment.	51%	44%	4%	1%
I have observed some teachers making fun of the way kids talk, look, or act.	<1%	25%	48%	27%

Responses also revealed that on average staff believed that their schools promote equity and acceptance of diversity. For instance, respondents indicated that steps toward multi-cultural education have been taken (74%), administrators supported staff in efforts to create harassment-free environments (92%), and students were asked to be involved in rule-setting and solving problems (76%). Furthermore, nearly all school staff (95%) responded that they would be accepting of gay, lesbian, and bisexual students. Interestingly, however, 26% of individuals surveyed noted that they had observed other teachers making fun of the way students talk, look, or act (although these individuals could be commenting on the same teachers).

Factor Analysis. Factor analysis provides a means by which to evaluate whether groups of questions/items exist with similar underlying characteristics. In this case, we were interested in whether questions assessed distinct attitudinal constructs because little research has addressed this area. As such, a principal axis factor analysis was conducted using the 28 questions about staff attitudes (refer to Kim & Mueller [1978] for a more technical discussion of factor analysis procedures). Results indicated that four attitudinal constructs (factors) existed (see Table 7.2). Items were retained for a factor when they had factor loadings of .40 or above on that factor and loadings under .40 on other factors. Higher factor loadings indicate a stronger relationship between the item and the factor. The resulting factors were named:

1. *Equity* (eigenvalue = 4.26), which accounted for 15% of the variance and consisted of 11 items assessing issues related to equality (e.g., staff speak out in favor of equality) and rule-setting (e.g., students help set rules),
2. *Hostile Climate* (eigenvalue = 3.41), which accounted for 12% of the variance and was composed of 10 items evaluating attitudes and behaviors consistent with a hostile environment (e.g., teachers joke about gay and lesbian students),
3. *Openness to Diversity* (eigenvalue = 7.01), which accounted for 7% of the variance and consisted of five items relating to acceptance of diverse students (e.g., students with disabilities often have talents), and
4. *Willingness to Intervene* (eigenvalue = 5.20), which accounted for 5% of the variance and included two questions inquiring about school staff willingness to stop people from making inappropriate jokes.

Alpha coefficients for the final scales were .88 for Equity, .83 for Hostile Climate, .71 for Openness to Diversity, and .78 for Willingness to Intervene, indicating that questions on each scale were reflective of a single attitudinal construct.

Interscale correlations were examined to determine how attitudinal constructs were related and findings supported the factor structure. Greater perceptions of equity were associated with less hostile environments ($r = -.54, p < .01$), more openness to diversity ($r = .33, p < .01$), and more willingness to intervene in situations in which inappropriate joking is occurring ($r = .22, p < .01$). In addition, a greater openness to diversity was related to a less hostile environment ($r = -.32, p < .01$) and more willingness to intervene when hearing jokes of a racial or sexual nature ($r = -.35, p < .01$). Finally, ratings indicating more hostile environments were associated with less staff willingness to tell people to stop making inappropriate jokes ($r = .29, p < .01$).

Means and Standard Deviations of Factors.   Means and standard deviations were then calculated for each scale resulting from the factor analysis: Equity ($M = 1.92$, $SD = 0.45$), Hostile Climate ($M = 2.94$, $SD = 0.44$), Openness to Diversity ($M = 1.54$, $SD = 0.42$), and Willingness to Intervene ($M = 2.14$, $SD = 0.65$). In the case of Equity, Openness to Diversity, and Willingness to

TABLE 7.2

Factor Analysis of Survey Items

Item Descriptor	Equity	Hostile Climate	Openness to Diversity	Willingness to Intervene
		Factor Loadings		
School makes all kinds of students feel welcome	.60			
Students are taught about diversity	.71			
Staff speak out in favor of equality	.50			
Administration supports staff in creating a harassment-free environment	.53			
Provided professional development to work with diverse populations	.57			
Students help set rules	.55			
School rules are clearly explained	.61			
School supports talk of diversity	.66			
Rules are enforced fairly	.60			
There are steps to provide multicultural education	.57			
Staff are trained to intervene about harassment	.57			
Teachers favor students of their own race		.61		
Teachers joke about gay and lesbian students		.56		
Students from families that don't have much money are joked about		.53		
Adults make jokes about race		.59		
People make hurtful, rude remarks about how you look		.55		
Teachers favor students of their own sex		.47		
Teachers make fun of the way students talk		.57		
Often hear students saying disrespectful things		.47		
Students are touched and pushed around		.47		
Staff make sexual jokes		.47		
Students with disabilities often have talents			.56	
Would rather work in school without disabled students			−.61	
Would rather work in school without diverse students			−.61	
Accept gay and lesbian students			.47	
Students with disabilities receive the same education			.47	
Tell people to stop if making racial joke				.89
Tell people to stop if telling sexual joke				.60

Intervene, mean values around 2 indicated that these values were thought to be promoted. With respect to Hostile Climate, a mean value close to 3 implies that respondents did not believe that their school environments were hostile. Overall, these mean values suggest that school staff described their schools as equitable, open to diversity, and welcoming. In addition, participants reported willingness to intervene in harassing situations.

Next, mean scale values were compared across (1) males and females, (2) school types, and (3) individual schools. Comparisons were made using ANOVAs, which provided a means by which to evaluate whether on average groups differed on the four attitudinal constructs. With respect to sex, results from a one-way ANOVA indicated that scale means did not differ for males and females (Equity, F (1, 768) = 1.67; Hostile Climate, F (1, 776) = 2.82; Openness to Diversity, F (1, 765) = 3.17; Willingness to Intervene in Teasing, F (1, 712) = 1.57). This suggested that male and female school personnel tended to maintain similar attitudes across these areas.

Teachers and aides/paraprofessionals were then classified into three categories according to the grades for which they were responsible to subsequently evaluate factor scores (i.e., attitudinal constructs) based on school type. These were: Elementary school (kindergarten through fifth grade), middle school (sixth through eight grade), and high school (ninth through twelfth grade). This classification system accounted for 83% of the participants; the remaining 17% either taught across multiple school types or did not report which grades they taught. One-way ANOVAs were then calculated and results indicated that mean differences existed across school types (see Table 7.3). As delineated in Table 7.3,

TABLE 7.3

Means, Standard Deviations, and One-way Analysis of Variance (ANOVA) for Effects of School Type on Scale Scores

	Elementary School (N = 338)		Middle School (N = 117)		High School (N = 198)		ANOVA	
	M	SD	M	SD	M	SD	F (2, 652)	η^2
Equity	1.79	0.39	1.83	0.48	2.11	0.44	6.64*	0.10
Hostile Climate	3.05	0.41	2.99	0.47	2.77	0.41	5.07	0.08
Openness to Diversity	1.51	0.41	1.56	0.44	1.58	0.43	1.61	0.01
Willingness to Intervene	2.25	0.66	2.10	0.67	1.98	0.62	10.57*	0.03

Note. For Equity, a Tukey post hoc test revealed that high school teachers rate their school environments as significantly more equitable than elementary and middle school teachers. For Willingness to Intervene, elementary school teachers are significantly more likely to intervene than high school teachers.

*$p < .01$.

school personnel differed on Equity and Willingness to Intervene. Broadly, this finding indicated that staff from the three school types held different attitudes with respect to Equity and Willingness to Intervene. To determine where specific differences existed Tukey post-hoc tests were conducted. With respect to Equity, high school staff rated equity significantly higher than elementary and middle school staff ($p < .01$). High school staff therefore viewed their schools as more equitable. For example, perhaps high schools include students in rule setting more often than elementary or middle schools. Conversely, high school staff was significantly less willing to intervene when hearing inappropriate jokes than elementary school staff ($p < .01$). This might be because high school staff interpret the jokes as less harmful to their students than elementary school staff do, or might feel less comfortable intervening because the students are older.

Finally, one-way ANOVAs were conducted to evaluate differences across the 18 schools surveyed on Equity, Hostile Climate, Openness to Diversity, and Willingness to Intervene. Results indicated that schools differed across the four attitudinal factors (Equity, $F (17, 753) = 11.68$; Hostile Climate, $F (17, 756) = 3.57$; Openness to Diversity, $F (17, 764) = 3.71$; Willingness to Intervene, $F (17, 700) = 3.05$). This suggested that members of the 18 schools maintained different attitudes influencing school climate. It is unclear why these differences emerged. Correlations between number of staff members in each school completing surveys and the scale factors were not significant, indicating that attitudes were not a function of the number of teachers responding to the survey in a given school. Given that additional potentially salient indicators about each school did not exist in the data set (e.g., location of school, total enrollment, total number of teachers in school), however, a more comprehensive evaluation of school-to-school differences was not possible.

Discussion

The central aim of this study was to evaluate school climate factors that potentially influence bullying among staff from 18 schools in the United States. Results indicated that four distinct attitudinal constructs were evident: Equity, hostile climate, openness to diversity, and willingness to intervene. On average, the school personnel surveyed maintained positive attitudes toward their students, believed that respect for diversity existed, and were generally willing to intervene when they witnessed inappropriate racial or sexual joking or heard a student make hurtful comments to a peer. In fact, school staff reported that they were more willing to intervene in teasing episodes than students were. This is counter to previous literature in which students have been surveyed; findings from these investigations have suggested that teachers are not as likely to intervene (e.g., O'Moore, Kirkham, & Smith, 1998). With respect to educational preparation, results indicated that the majority of individuals surveyed had received training on how to intervene appropriately in student-to-student harassment, a finding that is somewhat discrepant from previous literature suggesting that teachers do not receive adequate training (e.g., Boulton, 1997). It might be, however, that although respondents from these schools had obtained some training, if asked, they would respond that they desired additional training.

When comparing attitudes as a function of individual and school characteristics, a number of findings emerged. First, attitudes toward bullying did not differ for male and female staff. Previous findings on sex differences have been inconclusive, but these research endeavors have tended to focus on physical manifestations of bullying (e.g., Borg & Falzon, 1989; Boulton, 1997). As such, results from the current investigation suggest that males and females might be more likely to have similar attitudes when verbal rather than physical forms of bullying are under consideration. Second, attitudes differed across school types. Whereas high school staff perceived their educational environments to be more equitable than elementary and middle school staff they were less likely to intervene in inappropriate joking episodes than elementary school staff. This supports previous literature suggesting that willingness to intervene declines as students become older (e.g., O'Moore, Kirkham, & Smith, 1998). Perhaps teachers of more advanced students feel less responsible for their students' interactions than teachers of younger students who might view part of their jobs as teaching appropriate socialization skills. Third, equity, hostile climate, openness to diversity, and willingness to intervene differed across individual schools. Due to limitations of the current investigation, however, it is unclear why these differences exist. For example, it might be that school size or the existence of programming to create positive school environments influences staff attitudes.

Findings provide a preliminary understanding of staff attitudes influencing their respective school climates. This investigation was limited in some respects, however. Data were collected from only one state, and therefore efforts should be made to collect similar data in states with different characteristics. In addition, this investigation did not address the extent to which staff attitudes were linked to bullying behaviors, and this is a crucial factor to understand. For example, in schools in which teachers view bullying as problematic and are well-trained to intervene, are rates of bullying as reported by students lower than in schools in which teachers do not label many behaviors as teasing and have not had appropriate training? Furthermore, this survey was somewhat restricted in its definition of bullying, in that it mainly focused on verbal manifestations of bullying such as teasing. However, it is important to note that although teasing constitutes only one aspect of bullying, it is the most commonly observed and experienced form (Hoover et al., 1993). Finally, this study did not explore how staff attitudes toward school climate variables related to students' perceptions. Because the survey used in this investigation was also given to students we will be able to address this issue in future papers.

In sum, this study contributes to the field by presenting valuable information on school staff attitudes that likely influence the occurrence of bullying. Results are critical in informing essential training for teachers and other school personnel. As will be discussed in the following section, findings were influential in the design of a pilot bullying intervention for three of the schools surveyed.

Translating Research Into Practice: Implications for Bullying-Prevention and Intervention Programs

The role of school personnel is salient in ecologically-based interventions, which have proved to be effective in reducing bullying. Various approaches derived from this framework exist including the "whole-school approach," which involves teachers, students, parents, and outside agencies (e.g., Olweus & Alsaker, 1991; Smith & Sharp, 1994) and the systemic thinking approach (e.g., Sawatzky, Eckert, & Ryan, 1993), which relies on teachers, students, parents, and communities. Such comprehensive programs are necessary if bullying is to be adequately addressed. As noted by Siann and colleagues (1993), "Bullying should be regarded within a social context rather than from the point of view of individual pathology."

A first step in any successful prevention or intervention program involving school staff is training about bullying. Broadly, critical issues for preservice and in-service training include defining bullying and its signs, effects, and causes, highlighting preventive strategies, teaching skills for how to deal with bully/ victim problems, and encouraging the development of school policy to counter bullying (O'Moore, 2000). Unfortunately, not enough teachers are involved in comprehensive pre-service training or in-service educational programs. For instance, of 138 United Kingdom secondary school teachers surveyed, 87% desired additional training on bullying (Boulton, 1997). Specifically, these teachers either agreed or strongly agreed with at least one of the following two statements: "I would appreciate more training in how to deal with bullying" and "I would appreciate more training in how to prevent bullying." Similarly, only 5% of the 44 teachers surveyed at seven Dublin schools reported that their training had adequately equipped them to deal with bullying (Byrne, 1994). This perceived lack of training might be one reason why teachers do not always intervene when witnessing bullying (e.g., Espelage & Asidao, 2001) and often do not speak to bullies about their inappropriate behaviors (e.g., O'Moore, Kirkham, & Smith, 1998).

In sum, it is critical that school staff training be included in preservice training and bullying prevention and intervention programs. As noted by Olweus (1993), when school personnel acquire effective strategies with which to respond to bullying and implement their responses immediately, rates of bullying decrease.

Next, we turn to specific prevention and intervention programs that include school personnel.

Wisconsin Pilot Bullying-Intervention Program

A pilot bullying-intervention program, Keep It Safe is currently underway in three Wisconsin schools. The purpose of the Keep It Safe project is to develop a process for change in schools that will prevent sexual harassment and assault when students become adolescents and adults. The process and activities are designed to address bullying and harassment among younger children and the adults who teach and parent them. Along the way, another goal is to improve school climate so that, ultimately, student achievement is increased.

This project was informed by findings from the survey described above. Specifically, schools use the survey as an initial assessment and planning tool. In this manner, schools are able to tailor the intervention based on survey results from their particular school. Initial work with staff includes a review of the survey data and identification of areas most in need of improvement. In addition, three focal components are addressed in all schools: (1) school environment, including processes and policies, (2) adult behaviors, including modeling and response to bullying, and (3) student skill development. Although only the adult behavior component will be discussed thoroughly here, a more detailed explanation of this intervention can be obtained from K12 Associates LLC.

A basic premise of the intervention is that evaluating staff attitudes allows for a better understanding of what behaviors should be targeted. As such, the attitudinal constructs described above (e.g., hostile climate, equity, openness to diversity) are reflected in intervention themes. First, ways in which adult behaviors can contribute to a hostile climate are addressed. For example, adult modeling is a critical component that can exacerbate bullying and harassment in schools. Teachers who tease students in inappropriate ways provide reinforcement of verbal harassment and bullying among students. As part of the intervention adults therefore receive training in how to serve as effective role models. In addition, teachers are provided with information about curriculum addressing the prevention of bullying, harassment, and assault. By directly exploring these issues in the classroom teachers convey the message that bullying contributes to a hostile climate.

Second, educators are encouraged to consider their attitudes and behaviors related to equity. For example, through their actions adults might increase gender inequality by accepting gender-role stereotypes or assuming that girls are better students than boys. Adults also might encourage unhealthy competition by basing their instructional methods on hierarchical limitations (e.g., creating a hierarchy in which only the same few students are rewarded all the time) rather than modeling equity regardless of student characteristics. When this occurs, those who are "outsiders" or on the margins develop resentments, and those on the inside develop arrogance. Either way, bullying can develop because of the imbalance of perceived power. Teachers in the pilot schools have therefore been trained to promote cooperative work among students, with a focus on inclusiveness and equal treatment of all students.

A third intervention component highlights respect for diversity. Staff members attend a four-day training in the Tribes process that shows teachers how they can use inclusive activities and cooperative methods to create stronger positive relationships among students. Students learn that they are truly valued and can be successful because the teacher creates support and highlights how individual contributions from diverse students strengthens the community.

Thus far the intervention has had mixed results. Although teachers have welcomed information about new intervention strategies, they have been less able (and sometimes less willing) to make changes in the ways in which they intervene in bullying. The educators who have been open to examining their own words and actions, however, have found the subsequent changes in student behavior to be dramatic.

K12 Associates is now working to design more targeted curriculum for teachers and aides. In addition, they are instituting more comprehensive assessments of teachers after the intervention is implemented to determine the extent to which new instructional methods are used and more effective teacher-student interactions are evident.

Promoting Issues in Common (PIC) Model (Hazler, 1996)

The Promoting Issues in Common model was developed in the United States as a way to counsel bullies and victims who are in conflict (Hazler, 1996). As noted by Hazler (1996), the primary goal of this model is to assist "people with problematic relationships to deal directly with these relationships" (p. 66). As such, ultimately the bully and victim work together to resolve relationship conflict and to re-distribute power and control equally in the relationship. This therapeutic model requires that all participants (i.e., bullies and victims) perceive the counseling environment to be safer than the one in which conflict occurs. Primary steps in the model include (1) gaining control (e.g., insuring that students involved in counseling aren't physically fighting), (2) assessing the problem (e.g., determining what the bully/victim problems are), and (3) intervening directly.

The model relies on a multisystemic approach, in that all members of the system (e.g., schools, parents, bullies, bystanders) must be trained to deal with bullying and be involved in implementing interventions. The following are specific actions to be assumed by schools and communities that will create a climate that does not tolerate bullying: (1) provide clear and consistent enforcement of behavioral rules, (2) do not overlook acts that seem to be abusive, (3) provide support for bullies to deal with the problems that led them to bully, (4) educate bystanders about what they can do when the witness bullying episodes, (5) provide assistance to victims, (6) engage students, parents, teachers, and the community in cooperative activities, and (7) design activities in which diverse groups work toward common goals.

With respect to specific direct interventions for teachers, a classroom action plan can frame interventions, one that specifies ways in which bullying will be dealt with and one that all classroom members agree upon. This provides an opportunity for students to engage in cooperative work as well. Teachers should also integrate assertiveness training into lesson plans and modeling. Furthermore, by designing role-play situations in which students assume the roles of bullies, victims, and bystanders, students can develop an enhanced perspective of the feelings of all involved parties. Finally, Hazler (1996) suggests that teachers highlight historical figures that have bullied others (e.g., Adolph Hitler).

Bullies, victims, and bystanders are also provided with suggestions for action as part of this model. For instance, bullies should consider the myriad consequences of bullying, develop empathy for victims, and learn additional anger management skills. Victims, on the other hand, should consider being more assertive, strengthen friendships to discourage isolation, and ask for social support when necessary. Finally, bystanders should consider potential actions they might take when they observe bullying, such as speaking up against the bullying, providing support for victims, or soliciting help from adults.

Toronto Anti-Bullying Intervention
(Pepler, Craig, Ziegler, & Charach, 1994)

The Toronto Anti-Bullying Intervention began in the fall of 1991 (Pepler, Craig, Ziegler, & Charach, 1994). It was modeled after the Norwegian national bullying-intervention program, which stresses the need for a multisystemic approach to countering bullying (Olweus, 1991). As designed in Norway, the program included aims such as increasing knowledge about bullying across all relevant systems, encouraging teachers and parents to become involved in planning and implementing interventions, and delineating specific rules against bullying behaviors. The program requires schools, classrooms, students, school staff, and parents to be active contributors.

Whereas the Norwegian program was nationally mandated and well-funded by the Ministry of Education, and therefore included extensive training materials, the more modest Canadian program relied on program development by teachers and administrators who were less familiar with extant bullying literature. Nonetheless, through evaluating bullying dynamics within Canadian schools, an effective intervention was designed. Three common components—staff training, codes of behavior, improved playground supervision—were introduced in all four Canadian schools involved in the pilot intervention program, and individual schools also had the opportunity to tailor the program to their specific needs. These components were infused across the four levels of intervention: (1) the school level, (2) the parent level, (3) the classroom level, and (4) the individual bully and victim level.

With respect to the school level, a school conference on bullying and victimization was held for teachers to increase their knowledge in this area. In addition, adult supervision was increased in areas in which bullying commonly occurred (e.g., playgrounds). Furthermore, schools developed codes of behavior that specified unacceptable behaviors and additionally included the rights and responsibilities of all school members.

In terms of the parent level, parents were presented with information about the intervention program at pilot schools, and in the future will be provided with a booklet on bullying. In addition, parents were encouraged to engage their children in dialogue about bullying and to be cognizant of signs of victimization.

A variety of activities were implemented at the classroom level, including using literature highlighting bullying themes and providing safe contexts in which students could discuss real-life bullying incidents. Furthermore, a unique aspect of the Canadian program was its inclusion of a peer conflict-mediation program that provided a means through which students could resolve a range of interpersonal conflicts.

Finally, discussions with students in groups, with individual bullies, and with individual victims framed the individual bully and victim level. These discussions provided information about appropriate and inappropriate behaviors, and presented ways in which victims could attempt to counter bullying. School personnel also involved parents to ensure that victims received necessary support and bullies were disciplined for inappropriate behaviors.

Preliminary results from this pilot intervention program were somewhat positive, although researchers noted that bullying was still a problem within the four pilot schools (see Pepler et al., 1994 for a comprehensive discussion of results). Over the 18-month period from pre-test to evaluation, students reported an increase in teachers intervening in bullying episodes, and an increase in the frequency with which teachers spoke to bullies. The proportion of bullies and victims discussing the problem with their parents remained stable over the evaluation period (42% and 59% respectively for bullies and victims). At 18 month follow-up students were not more likely to intervene in bullying episodes, but there was a decrease in the amount of children who reported that they would join in bullying a peer. In addition, over the 18-month evaluation there was an increase in the proportion of children who reported engaging in bullying behaviors (over the term and within the past five days), but a decrease in the proportion of youth who indicated they had been victimized in the past five days.

Summary

Despite the high frequency with which bullying occurs in American elementary, middle, and high schools, school personnel often report lower prevalence rates than students (e.g., Stockdale et al., 2002). One way to increase awareness among school staff is through preservice and in-service training. A necessary component of this educational process is assessment. In particular, by evaluating school personnel's attitudes that influence school climate, researchers can develop a more thorough conceptualization of the environments in which youth are educated. For example, teachers might foster bullying by failing to promote respectful interactions among students, modeling disrespectful behaviors, or declining to intervene in bullying episodes. Evaluations of staff attitudes and behaviors in specific schools will allow for the development of targeted intervention programs highlighting school staff training that will in turn result in school climates that do not tolerate bullying.

REFERENCES

Alsaker, F. D., & Valkanover, S. (2001). Early diagnosis and prevention of victimization in kindergarten. In J. Juvonen & S. Graham (Eds.), *Peer harassment in schools: The plight of the vulnerable and victimized* (pp. 175–195). New York: The Guilford Press.

Anderson, C. A. (1982). The search for school climate: A review of the research. *Review of Educational Research, 52,* 368–420.

Bitters, B. A. (1997). *Glossary of terms for working with equity and diversity.* Wisconsin Department of Public Instruction, Madison, WI.

Borg, M. G., & Falzon, J. M. (1989). Primary school teachers' perception of pupils' undesirable behaviours. *Educational Studies, 15,* 251–260.

Boulton, M. J. (1997). Teachers' views on bullying: Definitions, attitudes, and ability to cope. *British Journal of Educational Psychology, 67,* 223–233.

Byrne, B. (1994). Bullies and victims in a school setting with reference to some Dublin schools. *The Irish Journal of Psychology, 15,* 574–586.

Craig, W. M., Henderson, K., & Murphy, J. G. (2000). Prospective teachers' attitudes toward bullying and victimization. *School Psychology International, 21,* 5–21.

Espelage, D. L., & Asidao, C. S. (2001). Conversations with middle school students about bullying and victimization: Should we be concerned? *Journal of Emotional Abuse, 2,* 49–62.

Espelage, D. L., Bosworth, K., & Simon, T. R. (2000). Examining the social context of bullying behaviors in early adolescence. *Journal of Counseling and Development, 78,* 326–333.

Hazler, R. J. (1996). *Breaking the cycle of violence: Interventions for bullying and victimization.* Washington, DC: Accelerated Development.

Hoover, J. H., & Hazler, R. J. (1994). Bullies and victims. *Elementary School Guidance and Counseling, 25,* 212–220.

Hoover, J. H., Oliver, R., & Thomson, K. (1993). Perceived victimization by school bullies: New research and future direction. *Journal of Humanistic Education and Development, 32,* 76–84.

Kim, J., & Mueller, C. (1978). *Factor Analysis: Statistical methods and practical issues.* Thousand Oaks, CA: Sage Publications, Inc.

Lagerspetz, K. M. (1982). Group aggression among school children in three schools. *Scandinavian Journal of Psychology, 23,* 45–52.

Leff, S. S., Kupersmidt, J. B., Patterson, C. J., & Power, T. J. (1999). Factors influencing teacher identification of peer bullies and victims. *School Psychology Review, 28,* 505–517.

Marini, Z., Fairbairn, L., & Zuber, R. (2001). Peer harassment in individuals with developmental disabilities: Towards the development of a multidimensional bullying identification model. *Developmental Disabilities Bulletin, 29,* 170–195.

Nansel, T. R., Overpeck, M., Pilla, R. S., Ruan, W. J., Simons-Morton, B., & Scheidt, P. (2001). Bullying behaviors among U.S. youth: Prevalence and association with psychosocial adjustment. *Journal of the American Medical Association, 285,* 2094–2100.

Newman, D., Horne, A., & Bartolomucci, C. (2000). *Bullybusting: A psychoeducational program for helping bullies and their victims.* Champaign, IL: Research Press.

Olweus, D. (1978). *Aggression in the Schools: Bullies and Whipping Boys*. Washington, DC: Hemisphere.

Olweus, D. (1991). Bully/victim problems among school children: Basic facts and effects of a school based intervention program. In D. Pepler & K. Rubin (Eds.), *The Development and Treatment of Childhood Aggression* (pp. 411–448). Chicago: University of Chicago Press.

Olweus, D. (1992). Bullying among schoolchildren: Intervention and prevention. In R. D. Peters, R. J. McMahon, & V. L. Quinsey (Eds.), *Aggression and violence throughout the life span* (pp. 100–125). London: Sage Publications.

Olweus, D. (1993). *Bullying at school: What we know and what we can do*. Cambridge: Blackwell.

Olweus, D. (2001). Peer harassment: A critical analysis and some important issues. In J. Juvonen & S. Graham (Eds.), *Peer harassment in schools: The plight of the vulnerable and victimized* (pp. 3–20). New York: The Guilford Press.

Olweus, D., & Alsaker, F. D. (1991). Assessing change in a cohort longitudinal study with hierarchical data. In D. Magnusson, L. Gergman, G. Rudinger, & B. Torestad (Eds.), *Problems and methods in longitudinal research* (pp. 107–132). New York: Cambridge University Press.

O'Moore, M. (2000). Critical issues for teacher training to counter bullying and victimization in Ireland. *Aggressive Behavior, 26*, 99–111.

O'Moore, M., Kirkham, C., & Smith, M. (1998). Bullying in schools and Ireland: A nationwide study. *Irish Educational Studies, 17*, 254–271.

Pepler, D. J., Craig, W. M., Ziegler, S., & Charach, A. (1994). An evaluation of an antibullying intervention in Toronto schools. *Canadian Journal of Community Mental Health, 13*, 95–110.

Pervin, K., & Turner, A. (1994). An investigation into staff and pupil knowledge, attitudes, and beliefs about bullying in an inner city school. *Pastoral Care in Education, 12*, 16–22.

Sawatzky, D. D., Eckert, C., & Ryan, B. R. (1993). The use of family systems approaches by school counsellors. *Canadian Journal of Counselling, 27*, 113–122.

Siann, G., Callaghan, M., & Lockhart, R. (1993). Bullying: Teachers' views and school effects. *Educational Studies, 19*, 307–21.

Smith, P. K., & Brain, P. (2000). Bullying in schools: Lessons from two decades of research. *Aggressive Behavior, 26*, 1–9.

Smith, P. K., & Sharp, S. (Eds.) (1994). *School bullying: Insights and perspectives*. London: Routledge.

Stein, N. (2001). Introduction – What a difference a discipline makes: Bullying research and future directions. *Journal of Emotional Abuse, 2*, 1–5.

Stockdale, M. S., Hangaduambo, S., Duys, D., Larson, K., & Sarvela, P. D. (2002). Rural elementary students', parents', and teachers' perceptions of bullying. *American Journal of Health Behavior, 26*, 266–277.

Swearer, S. M., & Doll, B. (2001). Bullying in schools: An ecological framework. *Journal of Emotional Abuse, 2*, 7–23.

Taguiri, R. (1968). The concept of organizational climate. In R. Tagiuir & G. H. Litwin (Eds.), *Organizational climate: Exploration of a concept*. Boston: Harvard University.

8

Bullying Among Young Children: The Influence of Peers and Teachers

Laura D. Hanish, Becky Kochenderfer-Ladd,
Richard A. Fabes, Carol Lynn Martin,
Donna Denning
Arizona State University

Bullying at school is a widespread problem, touching the lives of most children at some time or another. Investigators have shown how prevalent this problem is among school-aged children with estimates suggesting that approximately 5% to 10% of children repeatedly attack their peers (Olweus, 1984) and approximately 10% to 15% of children persistently serve as the target of peer harassment (Boulton & Smith, 1994; Kochenderfer-Ladd & Wardrop, 2001). Estimates are even greater when the number of children who report more sporadic involvement in bullying is considered. For example, when asked if they had ever been bullied during their school years, Hoover, Oliver, and Hazler (1992) found that 81% of male and 72% of female middle and high school students answered in the affirmative. Similarly, in a prospective study following children from kindergarten to third grade, Kochenderfer-Ladd and Wardrop (2001) found that about 60% of their sample could be classified as a victim at least once during the four years of the study. Such findings indicate that peer victimization is a fairly pervasive phenomenon. In fact, it appears that only a minority of students actually escapes being victimized during their school years.

Moreover, it is clear that such aggressive behaviors negatively impact the lives of the youngsters who are involved. Researchers have demonstrated that both bullies and victims are at risk for experiencing a diverse set of short- and long-term adjustment difficulties, including academic difficulties, emotional and behavioral problems, and disrupted social relationships (Hanish & Guerra, 2002; Kochenderfer & Ladd, 1996a, 1996b; Kochenderfer-Ladd & Wardrop, 2001; Schwartz, McFadyen-Ketchum, Dodge, Pettit, & Bates, 1998). Bullying may be an even more serious problem when it involves such behaviors as weapon-carrying, physical assaults, and sexual harassment.

As is evident from the foregoing discussion, preventing bullying is imperative for the safety and well being of our schoolchildren. As prevention research has repeatedly shown, programs tend to be most successful when delivered early, before stable behavioral and interactional patterns have had a chance to firmly solidify (Coie & Dodge, 1998; Kazdin, 1985). To successfully intervene with young children, however, requires an understanding of bullying in the early school years. Unfortunately, relatively little attention has been directed towards bullying in this age group.

The present chapter is intended to fill this niche by examining what is known about bullying in preschool and kindergarten children. Importantly, bullying is a social process, influenced by interactions with peers and involvement with teachers (Atlas & Pepler, 1998), making the classroom one of the most important and proximal contexts for the development and prevention of bullying. Therefore, the goal for this work is to consider how interactions with peers and teachers relate to the development of bullying in young children. We begin by providing an overview of bullying behavior among young children, and then we discuss how peer and teacher interactions relate to bullying in this age group.

To illustrate these ideas, we will also draw from a study that consists of data gathered on 167 preschoolers and kindergarteners (87 boys, 80 girls; average age = 51.9 months, $SD = 10.78$ months) who attended a university-sponsored school providing full day care for 5 days a week. Children represented ethnically diverse backgrounds: 67% non-Hispanic White, 11% Asian American, 9% Hispanic, 5% African American, and 8% other racial groups. These data were part of a larger, short-term longitudinal (over the course of the school year) study of young children's social, emotional, and behavioral functioning and early school readiness and success (see Fabes, Martin, Hanish, Anders, & Madden-Derdich, in press; Hanish, Ryan, Martin, & Fabes, in press). Multiple methods were used, including observational procedures and teacher ratings. Measures of interest focused on bullying experiences, as well as multiple aspects of peer and teacher relationships.

Bullying in Early Childhood

Prevalence and Developmental Trends.   Because aggressive behaviors are prevalent among young children, it is difficult to differentiate the early emergence of more serious bullying behavior from normative developmental trends in the expression of aggressive behavior during early childhood (Coie & Dodge, 1998). For example, peer-directed aggression has been observed in infants as young as 12 months of age (Caplan, Vespo, Pedersen, & Hay, 1991), and by the time children reach preschool and kindergarten age, peer-directed aggression is quite common (Alsaker & Valkanover, 2001; Crick, Casas, & Ku, 1999; Kochenderfer & Ladd, 1996a; 1996b; Olson, 1992; Patterson, Littman, & Bricker, 1967). Kochenderfer and Ladd (1996b) found that approximately one-fifth of kindergarteners reported being victimized frequently by peers. Moreover, because bullying is typically defined as unprovoked aggressive behavior that is persistently directed toward a weaker or younger child with the intention to harm, it becomes quite controversial to label young children as bullies given this definition. At best, we must rely on the frequency with which preschoolers and kindergarteners aggress against their peers and identify those who fall outside the normative range of aggressiveness for this age group. Thus, although we use the term "bully" to be consistent with other chapters in this volume, as well as to preserve the original language when discussing other investigators' studies, it is used interchangeably with "aggressive child" to remind the reader that who we have actually identified in our work are those children who are more frequently aggressive than their peers.

And, in fact, there are individual differences in the level of aggressive behavior displayed, with some young children exhibiting more frequent (i.e., several times per day and several days per week) or more intense (in terms of severity or potential for harm) aggression than others. For instance, Crowther, Bond, and Rolf (1981) reported that, among boys, 16.4% of 3-year-olds, 12% of 4-year-olds, and 6.9% of 5-year-olds aggressed against others at least several times per day (prevalence rates for girls were 8.6%, 6.3%, and 2.9% at ages 3, 4, and 5, respectively). This age-related change in prevalence estimates is not surprising given that physical and verbal aggressive behaviors peak in frequency during early childhood and subsequently decline, making them more common among young children than at any other age in the lifespan (Cummings, Iannotti, & Zahn-Waxler, 1989). Further, relational forms of aggression are also evident in early childhood, suggesting that children are relatively skilled at using sophisticated methods for harming their peers at a very early age (Crick et al., 1999; Crick, Casas, & Mosher, 1997). Moreover, children who direct relatively high rates of aggressive behaviors toward peers also tend to express a constellation of externalizing problems, including intense and poorly regulated anger and oppositional or disruptive behaviors, that make their behaviors particularly pervasive and problematic (Eisenberg et al., 2001; Loeber, Keenan, Lahey, Green, & Thomas, 1993).

Findings from our observational data of preschool and kindergarten children are consistent with these developmental trends in peer-directed aggression. Trained observers coded children's free-time play behaviors in their classrooms and on the playground every day over a 10-week interval during the fall semester.

Children were randomly observed in 10-second intervals, and any involvement in a physically or verbally aggressive interaction with one or more peers, whether as the aggressor or the victim, was recorded. Of the 167 children, 93 (56 boys; 37 girls; 56%) were observed in at least one aggressive exchange; yet it is still likely that our observations underestimated the number of children who were actually involved in aggressive exchanges because the chances were low that an aggressive interaction would occur during the brief 10 second observational period allotted to a single observation. Thus, we augmented our observational data with teachers' reports of children's propensity toward aggression and the extent to which they served as targets of peer aggression. However, because such data were gathered at a university-sponsored daycare facility where there was a very low teacher-child ratio (one teacher for every three children), the rates presented (from both the observations and teacher ratings) may be lower than what occurs in commercial, community-based daycare classrooms in which teacher-child ratios are likely to be higher and fewer teachers are available to supervise young children's peer interactions.

Items on the teacher measures were drawn from Crick et al. (1999) and Dodge and Coie (1987), and tapped three forms of aggression: (1) reactive aggression (e.g., "When this child has been teased or threatened, he or she gets angry easily and strikes back"); (2) proactive aggression (e.g., "This child gets other kids to gang up on a peer whom he or she does not like"); and (3) relational aggression (e.g., "This child tells peers that they won't be invited to their birthday party unless they do what the child wants") and three types of victimization: (1) physical victimization (e.g., "This child gets pushed or shoved by peers"), (2) verbal victimization (e.g., "This child is called mean names"), and (3) relational victimization (e.g., "This child gets left out of the group when someone is mad at them or wants to get back at them). Teachers rated the degree to which each descriptor was true of individual children on a 1.00 (never true) to 5.00 (always true) scale. The subtypes of aggression were highly correlated with each other ($rs > .67$), as were the subtypes of victimization ($rs > .68$; all $ps < .001$); thus, two constructs, aggression and victimization, were created by averaging across their respective forms. Additionally, both aggression and victimization were significantly ($ps < .001$) related to observers' ratings of children's involvement in aggressive interaction ($rs = .52$ and $.51$, respectively). Teachers' ratings revealed extensive child involvement in peer-directed aggression, with approximately 45% of children receiving average aggression scores greater than 2.00 and about 40% receiving victimization scores greater than 2.00 (a rating of 2.00 on the 5-point scale indicated a behavior was "rarely true" of the child; thus, at least one type of aggression (or victimization) had to be *at least* "sometimes" true of the child). Clearly, acting aggressively and being the target of peer aggression were relatively common occurrences among preschool and kindergarten children.

Compared to middle and late childhood, a striking characteristic of the bullying phenomenon in early childhood is the tendency for aggression and victimization to co-occur at relatively higher rates. In fact, in the present dataset, victimization and aggression were highly related ($r = .71$, $p < .001$), indicating a substantial relationship between young children's own propensity to aggress and the likelihood of being aggressed against. Such findings are consistent with the extant literature that shows that not only do highly aggressive preschoolers attack their peers, but they are often attacked (or counterattacked in response to their prior aggressive behavior) by them as well (Olson, 1992; Patterson et al., 1967). Similarly, in samples of young children, peer victimization tends to be related to externalizing characteristics, like aggressive behavior and anger (Hanish, Eisenberg, Fabes, Spinrad, & Ryan, 2002). In contrast, in studies of older children, the relations between victimization and externalizing characteristics are weaker (Boivin, Hymel, & Hodges, 2001). For instance, whereas Alsaker and Valkanover (2001) reported a prevalence rate of 10% for aggressive victims compared to 6% for nonaggressive victims in a sample of kindergarten children, Pellegrini, Bartini and Brooks (1999) and Schwartz (2000) reported estimates around 4.5% and 11% for aggressive and nonaggressive victims, respectively, in samples of fourth through sixth graders. These findings underscore a developmental trend that is of relevance for understanding bullying in young children; in early childhood, bullies and victims are often, though not always, one and the same. However, as may be culled from the above trends, the two groups tend to become more distinct as children get older. Thus, intervention efforts directed toward young children may need to take a different approach than those directed toward older children, with interventions for young children focusing primarily on mitigating aggressive attacks and counter-attacks.

Sex Differences. Although it has generally been accepted that boys are more likely than girls to be involved in aggression, this perception may be due to boys' more frequent use of physical aggression. In contrast, it is generally believed that girls rely more on subtle aggressive behaviors that are designed to harm others' social relationships (Crick & Grotpeter, 1995). For example, research has suggested that overt aggression is displayed more frequently among boys whereas relational aggression is more popular among girls (Crick & Grotpeter, 1995; Crick et al., 1997). Similarly, some studies have found that girls were more relationally victimized than boys (Crick et al., 1999).

However, data from our own and other research have not been wholly consistent with expected gender differences (Hart et al., 2000; Kochenderfer & Ladd, 1996b). For example, using the current dataset, tests conducted on teachers' ratings of overall aggression (e.g., composite of reactive, proactive and relational) did not indicate that either gender was more aggressive than the other ($t(163) = .63$; $p > .05$). Nevertheless, when examining subtypes of aggression, teachers did perceive boys ($M = 2.72$) to be significantly more reactively aggressive than girls ($M = 2.28$; $t(163) = 2.71$, $p < .01$); although the practical significance of this difference is questionable. Additionally, no gender differences emerged for relational ($t(163) = -1.79$; $p > .05$) or proactive aggression ($t(163) = -.05$; $p > .05$). Such findings are consistent with a recent meta-analysis of sex differences in relational aggression that found little difference between males and females (Knight, Guthrie, Page, & Fabes, 2002).

The tendency for boys to be more reactively aggressive than girls could be due to differences in either the type or frequency of their peer victimization experiences. In other words, boys may be provoked into responding to peers aggressively. We tested this hypothesis two ways: first by using a composite score consisting of all forms of victimization, and then by examining each form independently. In the first analysis, teachers did not rate either gender as being more victimized than the other, $t(163) = 1.57$, ns. However, when examining subtypes of victimization, teachers perceived boys ($M = 2.08$) to be more physically victimized than girls ($M = 1.69$), $t(163) = 3.04$, $p < .01$. This finding is consistent with those reported by other investigators who have also found that boys tend to experience more physical victimization than girls (e.g., McNeilly-Choque, Hart, Robinson, Nelson, & Olsen, 1996). However, whereas the above-cited researchers also found that boys were more likely to be verbally or relationally victimized, in our study, no gender differences emerged for verbal victimization, $t(163) = 1.39$, ns, or relational victimization, $t(163) = .92$, ns. Still, the fact that boys in this particular study were more likely to be *physically* victimized than girls may at least partially explain their somewhat greater use of reactive aggression. Because boys may be faced with more physically threatening abuse, it would not be unexpected for them to respond in overt ways that come to teachers' attention and are, consequently, perceived by teachers as reactively aggressive.

Clearly, there continues to be mixed findings regarding boys' and girls' involvement in aggression and victimization, and further investigation is needed to explore the conditions that might contribute to sex differences in aggression and victimization in early childhood. The basis for this may lie within the context of boys' and girls' interactions with same-, other-, and mixed-gender peer groups. Prior research has indicated that male and female peers differentially socialize children's behavior, with effects dependent upon children's own gender (Fabes, Martin, & Hanish, 2003). Because many questions remain about how gender contributes to involvement in peer-directed aggression, it is important for future research to examine the effects. Thus, we tested for gender differences in the analyses presented in remainder of the chapter, and gender differences are described when relevant.

School as a Context for the Development and Maintenance of Bullying Behavior

For many children, school is the primary context in which bullying occurs. This is because schools provide numerous opportunities to interact with peers. Few other settings provide children with as much exposure to peers on as regular a basis as do schools. Thus, efforts to understand bullying must consider the role of classmates and teachers because they are the key socialization agents in this setting, creating either supportive or stressful contexts in which children's adaptive functioning unfolds (Ladd, Kochenderfer, & Coleman, 1997). The importance of the school setting has been documented in research with elementary school-aged and older children (Hanish & Guerra, 2000). However, in research with younger children, the school context has been relatively overlooked. In this section, we describe what is known about the processes through which peers and teachers influence school bullying in early childhood.

Bullying is clearly embedded within the school context. When bullying occurs, many peers are often nearby and aware that it is happening. In fact, among elementary school students, peers are present, whether they are active participants or not, in approximately 85% of all bullying episodes (Atlas & Pepler, 1998). In contrast, because bullying frequently occurs in situations where children are not likely to be monitored by adults, teachers, at least during the elementary school years, are less often present or aware of bullying episodes. For instance, Atlas and Pepler (1998) found that elementary school teachers were aware of bullying in only 25% of the instances. However, in preschool and kindergarten classrooms, children's social interactions tend to be more closely supervised than those of their older schoolmates. This is due, in part, to the lower ratio of children to teachers in preschool and kindergarten classes, as well as to the increased emphasis on, and attention to, social development in the early school years. Consequently, young children's teachers are likely to be more closely involved with bullying than older children's teachers.

Peers' and teachers' awareness of, and involvement in, bullying likely are significant influences on the amount of peer-directed aggression that occurs in a classroom (Henry et al., 2000). Studies of elementary school-age children have shown that both peers and teachers can encourage or discourage aggression toward peers. Thus, peers and teachers play an important role in setting the overall tone of the classroom, thereby partially dictating the degree to which peer-directed aggression will occur. For example, Salmivalli (2001) demonstrated that others' responses to bullying behaviors may run the gamut from active discouragement of the behavior (e.g., telling the bullies to stop), to passive onlooking (e.g., watching, but doing little to intervene), to active encouragement (e.g., reinforcing the bullies' behavior). Consequently, when peers and teachers support peer-directed aggression (by elevating the social status of aggressive children and by failing to reprimand disruptive and aggressive behaviors), classmates evidence relatively large increases in aggression levels over time. In contrast, when peer groups and teachers denounce such aggression (by rejecting and punishing aggressors), classmates show less dramatic increases in aggression levels over time (Henry et al., 2000). Moreover, Olweus' (e.g., 1994) intervention research has demonstrated that when teachers become more aware of and actively involved in bullying situations, rates of bullying decrease significantly.

In summary, by being aware of and either encouraging or discouraging bullying behavior, peers and teachers play important roles in the occurrence of school bullying. Thus, individuals at school have a great deal of influence on the occurrence of bullying, and working with peers and teachers to promote a prosocial classroom context is a critical intervention goal. To do so, requires an understanding of the nature of the school-related relationships of bullies and victims. Relationships with peers and teachers may be conceptualized in terms of the type and quality of the overall relationship as well as in terms of the specific interaction patterns that develop over time. Much of the prior research has focused on the quality of relationships that aggressive and victimized children have with peers and teachers. This research has most often shown that many bullies and victims have interpersonal relationships that are characterized by less warmth and closeness as compared to those of their uninvolved peers, although there are also some interesting variations in these findings. In contrast, less research has focused on the types of specific interactions that characterize bullies' and victims' relationships with others. In the following sections, we first discuss the relationships and interactions bullies and victims have with peers. Then, we turn to the relationships they form with teachers and the nature of teacher-child interactions for those involved in bullying.

Bullies' and Victims' Peer Relationships

Social Status and Friendships.   Compared to non-bullies, bullies tend to be disliked by other children. For instance, aggressive behaviors are often perceived as disruptive and aversive by others, which, in turn, result in aggressive children's rejection by the mainstream peer group (Asher & Coie, 1990). Research findings with samples of children ranging in age from preschool through adolescence have consistently demonstrated negative correlations between social acceptance and aggressive behavior and positive correlations between social rejection and aggressive behavior (Asher & Coie, 1990; Parker & Asher, 1987). Moreover, evidence suggests that aggressive behavior and rejection by peers are temporally related to one another in children as young as preschool. That is, observational research has demonstrated that young children's acts of aggression are often followed by acts of rejection on the part of peers (Olson, 1992). This suggests that, even among young children, aggressive behaviors are aversive to peers and are associated with relationship difficulties.

Despite this diminished social status in the larger peer group, bullies may be liked by other, similarly aggressive, youngsters. Such findings suggest that bullies enjoy relatively good relationships with some peers. Indeed, aggressive children are often well integrated into friendship networks consisting primarily of other aggressive children (Cairns, Cairns, Neckerman, Gest, & Gariepy, 1988; Snyder, Horsch, & Childs, 1997). This selective aggressive affiliation begins at an early age, and has been documented in children as young as preschool age (i.e., approximately 4 years of age; Snyder et al., 1997). Moreover, these aggressive affiliations have been shown to have an effect on children's aggressive behavior, predicting increases in children's aggression over time (Snyder et al., 1997). Thus, by virtue of their relative isolation from nonaggressive peers and affiliation with aggressive peers, aggressive children are at risk for continued involvement in bullying as they get older.

Victimized children tend to have similar problems in their relationships with peers; that is, victims are often rejected by the peer group (Boivin, Hymel, & Bukowski, 1995; Crick et al., 1999; Ladd et al., 1997). Unlike bullies, however, victims tend to have few close friends (Hodges, Boivin, Vitaro, & Bukowski, 1999; Ladd et al., 1997). Nonetheless, when victims do have friends, their friends tend to have similarly low social status within the peer group, making it difficult for the friends to protect them from others' attacks (Hodges et al., 1999).

Although these findings seem to be ubiquitous for samples of school-aged children and adolescents, peer disapproval may be less important for understanding who is likely to be victimized in preschool. Indeed, our own recent research has demonstrated that, among 3- and 4-year-olds, there was no relation between victimization and social acceptance or between victimization and having friends (Hanish, Ryan, et al., in press). Instead, among these preschoolers, the more time spent with peers, particularly aggressive peers, the more likely they were to be victimized. Thus, although helping victimized youngsters to develop and maintain friendships may be a useful intervention strategy with older children, it may be of limited efficacy for very young children. Rather, managing aggressive behaviors within the peer group may be a more critical intervention strategy.

Peer Interaction Patterns. To further understand young bullies' and victims' social functioning, it is also important to consider the extent to which they interact with their peers and the kinds of interactions they have when they do interact. When children interact with peers, they may exhibit a variety of behaviors and emotions. We posit that these behaviors and emotions play a dynamic role in contributing to the development of children's involvement in bullying over time, as children respond to peers' interactions with particular behaviors or emotions that then elicit peers' subsequent reactions. Thus, children's individual characteristics and behaviors, as well as their peers' responses to those, should influence involvement in peer-directed aggression over time.

Time Spent With Peers. In a seminal observational study of the emergence of aggression among preschoolers, Patterson et al. (1967) found that 3- to 4-year-olds who were involved in more overall social interactions were also more likely to display aggressive behavior. Based on this finding, they argued that children who interact at higher rates with their peers were more likely to learn a variety of social behaviors, especially aggression. Our own data are consistent with their findings. Specifically, we found that the proportion of time children spent in social play was correlated, albeit only minimally, with teacher-rated aggression ($r = .16$, $p < .05$). Additionally, Patterson et al. (1967) discovered that aggressive children were more active in their interactions with peers, including more intense motor behaviors, louder verbal behaviors, and covering more area during play (e.g., moved about the room more). In our study, we found this link only for girls; that is, girls' activity level with peers was positively correlated ($r = .31$, $p < .001$) with teacher-rated aggression whereas it was not associated for boys ($r = -.02$). These findings for girls are notable because, compared to boys, girls are less likely to engage in high activity play (Maccoby, 1998). Thus, this finding may indicate that highly active girls are particularly prone to aggress against others. An alternative explanation is that the aggressive behaviors exhibited by highly active girls are more readily noticed by teachers than the aggressive behaviors exhibited by less active girls, perhaps because high activity levels are relatively atypical for girls.

Patterson and colleagues further argued that the correlation between aggression and activity levels was not merely a function of children's general activity level, but rather that such children were becoming highly responsive to peers' reinforcers; that is, their behavior was being *shaped* by their peers' responses to them. That is, when peers reinforced aggressive behaviors, those behaviors tended to be repeated. Certainly, peers play a critical role in shaping children's externalizing behaviors, and this shaping process is dependent upon children's own characteristics as well as the characteristics of the particular peers that children are most exposed to. For instance, Fabes, Shepard, Guthrie, and Martin (1997) found that temperamental characteristics, such as arousability moderated the relation between playing with same-gender peers and tendencies to display externalizing behaviors for preschool boys. Thus, arousable boys who played with other boys were particularly likely to exhibit aggressive tendencies. In contrast, arousable girls who played with other girls were not more likely to exhibit externalizing behaviors. Moreover, Martin and Fabes (2001) demonstrated that such peer effects are "dosage dependent," with the effects enhanced for the children who spent the most time engaged with same-gender peers. This suggests that peers affect children's involvement in bullying in a dynamic and time-dependent way, with peers having an increasing influence on behavior as children spend more time with them. Consequently, we would expect these effects to be further compounded if these social interaction patterns continue over long periods of time (i.e., across multiple school years). These findings highlight the importance of understanding how children's own individual (i.e., gender) and temperamental characteristics interact with those of their peers to shape and maintain bullying behaviors.

One characteristic that may be an important influence on peer interactions, in general, and the development of bullying, in particular, is children's emotionality. Certain emotional qualities characterize bullies' and victims' social interactions, and these appear to play a role in initiating and maintaining involvement in peer victimization. For instance, bullies and victims have been shown to have difficulty regulating emotions and to express frequent or intense negative affect in the forms of anger, anxiety, or sadness (Eisenberg et al., 2001; Hanish, Eisenberg et al., 2002; Kochenderfer-Ladd, under review; Schwartz & Proctor, 2000). The present data illustrate this clearly. Observers coded whether children expressed positive (happiness, joy, excitement) or negative (anger, anxiety, sadness) emotional expressions during peer interactions, and this was correlated with observed involvement in aggression, as well as teacher-rated aggression and victimization. Findings showed that children who expressed more anger, anxiety, and sadness during peer interactions were more likely to be involved in aggressive episodes ($r = .24$, $p < .01$) and to be rated by teachers as both aggressive ($r = .31$, $p < .001$) and victimized ($r = .23$, $p < .01$). They also evidenced increases in aggressive participation across time ($r = .28$, $p < .001$). In contrast, the expression of positive emotions during peer interactions was not necessarily associated with lower levels of aggressive behaviors; however, children whose interactions were more joyful were viewed by teachers as less likely to be victimized by peers ($r = -.22, p < .01$).

Time Spent Alone. It is also possible that young children who do not interact, or rarely interact, with their peers are denied the chance to learn positive social skills necessary for navigating through peer conflicts. Consequently, although they may not be involved frequently with peers, when they are, they might be expected to be more socially inept or incompetent. Thus, we were also interested in examining if the *absence* of social interaction might relate to involvement in peer-directed aggression. In other words, we examined if the proportion of time children spent in solitary activities was predictive of aggression or victimization.

Solitary activities are multifaceted, with some solitary play behaviors encompassing developmentally immature behaviors (known as solitary active play; e.g., repetitive movements such as bouncing a ball or pretend play activities that are best engaged in with others), whereas other types of play constitute activities that are viewed as solitary by nature (i.e., solitary passive play behaviors such as reading, drawing). Still other solitary behaviors may be manifested in unoccupied behaviors (such as wandering aimlessly and on-looking behaviors). Each of these forms of solitary interaction confers different developmental advantages and disadvantages (Rubin, 1982). In fact, solitary active behaviors have been most often associated with problematic peer functioning, with past research showing negative relations between solitary active play and social acceptance, social competence, and social problem solving abilities in preschoolers (Rubin, 1982).

Results from our study showed that solitary-active play was positively related to observed involvement in bullying ($r = .24$, $p < .01$) and teacher-rated victimization ($r = .28$, $p < .01$), but not to teacher-rated aggression. Instead, solitary-passive play and unoccupied play were negatively associated with teacher-rated aggression ($r = -.16$ and $-.31$, $ps < .01$, respectively). These relations suggest that, during early childhood, solitary play behaviors are associated with relatively high rates of victimization primarily when they are developmentally inappropriate. More appropriate solitary behaviors had little negative effect and, in fact, were associated with lower likelihood of bullying others. Thus, in early childhood, spending time alone is not, in and of itself, associated with high levels of involvement in bullying. Instead, the specific solitary activities that young children engage in are more important correlates of victimization than simply being alone. These findings contrast those from samples of older children that show that, in middle childhood, spending time along is an important risk factor for being victimized (Boivin et al., 1995). As such, teachers or interventionists working with young children should help preschoolers channel their solitary activities into developmentally appropriate tasks.

Bullies' and Victims' Relationships With Teachers

Similar to relationships between peers, teacher-child relationships are often problematic for children who are involved in bullying, although the extant research in this area is more limited than research on peer relations. Much of the work in this area is built on the foundation of attachment theory—highlighting the importance of relationship quality as opposed to more specific teacher-child interactions that aggressive and/or victimized children experience. By serving as a protective factor for the development of positive peer relationships, or by serving as a risk factor that contributes to involvement in bullying, the types of relationships that teachers and children form could shape children's day-to-day peer-related functioning at school.

Quality of the Teacher-Child Relationship. A number of studies have demonstrated that children who have low social competence, behavior problems, or problematic peer relationships also have relationships with teachers that are insecure, distrusting, distant, conflictual, overly dependent, or imbued with little warmth and positive affect (Howes, Matheson, & Hamilton, 1994; Pianta, 1994; Pianta & Steinberg, 1992). Given the relations between being socially unskilled and being involved in bullying, these children are likely to be those who are most involved in bullying interactions. Therefore, these findings hint that bullying and victimized youngsters tend to have poor relationships with their teachers.

Direct assessments of teacher-child relationships for children involved in bullying add support to this idea. For instance, Ladd and his colleagues (Birch & Ladd, 1998; Ladd & Burgess, 2001) examined the relations between children's aggressive behavior with peers and the extent to which their relationships with teachers are warm and close, conflictual, or overly dependent in samples of kindergarteners and first graders. They found that children's aggressive behavior predicted the quality of their concurrent and subsequent relationships with teachers. More specifically, children who were aggressive developed relationships with teachers that were seen by teachers as distant and conflictual. Similarly, Howes, Hamilton, and Matheson (1994) found that young children who had a history (beginning in infancy) of secure attachment relationships with their teachers and day care providers demonstrated less physical and verbal aggression toward peers at age 4 than their insecurely attached peers. Moreover, physical and verbal aggression was also found to be less common among 4-year-olds whose teachers had less often interrupted peer play without explanation, reprimanded or punished children's social interactions or separated children from peers. Thus, the findings of these studies indicate that the kinds of relationships that children have with their teachers, as well as the behaviors of teachers in the context of peer-to-peer interactions, are associated with the development of aggression. As such, it may be helpful for children showing early signs of bullying behavior to have warm relationships with teachers because the presence of a supportive relationship with an adult may serve as a foundation through which the child can develop more appropriate ways of interacting with others.

Less is known about the quality of victimized youngsters' relationships with teachers. In one study, Ladd and Burgess (2001) reported no significant correlations between kindergarteners' and 1st, 2nd, and 3rd graders' self-reports of victimization by peers and teachers' ratings of conflict and closeness in the teacher-child relationship. In another study, Hanish, Porter, Ryan, and Denning (2002) asked kindergarten, 1st, 2nd, and 3rd graders to report on their experiences of victimization by peers, as well as on their experiences of harassment by teachers. These variables were found to be positively related to one another, suggesting that victimized children experience at least some aspects of the teacher-child relationship as problematic. Future research is clearly needed to investigate young victims' relationships with teachers and to explore ways in which teacher-child relationships can be enhanced to provide more support to victimized children.

Teacher-Child Interaction Patterns.   Findings from our sample help to elucidate the nature of teacher-child interactions for those involved in bullying. Similar to the analyses conducted with peers, observations of the frequency (percent of time), emotional quality (positive and negative), and activity level of children's interactions with teachers were correlated with observed involvement in aggression as well as with teacher-rated aggression and victimization. No gender differences were found; thus, findings are presented in Table 8.1 for the sample as a whole. The proportion of time children spent with teachers was not a significant correlate of any of the measures of aggression or victimization; moreover, none of the qualities of the teacher-child interactions were associated with children's overall observed involvement. However, children who exhibited more happiness and joy while interacting with their teachers were viewed as less aggressive and less victimized by their teachers, whereas those who exhibited more

TABLE 8.1
Correlations of Teacher Interaction Variables With Observed Involvement
in Bullying and Teacher-rated Aggression and Victimization

Predictor	Observed Involvement	Teacher-rated Aggression	Teacher-rated Victimization
Proportion of time with teacher	.12	−.07	.03
Positive emotion with teacher	−.12	−.19*	−.35***
Negative emotion with teacher	.11	.37***	.20**
Activity level with teacher	.00	−.01	−.23**

*$p < .05$. **$p < .01$. ***$p < .001$.

anger, anxiety, and sadness during teacher-child interactions were rated higher on both aggression and victimization.

What is not clear from these data is whether the emotions exhibited in the context of teacher-child interactions were a function of children's responses in their interactions with teachers or their responses to prior events (e.g., peer conflict), thereby reflecting teacher intervention (e.g., disciplining, providing support), or their own personality characteristics (e.g., overall tendency to display negative affect). However, it is clear that aggressive and victimized youngsters were more likely to spend their time with teachers in relatively negative exchanges. Interestingly, intense activity level with teachers was negatively associated with being perceived as experiencing greater victimization. Thus, children who engaged in physically calm interactions with teachers (e.g., low rates of physical activity) were perceived as more victimized.

Next, we examined the frequency and quality of teacher-child interactions as predictors of systematic changes in children's involvement in aggression. Moreover, we also tested if the effects of negative and positive emotions and activity level were moderated by the proportion of time children with spent teachers. We anticipated that although negative emotions and high activity levels with teachers might predict increasing involvement in bullying, such effects would be moderated if such children rarely interacted with teachers. Thus, a series of regression analyses were conducted in which residualized gain scores in observed involvement in aggression were regressed on the proportion of time spent with teachers, observers' ratings of children's positive and negative emotions in teacher-child interactions, and observers' ratings of children's activity level during teacher-child interactions. Specifically, three moderation models were examined in which, for each equation, the proportion of time spent with teachers was entered simultaneously with one of the quality of interaction variables (i.e., positive emotion, negative emotion, or activity level) on the first step followed by the corresponding interaction term on the second step.

The overall equations including positive and negative emotional tone were significant: $F(3, 159) = 3.00, p < .05$ and $F(3, 159) = 9.20, p < .001$, respectively.

Main effects revealed that the proportion of time spent with teachers predicted increased involvement in aggression beyond positive emotions ($\beta = .17$, $p < .001$) and negative emotions ($\beta = .28$, $p < .001$). Additionally, both positive and negative emotions were unique predictors (βs $= -.16$ and $.38$, $p < .05$, respectively). However, a significant moderation effect emerged to qualify the main effect of negative emotional tone ($\beta = .22$, $p < .01$). A breakdown of the moderation effect was conducted by creating four groups based on scores $\pm .5\ SD$ on the relevant means for time spent with teachers and negative emotions. A one-way ANOVA on the residual aggression scores revealed significant group differences, $F(3,\ 74) = 5.80$; $p < .05$; Student-Neuman Keul's post hoc tests ($p < .05$) showed that children who interacted frequently and negatively with teachers evidenced greater increases in rates of aggressive peer interactions ($M = .87$) than all other groups. In fact, while these children were becoming more involved in bullying, children in the other groups became less so: for infrequent, but negative teacher interactions ($M = -.12$); frequent, but not negative ($M = -.39$) and infrequent and not negative ($M = -.65$).

These findings raise some interesting questions regarding the role of teacher-child relationships in bullying. Clearly, children who are aggressive and victimized experience negative relationships with teachers (just as they do with peers), however, the extent to which these relationships are a function of child attributes, teacher attributes, the interaction of the two, or the teacher's response to the functioning of all of the children in the classroom is as yet unknown. It may be that, just as peers shape the development of bullying in dynamic and multifaceted ways, teachers do as well.

Translating Research Into Practice: Implications for Bullying-Prevention and Intervention Programs

These research findings demonstrated the important role that peers and teachers play in the emergence of bullying behaviors in young children. When peer and teacher relationships were characterized by positive qualities, they provided supportive contexts for children that minimized the incidence of aggression and victimization. However, when peer and teacher relationships were characterized by negative qualities, the likelihood that children were involved in bullying increased.

As has been previously demonstrated, when negative interactional patterns persist over long periods of time, they are associated with increased risk for developmental problems (Hanish & Guerra, 2002; Kochenderfer-Ladd & Wardrop, 2001; Ladd & Burgess, 2001). Thus, we are particularly concerned about the developmental trajectories for those bullies and victims who experience repeated involvement in bullying along with enduring negative interactions with others at school. This is particularly worrisome for aggressive children in light of findings showing that aggression is a stable phenomenon from an early age (Cummings et al., 1989; Huesmann, Eron, Lefkowitz, & Walder, 1984). Thus, as young bullies get older, they are at continued risk for involvement in bullying (Espelage, Bosworth, & Simon, 2001). As bullies continue to be exposed to negative social environments at school, the problems associated with participation in this behavior may become compounded with feelings of being disenfranchised from school and the loss of interest in participating in academic activities. Over time, this negative cycle of increasing behavioral, social, and academic problems may become progressively more difficult to break as children get older. In contrast, young children's peer victimization tends to be only minimally stable over time. Thus, the risk for stable victimization, beginning in preschool or kindergarten, is relatively low. However, as children get older and move into and through elementary school, stability estimates rise (Hanish & Guerra, 2000); thus, intervention efforts need to be directed at every age level to stop victimization as soon as it begins.

Although many of the conclusions in this chapter are drawn from correlational (rather than experimental) data, they do provide tentative directions for intervention. In particular, establishing good relationships with teachers and peers early in life is likely to provide children with a set of critical experiences that lay the foundation for future social and academic functioning. Consequently, classroom management practices, programs, and policies that can help children, particularly those who are most often aggressive and victimized, develop positive relationships with others at school may be helpful in preventing involvement in bullying from becoming a persistent problem. Specific strategies will likely include helping young children to manage their own and peers' externalizing behaviors, assisting children to establish positively toned interactions with peers and teachers, and directing children's solitary activities into appropriate outlets and activities. To do so may also require providing assistance to teachers, in the form of guidance in the management of peer relations, support for their efforts to create positive interactions for the children who most often bully others or are victimized, or aid in creating a positive classroom climate. Creating such positive classroom environments may help children acquire the skills to interact competently with peers as well as help teachers to facilitate positive peer interactions and respond in nurturing ways to even their most challenging children.

ACKNOWLEDGMENT

This research was supported in part by a grant from the National Institutes of Mental Health (1 RO1 MH 60838) to Richard A. Fabes. We would like to thank our students, Stacie Leonard, Patti Ryan, Lisa Dinella, Tiffani Kisler, Kristina Kupanoff, Mary Anders, and Shana Schmidt and for their efforts on this project. Finally, special thanks go to school director, Bob Weigand, and the children, teachers, and parents for their participation in this project. Please address correspondence concerning this article to Laura Hanish at Arizona State University, Department of Family and Human Development, Box 872502, Tempe, AZ, 85287-2502. E-mail: Laura.Hanish@asu.edu.

REFERENCES

Alsaker, F. D., & Valkanover, S. (2001). Early diagnosis and prevention of victimization in kindergarten. In J. Juvonen & S. Graham (Eds.), *Peer harassment in school: The plight of the vulnerable and victimized* (pp. 175–195). New York: Guilford.

Asher, S. R., & Coie, J. D. (1990). *Peer rejection in childhood*. New York: Cambridge University Press.

Atlas, R. S., & Pepler, D. J. (1998). Observations of bullying in the classroom. *Journal of Educational Research, 92*, 86–99.

Birch, S. H., & Ladd, G. W. (1998). Children's interpersonal behaviors and the teacher-child relationship. *Developmental Psychology, 34*, 934–946.

Boivin, M., Hymel, S., & Bukowski, W. M. (1995). The roles of social withdrawal, peer rejection, and victimization by peers in predicting loneliness and depressed mood in children. *Development and Psychopathology, 7*, 765–785.

Boivin, M., Hymel, S., & Hodges, E. V. E. (2001). Toward a process view of peer rejection and harassment. In J. Juvonen & S. Graham (Eds.), *Peer harassment in school: The plight of the vulnerable and victimized* (pp. 265–289). New York: Guilford.

Boulton, M. J., & Smith, P. K. (1994). Bully/victim problems in middle-school children: Stability, self-perceived competence, peer perceptions, and peer acceptance. *British Journal of Developmental Psychology, 12*, 315–329.

Cairns, R. B., Cairns, B. D., Neckerman, H. J., Gest, S. D., & Gariépy, J-L. (1988). Social networks and aggressive behavior: Peer support or peer rejection? *Developmental Psychology, 24*, 815–823.

Caplan, M., Vespo, J., Pedersen, J., & Hay, D. F. (1991). Conflict and its resolution in small groups of one- and two-year-olds. *Child Development, 62*, 1513–1524.

Coie, J. D, & Dodge, K. A. (1998). Aggression and antisocial behavior. In W. Damon & N. Eisenberg (Eds.), *Handbook of Child Psychology, 5th Ed.: Social, Emotional and Personality Development* (pp. 779–862). New York: John Wiley & Sons, Inc.

Crick, N. R., Casas, J. F., & Ku, H-C. (1999). Relational and physical forms of peer victimization in preschool. *Developmental Psychology, 35*, 376–385.

Crick, N. R., Casas, J. F., & Mosher, M. (1997). Relational and overt aggression in preschool. *Developmental Psychology, 33*, 579–588.

Crick, N. R., & Grotpeter, J. K. (1995). Relational aggression, gender, and social-psychological adjustment. *Child Development, 66*, 710–722.

Crowther, J. H., Bond, L. A., & Rolf, J. E. (1981). The incidence, prevalence, and severity of behavior disorders among preschool-aged children in day care. *Journal of Abnormal Child Psychology, 9*, 23–42.

Cummings, E. M., Iannotti, R. J., & Zahn-Waxler, C. (1989). Aggression between peers in early childhood: Individual continuity and developmental change. *Child Development, 60*, 887–895.

Dodge, K. A., & Coie, J. D. (1987). Social-information-processing factors in reactive and proactive aggression in children's peer groups. *Journal of Personality and Social Psychology, 53*, 1146–1158.

Eisenberg, N., Cumberland, A., Spinrad, T. L., Fabes, R. A., Shepard, S. A., Reiser, M., Murphy, B. C., Losoya, S. H., & Guthrie, I. K. (2001). The relations of regulation and emotionality to children's externalizing and internalizing problem behavior. *Child Development, 72*, 1112–1134.

Espelage, D. L., Bosworth, K., & Simon, T. R. (2001). Short-term stability and prospective correlates of bullying in middle-school students: An examination of potential demographic, psychosocial, and environmental influences. *Violence and Victims, 16*, 411–426.

Fabes, R. A., Martin, C. L., & Hanish, L. D. (2003). Young children's play qualities in same-, other-, and mixed-sex peer groups. *Child Development, 74*, 921–932.

Fabes, R. A., Martin, C. L., Hanish, L. D., Anders, M., & Madden-Derdich, D. (in press). Early school adjustment: The roles of gender-segregated play and temperamental regulation. *Developmental Psychology.*

Fabes, R. A., Shepard, S. A., Guthrie, I. K., & Martin, C. L. (1997). Roles of temperamental arousal and gender-segregated play in young children's social adjustment. *Developmental Psychology, 33*, 693–702.

Hanish, L. D., Eisenberg, N., Fabes, R. A., Spinrad, T. L., & Ryan, P. (2002). *The expression and regulation of negative emotions: Risk factors for young children's peer victimization.* Manuscript submitted for publication.

Hanish, L. D., & Guerra, N. G. (2000). The roles of ethnicity and school context in predicting children's victimization by peers. *American Journal of Community Psychology, 28*, 201–223.

Hanish L. D., & Guerra, N. G. (2002). A longitudinal analysis of patterns of adjustment following peer victimization. *Development and Psychopathology, 14*, 69–89.

Hanish, L. D., Porter, M., Ryan, P., & Denning, D. (2002). Victimization in the school and neighborhood: Relations with school functioning. Paper presented in P. C. Rodkin & E. V. E. Hodges (Chairs), *Aggression and victimization in group and sociocultural context*, at the 9th Biennial Meeting of the Society for Research in Adolescence. New Orleans, LA.

Hanish, L. D., Ryan, P., Martin, C. L., & Fabes, R. A. (in press). The social context of young children's peer victimization. *Social Development.*

Hart, C. H., Nelson, D. A., Robinson, C. C., Olsen, S. F., McNeilly-Choque, M. K., Porter, C. L. & McKee, T. R. (2000). Russian parenting styles and family processes: Linkages with subtypes of victimization and aggression. In K.A. Kerns, J. M. Contreras, & A. M. Neal–Barnett (Eds.)., *Family and peers: Linking two social worlds.* Westport, CT: Praeger.

Henry, D., Guerra, N. G., Huesmann, R., Tolan, P. H., Van Acker, R., & Eron, L. (2000). Normative influences on aggression in urban elementary school classrooms. *American Journal of Community Psychology, 28*, 59–81.

Hodges, E. V. E., Boivin, M., Vitaro, F., & Bukowski, W. M. (1999). The power of friendship: Protection against an escalating cycle of peer victimization. *Developmental Psychology, 35*, 94–101.

Hoover, J. H., Oliver, R., & Hazler, R. J. (1992). Bullying: Perceptions of adolescent victims in the Midwestern USA. *School Psychology International, 13*, 5–16.

Howes, C., Hamilton, C. E., & Matheson, C. C. (1994). Children's relationships with peers: Differential associations with aspects of the teacher-child relationship. *Child Development, 65*, 253–263.

Howes, C., Matheson, C. C., & Hamilton, C. E. (1994). Maternal, teacher, and child care history correlates of children's relationships with peers. *Child Development, 65*, 264–273.

Huesmann, L. R., Eron, L. D., Lefkowitz, M. M., & Walder, L. O. (1984). Stability of aggression over time and generations. *Developmental Psychology, 20*, 1120–1134.

Kazdin, A. E. (1985). *Treatment of antisocial behavior in children and adolescents.* Homeword, IL: Dorsey Press.

Knight, G. P., Guthrie, I. K., Page, M. C., & Fabes, R. A. (2002). Emotional arousal and gender differences in aggression: A meta-analysis. *Aggressive Behavior, 28*, 366–393.

Kochenderfer, B. J., & Ladd, G. W. (1996a). Peer victimization: Cause or consequence of school maladjustment? *Child Development, 67*, 1305–1317.

Kochenderfer, B. J., & Ladd, G. W. (1996b). Peer victimization: Manifestations and relations to school adjustment in kindergarten. *Journal of School Psychology, 34*, 267–283.

Kochenderfer-Ladd, B. J. (2002). *Stability of peer victimization for aggressive and asocial children.* Manuscript submitted for publication.

Kochenderfer-Ladd, B., & Wardrop, J. L. (2001). Chronicity and instability of children's peer victimization experiences as predictors of loneliness and social satisfaction trajectories. *Child Development, 72,* 134–151.

Ladd, G. W., & Burgess, K. B. (2001). Do relational risks and protective factors moderate the linkages between childhood aggression and early psychological and school adjustment? *Child Development, 72,* 1579–1601.

Ladd, G. W., Kochenderfer, B. J., & Coleman, C. C. (1997). Classroom peer acceptance, friendship, and victimization: Distinct relational systems that contribute uniquely to children's school adjustment? *Child Development, 68,* 1181–1197.

Loeber, R., Keenan, K., Lahey, B. B., Green, S. M., & Thomas, C. (1993). Evidence for developmentally based diagnoses of oppositional defiant disorder and conduct disorder. *Journal of Abnormal Child Psychology, 21,* 377–410.

Maccoby, E. E. (1998). *The two sexes: Growing up apart, coming together.* Cambridge: Belknap.

Martin, C. L., & Fabes, R. A. (2001). The stability and consequences of young children's same-sex peer interactions. *Developmental Psychology, 37,* 431–446.

McNeilly-Choque, M. K., Hart, C. H., Robinson, C. C., Nelson, L. J., & Olsen, S. F. (1996). Overt and relational aggression on the playground: Correspondence among different informants. *Journal of Research in Childhood Education, 11,* 47–67.

Olson, S. L. (1992). Development of conduct problems and peer rejection in preschool children: A social systems analysis. *Journal of Abnormal Child Psychology, 20,* 327–350.

Olweus, D. (1984). Aggressors and their victims: Bullying at school. In N. Furde & H. Gault (Eds.), *Disruptive Behaviour in Schools* (pp. 57–76). New York: John Wiley & Sons.

Olweus, D. (1994). Annotation: Bullying at school: Basic facts and effects of a school-based intervention program. *Journal of Child Psychology and Psychiatry, 35,* 1171–1190.

Parker, J. G., & Asher, S. R. (1987). Peer relations and later personal adjustment: Are low-accepted children at risk? *Psychological Bulletin, 102,* 357–389.

Patterson, G. R., Littman, R. A., & Bricker, W. (1967). Assertive behavior in children: A step toward a theory of aggression. *Monographs of the Society for Research in Child Development, 32 (5, Serial No. 113).*

Pellegrini, A. D., Bartini, M., & Brooks, F. (1999). School bullies, victims, and aggressive victims: Factors relating to group affiliation and victimization in early adolescence. *Journal of Educational Psychology, 91,* 216–224.

Pianta, R. C. (1994). Patterns of relationships between children and kindergarten teachers. *Journal of School Psychology, 32,* 15–31.

Pianta, R. C., & Steinberg, M. (1992). Teacher-child relationships and the process of adjusting to school. *New Directions for Child Development, 57,* 61–80.

Rubin, K. H. (1982). Nonsocial play in preschoolers: Necessarily evil? *Child Development, 53,* 651–657.

Salmivalli, C. (2001). Group view on victimization: Empirical findings and their implications. In J. Juvonen & S. Graham (Eds.), *Peer harassment in school: The plight of the vulnerable and victimized* (pp. 398–419). New York: Guilford.

Schwartz, D. (2000). Subtypes of victims and aggressors in children's peer groups. *Journal of Abnormal Child Psychology, 28,* 181–192.

Schwartz, D., McFadyen-Ketchum, S. A., Dodge, K. A., Pettit, G. S., & Bates, J. E. (1998). Peer group victimization as a predictor of children's behavior problems at home and in school. *Development and Psychopathology, 10,* 87–99.

Schwartz, D., & Proctor, L. J. (2000). Community violence exposure and children's social adjustment in the school peer group: The mediating roles of emotion regulation and social cognition. *Journal of Consulting and Clinical Psychology, 68,* 670–683.

Snyder, J., Horsch, E., & Childs, J. (1997). Peer relationships of young children: Affiliative choices and the shaping of aggressive behavior. *Journal of Clinical Child Psychology, 26,* 145–156.

9

Classroom Ecologies That Support or Discourage Bullying

Beth Doll, Samuel Song, and Erin Siemers
University of Nebraska, Lincoln

This chapter will describe how contextual characteristics of elementary school classrooms can foster or discourage peer bullying. Classrooms are important contexts for understanding bullying because most bullying interactions occur among classmates (Salmivalli, Lagerspetz, Bjorkqvist, Osterman, & Kaukiainen, 1996). In particular, two features of classrooms' ecosystems are highly relevant to understanding bullying: (1) The quality of social relationships in the classroom including relationships among students, between students and teachers, and between families and the classroom; and (2) the support for human agency in the classroom including support for students' self-control, self-efficacy, and self-determination. By describing how these classroom characteristics relate to bullying, it will also be possible to describe natural anti-bully supports that can be infused into classroom routines and practices.

To explain the relation between classroom ecologies and bullying, this chapter will borrow from the rich developmental research that describes ecological influences on peer aggression. Bullying is a special type of aggressive peer interaction in which a powerful classmate repeatedly intimidates, exploits and victimizes a weaker classmate. The peer aggression research shows that bullying anchors one extreme of a continuum of peer aggression, where the continuum ranges from jostling or playful aggression at one end to repeated intimidation or bullying at the other. Framing bullying interactions as part of this continuum raises critical questions about the classroom participants' conceptual understanding of bullying, ability to encourage or discourage bullying, and their ability to distinguish between bullying and other forms of peer aggression.

A central premise of this chapter is that bullying may be more or less prevalent in classrooms depending upon such systemic characteristics as the level of overall peer aggression, the tolerance for the aggressive interactions that occur, and the participants' ability to parry aggressive overtures without dominating or being dominated. To insure that children's perspectives are well represented in this conceptual analysis, the chapter will supplement the research literature with survey information collected from two samples of elementary school students. The surveys will describe children's perspectives on the occurrence of problematic aggressive interactions in their classrooms, and features of their classrooms that facilitate or discourage these interactions.

Aggressive Interactions Among Classmates

Aggression is a normal part of childhood. Socially competent children routinely engage in aggressive interactions with peers, and these are not always detrimental (Pellegrini, 2002). For example, adolescent boys often engage in aggressive behaviors as a means to establish new relationships with peers (Pellegrini & Bartini, 2001). In other cases, aggressive interactions may be a way to establish or maintain social status within a peer group (Estell, Cairns, Farmer, & Cairns, 2002). Playful aggression that occurs between friends is described in the research literature as 'jostling' or 'rough and tumble play' (Pellegrini, 2002; Pellegrini & Bartini, 2001). Rough and tumble play includes the same verbally and physically aggressive behaviors that might comprise bullying but differs in that it is not intended to inflict harm, manipulate or dominate the other child. Instead, rough and tumble play occurs within reciprocal interactions, where friends take turns jostling each other both for entertainment and to strengthen the friendship. If they recognize that their rough and tumble play is transitioning into hurtful behavior, most children will cease the aggression.

These aggressive peer interactions are only described as 'conflicts' if they become problematic for children. In our earlier research, most children in elementary school classrooms reported that they struggled with conflicts involving teasing, name-calling, bad arguments or physical fighting in approximately 8% of all recesses (Doll, Murphy, & Song, 2003). Most of these aggressive peer conflicts do not represent bullying. When aggressive interactions occur between two classmates having equivalent social power, they can be instances of legitimate conflict. Classmates might have authentic disagreements about games to play, accidental injuries, jostling that has crossed the line into meanness, or innumerable other incidents. Aggressive peer interactions such as cheating or exploitation can also occur when children compete for classroom resources (Pellegrini, 1995). The majority of these authentic conflicts will occur among friends rather than non-friends (Grotpeter & Crick, 1996), and classmates who are friends will work to reconcile these social 'accidents' when they occur (Berndt & Das, 1987; Pellegrini, 2002). It is unresolved conflict, often occurring outside of friendship groups, that presents the most difficulty for children.

When legitimate conflicts are left unresolved, or simply because an opportunity presents itself, children may resort to intimidation in order to prevail over or dominate classmates. These interactions can be instances of bullying, an extreme form of peer aggression in which one student seeks to gain status or power by repeatedly harming and intimidating a vulnerable peer using physical and verbal aggression or social ostracism (Olweus, 1991; Pellegrini & Bartini, 2001; Smith & Boulton, 1990). The peer's inability to defend against the aggression adequately may be due to physical weakness or clumsiness, limited intellectual aptitude, ineffective verbal skills, or a lack of protective support from peers or the classroom teacher (Hazler, Miller, Carney, & Green, 2001; Hodges & Perry, 1999; Pellegrini, Bartini, & Brooks, 1999).

In Fig. 9.1, we have represented jostling, legitimate conflict and bullying as a continuum of aggressive peer interactions that extends from aggression with benevolent intentions at one extreme (jostling) towards aggression with malevolent intentions at the other (bullying). Although they differ in their intent, all of these interactions are characterized by the behaviors of physical or verbal

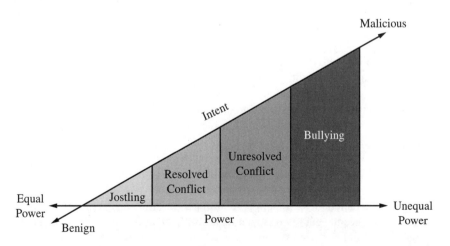

FIG. 9.1. A continuum of aggressive interactions.

aggression. When aggression is physical, it may be observed as behaviors of hitting, kicking, poking, pouncing, sneaking-up, picking-up, play fighting, chasing, holding, and pushing (Dodge, Coie, Pettit, & Price, 1990; Pellegrini, 1995). Verbal aggression like teasing, taunting, picking on, and making fun of is more difficult to observe directly, especially when the taunt is soft-spoken or occurs outside the hearing of adults. Even physical aggression can be difficult to observe if it occurs surreptitiously or in hidden corners of the classroom or playground. Consequently, researchers have found that self-reports and peer reports provide more accurate information about aggressive interactions than do teacher or researcher observations (Pellegrini & Bartini, 2001).

To distinguish among jostling, aggressive conflict and bullying, children must be able to detect and interpret the intention of the other child in the interaction. Because children are integral to the "kid society" that operates in their classrooms, they are frequently better than adults at judging whether an aggressive interaction is a form of jostling (and therefore appropriate behavior among friends), simple conflict or bullying. Being able to interpret and react appropriately to the intentions of other children during aggressive interactions is a critical social ability that influences children's vulnerability to bullying and intimidation.

This continuum of peer aggression hints at the kinds of strategies that might reduce bullying incidents within a classroom. For example, reducing the frequency of all aggressive interactions would likely reduce the frequency of bullying interactions at the extreme of the continuum. Alternatively, pulling more children into the friendship networks of the classroom would increase the likelihood that aggressive peer interactions, when they occur, will be among friends and so easier to resolve. It might be possible to diminish the frequency with which aggressive interactions escalate into bullying by increasing the successful resolution of peer conflicts before these escalate. Finally, it might be possible to discourage intimidation by equalizing the distribution of power in a classroom or providing the classroom's students with a protective sense of confidence. Thus, the continuum suggests that there might be multiple alternative pathways towards controlling bullying within a classroom.

In this chapter, descriptions of classroom characteristics that foster bullying will be drawn from developmental research that describes the emergence of social competence in vulnerable children, educational research that identifies the underpinnings of school success in high-risk urban children, and special education research that describes conditions for the successful inclusion of children with disabilities in general education classrooms (Doll, Zucker, & Brehm, 1999; Zucker, Brehm, & Doll, 2000). Interestingly, although all three lines of research grew from different purposes, their findings consistently identify two sets of classroom characteristics that support children's developmental competence. The first set describes the quality of social relationships that develop within the classroom including relationships among peers, between students and the teacher, and between the classroom and the students' families. The second set describes the strength of human agency[1] among students including their sense of self-efficacy, self-determination, and ability to control their behavioral conduct independent of excessive adult oversight. Careful examination of these characteristics can identify routines and practices that might discourage all peer aggression, and so limit bullying, in classrooms.

Classroom Relationships

Peer Inclusion.   Students who are socially included have someone to sit with on the bus, someone to play with at recess, someone to eat with at lunch, someone who chooses them for their team, and someone to talk to during free moments in a classroom. Having a friend in class makes it easier for students to enjoy daily activities in the classroom, easier to ask for assistance in times of stress, and much more likely that students will receive help when they ask (Heller & Swindle, 1983; Ladd & Oden, 1979). Classrooms in which more students are included show fewer conflicts, and those conflicts that do arise are less likely to escalate (Newman, Murray, & Lussier, 2001). Having a friend and having more friends have repeatedly been found to be protective factors against bullying (Boulton, 1999; Hodges, Malone, & Perry, 1997; Kochenderfer & Ladd, 1997; Schwartz, Dodge, Pettit, & Bates, 2000). Moreover, the type of friends can influence the protective effects of friendships. Specifically, friendships need to be made with children who are able and willing to protect the victim (i.e., defenders) rather than with children who are themselves victimized (Pellegrini et al., 1999).

In a typical classroom, approximately 4% of children are not included as a friend by any classmate (Asher, 1995). These are the children who are at risk for bullying and victimization (Hodges et al., 1997). Some of these children without friends are actively disliked by their classmates because they are frequent perpetrators of aggression and conflict (McFayden-Ketchum & Dodge, 1998). When they identify a student in class who can be intimidated, their aggressive interactions can become instances of bullying. Other children without friends are "overlooked" children who are withdrawn and passive. Bullies are more likely to victimize children who are isolated from their peer group because retaliation from peers is unlikely (Hodges et al., 1997). Passively isolated children are likely targets of bullies because they acquiesce in the face of physical fighting and are hypersensitive to arguing and teasing (Asher & Coie, 1990; Carlson, Lahey, & Neeper, 1984). Research has repeatedly shown that the vast majority of these victims are subsequently rejected by their peer group (Boulton & Smith, 1994;

---

[1]Human agency is a term used by Bandura (1982) to describe the mechanisms that people use to transform their knowledge into action. It incorporates judgments of personal competence combined with self-efficacy as these shape motivation and behavior.

Hodges et al., 1997; Salmivalli et al., 1996). Moreover, those victims who are most rejected become increasingly victimized over time (Hodges et al., 1997; Hodges & Perry, 1999).

Traditionally, schools have intervened with peer relationships one student at a time (Asher, 1995; Doll, 1996). However, a premise of this chapter is that a classroom's particular routines and practices have powerful influence over the degree to which all students in a class are included. Friendships emerge within a classroom when children have frequent opportunities to have fun together with classmates (Doll, Murphy, & Song, 2003; Renshaw & Asher, 1983). "Having fun" does not necessarily need to be divorced from learning or productive work. Instead, Rizzo (1989) suggests that schools create multiple roles for students to fill that, incidentally, force students into new interactions with each other. For example, an experienced 5th-grade teacher explained that she always gave classroom chore assignments to two students at a time, so that they would have an opportunity to work together. A fourth grader, new to her school, figured out that a good way to make friends was to volunteer to clear the cafeteria after lunch, because at least two students were assigned to work together.

A potentially powerful protective factor may be the number of children in the classroom (nonfriends and friends) who are willing to defend against bullying in general. Peers may encourage, discourage, or maintain bullying within the classroom (Salmivalli, 2001; Salmivalli et al., 1996). Peer roles may include "assistants" who join in the bullying directly, "reinforcers" who come around to watch or laugh when witnessing bullying, "defenders" who try to make the others stop bullying, and "outsiders" who are unaware of the bullying. The presence of large numbers of "defenders" in the peer group inhibits bullying, whereas "assistants" and "reinforcers" can increase its prevalence.

Further, cooperative learning strategies can facilitate friendships by providing children with opportunities to learn in non-competitive groups (Slavin, 1991). In cooperative learning classrooms, students work together in small groups to accomplish common tasks. Evaluations are earned by the group as a whole, and group members are expected to contribute to the work of the group and the learning of each group member. Delivering instruction within these cooperative groups modifies the classroom organization, the learning tasks that are assigned, the nature of the teacher's instruction and communication, and the academic and social behavior of students in the class (Hertz-Lazarowitz, 2001). Cooperative learning programs promote tolerance among peers and create a tranquil classroom environment where students practice listening and communicating with each other (Harris, Hopkins, & Wordsworth, 2001). When students are given opportunities to practice tolerance in the classroom, their emerging social skills can be generalized to areas outside of the classroom. To enhance the generalization of tolerance, teachers overtly praise students and the class when they demonstrate tolerance by using communication and listening skills that include all students (Olweus, 1993).

At recess, children are more likely to interact competently when multiple, highly attractive games are readily available (Doll, 1996). Still, it is not uncommon for schools to inadvertently limit recess games. For example, in one school where we have worked, upper elementary students had a single game to play—soccer—on a large field without marked goals or sidelines. The physical education teacher had been given the budget to purchase recess equipment and, when too many balls were lost, he stopped replacing them. The recess playground was left without tetherballs on the poles, a four-square court had been painted too small and was located on an incline, and there were no jump ropes or flying discs. A lack of developmentally-appropriate games leads to boring recess periods that are less likely to foster effective friendships. Alternatively, recess periods promote peer inclusion by providing games that are more fun with more children, do not depend on highly developed skills, and do not have winners and losers. In one 7th-grade classroom, the number of suspensions and office visits dropped dramatically once the classroom teachers purchased simple games for the students to take outside at lunch recess (Doll, Zucker, & Brehm, 1999).

To minimize peer conflicts, children can be taught to use problem solving strategies to avoid entering conflicts and to successfully remove themselves from conflicts that cannot be avoided (Peterson & Skiba, 2000; Roberts & Coursol, 1996). Classrooms are more likely to resolve aggressive interactions without adult assistance when students have been taught strategies to identify the conflict, describe both sides, brainstorm alternative solutions, and commit to a shared solution (Johnson & Johnson, 1994). It is particularly important that students learn not to withdraw or blame others instead of resolving conflicts effectively. Problem-solving instruction will be even more effective if the children are provided with 'linguistic cues' that adults can use in natural situations to remind the children of the steps (Soutter & McKenzie, 2000). For many children, the most difficult part of problem solving is generating multiple options (Johnson & Johnson, 1994). When classroom meetings engage all students in brainstorming multiple options for common peer conflicts, the number and frequency of a classroom's conflicts can be reduced (Murphy, 2002).

Teacher-Student Relationship.   Classrooms are safer places for students when the teacher is warm, engaged, responsive, and holds high expectations for students (Olweus & Limber, 1999; Pianta, 1999). The presence of caring and demanding teachers can improve students' sense of class membership and reduce peer conflict in the room (Barr & Parrett, 2001; Emmett & Monsour, 1996). On the face of it, the link between bullying and teacher-student relationships is easy to understand. When children believe that their teacher is caring and fair, they trust that teacher to protect them from victimization and intimidation in the classroom.

Teachers who are sensitive to their students respond swiftly and judiciously to bullying incidents thereby protecting students from bullying and providing a class-wide sense of security and comfort (Olweus, 1993; Olweus & Limber, 1999).

Their swift response demonstrates that bullying is unacceptable, contributing to an antibullying climate in the classroom and making it more likely that students will protect other students. Favorite teachers are powerful models for students (Werner & Smith, 1992), and the values and expectations that they convey for courtesy and fairness are deeply embedded within the classroom's social ecology. Some teachers choose to use this personal power to promote rules such as "you can't say you can't play" or "anyone can join the games in this class" (Paley, 1993).

Teacher monitoring is an especially important protection against bullying. Bullying is frequently covert because when students bully, they try to keep the victimization outside the notice of supervising adults. Conflicts are less likely to occur if teachers can heed the early warning signs of conflict, such as increases in verbal intimidation, voices getting louder, and tense physical reactions (Meese, 1997). When teachers are not alert to the possibility of victimizing interactions in their classroom, it is easy for them to overlook softly spoken taunts or assaults that occur in the hidden corners of the classroom or playground. From a distance a child may appear to be laughing carelessly with classmates, but an observer standing nearby would know that the child was struggling to look unconcerned while classmates taunted her with "baby" and "dumb."

A consistent finding is that school personnel including classroom teachers do not respond adequately to student reports of bullying (Boulton & Underwood, 1992; Hoover, Oliver & Hazler, 1992; Olweus, 1991). Either they fail to recognize bullying when it occurs or they fail to understand the importance of intervening to stop bullying (Hazler et al., 2001). In one study, playground supervisors intervened in only 4% of bullying conflicts (Craig & Pepler, 1997). Although the majority of teachers report that they consistently try to stop bullying in their schools, students reported that teachers usually do not intervene in bullying (Olweus, 1984; Pepler, Craig, Ziegler, & Charach, 1994). This discrepancy between student and teacher reports of intervention suggest that teachers may not be aware of the extent of bullying incidents and that students do not view teachers as effective interveners (Craig, Henderson, & Murphy, 2000).

In particular, a significant number of teachers only recognize physical bullying behavior, and require empathy training before recognizing more subtle, hidden forms of intimidation (Craig et al., 2000; Hazler et al., 2001). Other teachers acknowledge that bullying occurs in the classroom but minimize its importance, while still others believe it is helpful to ignore bullying (Stephenson & Smith, 1989). Teachers do not always recognize bullying in indirect intimidation such as social exclusion, spreading rumors, and name calling (Boulton, 1997). They sometimes choose not to intervene out of a misguided belief that the victim is responsible for overcoming the victimization (Olweus, 1993). In still other cases, victimized students deliberately hide the bullying from teachers and other adults. Victims explain that they do not tell teachers about bullying incidents because they fear retaliation from the bully or because they perceive teachers as inept, uncaring, or unable to protect them (Pepler et al., 1994). About half of victims do not report being bullied to any adult, but when they do, they are more likely to tell parents than teachers (Whitney & Smith, 1993).

The promotion of teacher responsiveness to bullying incidents is an essential component of Olweus' Bullying Prevention Program (Olweus & Limber, 1999). Specifically, Olweus suggests that teachers be alerted to the varying and subtle forms of bullying and be taught to respond quickly and decisively in the face of bullying. His evidence-based recommendations are reinforced by other experts, who suggest that responses to bullying should be confidential to protect victims from retaliation when they report an incident (Roberts & Coursol, 1996). Because adults may have difficulty distinguishing between bullying and other aggressive incidents, teachers should err on the side of intervening when in doubt, so that students know they can depend upon the teacher when they need protection or assistance. Teachers should also listen sympathetically to students who need support when they are victimized and mobilize peer assistance to identify effective ways to counter bullying (Rigby, 2001).

Further, efforts that alert teachers to the importance of bullying prevention must rest on a foundation of caring, trust, mutual respect, and understanding. The quality of teacher relationships with children is an essential cornerstone of effective classroom ecologies. One of the few evidence-based interventions to enhance teacher-student relationships is Pianta and Hamre's (2001) STARS Program. This is a consultation-based model in which a mental health consultant works together with the teacher to evaluate and strengthen the quality of relationships with students. Particular efforts of the intervention focus on understanding the nature of the teacher's relationships with students, and creating a 'bank' of positive experiences with students that will foster student trust and caring.

Parent-Classroom Relationships. Parents are rarely present when aggressive interactions occur. They hear about conflicts after-the-fact, and only when their children choose to discuss them. Indeed, parents are relatively unaware of bullying that occurs despite the fact that they are very interested in knowing about bullying in their children's classroom (Olweus, 1993; Olweus & Limber, 1999). Still, classroom anti-bullying interventions will be more effective when parents are aware and concerned about peer interactions and their children's experiences in the classroom (Roberts & Coursol, 1996). When their parents are actively involved in their classrooms, children copy their parents' positive, supportive attitudes towards classroom rules and routines (Curtner-Smith, 2000; Estrada, Arsenio, Hess, & Holloway, 1987; Shumow & Millert, 2001). Conversely, parental disengagement from, their children's education is associated with increased incidence of problem behaviors, discipline and suspension (National Center for Educational Statistics, 1992; Rumberger, 1995; Steinberg, 1996).

Parental values about social courtesies and resolving conflicts influence the behaviors that their children use when faced with conflicts in the classroom.

Children who experience harsh, punitive, stressful and violent home environments are more likely to be victimized by bullying in the classroom, especially if they have no friends (Schwartz et al., 2000). Conversely, children can learn bullying behaviors when parents model inappropriate discipline such as hitting or belittling (Curtner-Smith, 2000). Above all, children are more likely to intimidate and exploit if they believe that aggression and intimidation is necessary in order to "win", or if their families view aggression positively (Schwartz & Proctor, 2000).

At a minimum, classroom interventions that target peer aggression will need to include families by keeping them informed of the rules and social skills that will be used to govern children's interactions in the classroom. Optimally, parents will be actively courted as partners in classroom anti-bullying programs. Parents can participate in the development of a student code of conduct. By gaining input from parents, it is more likely that the code of conduct will reflect the values and beliefs of the community thereby increasing students' compliance with the code (Noonan, Tunney, Fogal, & Sarich, 1999).

Parents are integrated at all levels in Olweus' evidence-based Bullying Prevention Program (Olweus & Limber, 1999). At the school level, parents attend meetings to discuss what bullying looks like and the school's intervention plan, are members of bullying intervention committees, and are sent mailings about the school's efforts. In classroom meetings, parents are provided with information about bullying in general, incidents of bullying within their child's classroom, and recommendations for ways they can contribute to a classroom's anti-bullying intervention. In some cases, the classroom's students might also be invited to the meetings so that bullying can be discussed frankly and fully. Classroom meetings with parents are also important to discuss the school's intervention plan, how the parents can support the plan, and any individual bullying experiences. Parents of bullies and victims should be included in such conversations about expectations for student behavior, and should be encouraged to identify and report incidences of potential bullying or social exclusion. At the individual level, parents are invited to participate when their children have been directly involved in a bullying interaction.

Human Agency in the Classroom

Human agency refers to the collective self-systems that make it possible for children to become effective managers of their daily lives. In particular, children's social competence has been clearly related to their self-efficacy or self-identities as competent and effective people, their self-determination or ability to set and work towards self-selected goals, and self-control or ability to behave in ways that are appropriate and consistent with their goals. Each of these characteristics are most often framed as characteristics of individual children, but the developmental research clearly identifies caretaking practices that strengthen or diminish their presence within larger classroom groups.

Behavioral Self-control.   Teachers' systematic manipulation of behavioral antecedents and consequences can reduce serious problem behaviors (Walker, 1995). Unfortunately, studies show that teachers are unlikely to use their authority to interrupt or prevent bullying (Olweus, 1993). Further, strict external behavioral contingencies may not prepare students to control their behavior outside the presence of the adults who notice and cue it (Cole & Bambara, 1992). This is especially important for bullying, which generally occurs outside the notice of adults. Consequently, increasing emphasis is being placed on self-management strategies that empower students to change or maintain their own behavior, and so promote independence and behavioral competence in monitored and non-monitored school settings (Cole & Bambara, 1992; Mitchem & Young, 2001). Using strategies like self-monitoring, self-evaluation, and self-reinforcement, students can be taught to increase their behavioral self-control and decrease inappropriate behavior (Cole & Bambara, 1992).

The establishment of clarifying classroom rules that prohibit bullying and discourage onlooking are the single most important contribution to student self-control of bullying (Olweus, 1993). Three recommended rules include: we will not bully other students; we will try to help students who are bullied; and we will make it a point to include all students who are easily left out. The rules are even more effective in supporting self-control if they have been developed collaboratively with the classroom's students and operationally define bullying with student-generated examples of bullying. Olweus and Limber (1999) suggest rules be generated in a series of class meetings where students provide scenarios of bullying and then provide potential victim responses. We have used scenes from commercial videos or children's literature to prompt rich discussions of these rules. For example, one scene from the film *Little Man Tate* shows Fred Tate carefully handing out birthday party invitations to all of the children in his elementary school class, only to have the children throw the invitations on the ground before running in from recess. After viewing the scene, we have asked classes to consider, "Whose job is it to fix Fred Tate's problem? What should Fred do differently? What should the other children do differently? Do you know any Fred Tates that might need your help?" Such classroom conversations can foster student empathy through the exploration of the thoughts and feelings of victims. Weekly class meetings are important to integrate the rules into the class routines through discussions of how well students are following the rules and their overall satisfaction with school life.

In some cases, classrooms' physical environments can undermine behavioral self-control, even in the face of clear rules and good intentions. Overcrowded spaces, uncomfortable noise, dim or flickering lights, or rooms that are too hot or too cold can raise tensions in a classroom and make it more difficult for students to regulate their emotional responses to each other. Room arrangements can create corners of the classroom where misbehaviors are not easily monitored by the teacher or even by other students. Most peer conflicts are emotional experiences for children, and classrooms that build frustration can feed those conflicts. When such environmental hassles are unavoidable, those classrooms that actively educate children about how to communicate emotions will be more successful in curtailing and resolving conflict (Peterson & Skiba, 2000).

Just as important, a classroom's social ecology can enhance or disrupt behavioral self-control. In socially healthy classrooms, students have mastered routines and practices that promote rule-compliance. When conflicts or problems do occur, students know strategies for solving the problems or working around the disruption. Teachers explicitly model appropriate behaviors, students emulate them, and the natural consequences for appropriate behavior are embedded into the daily routines. The more self-controlled a classroom's students are, the more teachers can devote their energy to the students' other instructional needs.

A particular challenge in the face of bullying is to reinforce antibullying rules without setting the victims up for revenge by the bully. When adults use strict and punitive contingencies, they raise the risk of infuriating bullies who may, in turn, retaliate by further punishing the victim. To prevent retaliation, Maines and Robinson's (1998) 'No Blame Approach to Bully Prevention' works to induce empathy for the victim on the part of the onlookers and the bully. Once a bullying interaction has been identified in a classroom, they meet first with the victim to fully describe the bullying problem, who is involved, and the impact that the bullying has had on the victim's daily life. Next, they assist the victim in communicating their story about the bullying through a written note, picture or film. Then, and without the victim being present, they meet with a small group including the identified bullies and onlookers to discuss the bullying. They read the victim's note, talk about the tragic impact of the bullying on the victim's life, and ask the group to identify what they will do to stop the bullying. In Maines and Robinson's research, these 'no blame' meetings are sufficient to stop the bullying in 60% of all cases, by sensitizing the surrounding peer group to the serious harm that they are doing.

Self-efficacy.   Self-efficacy is the beliefs that students hold about their ability to learn and be successful in the classroom. It is a construct of self-fulfilling prophesies—children who expect to be successful take steps that make it likely that they will be, while those who expect to fail behave in ways that almost assure their failure (Bandura, 1986). Children who lack efficacy enter into challenging situations assuming that they will be unsuccessful. Faced with even minor difficulties, they give up their attempts and concede defeat. Further, they make the automatic assumptions that the failures are due to personal shortcomings and that those few successes that they encounter are accidental, and reflect no credit to themselves.

It is easy to see how this mindset can contribute to being victimized. Children without self-efficacy enter into aggressive interactions with diminished personal power, will be easier to dominate, and will concede to the bully without presenting substantial barriers. A longitudinal study by Olweus (1993) suggests that the alternative may also be true. That is, repeated victimization may cause children to feel inadequate and socially maladjusted. Moreover, because this pattern of victimization appears to persist as long as a child is part of that peer cohort, the feelings of inadequacy can persist for several years. Fortunately, there is evidence that once the victimization ceases, the individual's emotional equilibrium returns.

Although it is often represented as a characteristic of individual children, self-efficacy is clearly a product of the social context in several important respects (Bandura, 1986). It emerges out of opportunities to engage in complex peer interactions with social supports that raise the likelihood of success. It is also enhanced by seeing that other students like oneself are successful in similar social interactions. Perhaps most important, it is strengthened by early, persuasive feedback from the teacher and classmates that assures students that they are socially adept and likeable. Schunk and Zimmerman (1997) suggest that a classroom's modeling and social persuasion are most critical in the early grades when self-efficacy is first developing. While kindergartners think of themselves as successful and well-liked, third graders significantly underestimate their competence, and middle schoolers show an even more dramatic decline in estimating their own abilities.

In part, this declining efficacy might reflect children's growing maturity, as older elementary students have become more aware of their social shortcomings, and more accurate in judging their ability to succeed in difficult social interactions (Paris, Byrnes, & Paris, 2001). Still, the decline may also be due to the overwhelmingly derogatory comments that classmates make to one another about their work, their appearance, or their abilities. By the third grade, elementary school classrooms become a caucaphony of minor insults, put downs, and belittling peer comments that often go unconfronted by supervising adults, classmates, and even the targeted student. The collective impact of these comments is to create a social climate that emphasizes shortcomings over successes, and depresses the self-efficacy of students who learn there. In an ambitious line of research, Schunk and his colleagues have shown that teacher practices can raise the efficacy beliefs of the classrooms' students by promoting student awareness of their own actions, prompting students to reflect upon the conditions that increase their competence, and supporting students in planning and using strategies that will enhance their personal success (Zimmerman, Bonner & Kovach, 1996; Zimmerman & Schunk, 2001). Combined, these classroom practices shift responsibility for managing student behavior and learning away from the teacher onto the students themselves. In the same vein, Olweus (1993) recommends that teachers work to recognize student successes and consistently deliver generous praise to their students to bolster their sense of adequacy and worth.

Self-determination.   Self-determination refers to students' ability to be autonomous and self-directed in making daily life decisions. Self-determined students have goals for their behavior and their achievement. They make choices about daily actions that will advance themselves towards those goals, and routinely evaluate whether or not their progress towards goals is adequate. They are deliberate in revising and refining their actions to maintain consistency with these larger goals. Further, they are self-sufficient in their ability to set goals, make choices and evaluate progress. Although they may weigh the opinions and expectations of others, they are able to act as their own primary causal agent free from undue external influence or interference (Wehmeyer & Metzler, 1995).

Self-determination emerges within classroom settings that give students frequent and varied practice, feedback, and direct instruction in goal setting, decision making, problem solving, and self-evaluation of their skills and behavior (Sands, Spencer, Gliner, & Swaim, 1999; Zimmerman et al., 1996). Sharing responsibility for daily decision-making with students conveys a clear message that they are both capable of and expected to take charge of their daily actions, including their interactions with peers (Doll & Sands, 1998). In a self-determined classroom, students are accountable for their treatment of others and for the outcomes of their interactions. Self-determination is an empowering construct that is closely linked to self-efficacy. Students who practice self-determination gain a confidence in their ability to be self-sufficient, and so become more efficacious. Consequently, self determination is important for potential victims of bullying. Like self-efficacy, self-determination can inoculate students against victimization by countering passivity and inaction in the face of aggression. Instead, victims can learn to think about their actions as sources of control. For example, in our work with a small group of self-reported victims, we used problem solving strategies to help students identify what they could do to protect themselves from bullying.

Specific principles for integrating self-determination into the daily activities of classrooms can be found in Doll and Sands (1998) and Zimmerman et al. (1996). The primary emphasis of these principles is the provision of frequent and varied opportunities to use self-determination skills with adult guidance that supports but does not supplant the students' choices. Very recent research suggests that the most common impediments to the development of students' self-determination and autonomy are adult beliefs that students cannot make good decisions and adult constraints on student opportunities to be self-determined (Sands, Spencer, Gliner, & Swaim, 1999).

What Children Report

This review of classroom research has linked peer aggression to characteristics of the relationships and human agency that are integral to the classroom ecology. An important question is whether the children's perceptions of the classroom context also predict the peer aggression that they experience. To test this, we re-analyzed data from two samples in which we examined the impact of ecological aspects of the classroom on peer aggression (Doll, Siemers, & Brey 2003; Doll et al., 1999; Zucker, Brehm, & Doll, 2000). In both studies, students completed brief anonymous surveys describing classroom relationships (including peer aggression) and human agency. Results indicated that the scales on the survey yielded scores that were reliable and demonstrated factorial validity. Additionally, the scales related to self-efficacy, teacher-student relationships and self-determination demonstrated convergent validity as they were significantly related to key indices of school success including attendance, work completion and academic grades. Three items assessed aggressive peer interactions in both samples. Students were asked to rate (Sample 1–frequency; Sample 2–general perception): (1) problems with teasing and name-calling; (2) problems with hitting, pushing and shoving; and (3) problems with arguing. Thus, results of these surveys allow an analysis of the degree to which children's problems with peer aggression might be related to their classrooms' relationships and human agency.

Participants. Results are described for two samples. Sample 1 includes 190 2nd-through 5th-grade students from nine elementary classrooms in a large Western city. These children were predominantly white and middle class, and attended a year-round school located on the boundary where the city met the suburbs. Sample 2 includes 113 2nd-, 5th- and 6th-grade students from seven elementary classrooms in a small Great Plains city. The majority of these students were also white, and from working class families.

Surveys. All students completed anonymous surveys (Doll et al., 1999) that described the classrooms' social relationships and human agency. Items on the survey described positive attributes of the classroom ecology, and students rated each item by selecting 'yes', 'sometimes' or 'no.' Sample 1 was administered the earlier, 33-item version of the surveys with four 5–8 item subscales: Teacher Student Relationships, Peer Relationships, Academic Efficacy, and Self-Determination. Sample 1 participants were not given items assessing Self-Control. The Home-School Relationship items lacked sufficient internal consistency and so were excluded from further analysis. Internal consistency coefficients of the remaining four scales ranged from .84 to .90. These surveys are described in more detail in Zucker, Brehm, and Doll (2000).

Sample 2 was administered a refined, 40-item version of the survey with six subscales: Teacher Student Relationships, Peer Relationships, Home-School Relationships, Academic Efficacy, Self Determination, and Self-Control. The internal consistency for these refined scales ranged from .75 to .86. The Sample 2 surveys had slight variations in the wording of some items, reflecting refinements made in scale format and wording. For both Sample 1 and Sample 2 surveys, the Peer Relationship survey included the three peer aggression items (described above) and four items describing Peer Inclusion (having someone to play with, being allowed to join a group, having someone to eat lunch with, and having fun at recess). For these analyses, the three peer aggression items were combined into a composite index, and the remaining four items comprised a Peer Inclusion scale. Aggressive peer interactions were assessed differently for each sample. Sample 1's students reported whether the aggressive peer interactions had occurred or not occurred during a recent recess period, while students in Sample 2 rated how confident they were that peers would not be aggressive to them in their class. Both surveys were scored so that higher scores indicated more positive (less aggressive) behaviors or greater confidence that aggression would not occur.

Analyses.   Correlations of the classroom ecology scales with peer aggression are presented in Table 9.1. Results show that all bivariate correlations were positive and significant for both samples. Generally for Sample 1, greater peer inclusion at the classroom level and positive teacher-student relationships were associated with fewer occurrences of peer aggression. Few occurrences of peer aggression was also associated with high self-efficacy and self-determination. These same results emerged in Sample 2 in that these variables were associated with greater confidence that peer aggression would not occur in the classroom. This confidence was further associated with a positive home/classroom relationship and behavioral self-control.

TABLE 9.1

Means, Standard Deviations, Correlations and Regression Analysis
for Classroom Ecology Surveys Predicting Peer Aggression

Classroom Ecology Surveys	Mean	Standard Deviation	Bivariate Correlation	Partial Correlation	B	SEB	β
Sample 1 $F_{(4, 185)} = 12.77, R = .465**$							
Peer inclusion	1.562	.354	.356**	.276**	.318	.082	.266**
Teacher-student relationship	1.549	.439	.366**	.288**	.270	.066	.279**
Self-efficacy	3.409	1.511	.163*	.030	8.8E-03	.022	.032
Self-determination	3.104	1.172	.198**	.068	2.6E-02	.028	.072
Sample 2 $F_{(6, 106)} = 13.93, p = .0000, R = .66$							
Peer inclusion	1.596	.492	.582**	.482**	.634	.112	.479**
Teacher-student relationship	1.680	.408	.326**	−.061	−9.6E-02	.151	−.060
Home/classroom relationship	1.535	.433	.292**	.013	1.9E-02	.142	.013
Self-efficacy	1.574	.384	.476**	.252**	.475	.177	.280**
Self-determination	1.543	.394	.372**	−.112	−.219	.189	−.132
Behavioral self-control	1.575	.347	.443**	.193*	.397	.196	.211*

$*p < .05; **p < .01$

Subsequently, two multiple regression analyses were conducted to evaluate the relative contribution of these factors on the occurrence of peer aggression in Sample 1 and the confidence of not experiencing peer aggression in Sample 2. For both samples, Table 9.1 shows the predictor variables entered in each analysis. The model for Sample 1 was significant and the four predictor variables accounted for 22% of the variance in low peer aggression scores. However, only peer inclusion and teacher-student relationship were significantly associated with less aggression in the classroom. This demonstrates that although self-efficacy and self-determination are associated with peer aggression at the bivariate level, the association between these variables and peer aggression goes away when classroom level variables (peer inclusion, teacher-student relationship) are considered. Similarly, the model for Sample 2 accounted 37% of the variance in the students' confidence that they would not experience peer aggression in their classroom. While the entire model was significant, peer inclusion and self-efficacy were the only significant predictors to emerge. The results for Sample 1 and Sample 2 highlight the importance of classroom level factors on both the frequency reports of aggression and the confidence students' report about not seeing peer aggression in their classroom. However, these findings also suggest that self-efficacy remains related to confidence even after controlling for peer inclusion and teacher-student relations.

The results of this analysis confirm that children's perspectives link the ecological features of classrooms to the prevalence of aggression. The children's reports reinforce the findings reported in the research literature, emphasizing the importance of classroom characteristics in limiting peer aggression. Their reports also provide some evidence of the relative importance of the different ecological characteristics. That is, peer inclusion and teacher-student relationship were most strongly related to the frequency of peer aggression in Sample 1, while peer inclusion, self-efficacy, and self-control were most strongly associated with greater confidence that there would be peer aggression in the classroom in Sample 2. Children's ratings of the home-school relationships and of self determination were less closely related to peer aggression in both samples.

Translating Research Into Practice: Implications for Bullying-Prevention and Intervention Programs

Within the ecological perspective of this chapter, we are suggesting that shifts in classroom routines and practices can serve as a first line of defense against peer bullying. Students who bully or students who are victims are presumed to have the potential to interact effectively with peers, given the proper social context. Creating classroom contexts that discourage all aggression can reduce the frequency and the severity of bullying interactions that occur there.

The children's reports consistently emphasized the importance of peer inclusion as a defense against peer aggression. Decreased levels of social isolation in a classroom make it more likely that all students will have a supportive circle of friends, and friends provide an ever-present defense against bullying. Increased rates of peer inclusion in a classroom can be fostered by enhancing the number and enjoyability of opportunities for children to interact during play, work or learning. The addition of developmentally appropriate games during recess periods and cooperative learning activities during instruction are important contributions to the classroom's support for peer friendships. Peer friendships can be encouraged explicitly with classroom rules such as 'You can't say you can't play' and with curricular activities that prompt children to think about their roles in including or excluding classmates. Further, routines that encourage all children to become active 'directors' of their learning can carry over into social relationships, providing students with the social standing that they need to be an attractive play partner.

Aggressive peer interactions will also be reduced when teacher routines are altered to include more effective monitoring and more prompt and decisive responses to interactions that look like bullying. Effective monitoring may require that the classroom's physical environment be altered to include fewer hidden corners so that adult supervision is easier. The children's surveys emphasize that aggressive interactions will also be diminished when the relationship between teachers and their students is warm and trusting, modeling caring and cooperation for the class. Parents can also contribute to a reduction in aggressive interactions if they are provided with information about the nature of routines and rules in the classrooms, and the kinds of behaviors that are encouraged and discouraged there. Of course, students themselves can reduce the number of aggressive interactions that they initiate, and are more likely to do so in classrooms with clear rules founded with student input that discourage peer aggression.

The normal conflicts that do arise during a classroom's day can be resolved more quickly and effectively when the classroom's students understand conflict mediation strategies and have acquired the self-control to use them. The resolution of conflicts is strengthened when the classroom's teachers and parents model these same strategies. Conflict resolution can become a powerful 'habit' in a classroom when adults prompt students to use conflict resolution in response to any conflicts that emerge.

The use of intimidation and victimization can be reduced in classrooms where teachers model caring and trust, and victims are assured that adults will come to their defense if needed. Peers can also discourage victimization if they are explicitly instructed in their roles as 'defenders' and given concrete suggestions for ways to protect potential victims when bullying occurs. Parents who are informed about classroom incidents of bullying can contribute as well, discouraging the use of intimidating aggression in their family conversations with students. Strategies that raise the collective efficacy of a classroom's students or strengthen their self-determination essentially reduce the number of potential victims available for bullying. When these contextual interventions are not effective, incidents of bullying can be confronted directly using brief 'no blame' conferences with bullies and their onlookers.

Each of these contextual interventions recognize bullying as part of a continuum of peer aggression that occurs naturally within classrooms. The continuum is influenced by the perceptions of the adults and children who populate the classroom setting, as they have come to recognize and understand bullying and intimidation. Their collective perceptions and judgments about bullying can enhance or diminish natural supports for bullying in the classroom. This continuum of peer aggression suggests that classrooms can prevent bullying by first strengthening the natural supports for effective peer interactions.

An important contribution of this chapter has been to describe strategies for bullying prevention that alter the classrooms within which bullying occurs. Still, much of the research supporting this ecological model of bullying is drawn from literature that identified the predictors of bullying and victimization in individual children. There are far fewer efforts to identify the contextual predictors of bullying. A shift towards understanding bullying as an ecological phenomenon is thwarted in many subtle ways. For example, the language available to describe conceptual understandings of bullying includes terms for 'bullies,' 'victims' and 'onlookers' but has no single, meaningful term to refer to sites or contexts that predispose children to higher rates of bullying. More importantly, there are few measures available to evaluate the adequacy of bully-preventing contexts or identify the bully-preventing characteristics that might be missing or deficient in a classroom. Without practical and reliable measures describing relevant characteristics of bullying contexts, it will be difficult to evaluate the impact that prevention strategies have on shaping the more effective antibully ecologies within a class. Without new tools, research designs, and data analysis techniques that document the impact of interventions on bullying contexts, researchers and practitioners will continue to pay lip service to the ecological phenomenon of bullying while intervening to interrupt bullying one student at a time. This summary of the research has shown that failure to attend to the classroom contexts of bullying will be a missed opportunity to understand and prevent bullying in schools.

REFERENCES

Asher, S. R. (1995, June). Children and adolescents with peer relationship problems. A workshop presented at the Annual Summer Institute in School Psychology: Internalizing Disorders in Children and Adolescents, Denver, CO.

Asher, S. R., & Coie, J. D. (1990). *Peer rejection in childhood.* New York: Cambridge University Press.

Bandura, A. (1982). Self-efficacy mechanism in human agency. *American Psychologist, 37,* 122–147.

Bandura, A. (1986). *Social foundations of thought and action: A social cognitive theory.* Englewood Cliffs, N. J: Prentice-Hall.

Barr, R. D., & Parrett, W. H. (2001). *Hope fulfilled for at-risk and violent youth: K-12 programs that work* (2nd ed.). Boston: Allyn & Bacon.

Berndt, T. J., & Das, R. (1987). Effects of popularity and friendship on perceptions of the personality and social behavior of peers. *Journal of Early Adolescence, 7,* 429–439.

Boulton, M. J. (1997). Teachers' views on bullying: Definitions, attitudes, and ability to cope. *British Journal of Educational Psychology, 67,* 223–233.

Boulton, M. J. (1999). Concurrent and longitudinal relations between children's playground behavior and social preference, victimization and bullying. *Child Development, 70,* 944–954.

Boulton, M. J., & Smith, P. K. (1994). Bully/victim problems among middle school children: Stability, self-perceived competence, peer perceptions and peer acceptance. *British Journal of Developmental Psychology, 12,* 315–329.

Boulton, M. J., & Underwood, K. (1992). Bully/victim problems among middle school children. *British Journal of Educational Psychology, 62,* 73–87.

Carlson, C. L., Lahey, B. B., & Neeper, R. (1984). Peer assessment of the social behavior of accepted, rejected, and neglected children. *Journal of Abnormal Child Psychology, 12,* 189–198.

Cole, C. L., & Bambara, L. M. (1992). Issues surrounding the use of self-management interventions in the schools. *School Psychology Review, 21,* 193–201.

Craig, W. M., Henderson, K., & Murphy, J. G. (2000). Prospective teachers' attitudes toward bullying and victimization. *School Psychology International, 21,* 5–21.

Craig, W., & Pepler, D. J. (1997). Observations of bullying and victimization on the schoolyard. *Canadian Journal of School Psychology, 2,* 41–60.

Curtner-Smith, M. E. (2000). Mechanisms by which family processes contribute to school-age boy's bullying. *Child Study Journal, 30,* 169–186.

Dodge, K. A., Coie, J. D., Pettit, G. S., & Price, J. M. (1990). Peer status and aggression in boy's groups: Developmental and contextual analyses. *Child Development, 61,* 1289–1309.

Doll, B. (1996). Children without friends: Implications for practice and policy. *School Psychology Review, 25,* 165–183.

Doll, B., Murphy, P., & Song, S. (2003). The relationship between children's self-reported recess problems, and peer acceptance and friendships. *Journal of School Psychology, 41,* 113–130.

Doll, B., & Sands, D. (1998). Student involvement in goal setting and educational decision making: Foundations for effective instruction. In M. Wehmeyer & D. J. Sands (Eds.), *Making it happen: Student involvement in educational planning, decision making and instruction.* Baltimore: Paul H. Brookes.

Doll, B., Siemers, E. E., & Brey, K. (2003, August). ClassMaps Consultation: An ecological measurement of successful classroom contexts. A poster presented at the annual convention of the American Psychological Association, Toronto, ON, Canada.

Doll, B., Zucker, S., & Brehm, K. (1999, April). Reliability and validity of ClassMaps. A poster presentation at the annual convention of the National Association of School Psychologists, Las Vegas, NV. [ERIC Document Reproduction Services No. ED 435 934].

Emmett, J. D., & Monsour, F. (1996). Open classroom meetings: Promoting peaceful schools. *Elementary School Guidance and Counseling, 3,* 3–11.

Estell, D. B., Cairns, R. B., Farmer, T. W., & Cairns, B. D. (2002). Aggression in inner-city early elementary classrooms: Individual and peer group configuration. *Merrill-Palmer Quarterly, 48,* 52–76.

Estrada, P., Arsenio, W. F., Hess, R., & Holloway, S. (1987). Affective quality of the mother–child relationship: Longitudinal consequences for the child's school-relevant cognitive functioning. *Developmental Psychology, 23,* 210–215.

Grotpeter, J. K., & Crick, N. R. (1996). Relational aggression, overt aggression, and friendship. *Child Development, 67,* 2328–2338.

Harris, A., Hopkins, D., & Wordsworth, J. (2001). The implementation and impact of success for all in English schools. In R. E. Slavin & N. A. Madden (Eds.), *Research and reform in elementary education; success for all* (pp. 81–92). Mahwah, NJ: Lawrence Erlbaum Associates.

Hazler, R. J., Miller, D. L., Carney, J. V., & Green, S. (2001). Adult recognition of school bullying situations. *Educational Research, 43*, 133–146.

Heller, K., & Swindle, R. W. (1983). Social networks, perceived social support, and coping with stress. In R. D. Felner, L. A. Jason, J. N. Mortisugu, & S. S. Farber (Eds.), *Preventive psychology* (pp. 87–103). New York: Pergamon.

Hertz-Lazarowitz, R. (2001). Success for all: A community model for advancing Arabs and Jews in Israel. In R. E. Slavin & N. A. Madden (Eds.), *Research and reform in elementary education; success for all* (pp. 81–92). Mahwah, NJ: Lawrence Erlbaum.

Hodges, E. V. E., Malone, M. J., & Perry, D. G. (1997). Individual risk and social risk as interacting determinants of victimization in the peer group. *Developmental Psychology, 33*, 1032–1039.

Hodges, E. V. E., & Perry, D. G. (1999). Personal and interpersonal antecedents and consequences of victimization by peers. *Journal of Personality and Social Psychology, 76*, 677–685.

Hoover, J., Oliver, R., & Hazler, R. J. (1992). Bullying: Perceptions of adolescent victims in the Midwestern USA. *School Psychology International, 13*, 5–16.

Johnson, D. W., & Johnson, R. (1994). Effects on conflict resolution training on elementary school students. *Journal of Social Psychology, 134*, 803–818.

Kochenderfer, B. J., & Ladd, G. W. (1997). Victimized children's responses to peers' aggression: Behaviors associated with reduced versus continued victimization. *Development and Psychopathology, 9*, 59–73.

Ladd, G., & Oden, S. L. (1979). The relationship between peer acceptance and children's ideas about helpfulness. *Child Development, 50*, 402–408.

Maines, B., & Robinson, G. (1998). The no-blame approach to bullying. In D. Shorrocks-Taylor (Ed.), *Directions in educational psychology* (pp. 281–295). London: Whurr.

McFayden-Ketchum, S. A., & Dodge, K. A. (1998). Problems in social relationships. In E. J. Mash & R. A. Barkley (Eds.), *Treatment of childhood disorders* (2nd ed.), pp. 338–365. New York: Guilford.

Meese, R. L. (1997). Student fights: Proactive strategies for preventing and managing student conflicts. *Intervention in School and Clinic, 33*, 26–33.

Mitchem, K. J., & Young, K. R. (2001). Adapting self-management programs for classwide use: Acceptability, feasibility, and effectiveness. *Remedial and Special Education, 22*, 75–88.

Murphy, P. (2002). *The effect of classroom meetings on the reduction of recess problems: A single case design.* Unpublished doctoral dissertation, University of Denver, Denver, CO.

National Center for Educational Statistics (1992). (*Technical Report No. NCES 92-042*). Washington DC: U.S. Government Printing Office.

Newman, S. R., Murray, B., & Lussier, C. (2001). Confrontation with aggressive peers at school: Student's reluctance to seek help from the teacher. *Journal of Educational Psychology, 93*, 398–410.

Noonan, B., Tunney, K., Fogal, B., & Sarich, C. (1999). Developing student codes of conduct: A case for parent-principal partnership. *School Psychology International, 20*, 289–299.

Olweus, D. (1984). Aggressors and their victims: Bullying at school. In N. Frude & H. Gault (Eds.), *Disruptive behaviors in schools* (pp. 57–76). New York: Wiley.

Olweus, D. (1991). Bully/victim problems among school children: Basic facts and effects of a school based intervention program. In I. Rubin & D. Pepler (Eds.), *The Development and Treatment of Childhood Aggression*. Hillsdale, NJ: Erlbaum.

Olweus, D. (1993). *Bullying at school: What we know and what we can do.* Cambridge: Blackwell.

Olweus, D., & Limber, S. (1999). The Bullying Prevention Program. In D.S. Elliott (Ed.), *Blueprints for violence prevention*. Boulder, CO: Regents of the University of Colorado.

Paley, V. (1993). *You can't say you can't play.* Cambridge, MA: Harvard University Press.

Paris, S. G., Byrnes, J. P., Paris, A. H. (2001). Constructing theories, identities, and actions of self-regulated learners. In B. J. Zimmerman & D. H. Schunk, (Eds.), *Self-regulated learning and academic achievement: Theoretical perspectives* (2nd ed.) pp. 253–287. Mahwah, NJ: Lawrence Erlbaum.

Pellegrini, A. D. (1995). *School recess and playground behavior: Educational and developmental roles*. Albany, NY: State University of New York Press.

Pellegrini, A. D. (2002). Affiliative and aggressive dimensions of dominance and possible functions during early adolescence. *Aggression and Violent Behavior, 7*, 21–31.

Pellegrini, A. D., & Bartini, M. (2001). Dominance in early adolescent boys: Affiliative and aggressive dimensions and possible functions. *Merrill-Palmer Quarterly, 47*, 142–163.

Pellegrini, A. D., Bartini, M., & Brooks, F. (1999). School bullies, victims and aggressive victims: Factors relations to group affiliation and victimization in early adolescence. *Journal of Educational Psychology, 91*, 216–224.

Pepler, D. J., Craig, W. M., Ziegler, S., & Charach, A. (1994). An evaluation of an anti-bullying intervention in Toronto Schools. *Canadian Journal of Community Mental Health, 13*, 95–110.

Peterson, R., & Skiba, R. (2000). Creating climates that prevent school violence. *Preventing School Failure, 44*, 122–130.

Pianta, R. (1999). *Enhancing relationships between children and teachers*. Washington, DC: American Psychological Association.

Pianta, R. C., & Hamre, B. K. (2001). *STARS: Students, teachers and relationships support*. Lutz, FL: Psychological Assessment Resources.

Renshaw, P., & Asher, S. (1983). Children's goals and strategies for social interaction. *Merrill–Palmer Quarterly, 29*, 353–374.

Rigby, K. (2001). Health consequences of bullying and its prevention in schools. In J. Juvonen & S. Graham (Eds.), *Peer harassment in school*. New York: Guilford.

Rizzo, T. A. (1989). *Friendship development among children in school*. Norwood, NJ: Ablex.

Roberts, W. B., Jr., & Coursol, D. H. (1996). Strategies for intervention with childhood and adolescent victims of bullying, teasing and intimidation in school settings. *Elementary School Guidance and Counseling, 30*, 204–213.

Rumberger, R. W. (1995). Dropping out of middle school: A multilevel analysis of students and schools. *American Educational Research Journal, 32*, 583–625.

Salmivalli, C. (2001). Peer-led intervention campaign against school bullying: Who considered it useful, who benefited? *Educational Research, 43*, 263–278.

Salmivalli, C., Lagerspetz, K., Bjorkqvist, K., Osterman, K., & Kaukiainen, A. (1996). Bullying as a group process: Participant roles and their relations to social status within the group. *Aggressive Behavior, 22*, 1–15.

Sands, D. J., Spencer, K. C., Gliner, J., & Swaim, R. (1999). Structural equation modeling of student involvement in transition-related actions: The path of least resistance. *Focus on autism and other developmental disabilities, 14*, 17–27, 35.

Schunk, D. H., & Zimmerman, B. J. (1997). Social origins of self-regulatory competence. *Educational Psychologist, 32*, 195–208.

Schwartz, D., Dodge, K. A., Pettit, G. S., & Bates, J. E. (2000). Friendship as a moderating factor in the pathway between early harsh home environment and later victimization in the peer group. *Developmental Psychology, 36*, 646–662.

Schwartz, D., & Proctor, L. J. (2000). Community violence exposure and children's social adjustment in the school peer group: The mediating roles of emotion regulation and social cognition. *Journal of Consulting and Clinical psychology, 68*, 670–683.

Shumow, L., & Millert, J. D. (2001). Parents' at-home and at-school academic involvement with young adolescents. *Journal of Early Adolescence, 21*, 68–91

Slavin, R. E. (1991). Synthesis of research on cooperative learning. *Educational Leadership, 19*, 71–77.

Smith, P. K., & Boulton, M. (1990). Rough and tumble play, aggression, and dominance: Perception and behavior in children's encounters. *Human Development, 33*, 271–282.

Soutter, A., & McKenzie, A. (2000). The use and effects of anti-bullying and anti-harassment policies in Australian schools. *School Psychology International, 21*, 96–105.

Steinberg, L. (1996). *Beyond the classroom.* New York: Touchstone.

Stephenson, P., & Smith, D. (1989). Bullying in the junior school. In D. P. Tattum & D. A. Lane (Eds.), *Bullying in schools.* Stoke on Trent: Trentham.

Walker, Hill (1995). *The acting-out child: Coping with classroom disruption* (2nd ed.). Longmont, CO: Sopris West.

Wehmeyer, M. L., & Metzler, C. A. (1995). How self-determined are people with mental retardation? The National Consumer Survey. *Mental Retardation, 33,* 111–119.

Werner, E. E., & Smith, R. S. (1992). *Overcoming the odds: High-risk children from birth to adulthood.* Ithaca, NY: Cornell University Press.

Whitney, I. & Smith, P. K. (1993). A survey of the nature and the extent of bullying in junior, middle, and secondary schools. *Educational Research, 35,* 3–25.

Zimmerman, B. J., Bonner, S., & Kovach, R. (1996). *Developing self-regulated learners: Beyond achievement to self-efficacy.* Washington, DC: American Psychological Association.

Zimmerman, B. J., & Schunk, D. H. (2001). *Self-regulated learning and academic achievement: Theoretical perspectives.* Mahwah, NJ: Lawrence Erlbaum.

Zucker, S., Brehm, K., & Doll, B. (2000, March). ClassMaps: Making mentally healthy classrooms promotes academic success. A poster presented at the 32nd Annual National Convention of the National Association of School Psychologists, New Orleans.

IV

Beyond the Classroom: Considering School Climate, Family Relationships, Social Support, and Innovative School Partnerships

10

The Effects of School Climate on Changes in Aggressive and Other Behaviors Related to Bullying

Stephanie Kasen, Kathy Berenson,
Patricia Cohen, and Jeffrey G. Johnson
*Columbia University and
New York State Psychiatric Institute*

The school setting is the primary context in which most childhood bullying and victimization by peers occurs (Olweus, 1978). Moreover, intervention efforts undertaken by investigators to reduce or prevent bullying typically are implemented in the schools (U.S. Departments of Education and Justice, 1999). Whether considered individually or on a system-wide level, schools also are the preferred unit of analysis chosen by researchers when reporting rates of bullying and victimization (e.g., Boulton & Underwood, 1992; Olweus, 1993; Whitney & Smith, 1993). In a recent survey of more than 15,000 students in grades 6 through 10 in the United States, 29.9% reported either bullying others or being victimized by others, or both, at least some of the time during the current school term (Nansel et al., 2001). Middle and high school students have reported rates as high as 75% for being victimized at least once during the course of their school years (Hoover, Oliver, & Hazler, 1992). Björkqvist and Österman (1999) note that "bullying has probably occurred as long as there have been schools" (p. 57). There is clear evidence that schools do influence children's intellectual, emotional, and behavioral development; yet, to date, information about school context influences on bullying is limited. This chapter will focus on qualities of the social and emotional climate of the school and how they may be implicated in the facilitation or deterrence of school bullying.

Societal Expectations for Schools

In most modern countries, a central underlying rationale for compulsory school attendance by children between about 6 years old until at least 16 years of age is the attainment of knowledge, particularly in the academic subjects, through formal instruction. However, there are other cultural imperatives, the way of life in a society and its traditions, customs, and mores, that also are transmitted to each new generation via its educational institutions. Thus, schools function as a socializing agent of children: In addition to their intellectual development, schools are expected to address their moral, social, and behavioral development as well (Dreeben, 1968). Accordingly, elementary school curricula objectives include promoting the development of pro-social attitudes and behaviors, and increasing pupil awareness and acceptance of civic responsibilities. For example, in the New York State Education Department Resource Guide (2002), exploring lifestyles, beliefs, and traditions; knowing what it means to be a good citizen; and identifying/describing rules and responsibilities are among the social studies curriculum objectives indicated at the elementary school level.

The impact of the socializing role of the school has been recognized in the ecological model of childhood development (Bronfenbrenner, 1979), and in integrated theories of risk that implicate individual, familial, and social context influences on delinquent and other problematic behaviors in childhood and adolescence (Elliott, Huizinga, & Ageton, 1985; Tremblay et al., 1992). According to the tenets of social control theory, commitment to long-established conventional institutions within a society discourages acts of transgression and facilitates the internalization of norms and external constraints (Hirschi, 1969). Successful school bonding or commitment has been related empirically to enhanced student motivation and achievement (Bryk & Thum, 1989; Goodenow, 1993), and to decreased risk of student substance abuse, school dropout, and other maladaptive behaviors (Hawkins, Catalano, & Miller, 1992).

Due, in part, to the spiraling complexity of our society, educational institutions also are expected to address some of the broader social issues that affect the development of children. Schools have established specialized programs that target children considered to be at risk for academic failure, for example, children from families living in poverty, children from homeless or migrant families, and children with low English language proficiency (Reynolds, 1992). School-based intervention and prevention programs have been implemented to counteract high rates of depression, illicit drug use, and other categories of childhood morbidity (e.g., attention deficit disorders) (Pfeiffer & Reddy, 1998; Reeder et al., 1997), and to reduce the escalating rates of violence in the schools (Howard, Flora, & Griffin, 1999). The latter, as well as the rising incidence of national and world-wide terrorist activities, also has heightened the need for and use of school-based psychological services. Moreover, reporting of suspected child abuse and neglect by school personnel to official child protective services is mandatory in all 51 U.S. jurisdictions. However, although schools are the largest single source of abuse reports, the majority of cases go unreported; thus, there is a call for more intensive school-based programs to increase staff recognition of signs of abuse and neglect (Crenshaw, Crenshaw, & Lichtenberg, 1995).

Societal demands on U.S. schools were further expanded by federal passage of the Individuals with Disabilities Education Act, formerly named the Education of All Handicapped Children Act (Public Law 94-142), in 1975. Since then, it has been mandatory for schools to identify pupils with a physical or mental handicapping condition, for example, a sensory or speech impairment, a specific learning disability, a serious emotional disturbance, or an attention or hyperactivity problem, that interferes with or substantially limits their ability to benefit from a formal education. That task typically is accomplished by a school-based assessment that may entail educational, psychological, and medical evaluations, the results of which are used to determine the specific needs of the child. Schools are obligated to address those needs by making available essential intervention services that may include (but are not limited to) educational placement options with specially trained teachers; transportation services; speech therapy; occupational therapy; social work services; and counseling, psychological, or psychiatric services by mental health professionals. Individuals between 3 and 21 years old are eligible to receive services.

Clearly, schools are accountable to society and to parents for far more than academic distinction among students. Thus, it can be argued that the effectiveness of schools may be measured by more than academic success alone, but also by indicators of pupils' social competence, psychological well-being, and adequacy of long-term adult role functioning.

Early Empirical Evidence of School Influence on Children's Development

In the mid-1960s, large-scale school studies were conducted in the U.S. to identify ways in which schools could bridge the performance gap that existed between socially advantaged and disadvantaged students (Coleman, 1966; Jencks et al., 1972). The conclusions drawn from those studies, however, indicated that differences in academic attainment primarily were attributable to family circumstances and personal characteristics, regardless of variations in school resources (Jencks, 1979). That viewpoint was supported by others' findings that social background and ability level explained almost all student differences in achievement, whereas the contribution of the school was minimal (e.g., Ainsworth & Batten, 1974). Further confirmation of the limited independent influence wielded by schools on children came from attempts to counteract those inequities with preschool educational enrichment programs. Although the targeted population of pupils made immediate gains in cognitive development, gains were not maintained after the early elementary school grades (Bronfenbrenner, 1974). Consequently, the prevailing zeitgeist was that the negative impact of problematic family backgrounds or individual characteristics was immutable, and the schools ineffective.

Other findings, however, supported the argument that schools do indeed differ in how effective they are (e.g., Rutter, Maughan, Mortimore, Ouston, & Smith, 1979), and that the particular school attended can have significant long-term ramifications for students, especially low ability pupils. For example, schools serving students with similar backgrounds were shown to vary with regard to achievement scores, attendance rates, and rates of delinquency (e.g., Reynolds, Jones, St. Leger, & Murgatroyd, 1980; Rutter et al., 1979). Furthermore, associations between school factors and long-term educational, occupational, social, and personal benefits also were documented (e.g., Darlington, Royce, Snipper, Murray, & Lazar, 1980; Gray, Smith, & Rutter, 1980).

The failure of some investigations to explain differences in student outcomes as a function of variations in schools was attributed, in part, to limitations in the methodology or study design (Rutter, 1983). For example, student outcomes examined often were incidental to the aims and specific objectives of school curricula (e.g., change in verbal ability or IQ scores). In addition, the criterion used to evaluate school impact, the degree to which schools were able to eliminate student differences, was a poor indicator of school effectiveness. Individual and family characteristics exert substantial influence on capacities and behavior, and are independent of the impact of schooling. Consequently, despite very real effects of schooling on student outcomes, differences between students always will remain. Thus, increases in scholastic performance or declines in maladaptive behaviors within students may be more relevant criteria by which to estimate the effectiveness of schools. Finally, past studies may have failed to correctly identify the specific school features that do influence academic performance and behavioral outcomes of students.

What Characteristics of the School Do Matter?

Examination of school features of a physical or material nature (e.g., the size of the student body, condition of the physical plant; teacher to pupil ratios; expenditure per pupil) has indicated few systematic differences in student achievement (see review by Rutter, 1983). There has been a great deal of support, however, for associations between variations in achievement and other student outcomes and less tangible characteristics that reflect the internal life of the school. School policies, attitudes and behaviors of teachers, administrators, and the student body, and the overall atmosphere or school ethos, determine the internal life or social, emotional, and motivational climate of the school.

Variations in achievement levels have been attributed to social organization and motivational climate of the school (Ames, 1992; Goodenow, 1993; Griffith, 1995); to staff development, stability, and autonomy (Purkey & Smith, 1983); and to teacher attitudes and behaviors, the proportion of academically competent students in the student body, and the overall social climate (Rutter et al., 1979). Moreover, those effects sometimes had far reaching consequences for later employment status (Gray et al., 1980), and for career and marriage planning skills (Rutter, 1987). High levels of learning inspiration and ambition in high school students have been related to whether or not the school climate is perceived as supportive (Plucker, 1998). Variations in other nonacademic outcomes, including students' sense of well-being (Moos, 1979); dropout rates and interest in and commitment to schooling (Bryk & Thum, 1989); attendance rates and unruly behaviors (Rutter et al., 1979); truancy (Reynolds et al., 1980); and delinquency, criminal activities, drugs, and related maladaptive behaviors (Dubois, Felner, Brand, Adam, & Evans, 1992; Hawkins et al., 1992; Rutter et al., 1979), also have been linked to staff characteristics, achievement levels of other students, and overall social and emotional climate.

Kasen, Johnson, and Cohen (1990) examined the predictive effects of social and emotional school climate factors on changes in adolescent psychiatric disturbance over a $2\frac{1}{2}$ year period. Students who reported attending schools characterized by a high level of student-student and teacher-student conflict had significantly greater increases in attentional, oppositional, and conduct problems. In contrast, those who reported attending well organized harmonious schools that emphasized learning had significantly greater declines in oppositional, conduct, and alcohol problems. Moreover, adolescents who attended schools high in conflict were at increased risk for alcohol abuse and criminal conviction six years later in young adulthood, whereas adolescents who attended well organized harmonious schools were at less risk for dropping out of school, engaging in criminal activities, and having antisocial personality disorder (Kasen, Cohen, & Brook, 1998). Others have noted a protective effect of a positive school climate on the emergence of internalizing and externalizing problems over a one-year period among highly self-critical students and students low in efficacy (Kupermine, Leadbeater, & Blatt, 2001).

Variations in school climate also have been linked to student self-esteem and related outcomes. A substantial proportion of the research in this area has focused on the contrast between a motivational climate that emphasizes the intrinsic value of learning and uses within-student improvement to evaluate success versus a climate that pits students against each other in a competition for grades and other academic kudos (i.e., task goals versus performance goals, respectively). Pupils attending schools characterized by a competitive climate are more likely to attribute academic failure to a lack of ability; in contrast, those attending schools that focus on improvement within students are more likely to report higher self-efficacy and view failure as a transitory phenomenon due, for example, to not trying hard enough or forgetting to study (Ames, 1992; Elliot & Dweck, 1988). A competitive school climate also has been related to delinquency problems in students, for example, marijuana and other illicit drug use, truancy, early sexual intercourse, and petty stealing (Fiqueira-McDonough, 1986).

What Characteristics of the School Climate May Influence Bullying?

In contrast to the elementary school climate, the less structured climate of the junior high or middle school presents risks that may facilitate the occurrence of school bullying. Unlike the elementary school, the junior high or middle school implements a multiteacher instructional format, which leads to a more impersonal and less protective climate. That setting also permits more independent behavior and mobility among students, such as moving through the halls for classroom transfers several times a day, thus increasing the amount of unsupervised time that students are vulnerable to assault. More than 75% of assaults on middle and junior high school students by their classmates occur in the halls, restrooms, during lunch, and right before and after school; the classroom is by far the safest place (Safer, 1986). School bullying also tends to occur in unsupervised locations and during non-academic subject periods (Craig, Pepler, & Atlas, 2000; Olweus, 1993). Compared to pupils attending elementary schools, students attending junior high or middle schools experience a six-fold increase in rates of student assaults on other students, a 12- to 15-fold increase in rates of student suspensions, and higher rates of fear of victimization (Elias, Gara, & Ubriaco, 1985). With grade level held constant as a proxy for age, a comparison between junior high school seventh graders and seventh graders in a K-8 (i.e., kindergarten through eighth grade) elementary school indicated a higher rate of victimization (42% vs. 25%), more anonymity (44% vs. 4%), and less self-esteem (39% vs. 29%), in the junior high school seventh graders (Blyth, Simmons, & Bush, 1978).

There is a large body of literature that addresses corporal punishment in the schools, the deliberate infliction of physical pain in students for disciplinary purposes. Corporal punishment is banned in 27 states and permitted in 23 (National Coalition to Abolish Corporal Punishment in the Schools, 1997). States that endorse corporal punishment have higher rates of school shootings fatalities (Arcus, 2002) and higher assault rates by children (Strauss, 1994). There is widespread support in the literature that children who are abused subsequently abuse others (Ryan, Myoshi, Metzner, Krugman, & Fryer, 1996). Childhood victims of violence learn to devalue people and perpetrate the cycle of violence (Hyman & Perrone, 1998). Consequently, school authority figures who model punitive measures as an acceptable means by which to gain control of a situation may foster similar coercive aggressive behaviors in their pupils.

The Impact of Bullying on School Climate

School bullying creates a climate of fear and reduces the quality of life for all students and school personnel (Tremlow, Fonagy, & Sacco, 2001). To avoid being victimized, 22 percent of middle school and junior high school students reported avoiding three or more places on the school premises, and five percent reported staying home from school one or more times a month (Safer, 1986). Other reports indicate difficulties concentrating on schoolwork, sadness, and physical complaints in students as a consequence of being victimized by classmates (Sharp, 1995; Williams, Chambers, Logan, & Robinson, 1996). Failure by the school to address that problem cultivates a school climate that condones aggressive coercive-submissive interactions, and is associated with higher rates of school bullying (Craig et al., 2000; Olweus, 1993). Moreover, retaliatory actions taken by victims may sometimes result in devastating outcomes for the school as a whole (Tremlow, 2000). Finally, students who bully other students may experience very grave social and mental health problems as well, including increased risk of later criminal convictions and psychiatric illness (Baldry & Farrington, 2000); thus, they too may stand much to gain from effective school interventions.

Summary

School bullying is quite prevalent in our schools and a serious threat to healthy development in all children. It creates a climate of fear among students and teachers, condones aggressive coercive-submissive interactions between students, and may be a precursor to later violent and criminal activities, mental health problems, and sometimes tragic and fatal circumstances among bullies, victims, and bully-victims. Almost all childhood bullying and victimization occurs in the school setting. Prior research in the schools indicates that specific characteristics of the school context influence both academic and non-academic changes in student attitudes and behaviors, some of which are closely related to the occurrence of bullying. School features implicated in those changes are primarily those related to the internal life of the school or the school climate. For example, the use of corporal punishment by teachers and administrators, a school climate characterized by a high level of conflict between and among students and teachers, or one that pits students against each other for limited rewards, may operate to facilitate bullying, whereas a supportive and harmonious school climate or one that emphasizes within student improvement as opposed to competition between students may act as a deterrent. Schools play an important role in the social and emotional development of children, and may be an indispensable force for eliminating or reducing the threat of victimization by classmates.

Purpose of the Current Study

The effectiveness of school programs to eliminate or reduce bullying is contingent upon the identification and modification of features of the school climate (Swearer & Doll, 2001). To address that, we examine the effects of four

dimensions of school climate on concurrent behaviors (herein referred to as outcome behaviors) related to the bullying process in a longitudinal sample of over
500 youths attending over 250 schools. In order to attribute independent school
effects to actual changes in behavior, we include parallel baseline bullying measures obtained $2\frac{1}{2}$ years prior to bullying measures at outcome, and concurrent
measures of closeness of the relationship between youth and mother and parental
use of harsh, power-assertive punishment. Age, sex, and socioeconomic status
(SES) also are controlled. The data used to examine school bullying come from
the Children in the Community Study (CIC), an ongoing longitudinal investigation of individual, familial, and environmental childhood risks for behavioral and
emotional disturbances from childhood through early adulthood.

Method

Subjects

In 1975, 976 families were randomly selected on the basis of residence in one
of two New York upstate counties and having at least one child between ages
one and 10 in the household. Mothers were interviewed about family background characteristics, parenting practices, and the target child's temperament
and behavior. Mothers were re-interviewed and the target child interviewed in
three follow-up waves with an expanded protocol; data used in the current study
are drawn from the first follow-up (F1), conducted in 1983, and the second
follow-up (F2), conducted in 1985–1986, when the children were mean ages
13.5 and 16.0, respectively. In all, about 800 youths have been followed; this
sample is 51% female; 91% White and 8% African-American/Black; resides in
urban, suburban, and rural areas; and spans the entire range of socioeconomic
statuses. Demographic characteristics are representative of the population from
which sampling took place (Cohen & Cohen, 1996).

At F1, 721 youths were in school; by F2, 213 either had completed high
school (94.7%) or dropped out (5.3%). Only the remaining 508 youths (256 girls,
252 boys) still in school at F2 were included in the analyses. Mean ages of the
study sample at F1 (12.5 years, SD 1.78) and F2 (14.9 years, SD 1.93) correspond roughly to early and middle adolescence, respectively. The majority attended public schools (90%); the others were in attendance at private or
parochial schools. Grade levels ranged from 5 through 12 at F2.

Procedure

In both follow-ups, mothers and youths were interviewed separately but
simultaneously in their homes by trained lay interviewers. The study protocol
included an assessment of psychiatric disturbances, personality traits and disorders,

and parent-child interactions. Youths also were interviewed about their peer relationships, school context, and work experiences.

Measures

Demographic Controls.   All analyses were controlled for age at outcome, gender and family socioeconomic status (SES) at F1, the latter measured by an additive scale composed of both parents' level of education, fathers' occupational status, and family income; higher scores reflect higher SES.

Covariates.   Parental characteristics and child rearing methods have been associated with a high rate of bullying behaviors in childhood, in particular a lack of warmth, involvement, and support, and the use of harsh power assertive disciplinary actions (Bowers, Smith, & Binney, 1992, 1994; Farrington, 1993). To control for those concurrent influences on bullying behaviors, measures of closeness of the relationship between mother and youth and parental use of harsh punishment at F2 are included in the analyses. Maternal Closeness is a composite of four separate scales that combine mothers' and youths' responses: the 4-item Maternal Affection Scale ($\alpha = .72$ at F2) (e.g., shows love for child); the 5-item Maternal Communication Scale ($\alpha = .77$ at F2) (e.g., is easy to talk to); the 4-item Maternal Support Scale ($\alpha = .73$ at F2) (e.g., can be counted on to help out in any situation), and the 1-item Maternal Availability Scale (has time for me), all 14 items assessed on a 4-point Likert scale (1 = never to 4 = very often). Punishment is a composite of two separate scales that combine maternal self-reports and youth reports of the type of punishment/ discipline applied by both parents: the 7-item Power Assertive Scale ($\alpha = .67$ at F2) assessed frequency of harsh punishment methods used in the past month (e.g., smacked, threatened to punish); and the 5-item Discipline Scale ($\alpha = .58$ at F2) (e.g., withholds affection/ takes away privileges), assessed general parental style of disciplining on a 4-point Likert scale (1 = not at all like me/parent to 4 = very much like me/ parent). Scales were adapted from measures of similar constructs (Avgar, Bronfenbrenner, & Henderson, 1977; Schaefer, 1965) identified as influencing offspring behavior. Associations with difficult temperament, behavioral disturbances, and interpersonal problems in offspring support the predictive validity of the parenting scales (Cohen & Brook, 1987, 1995).

The third covariate, prior bullying and related behaviors, is probably the most salient covariate that can be utilized when investigating the influence of school climate on concurrent bullying behaviors. For every outcome measure obtained at F2, the parallel measure obtained at F1 is employed. These measures are described below in the *Outcome and baseline measures* section.

School Climate Predictor Scales.   At F2 youths responded to 45 items assessing social and emotional features of their school environment; items reflect the school process characteristics described by Rutter and colleagues

(Rutter et al., 1979) and Moos (1979). Principal factor analysis (see Kasen et al., 1990, for details) yielded four measures of the school climate, all of which are used in the current analyses.

A high score on the 15-item Conflict Scale ($\alpha = .82$ at F2) is indicative of a chaotic setting where teachers are ineffective in maintaining classroom control and students disregard authority (e.g., "Teachers often shout at students," "Students criticize or joke about the teachers a lot"). A high score on the 12-item Learning Focus Scale ($\alpha = .68$ at F2, formerly named Academic Focus) indicates a well-organized harmonious setting where learning is a priority for both students and teachers (e.g., "Most students are really interested in getting good grades," "Teachers really work hard to make the work interesting"). A high score on the 7-item Social Facilitation Scale ($\alpha = .44$ at F2) reflects a school ethos that fosters an open and informal atmosphere where personal concerns may be voiced and social ties encouraged (e.g., "Teachers lead discussions of emotional or family problems students may have," "There are many chances to spend time with friends around school outside of class"). A high score on the 6-item Autonomy Scale ($\alpha = .60$ at F2) is indicative of a school setting where students are encouraged to have a voice in school politics and in decisions about school programs (e.g., "Students here choose a lot of their own academic program," "Students are strongly encouraged to say whatever they think"). All items on the four school climate scales were assessed on a 3-point Likert scale (definitely true of my school, somewhat true, not true). Zero-order correlations among the school climate scales range from a high of $-.34$ (between Conflict and Learning Focus) to a low of $-.01$ (between Conflict and Autonomy). The school climate scales have been associated with changes in conduct and related problems (Kasen et al., 1990) and drug use (Brook, Whiteman, & Cohen, 1995) at adolescence, and to later deviant outcomes, including Antisocial Personality Disorder and criminal conviction, in early adulthood (Kasen et al., 1998).

Outcome and Baseline Measures. Definitions proposed for bullying typically include these features: (1) aggressive behavior, physical or verbal, (2) these behaviors are directed towards someone perceived to be physically or psychologically weaker, (3) there is an intention to harm psychologically or socially, or to inflict injury or discomfort, and (4) these behaviors occur over an extended period of time (Boulton & Underwood, 1992; Olweus, 1978). Specific behaviors include physical aggression; telling lies about the victim; intentional exclusion from social groups or ignoring the victim; making fun of or saying mean or unpleasant things about the victim; name-calling; breaking or taking belongings; threatening; and similar behaviors. Although peers are the primary targets of victimization, bullies often harass and are aggressive toward teachers and parents (however, teachers and parents also may bully students by the use of coercive power assertive behaviors and humiliation: Björkquist and Österman, 1999). Moreover, antisocial rule-breaking behavioral patterns, including fighting, pilfering, drunkenness, and truancy; a more positive attitude toward violence; a lack of empathy for others; and poor control over emotions and impulses, are typical of bullies. In addition, a child with an explosive or hotheaded temperament is considered to be at high risk of exhibiting bullying behaviors.

Although the primary goal of the CIC study was not the study of bullying, there are available extensive measures of childhood problems and behaviors that correspond to specific behaviors noted in the definition of bullying, or to characteristics associated with bullying. All scale items described in this section were administered at F1 and again at F2, and are used in the current study as covariates and outcomes, respectively. The bullying behavior scales described below reflect conduct disordered, aggressive, and bullying behavioral syndromes, and were drawn from others' measures of those same constructs (Achenbach & Edelbrock, 1981; Derogatis, Lipman, Rickels, Uhlenhuth, & Covi, 1974; Smith & Fogg, 1979). These scales have been associated with interpersonal difficulties and substance use along with long-term personality problems and maladaptive behavioral patterns (Brook, Whiteman, Gordon, & Cohen, 1986; Cohen, 1996).

Measures of bullying related behavior reported by youths included the 9-item School Problems Scale ($\alpha = .70$ at F1) (e.g., gets into trouble a lot, argues with teachers, tells lies in school), assessed on a 3-point Likert scale (yes, sometimes, no); the 5-item Deviance Scale ($\alpha = .65$ at F1) (e.g., truants, cheats, takes things from classmates' desks/lockers), frequency in current school term assessed (never to 5 or more times); the 8-item Rebelliousness Scale ($\alpha = .81$ at F1) (e.g., enjoys getting away with things, does not feel guilty, breaks rules); the 21-item Anger Scale ($\alpha = .79$ at F1) (e.g., angers others by teasing, quarrelsome, hotheaded, likes to show up others); and the 3-item Physical Aggression Scale ($\alpha = .50$ at F1) (e.g., threatens with physical harm, gets into a lot of fights), the three preceding scales assessed on a 4-point Likert scale (false, mostly false but not completely, mostly true but not completely, true).

Measures of bullying behaviors reported by mothers included the 4-item Teacher Harassment Scale ($\alpha = .71$ at F1, a shorter version of the School Problems Scale) (e.g., argues a lot with teachers, will talk back to teacher or walk out of class if angry), assessed on a 3-point Likert scale (often true, sometimes true, hardly ever or not true); the 5-item Noncompliance Scale taps resistance to maternal control ($\alpha = .88$) (e.g., often breaks rules, tries to get away with things, seldom follows orders), assessed on a 4-point Likert scale (very much like, somewhat like, a little like, not at all like); and the 25-item Externalizing Problems Scale (alpha .80 at F1), derived from the Child Behavior Check List (CBCL: Achenbach & Edelbrock, 1981) and reflecting aggressive, bullying, and delinquent syndromes (e.g., is mean and cruel, bullies others, threatens others, takes things that don't belong to him/her, is destructive, is impulsive, physically attacks others), assessed on a 3-point Likert scale (often true, sometimes true, hardly ever or not true).

We also examine school climate influences on internalizing problems, as reported by mothers. There is empirical evidence of more depression in bullies than in controls (Swearer, Song, Cary, Eagle, & Mickelson, 2000), of more depression and anxiety in bully-victims (i.e., those who are victimized by others and also bully others) than in controls (Swearer et al., 2000), and of more anxiety in victims than in bullies (Craig, 1998; Swearer et al., 2000). Insecurities, anxiety, depression, physical symptoms, and negative self-evaluations have been shown to be both a cause and a consequence of bullying (Salmon, James, & Smith, 1998); moreover, types of behaviors displayed by victims may determine the outcome of the bullying process (Salmivalli, Huttunen, & Lagerspetz, 1996). Therefore, it is useful to examine whether features of the school climate may influence those characteristics. The 11-item Internalizing Problems Scale ($\alpha = .78$ at F1), derived from the CBCL, reflects depressive and anxiety syndromes (e.g., is unhappy, sad, depressed, withdrawn), all items assessed on a 3-point Likert scale (*often true, sometimes true, hardly ever or not true*).

Data Analytic Design

Simultaneous regression analysis was used to examine the independent effects of concurrent school climate on each outcome scale. Partial regression coefficients are adjusted for age at outcome, sex, socioeconomic status, parallel baseline behavior, Maternal Closeness, Parental Punishment, and all four school climate dimensions (Conflict, Learning Focus, Social Facilitation, Autonomy). The size of the partial regression coefficient represents the unique effect of each independent variable on the dependent variable after partialing overlapping effects of all other independent variables in the equation. Scaled independent variables were standardized; thus, the increase or decrease in the dependent variable (i.e., as described by the partial regression coefficient) always corresponds to a one standard deviation (*SD*) change in each scaled independent variable. Both unstandardized (B) and standardized beta (β) regression coefficients are tabled to enhance interpretation of the findings. The latter is indicative of the effect size or change in standard deviation units of the dependent variable.

Hypotheses

The following hypotheses are based on the principles of ecological and social learning and control theories, and on prior findings of school climate effects (e.g., Brook et al., 1995; Kasen et al., 1990, 1998; Rutter et al., 1979). We expected adolescents attending schools high in conflict to show an increase in bullying-related behaviors and, because of the distress associated with ongoing exposure to conflict, an increase in internalizing problems. We expected adolescents attending schools high in learning focus to show a decrease in bullying-related behaviors, attributable to an increased sense of accomplishment and more teacher attention. We expected that adolescents attending schools that grant students a high degree of autonomy would show a decrease in bullying-related behaviors due to an increased sense of responsibility and growing maturity. Although close social ties with non-parental adults may benefit adolescents by increasing their support systems (Galbo, 1983), fostering social informality between teachers and students may not be appropriate in the school setting. Standards may become overly lax, and respect for teachers and their authority may diminish. Thus, we posited that adolescents attending schools high in social facilitation would experience an increase in bullying-related behaviors, and also in internalizing problems, the latter hypothesis based primarily on our finding of increased depression and anxiety in adolescents attending schools with a very open and informal social atmosphere (Kasen et al., 1990). Finally, we expected that a close maternal relationship would be associated with a decrease in bullying-related behaviors and internalizing problems, whereas harsh parental punishment would be associated with an increase.

Various aspects of a social climate also may interact; for example, an open informal atmosphere, as in a school with a high level of Social Facilitation, may heighten the disorganization and disharmony indicative of a school high in conflict. Thus, we hypothesized that adolescents attending a high conflict school with an open informal atmosphere would fare worse (i.e., show an increase in bullying-related behavior) than those in high conflict-low social facilitation schools. We also expected that autonomous functioning in schools where learning was not a priority would foster an increase in bullying-related behaviors due either to a lack of control and disorganization or unmotivated teachers or both.

Results

Associations Between Demographic Variables and Outcomes

Zero order correlations between outcomes and age and SES were as follows: Self-reports of deviant and rebellious behaviors increased with age ($r = .28$, $p < .001$ and $r = .13$, $p = .004$, respectively), whereas mother reports of noncompliance with rules decreased with age ($r = -.14$, $p = .001$). Higher levels of family SES were related to less self-reported school problems ($r = -.21$, $p < .001$) and anger ($r = -.13$, $p = .003$), and less mother-reported teacher harassment ($r = -.13$, $p = .003$), noncompliance with parental rules ($r = -.29$, $p < .001$), and externalizing ($r = -.23$, $p < .001$) and internalizing ($r = -.17$, $p < .001$) problems.

Compared to girls, boys had significantly higher scores on self-reported school problems, $F (1, 507) = 50.06$, $p < .001$, deviant behavior, $F (1, 507) = 27.42$, $p < .001$, rebelliousness, $F (1, 507) = 22.74$, $p < .001$), mother-reported teacher harassment, $F (1, 507) = 6.25$, $p < .05$, noncompliance with parental rules, $F (1, 507) = 6.91$ $p < .01$, and externalizing problems,

F (1, 507) = 5.46, $p < .05$. Compared to boys, girls had significantly higher scores on mother-reported internalizing problems, F (1, 507) = 16.23, $p < .001$.

Associations Between Covariates and Bullying

Table 10.1 shows the effects of the three covariates (baseline behaviors, mother closeness, parental punishment) on outcomes after partialing shared effects of age, sex, SES, and the other two covariates. Baseline measures of all bullying re-lated behaviors and of internalizing problems were highly predictive of the same outcomes $2\frac{1}{2}$ years later; on average, effect size was a 0.5 standard deviation (*SD*) (range 0.37 to 0.65 *SD*) unit change in the outcome. Thus, for internalizing problems and each bullying-related behavior examined, being 1 *SD* above the mean at baseline was associated with about a 0.5 *SD* increase in that problem or behavior $2\frac{1}{2}$ years later. Maternal closeness was significantly associated with a decrease in all bullying-related behaviors; however, compared to baseline behav-ior effects, effect sizes, on average 0.12 *SD* (range 0.20 *SD* to 0.07 *SD*), were lower. Harsh parental punishment was related to an increase in youth-reported physical aggression, and mother-reported noncompliance and externalizing and internalizing problems, average effect size 0.11 *SD* (range 0.15 to 0.07 *SD*).

School-Climate Predictors

Table 10.2 shows the effects of each school-climate scale (conflict, learning focus, social facilitation, autonomy) on outcomes after partialing the shared ef-fects of age, gender, SES, baseline behavior, mother closeness, parental punish-ment, and the other three school climate scales. The average school-climate effect size was 0.11 *SD* (range 0.20 *SD* to 0.07 *SD*). Independent effects of school climate were found for both youth and mother reports of outcomes, and, for the most part, in the direction hypothesized. Attendance at high-conflict schools was associated with an increase in youth-reported school problems, re-belliousness, anger, and physical aggression, and in mother-reported externaliz-ing problems. Attendance at well-organized harmonious schools that prioritize learning was associated with declines in youth-reported school problems, de-viance, and rebelliousness, and in mother-reported teacher harassment. Atten-dance at schools that encourage autonomous functioning among students was associated with declines in mother-reported noncompliance with parental rules and in externalizing and internalizing problems. However, attendance at schools with an open and informal atmosphere was associated with an increase in youth-reported school problems.

Interactions Between School Climate Scales

Mother reports of externalizing problems and teacher harassment increased significantly more over the $2\frac{1}{2}$ year interval among adolescents attending schools high in both conflict and social facilitation that in those attending high conflict/low

TABLE 10.1

Effects of Baseline Behavior, Maternal Closeness, and Parental Punishment on Bullying-related Behaviors and Internalizing Problems

	Baseline Behavior			Maternal Closeness			Parental Punishment		
	B	(B SE)	β	B	(B SE)	β	B	(B SE)	β
Youth Informants									
School problems	1.65	(.09)	.58***	−.21	(.09)	−.07*	.14	(.09)	.05
Deviance	2.34	(.16)	.55***	−.47	(.13)	−.11**	.19	(.14)	.04
Rebelliousness	2.37	(.13)	.56***	−.63	(.13)	−.15***	.18	(.13)	.04
Anger	1.82	(.19)	.35***	−.51	(.19)	−.10**	.30	(.20)	.06
Physical aggression	.66	(.06)	.37***	−.15	(.06)	−.08*	.23	(.07)	.13***
Mother Informants									
Teacher harassment	.50	(.04)	.41***	−.25	(.04)	−.20****	.02	(.05)	.02
Noncompliance	1.94	(.11)	.53***	−.70	(.11)	−.19****	.41	(.11)	.11***
Externalizing problems	4.17	(.18)	.65***	−.42	(.18)	−.07*	.96	(.18)	.15***
Internalizing problems	3.17	(.17)	.57***	−.32	(.17)	−.06	.39	(.18)	.07

Note. All coefficients adjusted for age, gender, SES, baseline behavior, maternal closeness, and parental punishment.

*p < .05. **p < .01. ***p < .001.

TABLE 10.2
Independent Effects of School Climate on Changes in Bullying-related Behaviors and Internalizing Problems

	School Conflict			Learning Focus			Social Facilitation			Autonomy		
	B	(B SE)	β	B	(B SE)	β	B	(B SE)	β	B	(B SE)	β
Youth Informants												
School problems	.38	(.11)	.12**	−.30	(.12)	−.10*	.29	(.11)	.09**	.01	(.12)	.00
Deviance	.27	(.17)	.07	−.82	(.18)	−.20***	.28	(.16)	.07	.20	(.17)	.05
Rebelliousness	.51	(.18)	.12**	−.49	(.20)	−.11*	.20	(.17)	.05	.22	(.18)	.05
Anger	.61	(.26)	.11*	−.11	(.27)	−.02	−.02	(.24)	.00	−.03	(.26)	.00
Physical aggression	.31	(.08)	.17***	.04	(.09)	.02	.12	(.08)	.06	−.10	(.09)	−.05
Mother Informants												
Teacher harassment	.08	(.05)	.06	−.12	(.06)	−.09*	.06	(.05)	.05	.01	(.06)	.01
Noncompliance	.02	(.14)	−.01	−.04	(.15)	−.01	.24	(.13)	.07	−.34	(.14)	−.09*
Externalizing problems	.46	(.23)	.07*	−.03	(.25)	.00	.18	(.22)	.03	−.47	(.23)	−.07*
Internalizing problems	.26	(.22)	.05	.06	(.24)	.01	.18	(.21)	.03	−.47	(.23)	−.08*

Note. All coefficients adjusted for age, gender, SES, baseline behavior, maternal closeness, parental punishment, and the four school-climate scales.
*p < .05. **p < .01. ***p < .001.

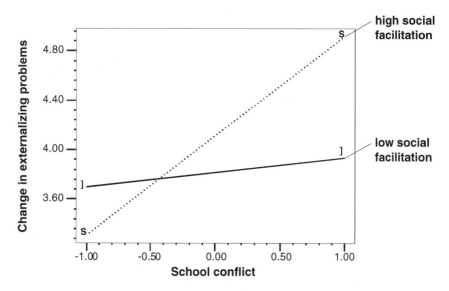

FIG. 10.1. Change in externalizing problems as a function of school conflict and social facilitation.

social facilitation schools. Thus, a high-conflict school setting that also is characterized by an informal, open, and sociable atmosphere operates to significantly worsen associations between a conflictual school climate and externalizing problems and teacher harassment. The effect on externalizing behavior problems is illustrated in Fig. 10.1. Note the steeper rise in externalizing problems over the $2\frac{1}{2}$ years among students in the high conflict-high social facilitation school setting; note also that, albeit not significant, high social facilitation within a low-conflict school setting was associated with less increase in externalizing problems than was low social facilitation within a low-conflict school setting.

There also was a significant interaction effect between learning focus and autonomy on rebelliousness and anger, however not in the expected direction. Rebelliousness and anger decreased significantly more in adolescents attending schools high in learning focus but low in autonomy than in adolescents attending schools high in learning focus and in autonomy. The effect on rebelliousness is illustrated in Fig. 10.2. Note the steeper decline in rebelliousness over the $2\frac{1}{2}$ years among students in the high learning focus-low autonomy school setting.

Discussion

Baseline rates of prior bullying-related behaviors and internalizing problems were highly predictive of those same behaviors $2\frac{1}{2}$ years later. These findings confirm others' reports of the stability of childhood aggressive, deviant, antisocial, and depressive syndromes in the psychiatric literature (e.g., Farrington, 1991;

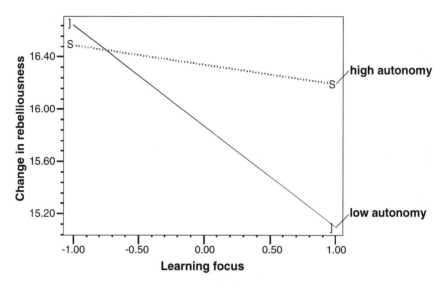

FIG. 10.2.   Change in rebelliousness as a function
of learning focus and autonomy.

Harrington, Fudge, Rutter, Pickles, & Hill, 1990; Tremblay, Pihl, Vitaro, & Dobkin, 1994). Thus, in order to evaluate the impact of school bullying interventions on student outcomes, it is essential to take into account the degree that students may manifest behaviors characterizing the bullying syndrome or may place them at risk of victimization. As hypothesized, there also was a strong association between parenting factors and changes in those outcomes. A warm supportive relationship with mothers was associated with a decline in all bullying-related behaviors and internalizing problems, whereas harsh parental punishment was related to increases in internalizing and externalizing problems and aggression. These findings support the consequential impact of parenting on problematic behavior and emotional disturbance in childhood found by others (e.g., Bowers et al., 1992, 1994); however, they also suggest that concurrent parenting influences on offspring may still be quite powerful in middle adolescence.

Dimensions of school climate were associated with changes in bullying-related behaviors and internalizing problems independent of the substantial effects of those same prior behaviors and problems, and concurrent parental influences. As expected, adolescents attending schools high in conflict and, albeit to a lesser extent, high in informality and social facilitation, increased in bullying-related behaviors over the $2\frac{1}{2}$-year interval; furthermore, the negative effects of high levels of conflict escalated in schools with high levels informality and social facilitation.

On the other hand, schools high in learning focus and high in granting autonomy to students were, in effect, a positive force, being associated with declines in bullying-related behaviors and, for autonomy, with a decline in internalizing problems. There was no evidence that granting students autonomy in schools where learning was not a priority would increase bullying behaviors; however, a high learning focus with minimal autonomy may be more effective when student rebelliousness or anger is problematic. Schools with a highly organized and supportive school climate where learning is a priority may be particularly advantageous for high-risk children with educational or psychosocial difficulties (Maughan, 1989).

Translating Research Into Practice: Implications for Bullying-Prevention and Intervention Programs

Overall, these findings provide support for increasing recognition of the school as a potential social and behavioral agent of change for student outcomes independent of highly influential individual and family characteristics. The student behaviors and characteristics that were amenable to change, for example, arguing with and threatening teachers (school problems, teacher harassment); frequent fighting and threatening behavior (physical aggression); enjoyment of and no guilt felt about transgressions (rebelliousness); teasing to anger, showing up others, and hotheadedness (anger); being mean, cruel, and bullying others (externalizing problems); and being sad, anxious, and withdrawn (internalizing problems), are in close accord with the behaviors and characteristics that describe bully, victim, and bully-victim statuses. Therefore, these findings also have more specific implications for school-based programs that may address the issue of bullying.

A subtle but perceptible imbalance of power pervades conflictual school settings. Frequent violent incidents and disciplinary referrals, poor student and teacher morale, teacher intimidation, little learning, and a general lack of organization create a school climate that condones aggressive and coercive patterns of interactions. In contrast, administrators and teachers who provide students with a structured and supportive environment that emphasizes learning and student motivation and responsibility foster achievement, self-esteem, and a no-tolerance policy toward disruptive influences. Thus, implementation of an effective bullying intervention or prevention program may be contingent upon the readiness of the school to assess those aspects of the school climate and, if necessary, undertake changes to enhance protective factors and eliminate or reduce risk factors that may be related to bullying or being victimized.

Based on the findings here, strategies to modify negative factors certainly might include changes in the overall school policy on disciplinary action in order to reduce or eliminate student-student and student-teacher conflict; increased teacher support and professional training to lift teacher morale, enhance classroom management skills, and heighten student motivation; and incorporating socializing concepts, for example, feeling empathy for others, responsibility to others, tolerance of differences, and understanding the consequences of one's behavior, into the academic curriculum. Others' findings indicate that a change in school policy to effect a less competitive school climate that focuses on individual improvement will increase students' self-esteem (Ames, 1992) and commitment to learning and school bonding (Goodenow, 1993), thus creating a climate unfavorable to bullying. Moreover, the use of fair and effective strategies by school authority figures for classroom control may provide desirable models of interpersonal interactions between students (Hyman & Perrone, 1998). Perhaps, the most essential element of an effective school-based bullying program is that it involves all school personnel and students, as all are concerned parties. In contrast to an individual or group approach to intervention (e.g., student-counselor or classroom, respectively), a school-based program that addresses a bullying problem is a system approach to intervention (or prevention). Thus, administrators, faculty, professional support personnel such as the school psychologist or guidance counselor, other nonteaching school personnel, and all students, as the latter may be potential bullies or victims, bully-victims, or bystanders, should be involved.

Certain limitations in the data should be addressed. First, the sample was predominantly White; thus, generalizability of findings to non-White populations is unknown. However, close similarity between the demographic characteristics of our sample and the demographic makeup of the northeastern region of the U.S. has been confirmed by 1980 census data (Cohen & Cohen, 1996), and indicates a significant target population. Second, there may be concern that students' perceptions of school climate dimensions are influenced by personal characteristics that may also relate to outcomes examined; however, that was reduced by the inclusion of baseline behaviors as a covariate and mother informant measures of behavior. Although more objective observations would eliminate that potential bias, this was not feasible given the large number of schools attended by this geographically dispersed random sample in which the individual and not the school was the unit of analysis. Moreover, compared to the objective social context, the perceived social context is reported to be more meaningful and more causally related to behavior (Jessor, 1983). Thus it may be useful to supplement studies based on more objective measures of the school climate with studies that use subjective assessments. Finally, as the original goals of this longitudinal study were not specific to the bullying process, we did not measure certain identified characteristics of bullying, for example power imbalance between bully and victim. We also were not able to examine the association between school climate and verbal aggression or passive bullying. Bullying takes many forms other than physical aggression and threats; name-calling, malicious rumors, lies and gossip, shunning, intentional exclusion from the group or ignoring, all are common forms of bullying, particularly for girls (Rivers & Smith, 1994). However, strengths of the study include the use of prospective longitudinal data collected from multiple informants in a randomly selected sample, and the inclusion of potentially relevant covariates (especially the highly predictive measures of baseline behaviors), and measures of school climate with established utility (e.g., Brook et al., 1995; Kasen et al., 1990, 1998).

REFERENCES

Achenbach, T. M., & Edelbrock, C. S. (1981). Behavioral problems and competencies reported by parents of normal and disturbed children aged four through sixteen. *Monograph of Social Research and Child Development, 46* (188), 1–82.

Ainsworth, M. E., & Batten, E. O. (1974). *The effects of environmental factors on secondary educational attainment in Manchester: A Plowden follow-up.* London: Macmillan Education.

Ames, C. (1992). Classrooms: Goals, structures, and student motivation. *Journal of Educational Psychology, 84*, 261–271.

Arcus, D. (2002). School shooting fatalities and school corporal punishment: A look at the states. *Aggressive Behavior, 28*, 173–183.

Avgar, A., Bronfenbrenner, U., & Henderson, C. R. (1977). Socialization practices of parents, teachers, and peers in Israel: Kibbutz, moshav, and city. *Child Development, 48*, 1219–1227.

Baldry, A. C., & Farrington, D. P. (2000). Bullies and delinquents: Personal characteristics and parental styles. *Journal of Community and Applied Social Psychology, 10*, 17–31.

Björkqvist, K., & Österman, K. (1999). Finland. In P. K. Smith, Y. Morita, J. Junger-Tas, D. Olweus, R. Catalano, & P. Slee (Eds.), *The nature of school bullying: A cross-national perspective* (pp. 56–67). London and New York: Routledge.

Blyth, D. A., Simmons, R. G., & Bush, D. (1978). The transition to early adolescence: A longitudinal comparison of youth in two educational contexts. *Social Education, 51*, 149–162.

Boulton, M. J., & Underwood, K. (1992). Bully/victim problems among middle school children. *British Journal of Educational Psychology, 62*, 73–87.

Bowers, L., Smith, P. K., & Binney, V. (1992). Cohesion and power in the families of children involved in bully/victim problems at school. *Journal of Family Therapy, 14*, 371–387.

Bowers, L., Smith, P. K., & Binney, V. (1994). Perceived family relationships of bullies, victims, and bully/victims in middle childhood. *Journal of Personal and Social Relationships, 11*, 215–232.

Bronfenbrenner, U. (1974). *Is early intervention effective? A report on the longitudinal evaluations of preschool programs.* Office of Child Development, U.S. Department of Health, Education, and Welfare. Washington DC: Government Printing Office.

Bronfenbrenner, U. (1979). *The ecology of human development: Experiments by nature and design.* Cambridge, MA: Harvard University Press.

Brook, J. S., Whiteman, M., & Cohen, P. (1995). Stages of drug use, aggression, and theft/vandalism: Common and uncommon risks. In H. B. Kaplan (Ed.), *Drugs, crime, and other deviant adaptations* (pp. 83–98). New York: Plenum.

Brook, J. S., Whiteman, M., Gordon, A. S., & Cohen, P. (1986). Dynamics of child and adolescent personality traits and adolescent drug use. *Developmental Psychology, 22*, 403–414.

Bryk, A. S., & Thum, Y. M. (1989). The effects of high school organization on dropping out: An exploratory investigation. *American Educational Research Journal, 26*, 353–383.

Cohen, P. (1996). Childhood risks for young adult symptoms of personality disorder: Method and substance. *Multivariate Behavioral Research, 31*, 121–148.

Cohen, P., & Brook, J. S. (1987). Family factors related to the persistence of psychopathology in childhood and adolescence. *Psychiatry, 50*, 332–345.

Cohen, P., & Brook, J. S. (1995). The reciprocal influence of punishment and child behavior disorder. In J. McCord (Ed.), *Coercion and punishment in long term perspectives* (pp. 154–164). Cambridge, England: Cambridge University Press.

Cohen, P., & Cohen, J. (1996). *Life values and adolescent mental health.* Hillsdale, NJ: Erlbaum Associates.

Coleman J. S. (1966). *Equality of educational opportunity.* Washington, DC: U.S. Government Printing Office.

Craig, W. (1998). The relationship among bullying, victimization, depression, anxiety, and aggression in elementary school children. *Personality and Individual Differences, 24*, 123–130.

Craig, W. M., Pepler, D., & Atlas, R. (2000). Observations of bullying in the playground and in the classroom. *School Psychology International, 21*, 22–36.

Crenshaw, W. B., Crenshaw, L. M., & Lichtenberg, J. W. (1995). When educators confront child abuse: An analysis of the decision to report. *Child Abuse & Neglect, 19*, 1095–1113.

Darlington, R. B., Royce, J. M., Snipper, A. S., Murray, H. W., & Lazar, I. (1980). Preschool programs and later competence of children from low income families. *Science, 203*, 202–204.

Derogatis, L. R., Lipman, L. S., Rickels, K., Uhlenhuth, E. H., & Covi, L. (1974). The Hopkins Symptom Checklist (HSCL). *Behavioral Science, 19*, 1–15.

Dreeben, R. (1968). *On what is learned in school.* Reading, MA: Addison-Wesley.

Dubois, D. L., Felner, R. D., Brand, S., Adam, A., & Evans, E. G. (1992). A prospective study of life stress, social support, and adaptation in early adolescence. *Child Development, 63*, 542–557.

Elias, M. J., Gara, M., & Ubriaco, M. (1985). Sources of stress and support in children's transitions to middle school: An empirical analysis. *Journal of Clinical and Child Psychology, 14*, 112–118.

Elliott, D. S., Huizinga, D., & Ageton, S. S. (1985). *Explaining delinquency and drug use.* Beverly Hills, CA: Sage.

Elliott, E. S., & Dweck, C. S. (1988). Goals: An approach to motivation and achievement. *Journal of Personality and Social Psychology, 54*, 5–12.

Farrington, D. P. (1991). Antisocial personality from childhood to adulthood. *Psychologist: Bulletin of the British Psychological Society, 4*, 389–394.

Farrington, D. (1993). Understanding and preventing bullying. In M. Tonry (Ed.), *Crime and justice: A review of research* (Vol. 17) (pp. 381–458). Chicago: University of Chicago Press.

Fiqueira-McDonough, J. (1986). School context, gender, and delinquency. *Journal of Youth and Adolescence, 15*, 79–98.

Galbo, J. (1983). Adolescents' perceptions of significant adults. *Adolescence, 18*, 417–427.

Goodenow, C. (1993). Classroom belonging among early adolescent students: Relationships to motivation and achievement. *Journal of Early Adolescence, 13*, 21–43.

Gray, J., Smith, A., & Rutter, M. (1980). School attendance and the first year of employment. In L. Hersov and I. Berg (Eds.), *Out of school: Modern perspectives in truancy and school refusal.* (pp. 343–370) New York: Wiley.

Griffith, J. (1995). An empirical examination of a model of social climate in elementary schools. *Basic and Applied Social Psychology, 17*, 97–117.

Harrington, R., Fudge, H., Rutter, M., Pickles, A., & Hill, J. (1990). Adult outcomes of childhood and adolescent depression, I: Psychiatric status. *Archives of General Psychiatry, 47*, 465–473.

Hawkins, J. D. Catalano, R. F., & Miller, J. Y. (1992). Risk and protective factors for alcohol and other drug problems in adolescence and early adulthood: Implications for substance abuse prevention. *Psychological Bulletin, 112*, 64–105.

Hirschi, T. (1969). *Causes of delinquency.* Berkeley: University of California Press.

Hoover, J. H., Oliver, R., & Hazler, R. J. (1992). Bullying: Perceptions of adolescent victims in the Midwestern U.S.A. *School Psychology International, 13*, 5–16.

Howard, K., Flora, J., & Griffin, M. (1999). Violence-prevention programs in schools: State of the science and implications for future research. *Applied and Preventive Psychology, 8*, 197–215.

Hyman, I. A., & Perrone, D. C. (1998). The other side of school violence: Educator policies and practices that may contribute to student misbehavior. *Journal of School Psychology, 36*, 7–27.

Jencks, C. (1979). *Who gets ahead?* New York: Basic.

Jencks, C., Smith, M., Aclund, H., Bane, M. J., Cohen, D., Gintis, H., et al. (1972). *Inequality: A reassessment of the effect of family and schooling in America.* New York: Basic.

Jessor, R. (1983). The stability of change: Psychosocial development from adolescence to youth adulthood. In D. Magnusson & V. Allen (Eds.), *Human development: An interactional perspective (pp. 321–341).* New York: Academic Press.

Kasen, S., Cohen, P., & Brook, J. S. (1998). Adolescent school experiences and dropout, adolescent pregnancy, and young adult deviant behavior. *Journal of Adolescent Research, 13*, 49–72.

Kasen, S., Johnson, J., & Cohen, P. (1990). The impact of school emotional climate on student psychopathology. *Journal of Abnormal Child Psychology, 18*, 165–177.

Kupermine, G., Leadbeater, B. J., & Blatt, S. J. (2001). School social climate and individual differences in vulnerability to psychopathology among middle school students. *Journal of School Psychology, 39*, 141–159.

Maughan, B. (1989). School experiences as risk/protective factors (pp. 200–220). In M. Rutter (Ed.), *Studies of psychosocial risk: The power of longitudinal data.* New York: Cambridge University Press.

Moos, R.H. (1979). *Evaluating educational environments.* San Francisco: Jossey-Bass.

Nansel, T. R., Overpeck, M., Pilla, R. S., Ruan, W. J., Simons-Morton, B., & Scheidt, P. (2001). Bullying behaviors among US youth: Prevalence and association with psychosocial adjustment. *Journal of the American Medical Association, 285*, 2094–2100).

National Coalition to Abolish Corporal Punishment in the Schools. (1997). *Corporal punishment factsheet.* Columbus, OH: Author. From http://www.stophitting.com/facts_about_corporal_punishment.htm

New York State Education Department Resource Guide (2002). Albany, NY: University of the State of New York. From http://www.emsc.nysed.gov/ciai/socst/ssrg.html

Olweus, D. (1978). *Aggression in the schools: Bullies and whipping boys.* Washington, DC: Hemisphere Press (Wiley).

Olweus, D. (1993). *Bullying at school: What we know and what we can do.* Cambridge, MA: Blackwell.

Pfeiffer, S. I., & Reddy, L. A. (1998). School-based mental health programs in the United States: Present status and a blueprint for the future. *School Psychology Review, 27*, 84–96.

Plucker, J. (1998). The relationship between school climate conditions and student aspirations. *Journal of Educational Research, 91*, 240–246.

Public Law 94–142. *Education for all handicapped children act,* November, 29, 1975.

Purkey, S. C., & Smith, M. S. (1983). Effective schools: A review. *Elementary School Journal, 83*, 427–452.

Reeder, G. D., Maccow, G. C., Shaw, S. R., Swerdlik, M. E., Horton, C. B., & Foster, P. (1997). School psychologists and full-service schools: Partnerships with medical, mental health, and social services. *School Psychology Review, 26*, 603–621.

Reynolds, D., Jones, D., St. Leger, S., & Murgatroyd, S. (1980). School factors and truancy. In L. Hersov & I. Berg (Eds.), *Out of school: Modern perspectives in truancy and school refusal* (pp. 85–110). New York: Wiley.

Reynolds, M. C. (1992). Students and programs at the school margins: Disorder and needed repairs. *School Psychology Quarterly, 7*, 233–244.

Rivers, I., & Smith, P. K. (1994). Types of bullying behavior and their correlates. *Aggressive Behavior, 20*, 359–368.

Rutter, M. (1983). School effects and pupil progress: Research findings and policy implications. *Child Development, 54*, 1–29.

Rutter, M. (1987). Psychosocial resilience and protective mechanisms. *American Journal of Orthopsychiatry, 57*, 316–331.

Rutter, M., Maughan, B., Mortimore, P., Ouston, J., & Smith, A. (1979). *Fifteen thousand hours: Secondary schools and their effects on children.* Cambridge, MA: Harvard University Press.

Ryan, G., Myoshi, T., Metzner, J., Krugman, R., & Fryer, E. (1996). Trends in a national sample of sexually abusive youths. *Journal of the American Academy of Child and Adolescent Psychiatry, 35,* 17–25.

Safer, D. J. (1986). The stress of secondary school for vulnerable students. *Journal of Youth and Adolescence, 15,* 405–417.

Salmivalli, C., Huttunen, J., & Lagerspetz, K. M. J. (1996). How do the victims respond to bullying? *Aggressive Behavior, 22,* 99–109.

Salmon, G., James, A., & Smith, D. M. (1998). Bullying in schools: Self-reported anxiety, depression and self esteem in secondary school children. *British Medical Journal, 317,* 924–925.

Schaefer, E. S. (1965). Children's report of parental behavior: An inventory. *Child Development, 36,* 413–424.

Sharp, S. (1995). How much does bullying hurt? The effects of bullying on the personal well-being and educational progress of secondary aged students. *Educational and Child Psychology, 12,* 81–88.

Smith, G. J., & Fogg, C. P. (1979). Psychological antecedents of teenage drug use. In R. Simmons (Ed.), *Research in community and mental health* (Vol. I) (pp. 87–102). Greenwich, CT: JAI Press.

Strauss, M.A. (1994). *Beating the devil out of them.* Lexington, MA: DC Health.

Swearer, S. M., & Doll, B. (2001). Bullying in schools: An ecological framework. *Journal of Emotional Abuse, 2,* 7–23.

Swearer, S. M., Song, S. Y., Cary, P. T., Eagle, J. W., & Mickelson, W. T. (2000). Psychosocial correlates in bullying and victimization: The relationship between depression, anxiety, and bully/victim status. *Journal of Emotional Abuse, 2,* 95–121.

Tremblay, R. E., Masse, E., Perron, D., LeBlanc, M., Schwartzman, A. E., & Ledingham, J. E. (1992). Early disruptive behavior, poor school achievement, delinquent behavior, and delinquent personality: Longitudinal analyses. *Journal of Consulting and Clinical Psychology, 60,* 64–72.

Tremblay, R. E., Pihl, R. O., Vitaro, F., & Dobkin, P. L. (1994). Predicting early onset of male antisocial behavior from preschool behavior. *Archives of General Psychiatry, 51,* 732–739.

Tremlow S. W. (2000). The roots of violence: Converging psychoanalytic explanatory models for power struggles and violence in schools. *Psychoanalytic Quarterly, 69,* 741–785.

Tremlow, S. W., Fonagy, P., & Sacco, F. (2001). An innovative psychodynamically influenced approach to reduce school violence. *Journal of the American Academy of Child and Adolescent Psychiatry, 40,* 377–379.

U.S. Departments of Education and Justice. (1999). *1999 Annual Report on School Safety.* Washington, DC: U.S. Department of Education, Education Publications Center.

Whitney, I., & Smith, P. K. (1993). A survey of the nature and extent of bully/victim problems in junior/middle and secondary schools. *Educational Research, 35,* 3–25.

Williams, K., Chambers, M., Logan, S., & Robinson, D. (1996). Association of common health symptoms with bullying in primary school children. *British Medical Journal, 313,* 17–19.

11

The Role of Social Support in the Lives of Bullies, Victims, and Bully-victims

Christine Kerres Malecki and
Michelle Kilpatrick Demaray
Northern Illinois University

The discussion of bullying within ecological theory (Swearer & Doll, 2001; Swearer & Espelage, this volume) provides a natural framework for a discussion of social support in the lives of children and adolescents involved in bullying behavior in schools. According to the ecological perspective, problems related to bullying stem from an interaction between the child and their environments (Swearer & Doll, 2001). Within the ecological model, the environments that may influence bullying behavior are broad, including the family, school, and community settings. One important contextual factor of these environments is social support.

The level of support that students perceive from significant individuals (e.g., peers, teachers, and parents) in their environments may influence bully and victim problems. Because social support is related to positive outcomes for students that possess it and negative outcomes for students that lack it, understanding how this aspect of the environment is related to bully and victim problems is important. Understanding how levels of social support in children's environments may influence bully behaviors may help us answer important questions. For example, do bullies perceive less support from peers; or do peers support bullies and their behaviors? Do victims perceive less social support from important people in their environments? If so, what are the consequences of low social support for victims? Do bullies perceive less support from teachers?

This chapter will provide a review of social support and the theoretical models of this construct that may lend support for past, present, and future empirical research on bullying and social support. A brief discussion of the measurement of social support will also be presented. An overview of the research on the perceptions of support for bullies and victims will be presented followed by the research on how social support relates to outcomes for bullies and victims. Limitations of the current research, implications, and future directions will be discussed.

Social Support

Social support has been defined in a number of ways, including Cobb's (1976) classic description of the three components of social support: feeling loved, feeling valued or esteemed, and belonging to a social network. These aspects of social support may differ for students that are bullies or victims. For example, victims may not feel valued by their peers or feel like they belong to a social network of peers, especially if it is their classmates that are bullying them. Bullies also may not feel loved or esteemed because their bullying behavior may, for example, make them less likable to teachers and peers.

Tardy (1985) defined five dimensions in the conceptualization of social support: direction, disposition, description/evaluation, content, and network (see Fig. 11.1). In this model, *direction* refers to whether social support is being *given* or *received*. *Disposition* refers to social support being *available* (accessible) or *enacted* (actually utilized). Tardy discussed whether an *evaluation* of an individual's social support is elicited or simply a *description* of that social support is assessed. *Content* refers to four types of social support based on House's (1981) categories including *emotional, instrumental, informational*, and/or *appraisal* support. Emotional support consists of support in the form of trust, love, and empathy. Instrumental support includes resources such as money, tangible resources, and time. Informational support is advice or information provided to someone. Appraisal support consists of evaluative feedback given to individuals. Finally, Tardy's *network* refers to the source(s) or the member(s) of an individual's support network. For children and adolescents this may include a variety of sources, such as parents, teachers, classmates, friends, club members, or school staff.

For students that are victims of bullying or for bullies, the content and networks of their social support may differ from other students. Victims may not receive the emotional support from peers or classmates that they would like. They may, however, seek out emotional support from others (e.g., parents, teachers, close friends)

SOCIAL SUPPORT

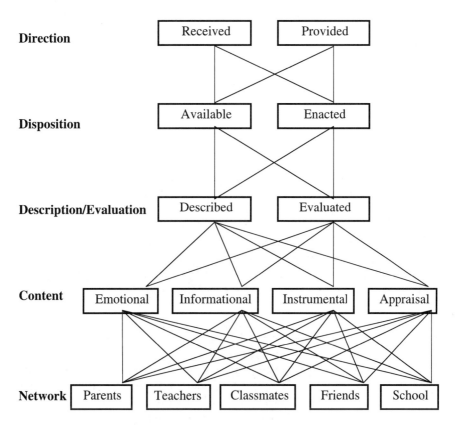

FIG. 11.1. Tardy's model of social support.

to help them cope with the bullying. Bullies also may not receive emotional support from a wide network. They may, for example, receive less emotional support from adults (e.g., parents and teachers) due to their negative behaviors.

Broad Theoretical Orientation: Stress-Buffering and Main Effect Theories

Throughout the literature, the relationship between perceived social support and children and adolescents' functioning can be explained by two primary theoretical orientations: the *stress-buffering model* and the *main effect* theory (Cohen, Gottlieb, & Underwood, 2000). The stress-buffering theory advocates that the positive benefits of social support primarily aid children who are at-risk or under stress (Barrera, 1986; Cohen et al., 2000; Cohen & Wills, 1985). For example, using the stress-buffering hypothesis, a researcher might examine the potential protective effects of social support for victims of bullying. Stress-buffering theory would posit that if students who are victims of bullying receive social support, that social support may buffer them from negative outcomes, such as anxiety, depression, and drug use.

The *main-effect model* advocates that social support has a positive benefit for *all* children and adolescents (Cohen et al., 2000; Cohen & Wills, 1985), regardless of stress levels or circumstances. The main-effect model presumes that access to social support improves one's overall psychological state (e.g., sense of worth and belonging, security, stability) and may provide the individual with support which in turn, reduces psychological problems (Cohen et al., 2000).

Both the stress-buffering and the main effect models may be used as tools in explaining the role of social support in the lives of bullies and victims. For example, according to the stress-buffering model, victims may be under greater stress and the presence of social support from significant people in their lives may buffer them from developing negative social or psychological outcomes (e.g., depression, anxiety) as a result of being bullied. On the other hand, according to the main effect model, social support may help all students, not just those under stress. Therefore, both bullies and victims may benefit from social support as an overall positive influence, regardless of the stress they may be under as a result of bullying behaviors.

In the general social support literature (using derivatives of the main-effect and the stress-buffering theory) a relationship has been clearly established between levels of social support in children and adolescents' lives and healthy outcomes. The literature in this area is too extensive to review for the purposes of this chapter. However, in general, social support has been related to healthy physical (Schwarzer & Leppin, 1991; Uchino, Cacioppo, & Kiecolt-Glaser, 1996), social and/or psychological (Bender & Losel, 1997; Compas, Slavin, Wagner, & Vannatta, 1986; Demaray & Elliott, 2001; Demaray & Malecki, 2002a, 2002c; Forman, 1988; Malecki & Elliott, 1999; Piko, 2000; Wenz-Gross & Siperstein, 1998), and educational (Gillock & Reyes, 1999; Levitt, Guacci-Franco, & Levitt, 1994; Malecki & Elliott, 1999; Malecki & Demaray, 2002b; Rosenfeld, Richman, & Bowen, 2000) outcomes. The stress-buffering and main effect models are not solely adequate to provide interpretation of these links between social support and more positive outcomes for children and adolescents. Thus, researchers have identified several specific theories that may help explain these relations between social support and outcomes for students.

Theoretical Frameworks on How Social Support Functions

Although most social support research can be categorized under the main effect or stress-buffering theories, these models constitute only two general approaches in examining social support. More specific theories provide explanations on the mechanics of *how* social support might bolster one's overall well-being or *how* social support acts as a protective factor under stressful situations. The specific theories discussed here include social-exchange theory, pro-social behavior theory, and social comparison theory.

Social-exchange Theory. Social support, at the very least, includes two people; the provider of support and the recipient (Shumaker & Brownell, 1984). A behavior directed toward someone may be perceived differently by those two parties. For example, despite the intentions of the provider, the recipient may perceive a behavior as being unhelpful or harmful. Relationships that continue without addressing the mismatch of perceptions become inequitable and the supportive behavior as perceived by the provider may actually begin to distress the recipient if their perceptions are different. Additionally, if someone is not communicating a need for support, they may not receive any support. Likewise, if a provider of support never sees benefits or reciprocation, they may withdraw further support. The social-exchange theory maintains that individuals try to maintain relationships that are mutually beneficial (Shumaker & Brownell, 1984; Stewart, 1989).

Social-exchange theory is important in the examination of social support and bullying. The nature of bullying and being victimized is a power differential resulting in an inequitable relationship. Additionally, research has suggested that bystanders are affected by bullying behavior and even if they are not directly involved in bullying, their involvement as a bystander may influence how much (if any) support they provide. Measures of social support and research in this area should take into account the *perceptions* surrounding supportive exchanges. Ideally both the provider and the recipients' perceptions should be examined.

Prosocial Behavior Theory. Important in the discussion of social support exchange is a discussion of the motive and intentions of providers of support. Shumaker and Brownell (1984) discussed factors that may influence the extent to which people will assist others. For example, in distress situations a recipient of support must communicate their need for support before others will intervene. It may be asking a lot to expect a student to publicly call for help in a bullying situation (Naylor, Cowie, & del Rey, 2001). Even when help is specifically elicited, a number of factors including level of social skills, setting, sense of right and wrong, and even mood affect whether or not a provider of support will act (Shumaker & Brownell, 1984). For example, other students may not feel adequate in intervening or may not feel they have the social status to comfortably intervene.

Additionally, prosocial behavior theory can assist us in thinking about the group dynamics that may come into play when examining the contextual role of social support in bullying. Latane and Nida (1981) found that the more bystanders present in a distress situation, the less likely that one of them will respond to help. However, they pointed out that the recipient might assume that having more bystanders present may make it *more* likely that someone will aid them. The presence of students at a bullying incident may diffuse the responsibility of intervening.

Social Comparison Theory.   Working in conjunction with pro-social behavior theory, social comparison theory focuses on the processes by which people compare themselves to peers and how those comparisons affect actions and emotions (Stewart, 1989). Stewart described social comparison theory as related to social support by focusing on appraisal support (evaluative feedback) as well as modeling appropriate behavior. Social comparison theory posits that people will try to emulate those that are of higher status (e.g., health status, social status). Thus, this research may be important in determining why bystanders will not aid the victim in a bullying situation. They may be focused on the higher status peer (the bully) rather than the lower status victim.

Measuring Social Support

Key to being able to examine the relations between social support and bullying behavior is having an appropriate measure of social support. Rating scales are one methodology available to assess students' perceptions of social support. Several of these will be briefly described.

Survey of Children's Social Support—Appraisals Scale (SOCSS-APP; Dubow & Ulman, 1989). The APP is a 31-item rating scale that measures perceived social support from children and adolescents' family, peers, and teachers. Students answer questions such as "Some kids have friends who like to hear their ideas, but other kids do not. Do your friends like to hear your ideas?" on a 5-point rating scale (1 = *Never* to 5 = *Always*). Items primarily reflect supportive behaviors in the form of caring, love, and feeling valued. Dubow and Ullman (1989) reported internal consistency evidence with a Cronbach's alpha of .88 on the total score. In addition, they reported a three to four week test-retest reliability coefficient of .75. Validity evidence for the APP has been demonstrated via a three-factor structure (family, teacher, and peer support) and via significant correlations (*r*s = .42 to .66) with the corresponding subscales on the *Social Support Scale for Children* (SSSC; Harter, 1985a). No information has been found on administration time, but from the present authors' experience, the APP requires approximately 10 to 15 minutes of children's time. The APP is one part of the *Survey of Children's Social Support* (Dubow & Ullman, 1989) which includes the *Scale of Available Behaviors* (SAB), the APP, and a measure of children's social network size (NET), all self-report measures. See Dubow and Ullman (1989) for more information.

Social Support Scale for Children (SSSC; Harter, 1985a).   The SSSC is a 24-item rating scale that assesses 8- to 12-year-old children's perceptions of social support from four sources (parents, teachers, classmates, and friends).

Children read two statements and decide which one is more like them. For example, "Some kids have parents who don't really understand them BUT other kids have parents who really do understand them." Students decide if the appropriate statement is sort of true or really true of them. The SSSC takes approximately 15 to 20 minutes to complete. The SSSC measures primarily social support in the form of positive regard from others. There is only one form (student self-rating) of the SSSC. Harter (1985a) has reported evidence for internal consistency with alpha coefficients of .72 to .82 on the four subscales in two elementary school samples and coefficients of .74 to .88 on the four subscales in two middle school samples. Furthermore, Harter has provided evidence of validity with correlations from .35 to .49 between the SSSC subscales and the Self-Perception Profile for Children (Harter, 1985b) total score. See Harter (1985a) for further details.

The Child and Adolescent Social Support Scale (CASSS; Malecki, Demaray, & Elliott, 2000). The CASSS measures the frequency and importance of perceived support from five sources: parents, teachers, classmates, close friends, and the school. "My parents understand me" is an example item. Frequency ratings consist of a 6-point Likert Scale (1 = *Never* to 6 = *Always*). Importance ratings consist of a 3-point Likert Scale (1 = *Not Important* to 3 = *Very Important*). The CASSS also contains items that tap each of the four types of support including emotional, informational, instrumental, and appraisal support. This self-report measure is designed for students in grades 3 through 12 and takes students approximately 15 minutes to complete.

Evidence for the reliability of scores on the CASSS have been demonstrated via alpha coefficients for the Total Frequency and Total Importance scores both being .97 (Malecki & Demaray, in press). Subscale scores have produced alpha coefficients ranging from .92 to .96 and .89 to .95 for the Frequency and Importance subscales, respectively. Test-retest reliability evidence has been demonstrated for the frequency scores with eight to ten week coefficient of .85 on the Total Frequency score (Malecki & Demaray, in press). Validity evidence in the form of correlations with similar measures of social support has been demonstrated. For example, the Total Frequency score on the CASSS has been related to total scores on the *Social Support Scale for Children* (Harter, 1985a), $r = .58$, and the *Social Support Appraisals Scale* (Dubow & Ullman, 1989), $r = .61$ (Malecki & Demaray, in press).

Using a measure such as the CASSS or other multidimensional measures in the research of social support and bullying behavior can help advance our understanding of social support as it relates to bullying.

Social Support and Bullying Behavior

Many researchers have overlooked social support perceived by bullies and victims. Yet, given the associations between the perceptions of social support and many of the positive outcomes mentioned above, understanding the levels of support that these students perceive is important. Several researchers have begun to investigate social support for bullies and victims; however, these have not been in depth investigations of the construct. The research that has been conducted on bully-victim problems and social support is focused on two main areas, which include (a) describing the perceptions of social support for students who are classified as victims or bullies, and (b) investigating the relationship of social support and various outcomes for students who are victims or bullies. The research in these two areas will be described below.

Perceptions of Social Support for Victims and Bullies

The previous literature on the perceptions of support of bullies and victims is very scarce. In fact, only two studies were found that focused on this topic. Furlong, Chung, Bates, and Morrison (1995) investigated the perceptions of social support for students who were the victims of school violence in a sample of 6,189 students in grades 5 to 12. For peer support, students were asked how many other students at school they consider to be a good friend. For teacher support they were asked how many teachers they would be able to talk with about their problems. Victims reported less teacher and peer support.

In order to get a better understanding of the perceptions of social support by students experiencing victim and bullying behaviors, Demaray and Malecki (2002b) investigated perceptions of support for victims, bullies, bully-victims, and a comparison group. This study included 499 students in grades six through eight in a predominately Hispanic and lower socioeconomic status sample.

Demaray and Malecki (2002b) investigated perceptions of both the frequency and importance of social support, assessed via the CASSS. It was found that the comparison group perceived more overall total support than all other groups (Bullies, Victims, and Bully-Victims). When comparing specific *sources* of support, again, significant differences were found among the groups. For parent support, comparison students reported perceiving more support from parents than bullies or bully-victims. With regard to teacher support, the comparison group perceived significantly more support from teachers than did bullies. Interestingly, *both* the comparison and the bully groups perceived more support from classmates than victims and bully-victims, with victims and bully-victims perceiving less support from their classmates. This makes sense given that the victims and bully-victims are on the receiving end of bullying behavior from peers in the school. Analyses indicated that there was not a significant difference in perceptions of close friend support by bully-victim status. Lastly, for school support, the comparison group reported significantly more support than the bully-victim group.

A very different pattern of results was found when investigating the differences in perceptions of the *importance* of social support by bully-victim status compared to the frequency results. The victim and bully-victim groups rated total social support as more important than the bully and comparison groups.

Significant differences on importance ratings were also found with regards to the various sources of support. Victims and bully-victims rated the importance of parent and teacher support as more important than the comparison group. The importance of classmate and close friend support was rated higher by the victim group than the bully group and the bully-victim group reported higher ratings of importance than the bully and comparison groups.

One of the major themes found in the comparisons of the groups' ratings of both frequency and importance of social support is that in general, victims and bully-victims reported less frequency of perceived social support; however, they placed greater importance on social support than the other groups. This is especially problematic because students who are highly valuing social support from specific sources reported that they are not receiving it.

Thus, although there have been few investigations of perceptions of support of bullies or victims, these studies demonstrate that there are differences in perceptions of social support from varying sources for students that are bullied or engage in bullying. Because higher perceptions of social support are linked to many positive outcomes for students (Bender & Losel, 1997; Compas et al., 1986; Levitt et al., 1994) it is important for researchers to investigate outcomes for bullies or victims in relation to their perceptions of support.

Social Support and Outcomes

Researchers have also investigated outcomes for students based on bully or victim status and their levels of perceived social support. Again, however, the literature on this topic is scarce. Rigby (2000) investigated the effects of victimization and perceived support on the overall well-being of 845 school-age (12 to 16 years old) children in Australia. Social support was assessed by asking children how much help they would get from their teacher, best friend, classmates, mother, and father if they were having a serious problem at school. The researchers found that both peer victimization and low levels of perceived social support contributed significantly to lower overall well-being. The researchers also investigated the possible buffering effect of social support for students who had positive general well-being scores despite having high victimization scores, however, no buffering effect was supported via analyses.

Rigby and Slee (1999) conducted similar research investigating the relationship among social support, bully-victim problems and suicidal ideation. These investigations included two studies on 1103 children (ages 12 to 18) and 845 children (ages 12 to 16). Social support was assessed in the same method as previously described. They found that bully and victim problems as well as social support made independent and significant contributions to suicidal ideation. However, interactions with bullying and social support and victim problems and social support were not significant in contributing to suicidal ideation. Thus, a moderating role of social support was not found.

Malecki and Demaray (2002a) investigated the role of social support in relationship to students' outcomes for victims in a sample of 100 students in sixth to eighth grade at an urban middle school in Illinois. The majority of the students were Hispanic and received free or reduced lunch prices. Social support was assessed via the CASSS. Using Baron and Kenny's (1986) process for investigating mediation, they found that students' perceptions of social support were partial mediators of the relationship between levels of victimization and several outcomes including students' personal adjustment, clinical maladjustment, and emotional symptoms. Students' levels of being victimized were related to personal adjustment, clinical maladjustment, and emotional symptoms, but after social support was taken into account, the predictive power of being victimized was reduced. Furthermore, evidence for pure mediation (for teacher social support) between victimization and school maladjustment was found. Specifically, the predictive power of being victimized was eliminated after social support was taken into account. These results provide evidence that social support may mediate the relation between students' victimization in schools and their adjustment.

Limitations to Previous Research

Only a handful of studies investigating social support and bully-victim behaviors have been published. Not only is there a small number of studies available, but what is available has some noteworthy limitations. Rigby (2000) and Rigby and Slee (1999) have begun to investigate social support and bully-victim behaviors, however, this research was conducted in Australian schools and needs to be replicated in U.S. schools. In addition, the majority of the researchers have investigated perceptions of social support for the victims of bullying (Furlong et al., 1995; Rigby, 2000), and have not included students classified as bullies or bully-victims. Another criticism of the previous research is that it did not include comprehensive measures of social support with well-documented psychometric properties. For example, Rigby (2000) and Rigby and Slee (1999) assessed social support via five questions about the support students received from five sources (one question per source). Students were asked how much help ("none or hardly any" to "a lot") they would get from each source (class teacher, best friend, students in your class, mother, and father) if they were having serious problems at school. Furlong et al. (1995) assessed social support network from peers via one question (how many students at school do you consider to be a good friend) and social support network from teachers via one question (how many teachers would you be able to talk with about their problems). Given the definition of social support and the various sources and types of support students may receive, researchers should broaden the measurement of social support in their research in order to more thoroughly investigate perceptions of social support and bully-victim behaviors for students.

Translating Research Into Practice: Implications for Bullying-Prevention and Intervention Programs

The research presented in this chapter on social support and bullying behavior provides many important implications for future research and practice in the schools. First, it is clear that there is a meaningful relationship between the social support students perceive and their involvement in bullying. For example, we have learned that students exhibiting bullying behavior perceived less parent and teacher support than other students but perceived similar amounts of classmate and friend support (Demaray & Malecki, 2002b). One could hypothesize that for a student, receiving less than adequate parental support may lead to negative behaviors including bullying. This behavior could result in lessened teacher support, thus leading to the student disengaging from the learning environment at school. Therefore, it may be reasonable to design prevention programs that have an ecological focus that have as one target parent-child relationships and parent involvement in schools. Getting teachers involved in facilitating these relations may also result in increased teacher support for the student.

As the social-comparison theory postulates, students' bullying behavior may actually increase (or at least not reduce) their peer support. That increased social support in response to bullying behavior may act to reward and therefore increase the bullying behavior. Prevention and/or intervention programs should seek to break this cycle and reduce the rewarding nature of bullying behavior with a focus on bystanders. Specifically, programs could involve changing students' perceptions about bullying behavior and teach bystanders to withhold or reduce support in response to bullying behavior. At the same time, students could be taught to increase social support for all students, particularly when students are engaging in positive alternatives to bullying.

Prevention or intervention programs could play upon the pro-social behavior theory and teach students social skills, communicate clear expectations and values regarding acceptable and unacceptable behavior in schools, and teach potential victims in schools how to seek help. If bullying becomes less acceptable and less powerful, the social environment of the school could start to discourage rather than remain passive or encouraging for bullies.

Several established prevention and intervention programs are being implemented and evaluated with a goal of decreasing the occurrence of bullying behavior in the schools. These programs consist of many of the elements discussed above. One example, the Bullying Prevention Program (Olweus, Limber, & Mihalic, 1999), involves school, classroom, and individual-level prevention and intervention components. At the school level, staff members are involved in actions such as creating a committee on bullying, assessing the problem at their school, developing school-wide rules against bullying (including rules such as "We shall try to help students who are bullied" and "We shall make it a point to include students who become easily left out"), and holding regular classroom meetings to encourage positive behavior. In the classroom, teachers hold regular classroom meetings to keep the issue on the minds of students and to model and encourage positive behavior. In addition, children who have been identified as bullies and/or victims are targeted for individual intervention. Specifically, teachers are encouraged to provide support for children who are victims of bullying by recruiting peers, creating opportunities to raise the students' status in the classroom, and by working with parents to ensure the students are receiving adequate support (Olweus et al., 1999). The Bullying Prevention Program has shown evidence of its effectiveness such as reducing bullying problems by 50% to 70%, reducing other negative behavior (e.g., fighting, truancy), and increasing student satisfaction at school (Olweus, 1991). Although social support is not an explicit target of the Olweus program, it is easy to see how many of the components of his program involve increasing social support in students' lives. For example, the example school rules stated above (try to help students who are bullied and try to include students who are left out) clearly involve increasing students' peer support.

A few programs have social support as an explicit component of the intervention. One such program implemented in the U.K. (particularly in England) has consisted of peer support systems. Peer support systems (Cowie, 2000) involve training peers to work toward preventing and intervening in bullying behavior in their schools. Four aspects of peer support systems are typically implemented: (a) providing peers with "everyday" support and friendship in typical interactions, (b) peer mediation/conflict resolution, (c) counseling students one on one over a period of time, and (d) mentoring in a one-to-one relationship with a peer of lower status (vulnerable or younger). Several studies of the peer support systems have been conducted including those by Naylor and Cowie (1999) and Cowie and Olafsson (2000). In general, these studies revealed that bullying behavior does not seem to decrease in response to the program. However, the studies were conducted in the short-term, either within one or two years of the program's implementation. In addition, the perceptions of the participants and recipients of the program were positive. Specifically, victims appear to tell someone that they are being bullied more often in peer support system schools than in non-program schools. In addition, victims report that when peers intervened on their behalf and befriended them, it was helpful to them.

Future research needs to be done on existing intervention programs as well as research that helps design programs that consist of a menu of research-based strategies that can be individualized according to the needs of a particular setting. In addition, although evidence for a mediating effect between bullying, social support, and various outcomes has been somewhat weak, there is simply not enough research examining different school settings, ages of students, school and student characteristics, and various outcomes to be able to discount mediating effects. Additionally, taking an ecological approach to studying bullying in schools will allow for other third-variable constructs to be taken into consideration that might account for the relationship between bullying behavior and social support. Much work remains to be done to complete our understanding in this area.

The current literature base on social support and its relation to bullying in schools provides much for us to learn. Bullying does not occur in a void, and there is more to the picture than just the bully and his or her victim and their characteristics. Rather, as this book describes, there are many contextual factors that must be taken into consideration when trying to understand bullying behavior as well as in planning, developing, or evaluating prevention or intervention programs. The contextual factor of social support appears to be important for both students that bully as well as the victims of bullying. Future research of this important element of bullying should take several directions. First, the nature of the relation between bullying behavior and social support (for both bullies and victims) should be further investigated. Second, using the theoretical approaches described in this chapter, researchers should examine other outcomes important to students and determine whether there is a stress-buffering mechanism in place for students who are victims. Research has shown that the stress-buffering model is relevant for some outcomes and for some populations more than others (Malecki & Demaray, 2002b). Thus, comprehensive research should not discount this theory even if evidence for it has not been shown when examining other outcomes. Finally, intervention planning and development should be undertaken with an ecological framework and should include social support as one of many contextual factors.

REFERENCES

Baron, R. M., & Kenny, D. A. (1986). The moderator-mediator variable distinction in social psychological research: Conceptual, strategic, and statistical considerations. *Journal of Personality and Social Psychology, 51*, 1173–1182.

Barrera, M. (1986). Distinctions between social support concepts, measures, and models. *American Journal of Community Psychology, 14*, 413–445.

Bender, D., & Losel, F. (1997). Protective and risk effects of peer relations and social support on antisocial behavior in adolescents from multi-problem milieus. *Journal of Adolescence, 20*, 661–678.

Cobb, S. (1976). Social support as a moderator of life stress. *Psychosomatic Medicine, 38*, 300–314.

Cohen, S., Gottlieb, B. H., & Underwood, L.G. (2000). Social relationships and health. In S. Cohen, L. G. Underwood, & B. H. Gottlieb (Eds.), *Social support measurement and intervention: A guide for health and social scientists* (pp. 3–25). New York: Oxford University Press.

Cohen, S., & Wills, T. (1985). Stress, social support, and the buffering hypothesis. *Psychological Bulletin, 98*, 310–357.

Compas, B. E., Slavin, L. A., Wagner, B. A., & Vannatta, K. (1986). Relationship of life events and social support with psychological dysfunction among adolescents. *Journal of Youth and Adolescence, 15*, 205–221.

Cowie, H. (2000). Bystanding or standing by: Gender issues in coping with bullying in English schools. *Aggressive Behavior, 26*, 85–97.

Cowie, H., & Olafsson, R. (2000). The role of peer support in helping the victims of bullying in a school with high levels of aggression. *School Psychology International, 21*, 79–95.

Demaray, M. K., & Elliott, S. N. (2001). Perceived social support by children with characteristics of attention-deficit/hyperactivity disorder. *School Psychology Quarterly, 16*, 68–90.

Demaray, M. K., & Malecki, C. K. (2002a). Critical levels of perceived social support associated with student adjustment. *School Psychology Quarterly, 17*, 213–241.

Demaray, M. K., & Malecki, C. K. (2002b). Perceptions of the frequency and importance of social support by students classified as victims, bullies, and bully/victims in an urban middle school. Manuscript submitted for publication.

Demaray, M. K., & Malecki, C. K. (2002c). The relationship between perceived social support and maladjustment for students at risk. *Psychology in the Schools, 39*, 305–316.

Dubow, E. F., & Ullman, D. G. (1989). Assessing social support in elementary school children: The survey of children's social support. *Journal of Clinical Child Psychology, 18*, 52–64.

Forman, E. A. (1988). The effects of social support and school placement on the self-concept of LD students. Learning Disability Quarterly, 11, 115–124.

Furlong, M. J., Chung, A., Bates, M., & Morrison, R. L. (1995). Who are the victims of school violence? A comparison of student non-victims and multi-victims. *Education and Treatment of Children, 18*, 282–298.

Gillock, K. L., & Reyes, O. (1999). Stress, support, and academic performance of urban, low-income, Mexican-American adolescents. *Journal of Youth and Adolescence, 28*, 259–282.

Harter, S. (1985a). *Manual for the Social Support Scale for Children.* Denver: University of Denver.

Harter, S. (1985b). *Manual for the Self-Perception Profile for Children.* Denver: University of Denver.

House, J. (1981). *Work stress and social support.* Reading, MA: Addison-Wesley.

Latane, B., & Nida, S. (1981). Ten years of research on group size and helping. *Psychological Bulletin, 89*, 308–324.

Levitt, M. J., Guacci-Franco, N., & Levitt, J. L. (1994). Social support achievement in childhood and early adolescence: A multicultural study. *Journal of Applied Developmental Psychology, 15*, 207–222.

Malecki, C. K. & Demaray, M. K. (in press). What type of support do they need? Investigating student adjustment as related to emotional, informational, appraisal, and instrumental support. *School Psychology Quarterly.*

Malecki, C. K., & Demaray, M. K. (2002a). *Does social support mediate student adjustment for victims of bullying in schools?* Manuscript submitted for publication.

Malecki, C. K., & Demaray, M. K. (2002b). *Social support as an academic enabler for students identified as at-risk, not at-risk, and resilient.* Manuscript submitted for publication.

Malecki, C. K., Demaray, M. K., & Elliott, S. N. (2000). *The Child and Adolescent Social Support Scale.* Northern Illinois University: DeKalb, IL.

Malecki, C. K., & Elliott, S. N. (1999). Adolescents' ratings of perceived social support and its importance: Validation of the Student Social Support Scale. *Psychology in the Schools, 36*, 473–483.

Naylor, P., & Cowie, H. (1999). The effectiveness of peer support systems in challenging school bullying: The perspectives and experiences of teachers and pupils. *Journal of Adolescence, 22*, 467–479.

Naylor, P., Cowie, H., & del Rey, R. (2001). Coping strategies of secondary school children in response to being bullied. *Child Psychology and Psychiatry Review, 6*, 114–120.

Olweus, D. (1991). Bully/victim problems among school children: Basic facts and effects of a school based intervention programme. In D. Pepler & K. Rubin (Eds.), *The development and treatment of childhood aggression* (pp. 411–448). Hillsdale, NJ: Lawrence Erlbaum.

Olweus, D., Limber, S., & Mihalic, S. F. (1999). *Blueprints for Violence Prevention, Book Nine: Bullying Prevention Program.* Boulder, CO: Center for the Study and Prevention of Violence.

Piko, B. (2000). Perceived social support from parents and peers: Which is the stronger predictor of adolescent substance use? *Substance Use & Misuse, 35*, 617–631.

Rigby, K. (2000). Effects of peer victimization in schools and perceived social support on adolescent well-being. *Journal of Adolescence, 23*, 57–68.

Rigby, K., & Slee, P. T. (1999). Suicidal ideation among adolescent school children, involvement in bully-victim problems, and perceived social support. *Suicide and Life-Threatening Behavior, 29*, 119–130.

Rosenfeld, L. B., Richman, J. M., & Bowen, G. L. (2000). Social support networks and school outcomes: The centrality of the teacher. *Child and Adolescent Social Work Journal, 17*, 205–226.

Schwarzer, R., & Leppin, A. (1991). Social support and health: A theoretical and empirical overview. *Journal of Social and Personal Relationships, 8*, 99–127.

Shumaker, S. A., & Brownell, A. (1984). Toward a theory of social support: Closing conceptual gaps. *Journal of Social Issues, 40*, 11–36.

Stewart, M. J. (1989). Social support: Diverse theoretical perspectives. *Social Science and Medicine, 28*, 1275–1282.

Swearer, S. M., & Doll, B. (2001). Bullying in schools: An ecological framework. *Journal of Emotional Abuse, 2*, 7–23.

Swearer, S. M., & Espelage, D. L. (in press). An ecological framework of bullying among youth. In D. Espelage and S. Swearer (Eds.), *A Social-Ecological Perspective on Bullying Prevention and Intervention in American Schools*. Mahwah, NJ: Lawrence Erlbaum and Associates.

Tardy, C. H. (1985). Social support measurement. *American Journal of Community Psychology, 13*, 187–202.

Uchino, B., Cacioppo, J., & Kiecolt-Glaser, J. (1996). The relationship between social support and physiological processes: A review with emphasis on underlying mechanisms and implications for health. *Psychological Bulletin, 119*, 488–531.

Wenz-Gross, M., & Siperstein, G. N. (1998). Students with learning problems at risk in middle school: Stress, social support, and adjustment. *Exceptional Children, 65*, 91–100.

ACKNOWLEDGMENT

Correspondence concerning this chapter should be addressed to Christine K. Malecki, Northern Illinois University, Department of Psychology, DeKalb, IL 60115. E-mail: cmalecki@niu.edu.

12

The Impact of Family Relationships on School Bullies and Victims

Renae D. Duncan
Murray State University

Stocker and Youngblade (1999) emphasize the importance of family relationships in helping children develop the skills necessary for positive peer interactions. They argue that because the family is where the child first sees and experiences relationships, it is through the family that the child will learn what to expect in relationships, how to behave in relationships, and the interpersonal skills to be used in relationships. As seen in previous chapters, research indicates clear differences in the characteristics and behaviors of bullies (those who bully others), victims (those who are victimized by others), bully-victims (those who both bully and are victimized by others), and children not involved in bullying. Thus, it is likely that at least some of the characteristics that predispose children to becoming victims or bullies develop before the child enters school and that some of these characteristics are developed through experiences within the family. This chapter will examine the parents and siblings of children involved in bullying and will highlight several theories which explain the link between family characteristics and school bully involvement.

Impact of the Family
on Peer Relationships

In an excellent review of the literature examining the link between family and peer relationships, Ladd (1992) describes pathways by which a child's experiences in the family shape the child's relationships with peers. Ladd states that these pathways can be either direct or indirect. For example, a parent who refuses to let a child join after-school activities is having a direct influence on the child's interactions and relationships with peers. In contrast, a parent who uses harsh physical discipline with a child has an indirect influence on the child's peer relationships. This harsh parental behavior has an indirect effect on peer relationships because the abused child fails to learn appropriate problem-solving skills from the parents, which in turn leads to conflictual relationships with peers. Various models have been proposed which attempt to explain the indirect pathways by which family and parent-child relationships affect the child's interactions with peers. In this section of the chapter we will examine how attachment theory, social learning theory, family systems theory, and the research on parenting styles explain the influence of parents and family on the behaviors of children involved in bullying.

Attachment Theory.   Bowlby (1969) proposes that during the first few years of life, the interactions between caregiver and child lead to the child's development of an internal working model of relationships. A child raised by a caring and responsive caregiver develops a secure attachment to that person and learns to handle new situations with confidence. In contrast, the child raised by an unresponsive, inconsistent and insensitive caregiver develops an insecure attachment style. The insecurely attached child handles new situations with distress and discomfort and may learn to behave aggressively in order to gain attention from that caregiver. The theory also states that the attachment style developed between the caregiver and child serves as the foundation (working model) for the child's relationships with others because the child has learned to expect either consistent and sensitive interactions or inconsistent and insensitive interactions with others.

The link between early attachment styles and relationships with siblings was noted in a longitudinal study of first-born children in which Volling and Belsky (1992) found that an insecure infant-mother attachment was predictive of later aggression with the sibling. Similarly, Teti and Ablard (1989) found that older siblings with secure attachments were more likely than those who did not have secure attachments to try to soothe and take care of their distressed younger siblings.

The apparent impact of attachment style continues once the child enters the school setting. Ladd's review (1992) cites several older studies in which preschool children with insecure attachment styles displayed "withdrawn or negative" peer interactions and had more behavior problems than their more securely attached peers. In contrast, securely attached preschoolers had healthier and more pleasant peer relationships and were more cooperative and sociable with their peers.

Perry, Hodges, and Egan (2001) point out that the characteristics typically seen in children with anxious/resistant attachment styles are those same characteristics that bullies tend to target. Specifically, these children "tend to be manifestly anxious, to cry easily, and to explore little" (p. 83). Perry et al. also suggest that resistantly attached children have self-concepts defined by feelings of helplessness and incompetence, which again make them likely targets of bullies. As would be expected, Troy and Sroufe (1987) found that children who had insecure, anxious-avoidant, or anxious-resistant attachments at 18 months were more likely than those with secure attachments to become involved in bullying when four to five years of age. Troy and Stroufe also found that bullying took place only when an anxious-resistant child was paired with an anxious-avoidant child, and that the securely attached children simply avoided becoming involved in bullying.

Although few studies have examined attachment styles and involvement in bullying, this theory appears to have promise in helping to explain how early parent-child relationships can play a role in determining why some children become victims, why others become bullies or bully-victims, and why even more children are able to avoid involvement in bullying. Future research will help us better understand which aspects of early attachment to caregivers most strongly influence the child's later peer interactions, and whether there are characteristics of the child or family that encourage or discourage involvement in bullying at school.

Social Learning Theory.   Social learning theory posits that children learn by modeling the behaviors of others and through reinforcement of these behaviors. Thus, research which notes that toddlers who were physically abused by parents are more aggressive toward peers and caregivers (George & Main, 1979), and that abused children respond to aggression with aggression (Howes & Eldredge, 1985), may be evidence that abused children model their own aggressive behavior after the behavior of their parents. A link between physical abuse by parents and bullying of peers has been supported by Olweus (1994) and Strassberg, Dodge, Pettit, and Bates (1994) who note that parents of bullies are often physically and emotionally aggressive in their interactions with their children. Similarly, Schwartz, Dodge, Pettit, and Bates (1997) examined boys and their families in preschool and again in the third and fourth grades. The researchers found that those boys identified as bully-victims (those who both bully and are victimized by their peers) in the third and fourth grades were likely to have had a negative home environment during preschool. The researchers also found that during preschool, these boys were likely to have experienced physical abuse, witnessed marital violence, and to have had a hostile mother who used restrictive discipline with the child. Schwartz et al. (1997) propose that physical abuse and domestic violence teach the child to use aggression as a tool to gain what is wanted by the child. Thus, bullies and bully-victims may model their aggressive behaviors from what they see (and experience) in the behavior of their parents.

Early research examining peer relationships of children who had been abused by parents also supports the link between child abuse and bullying. It has been found that toddlers who were physically abused by parents were aggressive toward peers and caregivers (George & Main, 1979) and that abused children responded to aggression with aggression, which caused the inappropriate behavior to escalate (Howes & Eldredge, 1985). Perhaps of more importance in understanding bullying behavior, Howes and Eldredge (1985) and Main and George (1985) found that when faced with a peer in distress, abused children responded to that peer's distress with aggression. Interestingly, Perry, Williard, and Perry (1990) found that bullies target children who openly display distress as a response to being humiliated or physically harmed by the bully and that bullies are rewarded by the victim's suffering.

Modeling also plays an important role in Patterson's (1982) coercive theory which suggests that parents unwittingly reinforce children's oppositional and aggressive behavior and that children's undesired behaviors then elicit coercive and punitive behavior from the parents. This coercive cycle is reflected in the following example: The mother asks the child to perform a task. The child refuses to do the task as requested by the mother, so the mother yells in response. The child yells in return and eventually the argument escalates to the point where the parent does the task herself out of sheer frustration. When this pattern occurs across time, the child has learned that "If I become oppositional enough, I do not have to do anything I don't want to do." The child has learned that aggression and coercion bring rewards, thus the child learns to use these negative behaviors to gain what is desired. Patterson (1984) found that children were even more likely to become involved in these coercive cycles with their siblings than with their parents and that younger children enter this coercive cycle by modeling the behavior of the older sibling. Thus, both reinforcement and modeling of the aggressive, oppositional, and coercive behaviors ensures that these behaviors will continue. MacKinnon-Lewis, Starnes, Volling, and Johnson (1997) suggest that the relationship with mothers and siblings acts as a "training ground" for the child in that children who are aggressive with peers are "trained" to behave in such a manner through their interpersonal interactions at home. If indeed the family is where children develop the skills they will use in their future interactions with peers, it is easy to see how the behaviors noted in Patterson's coercive cycle could help explain the behaviors exhibited by bullies and bully-victims.

Family Systems Theory.   Family Systems Theory proposes that the family is a single unit made up of a variety of interconnected relationships. Thus, a child's (or adult's) emotional or behavioral difficulties reflect problems within the family unit rather than being evidence of something that is "wrong" with the child. The family systems model was one of several presented by Ingoldsby, Shaw, and Garcia (2001) to explain the link between intrafamilial aggression and peer aggression. This model focuses on conflict within family subsystems such that when conflict occurs in one subsystem, the other subsystems and the emotional climate of the family are necessarily impacted. Ingoldsby et al. (2001) noted that conflict in only one subsystem within a family (parent-parent, parent-child, child-sibling) is only weakly related to conflict with teachers and peers. However, when conflict occurs in more than one of these intrafamily relationships the likelihood of conflict with teachers and peers increases. Similarly, Garcia, Shaw, Winslow, and Yaggi (2000) found that although destructive sibling conflict and a rejecting parenting style were highly predictive of aggressive behavior in young boys, children who experienced problems in only one subsystem (parent-child or sibling-child) were less likely to display aggressive behavior than were children who experienced difficulties in both the sibling and parent relationships. Also, Stocker, Burwell, and Briggs (2002) found that sibling conflict was predictive of increases in children's anxiety, depressed mood, and delinquent behavior above that already accounted for by mother's and father's hostility and marital conflict.

Conflict within the husband-wife subsystem also impacts the child's peer relationships. Stocker and Youngblade (1999) found that marital conflict was related to children's difficulties in both sibling and peer relationships. Katz and Woodin (2002) found that children of parents who handle marital conflict with hostility and withdrawal displayed more negative affect and noncompliance with peers than did children whose parents handled conflict in a more healthy manner.

The importance of examining the family as a whole was also reflected in the research of Katz and Gottman (1996) and McHale, Johnson, and Sinclair (1999) in which low levels of family warmth, accord, and mutuality and high levels of competitiveness and conflict were found to be predictive of poor peer relationships in children. Similarly, MacKinnon-Lewis et al. (1997) found that adding the sibling relationship into their prediction model explained more variance in peer aggression and peer acceptance than did the parent-child relationship alone. The authors noted that the sibling relationship appeared to act as a mediator between rejecting relationships with mothers and aggressive interactions with peers.

Although few studies have directly examined the families of children involved in bullying, the research that has been conducted supports the theory that a child's behavioral problems are symptoms of a dysfunctioning family system. For example, Berdondini and Smith (1996) and Bowers, Smith, and Binney (1992) described the families of victims as cohesive yet enmeshed. Additionally, in several examinations of the families of children involved in bullying, it was found that bullies were less likely than other children to have a father in the home (Berdondini & Smith, 1996; Bowers et al., 1992; Bowers, Smith, and Binney, 1994). Families of bullies were also characterized as having low cohesion (Berdondini & Smith, 1996; Bowers et al., 1992, 1994) and little warmth, yet all family members were viewed as having high needs for power (Bowers et al., 1992, 1994). Indeed, Bowers et al. (1994) state, "It is as if these bullies are developing a general model of relationships as lacking warmth, and concerned with power . . ." (p.228).

Parenting Styles. Ladd (1992) summarized early research on the impact of parenting styles on children by stating that parents' child-rearing behaviors serve as a model upon which children base their behavior and expectations of future relationships. Early research on parenting styles focused primarily on four parenting types: authoritarian, authoritative, indulgent, and indifferent-uninvolved (Maccoby & Martin, 1983). Authoritarian parents are demanding and unresponsive to the child, authoritative parents are demanding and responsive, indulgent parents are responsive yet undemanding, and indifferent-uninvolved parents are undemanding and unresponsive to the child. Ladd's (1992) review of the literature clearly indicates that children with authoritarian, indulgent, or indifferent-uninvolved parents display more behavior problems than do children raised by authoritative parents. Specifically, children whose parents use authoritarian styles tend to be either aggressive toward their peers or dominated by peers. Similarly, children whose parents are permissive tend to be aggressive, especially when their parents fail to place limits on aggressive behaviors, and the children of uninvolved parents are likely to display aggressive and delinquent behavior. In contrast, children whose parents use more authoritative styles tend to be independent and to have strong social skills.

Baldry and Farrington (1998) found that children involved in bullying (whether as bullies, victims, or both) tended to have relatively authoritarian parents. However, other research examining the parent-child relationships of children involved in bullying finds differences between these groups which more closely parallel the parenting types discussed above. For example, parents of bully-victims seem to display those characteristics evident in the indifferent-uninvolved parenting style. Specifically, bully-victims report that they are both neglected by and inconsistently monitored by their parents (Bowers et al., 1994). However, bully-victims have also described their parents as authoritarian, punitive, and unsupportive (Baldry & Farrington, 1998). Parents of bullies also display characteristics of both the authoritarian and indifferent-uninvolved styles. For example, parents of bullies appear to be both physically and emotionally aggressive with their children (Olweus, 1994; Strassberg et al., 1994) while at the same time being overly indulgent of them (Olweus, 1994). In contrast, Baldry and Farrington (1998) found that bullies reported fewer negative parental behaviors than did children who were victims or bully-victims.

Parenting styles used by parents of victims are more difficult to fit into the classification system discussed above, though aspects of the authoritarian style are evident. Specifically, research consistently indicates that mothers of victims are overly controlling of their children (Ladd & Ladd, 1998; Olweus, 1992; Rigby, 2002).

This excessive control of the child may reflect the unresponsive and demanding styles seen in authoritarian parents. As mentioned above, children raised by authoritarian parents tend to be either aggressive toward or dominated by their peers. Thus, it is possible that overly controlling and authoritarian parenting leads to an inhibition of the child's sense of autonomy. Interestingly, Putallaz (1987) found that children whose autonomy was restricted by their mothers were less assertive with peers than were those whose mothers allowed more autonomy. In addition, Perry et al. (2001) suggest that the controlling style seen in parents of victims leads the child to feel as if his or her feelings and thoughts are wrong, which in turn can lead to a variety of internalizing symptoms and behaviors commonly seen in victims of bullying. These internalizing symptoms and weak assertiveness skills may then place the child at risk for victimization at the hands of their peers.

Parent and Sibling Characteristics

It is evident from the examination of Attachment Theory, Social Learning Theory, Family Systems Theory, and the research on parenting styles that early family and parent/child experiences may result in the child becoming involved in unhealthy peer relationships at school. This section will take a less theoretical approach to understanding the impact of the family on the child's peer relationships by exploring the literature which describes the characteristics of parents and siblings of children who are bullies, victims, and bully-victims.

Parents of Victims. A fairly consistent pattern in the relationships between victims and their parents is evident in the research literature. For example, parents of victims are described as being overly intense and overinvolved in their children's lives (Bowers et al., 1994). Similarly, the mothers of male victims have been found to be overprotective (Olweus, 1993), controlling and restrictive, and to coddle their sons (Olweus, 1992). Olweus (1994) also found that although male victims report a close and positive relationship with their mothers, the boys' teachers believed the mothers were overprotective. This same control and warmth in the male victim/mother relationship was found in videotaped interactions between kindergarten children and their mothers in which Ladd and Ladd (1998) found that mothers of victimized children tended to be overly controlling of their children while at the same time the mother-child relationship was characterized as more emotionally close than typically seen.

Finnegan, Hodges, and Perry (1998) found that the maternal overprotectiveness discussed above was true only for male victims. In addition, it was found that those boys who had both a fearful coping style and overprotective mothers were the boys most likely to be victimized by peers. Interestingly, male victims were more likely than other boys to report that their mothers allowed the boys to express themselves during family arguments. The authors suggest that the "animated, positively toned discussions, even lively debates" (p. 1082) between mother and son is evidence of the enmeshed relationships found in other studies. This overinvolvement in their children's lives is also evident in a survey of 15,686 U.S. school children, in which Nansel et al. (2001) found that the parents of victims were highly likely to be involved in their children's schools. The authors propose that this parental involvement may reflect concern the parents have about the difficulties their children are experiencing with their peers. However, they also suggest that the parental involvement may reflect the notion that victims are less independent than their peers which may leave them more vulnerable to attacks.

Although the mothers of victimized males appear to be overly protective, perhaps even overcontrolling, researchers have found fathers of victims to be distant and critical (Olweus, 1993) or absent (Fosse & Holen, 2002). Indeed, Fosse and Holen found that among male outpatients, those who were bullied were less likely than the nonbullied males to have grown up without their biological parents or their biological fathers. The authors theorize that boys learn from their fathers how to interact with other males and how to keep themselves safe from bullies. Thus, fatherless boys do not develop these skills to the same degree as do boys raised by their fathers. This is supported by early research which found that boys' popularity with peers was related to physically playful and affectionate interactions with the father (MacDonald & Parke, 1984).

A different pattern has been noted in the parent-child relationships of female victims. Whereas mothers of victimized boys tend to be overly protective of their sons, victimized girls report having a more negative attitude toward their mothers than do nonvictims (Rigby, 1993). In addition, female victims are more likely to experience poor family functioning, inadequate family communication, and lower family affect than nonvictims of bullying (Rigby, 1994). These poor family relationships and negative mother-child relationships were not reported by male victims (Rigby, 1993, 1994).

Further evidence of the unhealthy female victim/parent relationship is reflected in an examination of persons seeking outpatient mental health treatment. It was found that female outpatients with histories of bully victimization were more likely than nonbullied female outpatients to have been abused or neglected by their parents (Fosse & Holen, 2002). Similarly, Finnegan et al. (1998) found that female victims described their mothers as hostile and rejecting and described mothers who would withdraw their love and threaten to reject and abandon the girls when they misbehaved. They further stated that the parenting behaviors used by the mothers were "likely to threaten girls' need for communion and their development of the social skills needed to relate closely and effectively with others" (p. 1082).

Finnegan et al. (1998) hypothesized that the behaviors of mothers have a differential impact on children depending on the sex of the child such that if the mother hinders the development of autonomy in boys or connectedness in girls, these children are likely to become victims. Perry et al. (2001) suggest that because of the mother's overprotective parenting style, the male child has difficulty exploring and experiencing new situations alone or with peers. Because the child is sheltered from potentially negative experiences, those skills necessary to handle conflict and discomfort are not developed. Further, Finnegan, et al. (1998) suggest that the overprotected male child is unable to develop the autonomy necessary to obtain and maintain status in the peer group. Thus, the overprotected boy (who may already be rejected by other boys) feels helpless and anxious when he encounters a difficult situation involving peers because he has not learned the skills necessary to handle these situations effectively.

In contrast to the overprotective parenting style exhibited by mothers of male victims, the mothers of female victims are described as emotionally abusive, hostile, and rejecting of their daughters. Finnegan et al. (1998) propose that this hostile and rejecting parenting style leads to the development of depression, anxiety or other internalizing symptoms in the child. Additionally, because the mother fails to model healthy interpersonal skills, the daughter has difficulty learning those skills necessary for developing relationships with other girls. Finnegan et al. suggest that these girls become victims of bullying because they have difficulty regulating their emotions, feeling or expressing empathy, and communicating effectively, all of which may make them easy targets for victimization by peers.

In his discussion of an unpublished paper (Rigby, Slee, & Martin, 1999, as cited in Rigby, 2002), Rigby stated that when parents provided a healthy level of care to their children the children were unlikely to be involved in bullying, yet when parents were overly controlling, the children were more likely than their peers to become involved in bullying. However, Rigby was careful to point out the fact that the study was correlational in nature. Although the data might suggest that parents' controlling behavior causes involvement in bullying, the data might just as easily reflect a situation in which the parents are more controlling in response to the behavior of the child.

Interestingly, Rigby reports that when the children's level of extraversion and mental distress were statistically controlled in the analysis, the influence of parental care was negligible for boys. However, girls who reported a high level of parental control and a low level of parental care were likely to bully others and girls who reported a high level of parental control only were more likely than their peers to be victims. If we use the definition of psychological control offered by Perry et al. (2001) in which "Psychological control involves attempts by the parent to constrain, invalidate, or manipulate the child's thoughts and feelings," it would appear as if the controlling behavior noted by Rigby and others can be emotionally abusive to the child.

This abusive parenting style was also found in a study in which college students were asked about their childhood experiences at home and at school (Duncan, 1999a). It was found that victims were significantly more likely than nonvictims of bullying to have been mistreated by their parents. Victims reported a significantly higher frequency of physical and emotional abuse by parents than did nonvictims of bullying. Specifically, victims reported more maternal slapping, kicking, yelling, insulting, criticizing, embarrassing, and ridiculing or humiliating than did nonvictims of bullying. Victims also reported higher levels of paternal slapping and yelling and were more likely than nonvictims of bullying to report that their mothers and fathers made them feel guilty and made them feel like a bad person. Additionally, 29% of the victims versus 9% of nonvictims had been sexually assaulted in childhood. It is important to note however that the sexual assault percentages also include assaults committed by persons outside the family.

Child abuse may contribute to the development of interaction styles seen in individuals targeted by bullies. For example, Finkelhor and Browne (1985) proposed that children who are abused may learn that they are powerless, they become less self-confident and are less able to assert their needs. Additionally, abused children lose the ability to determine whether others are trustworthy. Because of this lack of assertiveness, poor judge of character, sense of powerlessness, and lack of confidence abused children come to expect to be harmed and fail to recognize danger and are thus less able to protect themselves when encountered by others who might be dangerous. Therefore, the child abuse victim is targeted by the bully, who sees a vulnerable child who will not retaliate when attacked. Research indicates that children with low self-esteem (Sharp, 1996), passive response styles (Bernstein & Watson, 1997; Sharp, 1996), and who are submissive and unassertive with peers (Schwartz, Dodge, & Coie, 1993)—all of which are characteristics common in child abuse survivors—are bullied more than others. Perry et al. (1990) found that children easily detect which of their peers are most submissive and fail to assert their needs. The children expect that these submissive peers will not retaliate and will show more suffering when picked on by bullies, which in turn, rewards the bully's behavior.

Parents of Bullies and Bully-victims.   A need for power is evidenced in the prevalence of physical and emotional aggression used by parents of bullies in their interactions with the child (Olweus, 1994; Strassberg et al., 1994). Olweus (1994) notes that parents of bullies fail to place limits on their children's aggressive behaviors and are "generally permissive and tolerant" of aggression toward others. Bullies also report poor relationships with their parents and unhealthy family functioning (Rigby, 1993) and rate their families as high in negative affect while providing little emotional support (Rigby, 1994).

Somewhat similar patterns emerge in the parents of bully-victims (those who both bully and are victimized by their peers). For example, Bowers et al. (1994) found that bully-victims report troubled relationships with their parents, poor parental warmth, abusive and inconsistent discipline and monitoring, and neglect. Bully-victims also viewed their mothers as relatively powerless, perhaps as a result of domestic violence that occurs more often in these families than in the families of other children.

Sibling Characteristics. Numerous studies have shown that the most prevalent form of violence within the family occurs between siblings (for example, Gelles & Straus, 1988; Goodwin & Roscoe, 1990; Roscoe, Goodwin, & Kennedy, 1987; Steinmetz, 1977; Straus, Gelles, & Steinmetz, 1980). Roscoe et al. (1987) found that close to 100% of the 244 junior high school students surveyed had been a victim of physical aggression at the hand of a sibling within the past year. Roscoe et al. also found that 96% of females and 85% of males acknowledged having physically assaulted a sibling within that same year. In a study in which 375 rural middle school students were surveyed, Duncan (1999b) found that 30% of the 336 children with siblings were frequently victimized by their siblings. Twenty-two percent of the children reported that they were often hit or pushed around by a sibling, 8% reported that they were often beaten up by a sibling and 8% agreed with the statement "I'm scared that my brother or sister will hurt me bad someday." Even more children reported that they often bully their siblings (42%), with 24% admitting that they often hit or push around their siblings and 11% stating that they often beat up their brothers and sisters. Duncan (1999b) also found that children involved in bullying at school were also likely to be involved in bullying at home with their siblings. For example, 57% of children who bullied their peers and 77% of bully-victims also bullied their siblings, whereas only 38% of victims and 32% of those not involved in bullying admitted to bullying their siblings. In addition, a minority of victims (36%), bullies (29%), and those not involved in bullying (23%) reported frequent victimization by their siblings, whereas the majority of bully-victims (60%) reported that their siblings frequently victimized them.

The relation between sibling violence and school aggression is supported by the research of Berndt and Bulleit (1985) who found that preschoolers who were aggressive with their siblings were most likely to be aggressive with peers. Also, Stormshak, Bellanti, and Bierman (1996) found that children with high sibling conflict were rated by teachers as displaying high aggression and low social competence at school. A similar pattern of unpleasant sibling relationships was noted in several studies conducted by Bowers, Smith, and Binney, who found that bullies had ambivalent and somewhat negative relationships with their siblings (Bowers et al., 1994) and viewed their siblings as being more powerful than themselves (Bowers et al., 1992, 1994). This is in contrast to victims who reported positive and enmeshed relationships with their siblings (Bowers et al., 1994).

The link between sibling and peer aggression suggests that the maladaptive social interactions of bullies and victims may be related to problems within the sibling relationship. East and Rook (1992) found that isolated/sensitive children who had a supportive sibling displayed less anxiety and immaturity than those without such a sibling. This suggests that siblings may provide the isolated child some compensation for the support they are unable to receive from peers. However, East and Rook also hypothesize that if isolated children feel they are close to and are receiving a high level of support from siblings, they may feel no drive to seek such closeness and support from peers, thus furthering their isolation. This potentially damaging aspect of extreme sibling closeness was also addressed by Bowers et al. (1994) who noted that victims report extremely close, if not enmeshed, relationships with their siblings.

One might suspect based on the research that children who are aggressive with siblings are likely to be aggressive with peers, that sibling conflict would have a purely negative impact on children. However, Stormshak et al. (1996) found that children who had moderately conflictual and moderately warm relationships with their siblings displayed more social competence and emotional control at school than children who had more negative or more warm sibling relationships. In contrast, those with high sibling conflict and low sibling warmth were more disliked by peers than the other children. The authors suggest that experiencing conflict with a sibling who is also supportive, helps the child learn to regulate emotions and behaviors. When the warmth is not present, the child is likely to be aggressive, but when there is warmth with no conflict, the child may not learn the skills necessary to handle uncomfortable interpersonal interactions with peers.

Similarly, Stocker and Dunn (1990) found that those children who were competitive and controlling with siblings had positive friendships while those with hostile sibling relationships were closer to their friends than any of the other children in the study. The researchers suggest that children who have unpleasant relationships with siblings compensate by developing particularly close relationships with their friends. However, Stocker and Dunn also propose that it is through sibling conflict that children develop the skills necessary to handle the ambiguities and stressors which occur in friendships. This notion is supported by Bank and Kahn (1982) who also suggest that it is through conflict that a child learns those skills necessary to resolve conflict. Sibling conflict also helps the child learn to manage aggressive advances by others without losing face or humiliating the other child. The authors also propose that sibling conflict can foster loyalty and help the child learn to develop more appropriate ways to express aggressive feelings.

Lockwood, Kitzmann, and Cohen (2001) discuss two models that explain the connection between sibling and peer relationships. The carryover model states that peer relationships mirror sibling relationships. Thus, according to this model a child who has warm relationships with siblings will also have warm relationships with peers and the child who is most aggressive with siblings will also be aggressive with peers. In contrast, the compensation model proposes that sibling and peer relationships balance each other. Thus, a child who is being victimized or rejected by peers is likely to report a close and warm relationship with siblings. Based on their research with 8- to 13-year-old children and their families,

Lockwood et al. found evidence to support both models. The authors noted that children whose relationships with siblings are characterized by high levels of warmth had the most positive relationships with peers. In addition, the children with high levels of sibling warmth were less likely than other children to be viewed as victims or as rejected by peers. The authors propose that children in these warm sibling relationships are able to learn and practice healthy interpersonal skills through interactions with the sibling and that children who have positive relationships with peers may take these positive interactions back into the sibling relationship, which then encourages even more sibling warmth.

In contrast to previous studies, Lockwood et al. (2001) found that sibling warmth did not mediate the likelihood of peer aggression when the siblings also engaged in high levels of conflict. However, the authors noted that sibling conflict has both risks and benefits for children. Children who experience low levels of sibling conflict had a lower social status among peers and were more likely to be victimized than other children. At the same time, children from homes with high levels of sibling conflict were more likely than the other children to be rejected by their peers and were somewhat more aggressive than the low sibling conflict children. The authors propose that children who experience little sibling conflict fail to develop the social skills necessary to successfully interact with peers in the school setting. Additionally, Lockwood et al. (2001) suggest that children who experience high levels of sibling conflict develop a negative attributional bias, which predisposes the child to handling uncomfortable peer interactions with aggression.

Summary of the Research Examining Parent and Family Characteristics

Although the research examining families of children involved in bullying is sparse, several interesting patterns are apparent (see Tables 12.1 and 12.2). Specifically, the families of male victims appear to be overly close, with mothers who coddle and overprotect their sons. Additionally, victims seem to have relationships with siblings characterized by a similar level of closeness. The overly close sibling relationships and overinvolvement in their son's lives by mothers appear to stifle autonomy and to inhibit the boys' ability to develop skills necessary for involvement in healthy peer relationships.

Female victims appear to come from families very different from those of male victims. Whereas the boys' families seem almost too good, families of female victims are characterized as emotionally abusive and unhealthy. Indeed, the mothers have been described as withdrawing love and threatening abandonment of the girls when the girls do not follow their mothers' directives. Because the girls are unable to model appropriate interpersonal behaviors from their mothers, they are left without the skills needed to become involved in healthy friendships with other girls. Additionally, the emotionally abusive behaviors directed toward

TABLE 12.1
Family and Parent Characteristics
of Male and Female Victims

Male Victims		Female Victims	
Mothers	*Fathers*	*Mothers*	*Fathers*
Overprotective	Distant	Hostile	No data
Controlling	Critical	Rejecting	
Restrictive	Absent	Withdraw Love	
Coddling		Threatening	
Overinvolved		Controlling	
Warm			
Family Characteristics		*Family Characteristics*	
Male Victims		*Female Victims*	
Cohesive		Poor Functioning	
Enmeshed		Low Communication	
Warm		Low Affect	
		Abuse & Neglect	

TABLE 12.2
Family Characteristics of Bullies
and Bully-Victims

Bullies	*Bully-victims*
Absent Father	Physical Abuse
Low Cohesion	Domestic Violence
Little Warmth	Hostile Mother
High Power Needs	Powerless Mother
Permit/Encourage Aggression	Indifferent/Uninvolved Parents
Physical Abuse	Neglect
Poor Family Functioning	Low Warmth
Negative Affect	Inconsistent Discipline
Authoritarian Parenting	Negative Environment
Harsh Physical Punishment	

the daughter may lead the girl to develop depression and anxiety which when paired with poor interpersonal skills, leaves the child at risk for rejection and victimization.

Families of bullies are often characterized by a lack of warmth, a lack of closeness, and as focused on power. Bullies are likely to grow up in homes without a father figure and are also likely to have been physically and emotionally maltreated while growing up. Bullies also acknowledge that they frequently mistreat their siblings, which parallels the aggression they perpetrate on their peers. Similarly, the families of bully-victims are often high in aggression and violence and low in warmth. The parents are likely to provide inconsistent discipline and are unlikely to monitor the behavior of their children. In fact, mothers tend to be described as neglecting their children and are often viewed as relatively powerless. A high level of sibling violence is often found in the homes of bully-victims, with the majority of bully-victims admitting that they both bully and are victimized by their siblings.

Translating Research Into Practice: Implications for Bullying-Prevention and Intervention Programs

Research examining parents and families of bullies, victims, and bully-victims finds behaviors within the families which may predispose children to involvement in bullying. Therefore, it is likely that the most successful intervention and treatment programs would involve not only the child, but the parents and siblings as well. Thus, future research examining the inclusion of family members in bully prevention programs would be invaluable.

Additionally, it may benefit educators to be mindful of the family environment when attempting to modify the problematic behavior of their students. Thus, school counselors might find that helping the bully *and* his or her parents find more appropriate outlets for their power needs will decrease the child's level of aggression toward peers and siblings. Also, teaching the parents to use alternative (nonviolent) forms of punishment will in turn teach the bully and his or her siblings to handle discomfort without aggression. Similarly, helping the parents recognize the inappropriateness of their children's aggressive behaviors may enable them to actively discourage bullying by their children both at school and at home. Overall, it is expected that changing the aggressive and power-focused climate of the family will result in changes in the bully's interactions with siblings and peers.

Similarly, a change in the family environment of male victims may help the victim stand up for himself when faced with conflict. School counselors and teachers might find it beneficial to encourage mothers of male victims to allow more risk-taking and autonomous behaviors in their sons. At the same time, helping the father to develop a closer and less critical relationship with the son will better enable the male victim to learn healthier ways to handle conflict with peers and may encourage the child to become more independent. Counselors will also need to ensure that siblings are not enabling the male victim to remain isolated by serving as his only friend. While sibling warmth is important, counselors should be careful to ensure that siblings allow and even encourage the victim to take chances with developing new friendships. In addition to involving the parents and siblings in the male victim's treatment, it would be beneficial for teachers and counselors to help the male victim learn to respond to bullying in a more controlled and less emotional manner. Responding to teasing and harassment in a calm, unemotional manner will remove some of the fodder which fuels the bully's behavior.

Intervention with female victims and bully-victims may need to be somewhat similar. In both groups of children we are likely to see emotionally abusive and perhaps physically abusive behavior by parents, and it will not be unusual to find domestic violence in the homes of bully-victims. Thus, if abuse is present, local Social Services agencies will need to be involved. Additionally, intervention by mental health professionals trained specifically in the treatment of child abuse will be important. Counselors should also help the parents become more nurturing and accepting of their children while also teaching them to handle their children's misbehavior with more consistent and appropriate consequences. Finally, assessing and treating symptoms of psychological distress in the victim and bully-victim will be vital. As with the male victim, helping the female victim and bully-victim face harassment without becoming overly emotional will remove at least some of the reinforcement the bully receives from victimizing his or her peers.

REFERENCES

Baldry, A. C., & Farrington, D. P. (1998). Parenting influences on bullying and victimisation. *Criminal and Legal Psychology, 3*, 237–254.

Bank, S. P., & Kahn, M. D. (1982). *The Sibling Bond*. New York: Basic Books.

Berdondini, L., & Smith, P. K. (1996). Cohesion and power in the families of children involved in bully/victim problems at school: An Italian replication. *Journal of Family Therapy, 18*, 99–102.

Berndt, D. J., & Bulleit, T. N. (1985). Effects of sibling relationships on preschoolers' behavior at home and at school. *Developmental Psychology, 21*, 761–767.

Bernstein, J. Y., & Watson, M. W. (1997). Children who are targets of bullying: A victim pattern. *Journal of Interpersonal Violence, 12*, 483–498.

Bowers, L., Smith, P. K., & Binney, V. (1992). Cohesion and power in the families of children involved in bully/victim problems at school. *Journal of Family Therapy, 14*, 371–387.

Bowers, L., Smith, P. K., & Binney, V. (1994). Perceived family relationships of bullies, victims and bully/victims in middle childhood. *Journal of Social and Personal Relationships, 11*, 215–232.

Bowlby, J. (1969). *Attachment and loss* (Vol. 1). New York: Basic Books.

Duncan, R. D. (1999a). Maltreatment by parents and peers: The relationship between child abuse, bully victimization and psychological distress. *Child Maltreatment, 4*, 45–55.

Duncan, R. D. (1999b). Peer and sibling aggression: An investigation of intra- and extra-familial bullying. *Journal of Interpersonal Violence, 14*, 871–886.

East, P. L., & Rook, K. S. (1992). Compensatory patterns of support among children's peer relationships: A test using school friends, nonschool friends, and siblings. *Developmental Psychology, 28*, 163–172.

Finkelhor, D., & Browne, A. (1985). The traumatic impact of child sexual abuse: A conceptualization. *American Journal of Orthopsychiatry, 55*, 530–541.

Finnegan, R. A., Hodges, E. V. E., & Perry, D. G. (1998). Victimization by peers: Associations with children's reports of mother-child interaction. *Journal of Personality and Social Psychology, 75*, 1076–1086.

Fosse, G. K., & Holen, A. (2002). Childhood environment of adult psychiatric outpatients in Norway having been bullied in school. *Child Abuse & Neglect, 26*, 129–137.

Garcia, M. M., Shaw, D. S., Winslow, E. B., & Yaggi, K. E. (2000). Destructive sibling conflict and the development of conduct problems in young boys. *Developmental Psychology, 36*, 44–53.

Gelles, R. J., & Straus, M. A. (1988). *Intimate violence.* New York: Simon and Schuster.

George, C., & Main, M. (1979). Social interactions of young abused children: Approach, avoidance, and aggression. *Child Development, 50*, 306–318.

Goodwin, M. P., & Roscoe, B. (1990). Sibling violence and agonistic interactions among middle adolescents. *Adolescence, 25*, 451–467.

Howes, C., & Eldredge, R. (1985). Responses of abused, neglected, and non-maltreated children to the behaviors of their peers. *Journal of Applied Developmental Psychology, 6*, 261–270.

Ingoldsby, E. M., Shaw, D. S., & Garcia, M. M. (2001). Intrafamily conflict in relation to boy's adjustment at school. *Development and Psychopathology, 13*, 35–52.

Katz, L. F., & Gottman, J. M. (1996). New directions for child development: No. 74. *Spillover effects of marital conflict: In search of parenting and co-parenting mechanisms* (pp. 57–76). San Francisco: Jossey-Bass.

Katz, L. F., & Woodin, E. M. (2002). Hostility, hostile detachment, and conflict engagement in marriages: Effects on child and family functioning. *Child Development, 73*, 636–652.

Ladd, G. W. (1992). Themes and theories: Perspectives on processes in family-peer relationships. In R. D. Park, & G. W. Ladd (Eds.), *Family-peer relationships: Modes of linkage* (pp. 3–34). Hillsdale, NJ: Lawrence Erlbaum Associates.

Ladd, G. W., & Ladd, B. K. (1998). Parenting behaviors and parent-child relationships: Correlates of peer victimization in kindergarten. *Developmental Psychology, 34*, 1450–1458.

Lockwood, R. L., Kitzmann, K. M., & Cohen, R. (2001). The impact of sibling warmth and conflict on children's social competence with peers. *Child Study Journal, 31*, 47–69.

Maccoby, E. E., & Martin, J. A. (1983). Socialization in the context of the family: Parent-child interaction. In P. Mussen (Series Ed.) & E. M. Hetherington (Vol. Ed.), *Handbook of child psychology: Vol 4. Socialization, personality, and social development* (4th ed.), pp. 1–102. New York: Wiley.

MacDonald, K., & Parke, R. D. (1984). Bridging the gap: Parent-child play interaction and peer interactive competence, *Child Development, 55*, 1265–1277.

MacKinnon-Lewis, C., Starnes, R., Volling, B., & Johnson, S. (1997). Perceptions of parenting as predictors of boy's sibling and peer relations. *Developmental Psychology, 33*, 1024–1031.

Main, M., & George, C. (1985). Responses of abused and disadvantaged toddlers to distress in agemates: A study in the day care setting. *Developmental Psychology, 21*, 407–412.

McHale, J. P., Johnson, D., & Sinclair, R. (1999). Family dynamics, preschoolers' family representations, and preschool peer relationships. *Early Education and Development, 10*, 373–401.

Nansel, T. R., Overpeck, M., Pilla, R. S., Ruan, W. J., Simons-Morton, Bruce, B., & Scheidt, P. (2001). Bullying behaviors among U.S. youth: Prevalence and association with psychosocial adjustment. *Journal of the American Medical Association, 285*, 2094–2100.

Olweus, D. (1992). Victimization by peers: Antecedents and long-term consequences. In K. H. Rubin & J. B. Asendorph (Eds.), *Social withdrawal, inhibition, and shyness in childhood* (pp. 315–341). Hillsdale, NJ: Lawrence Erlbaum.

Olweus, D. (1993). *Bullying at school.* Cambridge, MA: Blackwell publishers.

Olweus, D. (1994). Annotation: Bullying at school: Basic facts and effects of a school-based intervention program. *Journal of Child Psychology and Psychiatry, 35*, 1171–1190.

Patterson, G. R. (1982). *Coercive family process.* Eugene, OR: Castalia Press.

Patterson, G. R. (1984). Siblings: Fellow travelers in coercive family processes. In R. J. Blanchard (Ed.), *Advances in the study of aggression* (pp. 174–213). New York: Academic Press.

Perry, D. G., Hodges, E. V. E., & Egan, S. K. (2001). Determinants of chronic victimization by peers. In J. Juvonen & S. Graham (Eds.), *Peer Harassment in Schools: The Plight of the Vulnerable and Victimized* (pp. 73–104). New York: Guilford Press.

Perry, D. G., Williard, J. C., & Perry, L. C. (1990). Peers' perceptions of the consequences that victimized children provide aggressors. *Child Development, 61*, 1310–1325.

Putallaz, M. (1987). Maternal behavior and children's sociometric status. *Child Development, 58*, 324–340.

Rigby, K. (1993). School children's perceptions of their families and parents as a function of peer relations. *The Journal of Genetic Psychology, 154*, 501–513.

Rigby, K. (1994). Psychosocial functioning in families of Australian adolescent schoolchildren involved in bully/victim problems. *Journal of Family Therapy, 16*, 173–187.

Rigby, K. (2002). *New Perspectives on Bullying.* Philadelphia, PA: Jessica Kingsley Publishers.

Rigby, K., Slee, P. T., & Martin, G. (1999).The mental health of adolescents, perceived parenting and peer victimisation at school. Unpublished paper.

Roscoe, B., Goodwin, M. P., & Kennedy, D. (1987). Sibling violence and agonistic interactions experienced by early adolescents. *Journal of Family Violence, 2*, 121–137.

Schwartz, D., Dodge, K. A., & Coie, J. D. (1993). The emergence of chronic peer victimization in boys' play groups. *Child Development, 64*, 1755–1772.

Schwartz, D., Dodge, K. A., Pettit, G. S., & Bates, J. E. (1997). The early socialization of aggressive victims of bullying, *Child Development, 68*, 665–675.

Sharp, S. (1996). Self-esteem, response style and victimization: Possible ways of preventing victimization through parenting and school-based training programmes. *School Psychology International, 17*, 347–357.

Steinmetz, S. K. (1977). *The cycle of violence: Assertive, aggressive, and abusive family interaction.* New York: Praeger.

Stocker, C., & Dunn, J. (1990). Sibling relationships in childhood: Links with friendships and peer relationships. *British Journal of Developmental Psychology, 8*, 227–244.

Stocker, C. M., Burwell, R. A., & Briggs, M. L. (2002). Sibling conflict in middle childhood predicts children's adjustment in early adolescence. *Journal of Family Psychology, 16*, 50–57.

Stocker, C. M., & Youngblade, L. (1999). Marital conflict and parental hostility: Links with children's sibling and peer relationships. *Journal of Family Psychology, 13*, 598–609.

Stormshak, E. A., Bellanti, C. J., & Bierman, K. L. (1996). The quality of sibling relationships and the development of social competence and behavioral control in aggressive children. *Developmental Psychology, 32,* 79–89.

Strassberg, Z., Dodge, K. A., Pettit, G. S., & Bates, J. E. (1994). Spanking in the home and children's subsequent aggression toward kindergarten peers. *Development and Psychopathology, 6*, 445–461.

Straus, M. A., Gelles, R. J., & Steinmetz, S. K. (1980). *Behind closed doors: Violence in the American family.* Garden City, NY: Anchor Books.

Teti, D. M., & Ablard, K. E. (1989). Security of attachment and infant-sibling relationships: A laboratory study. *Child Development, 60*, 1519–1528.

Troy M., & Sroufe, L. A. (1987). Victimization among preschoolers: Role of attachment relationship history. *Journal of the American Academy of Child and Adolescent Psychiatry, 26*, 166–172.

Volling, B. L., & Belsky, J. (1992). The contribution of mother-child and father-child relationships to the quality of sibling interaction: A longitudinal study. *Child Development, 63*, 1209–1222.

13

Home-school Collaboration and Bullying: An Ecological Approach to Increase Social Competence in Children and Youth

Susan M. Sheridan, Emily D. Warnes, and Shannon Dowd
University of Nebraska-Lincoln

Bullying and other forms of violence among children and youth is a prevalent concern among educators, psychologists, and families alike. Families and schools represent the primary systems in children's lives, and schools and homes are their primary learning contexts. These ecological contexts provide important frameworks within which development occurs. Healthy development occurs most seamlessly when there are congruent and consistent messages delivered across contexts, and healthy and constructive relationships among them. The development of meaningful partnerships among these systems on behalf of children and youth is particularly important to produce positive, lasting outcomes. Thus, an optimal focus for interventions aimed at bullying and victimization exists in the cross-setting contexts of home and school.

This chapter will focus on consultation processes for working across home and school ecologies to address concerns related to bullying and social competence. Included is information on (a) consultation strategies aimed at developing partnerships among parents and educational professionals to help develop social competence in children (i.e., bullies, victims, bystanders); (b) procedures for assessing the child and environment to identify sources of difficulties as well as facilitators to support social skillfulness; and (c) strategies for implementing interventions across home and school settings to enhance social competence.

ECOLOGICAL SYSTEMS THEORY

According to ecological-systems theory (Bronfenbrenner, 1979), and as articulated in an earlier chapter (Swearer & Espelage, Chapter 1), a child is an inseparable part of a small social network comprised of multiple interrelated systems. The microsystem describes the relation of the child with an immediate ecosystem and setting (e.g., home *or* school). The mesosystem describes interrelations among major ecosystems in the child's life (e.g., home *and* school), and focuses on the interface of contexts for children's behaviors and performance. The exosystem and macrosystem represent influences from broader and more diffuse contexts including settings in which a child does not directly participate, and overall cultural or subcultural patterns, respectively.

In their Contextual-Systems Model, Pianta and Walsh (1996) denote a clear understanding of systems influences and children at risk. These authors extend the discussion of risk variables beyond status characteristics inherent to the child or family (e.g., poverty). They articulate the importance of the quality of family-school relationships, or lack thereof, as a primary contributing factor to level of child risk. Thus, children can be considered at greater risk of developing unhealthy or nonproductive patterns of behaviors if the major support systems in their lives (family members, school personnel, community contexts) are operating at odds with each other. That is, high-risk circumstances occur when children derive meanings from home or school that result in conflicting emotions, motivations or goals. Alternatively, children develop in low-risk circumstances if the child/family and school systems communicate, and provide children with congruent messages about expectations and standards for behavior. A major premise of this chapter is that relationships among the systems are central in addressing issues faced by children at risk for serious social or emotional problems, or who demonstrate serious behavioral problems (such as aggression, violence, or gang-related episodes).

Research Support for Home-School Partnerships

In recent decades, numerous studies have demonstrated unequivocally that the establishment of productive, constructive, collaborative relationships between parents and teachers is essential for maximizing a student's potential. Parent involvement in their children's educational experiences is positively associated with benefits for students. When parents are involved, students show improvement in academic domains such as grades (Fehrmann, Keith, & Reimers, 1987), reading test scores (Clark, 1988; Comer, 1988; Epstein, 1991; Stevenson & Baker, 1987), math achievement (Epstein, 1986), attitude toward schoolwork (Kellaghan, Sloane, Alvarez, & Bloom, 1993), completion of homework (Clark, 1993; Epstein & Becker, 1982), academic perseverance (Estrada, Arsenio,

Hess, & Holloway, 1987), and participation in classroom learning activities (Collins, Moles, & Cross, 1982; Sattes, 1985). Also improved are behaviors (Comer & Haynes, 1991; Steinberg, Mounts, Lamborn, & Dornbusch, 1991) and self-esteem (Collins et al., 1982; Sattes, 1985). Additionally, benefits for students include fewer placements in special education (Lazar & Darlington, 1978), greater enrollment in post secondary education (Baker & Stevenson, 1986; Eagle, 1989; Marjoribanks, 1988), higher attendance rates (Collins et al., 1982), lower dropout rates (Rumberger, 1995), fewer suspensions (Comer & Haynes, 1991), and realization of exceptional talents (Bloom, 1985). Furthermore, findings from the National Longitudinal Study on Adolescent Health revealed that adolescents have a higher probability of avoiding high-risk behavior (e.g., substance abuse, violence) when they feel connected to their families and their parents are involved in their lives (Resnick et al., 1997).

Parent participation in education also benefits teachers and parents. When parents are actively involved, they report enhanced interpersonal and teaching skills among their child's teachers. Likewise, parent participation has been associated with higher ratings of teaching performance by principals, and greater job satisfaction of teachers (Christenson, 1995). Parent benefits include an increased sense of self-efficacy regarding parenting practices (Davies, 1993; Kagan & Schraft, 1982), increased understanding of programs for their child (Epstein, 1986), greater appreciation for the role they play in their children's education (Davies, 1993), improved communication with their children (Becher, 1984), and greater involvement in home learning activities (Epstein, 1995). In sum, the more clearly and explicitly parents and educators communicate and collaborate in their work with children, the greater the probabilities for success of interventions (Conoley, 1987; Hansen, 1986). One model by which parents and service providers can communicate and collaborate on behalf of children at risk is conjoint behavioral consultation (CBC; Sheridan, Kratochwill, & Bergan, 1996).

CONJOINT BEHAVIORAL CONSULTATION

Conjoint behavioral consultation (CBC) is a structured indirect model of service delivery designed to bring parents and teachers together to address the academic, social, and behavioral needs of a student for whom all parties bear some responsibility (Sheridan et al., 1996). CBC is embedded within an ecological systems framework, which emphasizes (a) reciprocal interactions between the child and the primary systems in his/her life, and (b) collaborative problem solving and decision making across those systems. Participants are parents, teachers, and other caregivers, with structure and guidance provided by a consultant (i.e., a specialist such as a school psychologist).

The foundation of CBC in ecological-systems theory provides several advantages. First, the reciprocal nature of interactions between the child and environment, as well as the interrelations among systems allows for an integrated assessment of the factors that influence the child, thereby enhancing diagnosis and treatment (Sheridan et al., 1996). In addition, CBC provides an opportunity for an interactive partnership between home and school systems that emphasizes mutual responsibility and support. Finally, the structured problem solving process encourages the primary caregivers in the child's life to become actively involved in decision-making (Christenson & Sheridan, 2001).

To facilitate collaborative partnerships, CBC engages parents and teachers in a joint problem solving process. The structured model consists of four-stages: including problem identification, problem analysis, treatment implementation and treatment evaluation.

Problem Identification

The first stage of CBC is problem identification (Sheridan et al., 1996). During this stage, parents and teachers work together with a consultant to identify the specific social concerns for which consultation services are sought. Two primary goals are met through problem identification. First, a thorough assessment of the presenting social concerns is conducted. Second, a specific behavior is selected for intervention (e.g., resolving arguments, accepting "no," cooperating with peers). The goals are considered within the context of the broader ecology within which these issues present. That is, identification of a "problem" is always considered in relation to a broad range of ecological conditions. These include intrapersonal (within person), interpersonal (person-person), and contextual (person-setting) conditions. To address each of these objectives, parents and teachers are involved through mutual and collaborative means.

Ecological Assessment of Social Concerns

In assessing the social concerns of children and youth, the consultation team focuses attention on three distinct areas that effect social functioning. These include (a) child characteristics, (b) contextual variables, and (c) the match or "fit" between the child and his or her context. Each of these areas contributes to children's abilities to function in a socially competent manner within their environment.

Child Characteristics. When assessing social functioning through the consultation process, the behavioral, interpersonal, and cognitive characteristics that contribute to a child's social competence are considered. Assessment of social functioning can be completed using methods such as direct behavioral observations, parent and teacher reports, and child self-reports (Sheridan & Elliott, 1991; Sheridan & Walker, 1999).

Direct behavioral observations allow for assessment of behaviors in a social context (Elliott & Busse, 1991; Hops, Walker, & Greenwood, 1988;

Merrell & Gimpel, 1998; Sheridan & Elliott, 1991; Sheridan & Walker, 1999). Direct observations provide opportunities to examine a child in multiple natural settings (e.g., home and school) and assess the frequency with which he/she interacts with peers and the range of appropriate and inappropriate behaviors in his or her repertoire. Specific social behaviors that either impede or facilitate social functioning also can be determined through direct observations. For example, a child may be observed to exhibit numerous aggressive behaviors that decrease the likelihood that peers invite the child to play. Likewise, observations may indicate that a child is particularly outgoing and approaches others without trepidation. Although such disinhibition may be considered a particular strength in some contexts, qualitative aspects of the approach (e.g., running into an existing game or activity, yelling at other children) may be viewed as inappropriate or unacceptable by peers, leading to lack of social acceptance and possible victimization by others. Another child may be observed to be the recipient of taunting and teasing, and his/her responses identified as a target for intervention.

Finally, direct observations in naturalistic settings allow for comparison of social behavior within a peer-based context. Observers can determine the types of behaviors that are considered "typical" or socially acceptable in the peer group and compare the rate or frequency of a child's behaviors to that of the norm group, thus allowing for a focused direction for skill development.

Parent and teacher report is another method of assessing child characteristics that contribute to social functioning (Elliott & Busse, 1991; Merrell & Gimpel, 1998; Sheridan & Elliott, 1991; Sheridan & Walker, 1999). Rating scales are based on the assumption that parents and teachers are knowledgeable and capable of providing accurate information regarding a child's interaction with peers and others in the social environment. Data from rating scales provide information regarding a target child's social strengths, as well as performance or skill deficit areas. Standardized scales such as the Social Skills Rating System (SSRS; Gresham & Elliott, 1990) and the Walker-McConnell Scale for Social Competence and School Adjustment (WMS; Walker & McConnell, 1988) allow for a developmental and norm referenced perspective of a child's social behaviors.

Finally, child self-report is a method of assessing individual variables that contribute to social functioning (Bracken, 1993; Elliott & Busse, 1991). Although the aforementioned assessment strategies help define the particular behaviors that may be exhibited in social environments, intrapersonal conditions (specific social cognitions such as interpretations, expectations, attributions, self-efficacy) are not accounted for through these methods. Child interviews and self-reports provide information regarding cognitions and perceptions regarding the social environment (Sheridan & Walker, 1999). The manner in which a child conceptualizes and interprets his/her own social behaviors and those of peers may affect the type of social strategies used to interact with others (Crick & Dodge, 1994). Different cognitions about social information can lead to a variety of actions and reactions in social situations, encouraging utilization of a range of strategies (some effective and some ineffective). Child interviews can be useful to inquire about self-perceptions of social status and peer responses. These reports provide valuable information regarding a child's social cognitions (i.e., the manner in which he/she views the social world) that can be obtained only from a child him or herself.

Ecological/Contextual Variables. Not only do individual variables influence a child's social behavior, but the environmental context greatly affects that child's social functioning. Intervention efforts must rely on a thorough understanding of the complexity of the contextual variables that reinforce and/or inhibit social behavior (Haring, 1992). Thus, it is important that contextual and environmental variables that contribute to social competence be assessed. This can be done through techniques such as ecological observations and structured behavioral interviews with parents and teachers (Sheridan, Hungelmann, & Maughn, 1999; Sheridan & Walker, 1999).

Key to understanding social context is a careful analysis of various factors within the environment that support social interactions, including a determination of the types of behaviors that are normative in social contexts (Sheridan et al., 1999). Observations of the ecological context provide an opportunity to monitor qualitative aspects of the behavior of socially competent peers and identify the strategies used by such children to interact effectively with others. As mentioned previously, a target child's behavior can then be compared to that of the norm group, allowing for focused intervention in skill areas where the child is experiencing relative difficulties. Hoier and colleagues (e.g., Hoier & Cone, 1987; Hoier, McConnell, & Pallay, 1987) promoted the use of "template matching," wherein behavioral profiles (templates) of socially competent peers are constructed, creating behavioral norms among relevant peer groups. Using this procedure, the behaviors of socially skilled children are thoroughly assessed and incorporated into a template that characterizes social competence. This behavioral template can then be compared to the profiles of a target child to identify areas of social-behavioral strengths and weaknesses. Comparing qualitative aspects of a target child's social behavior to that of competent peers allows for a focus on socially valid and meaningful areas for intervention.

Ecological observations are also helpful in identifying various stimuli in the environment that reinforce or discourage specific social behaviors (Elliott & Busse, 1991; Sheridan et al., 1999; Sheridan & Walker, 1999). Consideration of these variables allows for a functional assessment, conducted to understand the purpose of specific behaviors engaged in by a child. Specifically, antecedents, consequences, and situational events surrounding the child's social behavior can be discerned through direct observation. These are often interpersonal (person-person) in nature.

Antecedents are events, actions, or conditions that establish the context for negative behavior to occur. Understanding precipitants to aggression is an important aspect of the problem-solving process for two reasons. First, examination of events that precipitate violence will help consultants identify factors that may be under their control (Keller & Tapasak, 1997). These include antecedents to violence or aggressive acts such as wearing a certain type of clothing or using certain forms of provocative language. Second, the identification of distal antecedents that may occur outside of the primary intervention setting, such as teasing on the bus or lack of supervision at home (Keller & Tapasak, 1997) may broaden the focus of intervention in a comprehensive approach to the problem.

Consequences are events or responses to actions that reinforce or maintain a behavior. For example, a student who has an expectation of retaliation by another peer for reporting observed aggressive behaviors may lead that child to "stand by" and refrain from assisting another peer who is being teased. Similarly, a child may provide significant attention (positive or negative) for disruptive actions. For some, this may serve to reinforce socially unacceptable behavior if positive attention for pro-social behaviors is not experienced.

Ecological or situational events are person-setting conditions in the environment that encourage or maintain the occurrence of a prosocial or antisocial behavior. For example, the physical make-up of a school building, playground, or lunchroom can be considered ecological conditions. Bullying and aggressive behavior tends to occur in crowded areas such as stairways, cafeterias, and hallways. Other common ecological conditions include bathrooms, locker areas and entrances and exits to the building. Finally, periods of transition have been shown to increase the occurrence of violence in a school building (Goldstein, Harootunian, & Conoley, 1994).

Like ecological observations, structured behavioral interviews provide a method for gathering information about the functions of a child's social behavior (Elliott & Busse, 1991; Sheridan & Elliott, 1991; Sheridan & Walker, 1999). Interview questions with parents and teachers can be tailored to inquire about the antecedents, consequences, and sequential conditions surrounding a child's behaviors in different social settings (e.g., home and school). The structured interview format used in CBC allows for a thorough examination of these variables (Sheridan et al., 1996). Through the interview process, an identification of the functions or purpose of social behavior is possible. This information then can be used to create meaningful prosocial interventions for the child.

Match or "Fit" Between the Child and Context. Following careful analysis of the individual child and contextual variables that influence social functioning, the "fit" or match between the child's behavior and his or her social environment can be determined. Certain social behaviors may be adaptive and functional in some social settings, but not in others (Haring, 1992; Sheridan et al., 1999). Expectations and normative behaviors vary across contexts; thus, what is appropriate in one setting may not be socially acceptable in another. For example, it may be acceptable for a child to lick his fingers during meals while at home; however, this same behavior may not be viewed as socially appropriate in the school cafeteria and lead to taunting and teasing from peers. Likewise, high energy and roughhouse play may be acceptable on the playground, but is clearly not appropriate in the classroom setting during free play opportunities. In addition to the variations in expectations and normative behaviors among social settings, a child's behavior may be reinforced differentially depending on the context. For example, a child may be encouraged by school staff to socialize with his or her peers while at school, although this same child may not be expected to socialize outside of the family system and may have limited opportunities to play with peers when at home. In a similar vein, direct verbal conflict management strategies may be reinforced at school, whereas in a particular family context, aggressive or other physical means for asserting one's rights may be taught. In the context of home-school partnerships, differences among the child's social settings can be explored, and the apparent match or mismatch between the child's behavior and his or her environments can be identified.

Selection of a Target Behavior

The second goal of the problem identification stage of CBC includes the selection of a target behavior for intervention (Sheridan et al., 1996). It is important that the target behavior selected in consultation leads to meaningful treatment outcomes. Central to this discussion is the construct of social validity, which is defined as the degree to which therapeutic changes are socially important or meaningful to a client (Kazdin, 1977). Specifically, socially valid target behaviors are those that, when modified, bring about changes that influence a child's ability to function effectively within his or her social network. Analysis of existing social behaviors and the contextual environments allows for identification of appropriate and meaningful areas for intervention. The assessment techniques mentioned above (e.g., child and ecological observations, behavioral interviews, and parent and teacher report) provide for this type of analysis.

Meaningful targets for intervention are those that will be naturally reinforced in the social environment, such that the behavior or skill that is learned will be maintained over time in the absence of formal intervention. For example, teaching a child to organize play activities, give genuine compliments, or problem solve will likely lead to a positive response from peers, thus encouraging future instances of similar prosocial behaviors. Template matching (Hoier & Cone, 1987), as described earlier, yields an objective means for identifying normative expectations that can be naturally reinforcing.

Once a target behavior has been selected, it is important to develop a clear operational definition (Sheridan et al., 1996) that is concrete, observable, specific, and objective. These criteria allow parents, teachers, and the consultant to specify clearly the problem being addressed in consultation, and to collect relevant data throughout the course of consultation. These data are used to monitor treatment effects over time and make decisions regarding the goals for consultation and the modification of interventions.

Problem Analysis

Problem analysis is the second stage in the CBC process. The primary objectives of this stage are to (a) conduct a functional assessment of the behavior, and (b) develop a cross-setting treatment plan (Sheridan et al., 1996).

Functional Assessment

Functional assessment is conducted to evaluate the purpose or function of specific behaviors (such as aggression or withdrawal) engaged in by the child. Through structured assessment of the environmental factors surrounding the child's behaviors, it is possible to identify and influence variables that reinforce and thereby maintain the behavior. Although environmental factors are initially assessed through observation during the problem identification stage of consultation, similar conditions are re-assessed in a structured way across home and school settings during the problem analysis stage.

Functional assessments designed to increase social competence should include assessment across all social settings. Social behaviors might be topographically similar (e.g., arguing with peer), yet serve different functions in different contexts (e.g., escape a task or demand in the classroom, receive attention on the playground). Similarly, topographically dissimilar behaviors (e.g., arguing, helping a peer) may serve the same function (e.g., attention) across multiple settings. Therefore, hypotheses regarding the function of social behaviors should be tested via direct manipulation of environmental variables (Sheridan et al., 1999). Making deliberate changes in reinforcement contingencies and environmental structure can help identify variables that impact behavior. Utilizing findings from functional assessment to provide direct linkages between assessment of ecological stimuli and intervention strategies is crucial.

Plan Development

The second objective of the problem analysis stage in CBC is to develop a cross-setting plan including specification of environmental conditions to be manipulated (Sheridan et al., 1996). An important consideration for this stage is treatment acceptability, or consultees' (parents' and teachers') perceptions regarding social intervention procedures. Interventions that promote a philosophy contrary to parent and teacher belief systems may be viewed as unacceptable and may not be implemented, or may be implemented incorrectly. For example, a behavioral strategy such as positive reinforcement may be perceived as "bribery" and thereby implemented sporadically or not at all. Early research on treatment acceptability has suggested that interventions that are seen as high in cost (e.g., in terms of time, money, or resources) may be viewed as undesirable, and result in reduced implementation (Witt, Martens, & Elliott, 1984). Conversely, plans that incorporate positive rather than aversive components may be viewed more favorably. Finally, interventions that target more severe concerns are generally rated as more acceptable (Witt et al., 1984).

Lewis, Sugai and Colvin (1998) designed and implemented a school violence intervention program that was intended to increase acceptability in natural settings. Variables such as teacher time for planning, amount of teacher expertise, and time available for intervention supervision were considered. Based on these considerations, the authors purposefully left some variables uncontrolled to allow for a fit of the intervention within the parameters of daily school operations. There were no systematic efforts to ensure intervention integrity outside of informal staff contacts, and loose criteria to reward students were established (Lewis et al., 1998), yet generally positive results were found.

Strategies for Increasing Social Competence

In addition to developing a plan that is acceptable to all parties, it is crucial that the intervention has evidence of efficacy for similar target behaviors and situational contexts (Kratochwill & Stoiber, 2002). The development of effective interventions must consider internal (i.e., child-related) and external (i.e., environmental or contextual) factors. For example, teaching a child discrete steps to use self-control, manage conflicts, or assert oneself is important to ensure he/she has the skills to perform these behaviors. However, social interactions do not occur in isolation. Variables of other peers with whom problem solving will occur will be important to address. These variables may include interaction styles, skills, behaviors and goals of the other students (Sheridan & Walker, 1999). Several child-focused (within-person) strategies and environmental/contextual (person-person and person-setting) strategies have been developed that successfully increase social competence in children and adolescents. These are reviewed next.

Child-focused Strategies. Child-focused interventions are designed to promote skill acquisition and encompass several strategies including modeling, coaching and social problem-solving (Sheridan & Walker, 1999). One of the most effective strategies is *modeling*, or the process by which a new behavior is learned through observing another person engage in that behavior (Gresham, 2002). Modeling can be viewed as a three-step process. The first step, skill instruction, includes a rationale for the behavior and presentation of the sequence of actions involved in the skill. Demonstration of the skill by a trainer, therapist, parent or peer is the second step of the process. The third step is skill performance, in which there is an opportunity to perform the newly learned behavior in a structured, supportive, and responsive setting, such as a role-play (Gresham, 2002; Sheridan & Walker, 1999).

Coaching is another empirically supported strategy for improving social competence in children and adolescents (Gresham & Nagle, 1980; Mize, 1995). Coaching procedures use direct verbal instruction as a means to teach social skills. The coaching procedure involves three steps: (a) presentation of rules or steps for the behavior, (b) an opportunity to practice, and (c) specific feedback regarding skill performance (Gresham, 2002).

Social problem solving (SPS) is a third strategy that has received support. SPS interventions target thoughts, emotions, and behaviors associated with social interactions. Frequently, aggressive youth demonstrate deficiencies in problem-solving skills (Goldstein et al., 1994). When a problem arises, social cues are interpreted incorrectly or responded to in an emotional, rather than intellectual manner (Elias & Tobias, 1996). Several problem solving approaches aim to address these deficits by teaching children how to solve social problems though a series of steps including: (a) becoming aware of feelings, (b) recognizing problematic situations, (c) generating alternate solutions to problems, (d) evaluating consequences, (e) selecting a strategy, (f) engaging in the strategy, and (g) evaluating and modifying the strategy (Elias & Tobias, 1996; Sheridan & Walker, 1999).

Although such procedures have been shown to increase knowledge about appropriate social behaviors, the positive gains are short-term and behavioral generalization has not been demonstrated typically (Goldstein et al., 1994). Further, despite advances in problem solving thinking skills, little research has addressed the effect upon students' aggressive behaviors (Keller & Tapasak, 1997).

Other-focused Strategies. In addition to interventions focusing on the child, there are several strategies that target other individuals, such as parents or peers. These interventions include parent training, peer-based interventions, and school-wide programs.

Parent training is a useful strategy for social skills training because parents are in many situations where they can observe and help their child improve social interactions. Parental involvement may take several forms. First, parents may be involved directly with social skill instruction. For example, they can participate in parent groups that provide important information regarding specific problematic and nonproblematic social situations (Sheridan, 1995; Sheridan, Dee, Morgan, McCormick, & Walker, 1996). Second, parents can help set the stage for positive social interactions by providing opportunities for skill utilization as well as recognizing and discussing feelings surrounding their child's friendships (Sheridan, 1998). Finally, parents can provide supplemental training in natural settings via cueing, prompting, modeling and reinforcement of cooperative and pro-social behaviors (Sheridan et al., 1996).

Peer-based interventions present additional opportunities to increase pro-social behaviors. According to Gresham (2002), one type of peer-based strategy is peer-initiated contact. Peer initiated contact involves confederate peers who are used to begin and maintain interactions with a target child. Peers may be trained by teachers to approach a target child and initiate conversations or ask him or her to play. Peer-initiated contact appears to be especially effective for socially withdrawn children (Gresham, 2002).

Cooperative learning, another peer-based strategy, may prevent aggressive behavior in the classroom (Keller & Tapasak, 1997). This approach involves a group of students working together on an academic task. Although each student in the group has a specific role, which promotes accountability, praise and reinforcement is based on group performance, thereby enhancing interdependence. Goals of cooperative learning strategies include improving peer relationships, classroom climate, inter-racial relationships and academic achievement (Slavin, 1990). To be effective in cooperative learning groups, a number of subskills are required, including: (a) getting started, (b) requesting assistance, (c) responding to requests, (d) providing assistance, and (e) verbalizing supportive statements (Cartledge & Johnson, 1997).

Modeling and reinforcement of cooperative techniques is vital (Cartledge & Johnson, 1997). CBC provides an opportunity for both home and school contexts to communicate congruent messages regarding the importance of cooperative, rather than competitive behaviors. Further, it increases the likelihood that modeling and systematic reinforcement of cooperative actions will occur across the respective settings (Sheridan & Walker, 1999).

Ecological Strategies. Ecological interventions improve social competence by targeting the child's social environment. Examples of ecological strategies include the manipulation of antecedents and consequences, and school-wide interventions. *Manipulation of antecedents*, or events that precede desired social interactions, can create an environment that promotes pro-social behavior. In essence, it sets the stage for positive interactions. Examples of interventions that manipulate antecedents include cueing, prompting the child to use learned pro-social behaviors, and peer-based strategies (Sheridan & Walker, 1999).

Similarly, *manipulation of consequences* can effectively increase social competence by reinforcing pro-social behaviors. Contingent social reinforcement and differential reinforcement are two of the most commonly used procedures. Contingent social reinforcement is used typically for performance deficits and requires that the child possess requisite skills in his/her repertoire. The goal is for parents and/or teachers to provide praise or rewards when the child engages in socially appropriate behavior (Sheridan & Walker, 1999).

Differential reinforcement procedures are used to decrease the frequency of undesired behaviors (Hansen, Nangle, & Meyer, 1998; Sheridan & Walker, 1999). It can be accomplished through differential reinforcement of other behaviors (DRO), differential reinforcement of low rates of behaviors (DRL), and differential reinforcement of incompatible behaviors (DRI). Differential reinforcement of other behaviors (DRO) provides reinforcement for any behavior except the target behavior. For example, a child who engages in teasing behavior on the playground may be reinforced for all instances of non-teasing behavior (e.g., playing alone, playing cooperatively with peers, keeping hands and feet to self). The effect is a reduction in the inappropriate target behavior as well as an increase in other prosocial behaviors (Gresham, 2002).

Differential reinforcement of low rates of behavior (DRL) delivers reinforcement for reduced rates of the target behavior. In the example above, a child who typically exhibits high levels of teasing behavior with peers may be reinforced for demonstrating lowered levels of the behavior. DRL procedures decrease the frequency of inappropriate social behaviors, however they rarely increase the frequency of positive behavior. Therefore, DRL strategies may be most helpful when paired with another strategy that teaches prosocial skills to replace the target behavior (Sheridan & Walker, 1999).

Differential reinforcement of incompatible behaviors (DRI) refers to the delivery of reinforcement for behaviors that are incompatible with the target behavior. Unlike DRO and DRL strategies, which primarily attempt to decrease negative behaviors, DRI attempts to increase the frequency of prosocial behaviors. For example, a prosocial behavior that is incompatible with teasing (e.g., giving a compliment) might be reinforced (Gresham, 2002).

School-based programs can effectively prevent and reduce challenging behaviors. School-wide interventions include several components such as monitoring discipline procedures, stressing pro-social skill development, reducing the frequency of negative consequences, and emphasizing early school success (Lewis et al., 1998). School-based procedures are preventive in nature and therefore are implemented in large groups of students, only some of whom may be targeted as needing skill instruction. These approaches increase the likelihood that both the target child and his or her peers will obtain the knowledge and skills necessary to engage in pro-social interactions (Sheridan & Walker, 1999). There are several commercial school-wide intervention/prevention programs available, such as "The Expect Respect Project," "Bully Busters," and the "Olweus Bullying Prevention Program." For comprehensive reviews of these programs, readers are referred to Whitaker et al. (see Chapter 16), Horne and Orpinas (see Chapter 15), and Limber (see Chapter 17).

Treatment Implementation

The third stage of the CBC process is treatment implementation. The primary objective of this stage is to implement the plan developed through the functional assessment across the home and school setting (Sheridan et al., 1996).

A central issue during treatment implementation is treatment integrity, which is defined as the degree to which an intervention is implemented as designed (Gresham, 1989). Adherence to established treatment components may affect intervention outcomes; therefore treatment integrity across home and school is important. School violence intervention integrity may be problematic for numerous reasons. Surveillance of larger areas such as school corridors and stairwells, extensive teaching loads and participation in specialized training may overburden intervention agents. Similarly, distractions and emergencies can sidetrack participants, thereby hindering treatment integrity (Goldstein, 1997).

Several procedures increase treatment integrity of school violence interventions. Procedures such as (a) providing a specific written plan containing intervention steps and responsibilities, (b) conducting direct observations of treatment implementation, (c) arranging times to meet or discuss plan components and modifications, and (d) encouraging consultees to self-monitor intervention implementation (Gresham, 1989) are all possible to effect integrity positively.

An additional consideration for the treatment implementation stage is data collection procedures. Data should continue to be gathered throughout the treatment phase and identical collection procedures are utilized to ensure comparability of baseline and treatment data. To enhance the reliability of data collection, procedures should be simple and easy to use. In addition, it is helpful to provide consultees with collection forms indicating the day and time data are to be gathered (Sheridan et al., 1996).

Treatment Evaluation

The fourth and final stage of CBC is treatment evaluation. There are two main goals of this stage: (a) evaluating treatment effectiveness, and (b) programming for generalization and maintenance (Sheridan & Elliott, 1991; Sheridan et al., 1996).

Evaluating Treatment Effectiveness

Identical assessment methods used throughout the aforementioned stages of CBC (e.g., behavioral observations, parent and teacher ratings) are used to evaluate the effectiveness of the treatments implemented in CBC. The effectiveness of a social intervention is determined by several factors including the degree of behavior change, immediacy of change once treatment is implemented, and maintenance and generalization of behavior change once intervention strategies are no longer in place (Sheridan & Elliott, 1991). Each of these indices of treatment effectiveness can be assessed from direct observational data over the course of treatment. Visual and statistical analyses (e.g., trend, stability, effect sizes) can be conducted to assess the change in the target behavior throughout baseline, treatment, and follow-up phases of the intervention, thereby providing a clear picture of treatment effectiveness.

Additional indices of treatment effectiveness include measures of social validity (Kazdin, 1977; Sheridan & Walker, 1998). Parent and teacher perceptions of social-behavioral change is one outcome measure that accounts for the social validity or meaningfulness of the intervention and consequent behavior change within the child's social environments. Consultee perception data are gathered via direct interviews with the consultant and through rating scales that measure the child's social behavior. Parents and teachers can provide information regarding relationships with peers and perceptions of social status. Consultee reports of behavior change and improved social standing indicate that the treatment implemented in consultation was effective.

Peer comparison is another way to assess the meaningfulness of behavioral change. Observations of not only the target child, but his or her peers, can provide information regarding social behavior in comparison in a normative social context. Data indicating that the child's behavior approximates that of peers provides support for the social skills treatment procedures utilized in consultation.

Programming for Generalization and Maintenance

A second goal of treatment evaluation is concerned with assessing and planning for the generalization and maintenance of treatment effects. Effective social skills treatment programs are those that promote generalization across settings, time, and behaviors. In contrast to a "train and hope" philosophy (whereby social behaviors are taught in decontextualized conditions and are expected to generalize naturally to the criterion environment; Stokes & Baer, 1977), active generalization programming is generally required to promote skill use in natural social settings. Some important generalization strategies that have been documented include: (a) teaching behaviors that are likely to be maintained by naturally occurring contingencies; (b) training across stimuli (e.g., persons and setting); (c) fading response contingencies to approximate naturally occurring consequences; (d) reinforcing application of skills to new and appropriate situations; and (e) including peers in training (Michelson, Sugai, Wood, & Kazdin, 1983; Stokes & Baer, 1977). A foundation for each of these strategies is the notion of developing training experiences that closely approximate the "real world" (Sheridan et al., 1999). It is possible that incorporating real world stimuli, contingencies, and experiences into training procedures will facilitate generalized use of social behaviors, although more research is needed to evaluate this assumption. Likewise, implementation of programs in naturalistic settings and contexts (such as cooperative learning, schoolwide interventions, in vivo conflict mediation, and structured recess programs) is expected to minimize the disconnect between training and criterion settings and thus facilitate generalized skill use.

Generalization between school and home settings is an additional concern in comprehensive social intervention programs, and such procedures are inherent within the CBC model. CBC facilitates generalization through involvement of individuals from both environments in the problem solving process, allowing for comprehensive information gathering, as well as consistent programming and reinforcement across both home and school. Similarly, parents and teachers are in an excellent position to monitor unplanned or undesired intervention effects (Sheridan et al., 1996).

TRANSLATING RESEARCH
INTO PRACTICE: IMPLICATIONS
FOR BULLYING PREVENTION
AND INTERVENTION PROGRAMS

The advantages of using CBC to address concerns related to social competence and bullying in children and adolescents can be illustrated through a case study. The case highlights several key aspects of the process. First, it represents the importance of using a variety of assessment tools to obtain comprehensive data regarding a child's social skills and problems across several settings. Second, it illustrates the utility of linking information gained from assessment to plan development. Third, systematic evaluation of the case is demonstrated. Finally, the process was conducted in the child's natural setting to promote generalization and maintenance of social gains.

Background Information

Matthew was an 8-year-old, third grade male with average intellectual and language abilities who attended a Midwestern parochial school. He displayed an awkward social interaction style, which resulted in teasing and bullying from classmates. Matthew responded to the taunts by becoming physically aggressive with his peers, thereby extending the conflict. He also had a negative reputation with teachers due to his frequent altercations with peers. Matthew's mother initially referred her son to CBC for difficulty developing peer relationships and aggressive behavior. She indicated that he was socially withdrawn and tended to isolate himself from the group.

Problem Identification

Several assessment methods were utilized to gather information regarding Matthew's social interactions and to define the target behavior. Procedures used to assess microsystemic influences included standardized behavior rating scales (Parent and Teacher forms of the Social Skills Rating Scale [SSRS]; Gresham & Elliott, 1990), self-report scales (SSRS—Self Report; Gresham & Elliott, 1990) and direct observations across home and school settings. The combination of measures provided information on Matthew's social interactions, such as responses to bullying and aggressive behavior as well as reactions from others (peers, teachers, parents) across home and school settings.

A Conjoint Problem Identification Interview was conducted to establish a positive working relationship between Matthew's mother and teacher and to prioritize behavioral difficulties. During the meeting, his mother and teacher shared several concerns regarding Matthew's ability to read social cues appropriately. Specific target areas included knowing when another child was interested in the topic of conversation, how to end a conversation, responding to problem situations in a non-aggressive manner, and initiating positive social interactions with peers. Through problem exploration and dialogue, Matthew's mother, teacher, and the consultant determined that the most important behavior (i.e., priority) for the home and school settings was initiation of positive social interactions with peers.

Behavior checklists (SSRS-P, SSRS-T) indicated that Matthew demonstrated poor social initiation skills. Specific items that were rated as never or sometimes true by Matthew's mother and or teacher included "Invites others to join in," "Joins ongoing activity or group without being told to do so," "Introduces himself to new people without being told," and "Invites others to your home." The self-report checklist (SSRS) also demonstrated difficulty with peer interactions. Specific items rated as never or sometimes true by Matthew included "I start talks with class members" and "I make friends easily."

Consultees conducted direct observations of Matthew's social interactions with peers. Specifically, observations were made on Matthew's initiation of pro-social contact with classmates. Direct measures were also utilized. An independent observer conducted twenty-minute direct observations three times per week throughout the process to examine Matthew's social interactions across time and setting.

Problem Analysis

A Conjoint Problem Analysis Interview was conducted to review baseline data, conduct a functional assessment and develop a treatment plan. During the data collection period, direct observations indicated that Matthew initiated one social interaction per day. Observations conducted by Matthew's teacher revealed that Matthew initiated one social interaction in the school setting. Similarly, Matthew's mother reported that her son initiated two social interactions with neighbors each day. It was noted that Matthew was passive in social situations with peers (i.e., he tended to observe play from outside the peer group rather than participate actively). Observations and a review of conditions surrounding his passive behaviors suggested that he was lacking the necessary prerequisite skills to develop appropriate assertive behavior. Based on the data collected, the consultation goal was set at the initiation of two social interactions per day.

Because Matthew did not appear to have the necessary pro-social interaction skills within his repertoire, the team developed a treatment plan geared toward teaching appropriate initiation and maintenance of positive interactions with peers. The plan, implemented across home and school settings, consisted of two components: (a) a social skills training program for Matthew that included modeling, coaching and behavioral rehearsal; and (b) instruction for the parents and teacher to prompt consistent and appropriate social interactions.

The *social skills program* was presented to Matthew and three of his peers. Within the program, discrete skills were taught for initiating conversations and joining into ongoing group activities. The program facilitator modeled the sequence of behavior necessary to perform the social skill. Matthew was encouraged to practice the newly learned social skills by role-playing with his peers. The role-plays took place in a nearby classroom to ensure a structured and safe practice setting. Once Matthew demonstrated skill acquisition, he was provided with opportunities to practice in more natural settings, such as the classroom and on the playground. Skill acquisition occurred when Matthew successfully completed eight sub-steps comprising the initiation skill (see *Appendix*).

Prompting from Matthew's parents and teachers served as the second component of the program. To address mesosytemic issues, Matthew's family, teacher and the consultant identified socially appropriate initiation behaviors as well as appropriate responses to bullying or aggression from peers. It was important to ensure both home and school settings were providing consistent messages on how to initiate contact with peers and how to respond when peers engaged in bullying behavior. The program leader taught the parents and teacher specific in vivo cueing procedures that would facilitate pro-social interactions. Matthew's mother and teacher were encouraged to observe Matthew's social behaviors and approach him in situations when he could use an appropriate social skill, but failed to do so. They made a statement reminding Matthew of the specific social skill steps and suggested that he use those steps in the current situation. Examples of prompts included "Matthew, today at recess would be a good place to practice your skill of . . ." In addition, Matthew's parents and teachers provided specific praise and feedback regarding Matthew's performance of the skill. Praise procedures were based on the IFEED acronym (i.e., praise was delivered Immediately, Frequently, with Enthusiasm, with Eye contact, and Descriptively; Rhode, Jenson, & Reavis, 1992; Sheridan, 1998). An example of an effective praise statement is "Matthew, you did a great job starting a conversation with Sally!"

Treatment Evaluation

During the Treatment Evaluation stage, behavioral rating scales and direct observations were used to evaluate the effectiveness of the treatment plan. The SSRS-Parent Form, SSRS-Teacher Form, and SSRS-Self Report were re-administered following the treatment plan. Improvements were noted on parent, teacher and self-ratings of initiation of social interactions.

Observations from Matthew's mother and teacher revealed improvement in Matthew's social interactions with peers (see Fig. 13.1). Matthew's mother reported that her son improved his rate of initiating conversations to an average of five times per day. The teacher reported that Matthew increased his initiation of social interactions with peers to four times per day. Independent observations in the school setting were consistent with teacher observations. Evaluation of the plan indicated that the goal had been exceeded. Matthew's parents and teachers

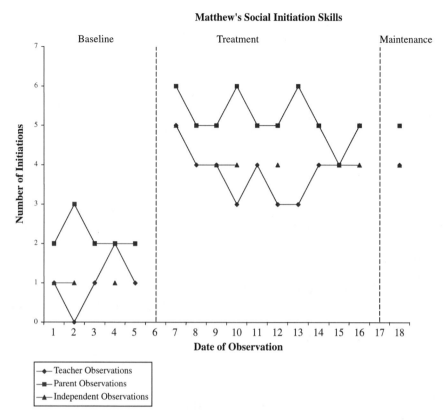

FIG. 13.1. Matthew's social-initiation behaviors
across home and school settings.

continued to provide Matthew with opportunities to practice his skills in natural environments to promote generalization. Maintenance of treatment gains was facilitated by a gradual fading of specific praise on Matthew's performance. Specifically, Matthew's parents and teacher began to provide intermittent praise and feedback following a prosocial interaction with peers.

Despite improvement in Matthew's social interactions with peers, some challenges were encountered during implementation of the plan. Time involvement on behalf of the parents, teacher and consultant was a challenging aspect of the case. The consultation team met bimonthly for several months. Each meeting lasted approximately one hour. Although regularly scheduled meetings provided opportunities for ongoing communication and plan modifications, it required flexibility with schedules, numerous hours spent within the school building and high levels of investment on the part of the parents and teacher. Whereas these were deemed necessary and appropriate for Matthew's case, the nature of involvement may look different for each school and family.

Summary

Bullying and victimization among children and youth are common concerns of families and schools today. An ecological approach to address such issues encourages conceptualization of issues and interventions at multiple ecological levels, including the child in his/her immediate setting, adults within multiple environments, and importantly, relationships among those environments. The focus of this chapter was interventions at the mesosytemic level through the development of meaningful and supportive partnerships between home and school contexts. Conjoint behavioral consultation (CBC) is one method by which homes and schools can work together to promote healthy social development of children and youth. Through this model of consultation, a range of ecologically relevant variables that effect children's social functioning in home and school are explored. Such analyses provide relevant contextual information that contributes to the design, implementation, and evaluation of effective interventions at the child, adult, or system level. Continued collaboration among home and school systems is essential and can be promoted by involving parents and teachers in a joint problem-solving process, allowing for comprehensive and on-going attention to address bullying and victimization concerns for children.

REFERENCES

Baker, D. P., & Stevenson, D. L. (1986). Mothers' strategies for children's school achievement: Managing the transition to high school. *Sociology of Education, 59,* 156–166.

Becher, R. M. (1984). *Parent involvement: A review of research and principles for successful practice.* Urbana, IL: ERIC Clearinghouse on Elementary and Early Childhood Education. (ERIC Document Reproduction Service No. ED 247–032).

Bloom, B. S. (1985). *Developing talents in young people.* New York: Ballantine Books.

Bracken, B. A. (1993). *Assessment of interpersonal relations.* Austin, TX: Pro-Ed.

Bronfenbrenner, U. (1979). *The ecology of human development.* Cambridge, MA.: Harvard University Press.

Cartledge, G., & Johnson, C. T. (1997). School violence and cultural sensitivity. In A. P. Goldstein, & J. Conoley (Eds.), *School violence intervention: A practical handbook* (pp. 391–425). New York: Guilford Press.

Christenson, S. L. (1995). Supporting home-school collaboration. In A. Thomas & J. Grimes (Eds.), *Best practices in school psychology III* (pp. 253–267). Washington, DC: National Association of School Psychologists.

Christenson, S. L., & Sheridan, S. M. (2001). *Schools and families: Creating essential connections for learning.* New York: Guilford Press.

Clark, R. M. (1988). Parents as providers of linguistic and social capital: How do the literacy skills of low achievers and high achievers differ, and how do parents influence these differences? *Educational Horizons, 66*(2), 93–95.

Clark, R. M. (1993). Homework-focused parenting practices that positively affect student achievement. In N. F. Chavkin (Ed.), *Families and schools in a pluralistic society* (pp. 85–105). Albany: State University of New York Press.

Collins, C. H., Moles, O., & Cross, M. (1982). *The home-school connections: Selected partnership programs in large cities.* Boston, MA: Institute for Responsive Education.

Comer, J. P. (1988). Educating poor minority children. *Scientific American, 259*(5), 2–8.

Comer, J. P., & Haynes, N. M. (1991). Parent involvement in schools: An ecological approach. *Elementary School Journal, 91*(3), 271–278.

Conoley, J. C. (1987). Schools and families: Theoretical and practical bridges. *Professional School Psychology, 2,* 191–203.

Crick, N. R., & Dodge, K. A. (1994). A review and reformulation of social information-processing mechanisms in children's social adjustment. *Psychological Bulletin, 115,* 74–101.

Davies, D. (1993). Benefits and barriers to parent involvement: From Portugal to Boston to Liverpool. In N. F. Chavkin (Ed.), *Families and schools in a pluralistic society* (pp. 53–72). Albany: State University of New York Press.

Eagle, E. (1989, April). *Socioeconomic status, family structure, and parental involvement: The correlates of achievement.* Paper presented at the annual meeting of the American Educational Research Association, San Francisco. (ERIC Document Reproduction Service No. ED 307 332)

Elias, M. J., & Tobias, S. E. (1996). *Social problem solving: Interventions in the schools.* New York: Guildford Press.

Elliott, S. N., & Busse, R. T. (1991). Social skills assessment and intervention with children and adolescents: Guidelines for assessment and training procedures. *School Psychology International, 12,* 63–83.

Epstein, J. L. (1986). Parents' reactions to teacher practices of parent involvement. *Elementary School Journal, 86,* 277–294.

Epstein, J. L. (1991). Effects on student achievement of teachers' practices of involvement. In B. S. Silvern (Ed.), *Advances in reading/language research: Vol. 5. Literacy through family, community, and school interaction* (pp. 261–276). Greenwich, CT: JAI Press.

Epstein, J. L. (1995). School/family/community partnerships: Caring for the children we share. *Phi Delta Kappan, 76,* 701–712.

Epstein, J. L., & Becker, H. J. (1982). Teacher practices of parent involvement. *The Elementary School Journal, 83,* 103–113.

Estrada, P., Arsenio, W. F., Hess, R. D., & Holloway, S. (1987). Affective quality of the mother-child relationship: Longitudinal consequences for children's school-relevant, cognitive-functioning. *Developmental Psychology, 23,* 210–215.

Fehrmann, P. G., Keith, T. Z., & Reimers, T. M. (1987). Home influences on school learning: Direct and indirect effects of parent involvement on high school grades. *Journal of Educational Research, 80,* 330–337.

Goldstein, A. P. (1997). Controlling vandalism: The person-environment duet. In A. P. Goldstein & J. C. Conoley (Eds.), *School violence intervention: A practical handbook* (pp. 290–321). New York: Guilford Press.

Goldstein, A. P., Harootunian, B., & Conoley J. C. (1994). *Student aggression: Prevention, management, and replacement training.* New York: Guilford Press.

Gresham, F. M. (1989). Assessment of treatment integrity in school consultation and prereferral intervention. *School Psychology Review, 18,* 37–50.

Gresham, F. M. (2002). Best practices in social skills training. In A. Thomas & J. Grimes (Eds.), *Best practices in school psychology – IV* (pp. 1029–1040). Washington D.C.: National Association of School Psychologists.

Gresham, F. M., & Elliott, S. N. (1990). *Social Skills Rating System: Manual.* Circle Pines, MN: American Guidance Services.

Gresham, F. M., & Nagle, R. J. (1980). Social skills trained with children: Responsiveness to modeling and coaching as a function of peer orientation. *Journal of Consulting and Clinical Psychology, 48*, 718–729.

Hansen, D. A. (1986). Family-school articulations: The effects of interaction rule mismatch. *American Educational Research Journal, 23*, 643–659.

Hansen, D. J., Nangle, D. W., & Meyer, K. A. (1998). Enhancing the effectiveness of social skills interventions with adolescents. *Education and Treatment of Children, 21*, 489–513.

Haring, T. G. (1992). The context of social competence: Relations, relationships, and generalization. In S. L. Odom, S. R. McConnell, & M. A. McEvoy (Eds.), *Social competence of young children with disabilities: Issues and strategies for intervention* (pp. 307–320). Baltimore, MD: Brookes.

Hoier, T. S., & Cone, J. D. (1987). Target selection of social skills for children: The template-matching procedure. *Behavior Modification, 11*, 137–163.

Hoier, T. S., McConnell, S., & Pallay, A. G. (1987). Observational assessment for planning and evaluating educational transitions: An initial analysis of template matching. *Behavioral Assessment, 9*, 5–19.

Hops, H., Walker, H. M., & Greenwood, C. R. (1988). *Procedures for establishing effective relationship skills (PEERS): Manual for consultants.* Delray, FL: Educational Achievement Systems.

Kagan, S. L. & Schraft, C. M. (1982). *When parents and schools come together: Differential outcomes of parent involvement in urban schools.* Boston, MA: Institute for Responsive Education. (ERIC Document Reproduction Service N. ED 281-951)

Kazdin, A. E. (1977). Assessing the clinical or applied importance of behavior change through social validation. *Behavior Modification, 1*, 427–452.

Kellaghan, T., Sloane, K., Alvarez, B., & Bloom, B. S. (1993). *The home environment and school learning: Promoting parental involvement in the education of children.* San Francisco: Jossey-Bass.

Keller, H. R., & Tapasak, R. C. (1997). Classroom management. In A. P. Goldstein, & J. C. Conoley (Eds.), *School violence intervention: A practical handbook* (pp. 107–126). New York: Guilford Press.

Kratochwill, T. R., & Stoiber, K. C. (2002). Evidence-based interventions in school psychology: Conceptual foundations of the procedural and coding manual of Division 16 and the Society for the Study of School Psychology task force. *School Psychology Quarterly, 17*, 341–389.

Lazar, L., & Darlington, R. B. (1978). *Summary: Lasting effects after preschool.* Ithaca, NY: Cornell University Consortium for Longitudinal Studies. (ERIC Document Reproduction Service No. Ed 175–523)

Lewis, T. J., Sugai, G., & Colvin, G. (1998). Reducing problem behavior through school-wide system of effective behavioral support: Investigation of a school-wide social skills training program and contextual interventions. *School Psychology Review, 27*, 446–459.

Marjoribanks, K. (1988). Perceptions of family environments, educational and occupational outcomes: Social-status differences. *Perceptual and Motor Skills, 66*, 3–9.

Merrell, K. W., & Gimpel, G. A. (1998). *Social skills of children and adolescents: Conceptualization, assessment, treatment.* Mahwah, NJ: Lawrence Erlbaum Associates.

Michelson, L., Sugai, D. P., Wood, R. P., & Kazdin, A. E. (1983). *Social skills assessment and training with children: An empirically based approach.* New York: Plenum.

Mize, J. (1995). Coaching preschool children in social skills: A cognitive-social learning curriculum. In G. Cartledge & J. F. Milburn (Eds.), *Teaching social skills to children and youth: Innovative approaches* (3rd ed., pp. 237–261). Boston: Allyn & Bacon.

Pianta, R., & Walsh, D. (1996). *High risk children in schools: Constructing sustaining relationships.* New York: Routledge.

Resnick, M. D., Bearman, P. S., Blum, R. W., Bauman, K. E., Harris, K. M., Jones, J., Tabor, J., Beuhring, T., Sieving, R. E., Shew, M., Ireland, M., Bearinger, L. H., & Udry, J. (1997). Protecting adolescents from harm: Findings from the National Longitudinal Study on adolescent health. *The Journal of the American Medical Association, 278*, 823–832.

Rhode, G., Jenson, W. R., & Reavis, H. K. (1992). *The tough kid book*. Longmont, CO: Sopris West.

Rumberger, R. W. (1995). Dropping out of middle school: A multilevel analysis of students and schools. *American Educational Research Journal, 32*, 583–625.

Sattes, B. (1985). *Parent involvement: A review of the literature* (Report No. 21). Charleston, WV: Appalachia Educational Laboratory.

Sheridan, S. M (1995). *The tough kid social skills book*. Longmont, CO: Sopris West.

Sheridan, S. M. (1998). *Why don't they like me? Helping your child make and keep friends*. Longmont, CO: Sopris West.

Sheridan, S. M., Dee, C. C., Morgan, J. C., McCormick, M. E., & Walker, D. (1996). A multimethod intervention for social skills deficits in children with ADHD and their parents. *School Psychology Review, 25*, 57–76.

Sheridan, S. M., & Elliott, S. N. (1991). Behavioral consultation as a process for linking the assessment and treatment of social skills. *Journal of Educational and Psychological Consultation, 2*, 151–173.

Sheridan, S. M., Hungelmann, A., & Maughan, D. (1999). A contextualized framework for social skills assessment, intervention, and generalization. *School Psychology Review, 28*, 84–103.

Sheridan, S. M., Kratochwill, T. R., & Bergan, J. R. (1996). *Conjoint behavioral consultation: A procedural manual*. New York: Plenum Press.

Sheridan, S. M., & Walker, D. (1999). Social skills in context: Considerations for assessment, intervention, and generalization. In C. R. Reynolds & T. B. Gutkin (Eds.), *The handbook of school psychology* (3rd ed., pp. 686–708). New York: Wiley & Sons.

Slavin, R. E. (1990). Research on cooperative learning: Consensus and controversy. *Educational Leadership, 47*, 52–54.

Steinberg, L., Mounts, N. S., Lamborn, S. D., & Dornbusch, S. M. (1991). Authoritative parenting and adolescent adjustment across varied ecological niches. *Journal of Research on Adolescence, 1*(1), 19–36.

Stevenson, D., & Baker, D. (1987). The family-school relation and the child's school performance. *Child Development, 58*, 1348–1357.

Stokes, T., & Baer, D. (1977). An implicit technology of generalization. *Journal of Applied Behavior Analysis, 19*, 349–367.

Walker, H., & McConnell, S. (1988). *Walker-McConnell Scale of Social Competence*. Austin, TX: Pro-Ed.

Witt, J. C., Martens, B. K., & Elliott, S. N. (1984). Factors affecting teachers' judgments of the acceptability of behavioral interventions: Time involvement, behavior problem severity, and type of intervention. *Behavior Therapy, 15*, 204–209.

APPENDIX: STEPS OF SOCIAL ENTRY

_____ 1. Faces the other person (i.e., body is square to the other when appropriate, or head turns toward other when in conversation). To receive credit, this behavior must occur for the majority of the interaction.

_____ 2. Uses eye contact (i.e., eyes look into face of other in a comfortable and appropriate manner, rather than on floor, out window, or staring inappropriately). To receive credit, this behavior must occur for the majority of the interaction.

_____ 3. Maintains appropriate physical space (i.e., approximately two arms lengths away when in conversation, or appropriately closer or further when the situation calls for it such as when whispering or playing a team sport). To receive credit, this behavior must occur for the majority of the interactions.

_____ 4. Maintains a neutral body posture (i.e., hands, arms and legs appear loose and relaxed, fists are not clenched). To receive credit, this behavior must occur for the majority of the interaction.

_____ 5. Uses an appropriate voice (i.e., voice is audible to those in immediate proximity but not to persons at a distance of 10 feet or more unless situation calls for it, inflection in voice is appropriate to the conversation rather than sarcastic or snide). To receive credit, this behavior must occur for the majority of the interaction.

_____ 6. Waits for a good time (i.e., does not interrupt on-going conversation or activity such that behavior evokes negative reaction from others; allows no more than 5–7 seconds to elapse before making a clear verbal initiation).

_____ 7. Makes opening statement (i.e., uses appropriate voice tone and emotional tone and appropriate greeting to initiate interaction such as "Hello!," "Hi!," "How are you doing?," states the other child's name).

_____ 8. Appropriately initiates interaction or asks to join (i.e., uses appropriate voice and emotional tone, and spontaneously makes a statement or gesture clearly requesting another to engage in a mutual activity or conversation).

_____   Total

14

Outcome Measures to Assess the Effectiveness of Bullying-prevention Programs in the Schools

Stephen S. Leff, Thomas J. Power,
and Amy B. Goldstein
*The Children's Hospital of Philadelphia
and The University of Pennsylvania
School of Medicine*

There are numerous innovative bullying and aggression-prevention programs being used in schools across the country and worldwide. Due to the infancy of applied research in this area, many of these programs lack appropriate data collection procedures, well-validated and community-responsive outcome measures, and procedures to ensure consistent program implementation (Leff, Power, Manz, Costigan, & Nabors, 2001). This chapter presents a review of the most commonly used sets of measures to identify aggressors and bullies and to determine the effectiveness of bullying and aggression prevention programs. The review will focus on the strengths and limitations of each set of measures. In addition, the chapter describes how our research team has collaborated with the adults who supervise students on the playground and in the lunchroom to develop and validate several innovative community-responsive questionnaires that can be used in conjunction with other methods to evaluate the effectiveness of bullying prevention and intervention efforts. The chapter concludes by discussing how to translate research to practice in the development outcome measures designed to evaluate the effectiveness of school-based bullying prevention programs.

Definition of School Bullying

Prior research on peer bullying has focused primarily upon understanding the characteristics and comorbidities associated with physical forms of bullying (i.e., hitting, pushing, fighting). Much of this research has been with boys who exhibit aggression in a direct and physical manner towards their peers (e.g., Block, 1983). However, more recent research has found that children can express their aggression, and bully others, in multiple ways (e.g., Crick & Grotpeter, 1995; Rys & Bear, 1997). For example, research has found that boys' and girls' overall aggression levels are actually somewhat similar, but that girls only occasionally display overtly aggressive behaviors (e.g., Crick & Grotpeter, 1995). Instead, girls are much more likely to use relational aggression, defined as "harming others through purposeful manipulation and damage of their peer relationships" (Crick & Grotpeter, 1995, p. 711). This type of aggression often takes the form of gossiping, leaving others out on purpose, or threatening to withdraw friendships.

In the current chapter, bullying is defined as "the systematic abuse of power" (Smith & Sharp, 1994, p. 2). More specifically, bullying behavior is thought to be a dynamic process that occurs within the context of a relationship, such that three key criteria are met. First, the bully exhibits behavior directed towards the victim that is designed to hurt, harm, or damage the victim physically, socially, or emotionally. Second, this behavior occurs only when there is an imbalance of power between the bully and victim (Smith & Sharp, 1994) such that the bully has more power and authority than the victim. An imbalance of power can be physical (i.e., the bully may be physically stronger or larger than the victim) or psychological (i.e., the bully may have higher social status than the victim or be able to readily damage the victim's social status) in nature. Third, the bullying behavior happens repeatedly over time. Thus, bullying does not occur when two children of equal strength or power become involved in an occasional argument or conflict (Olweus, 1984). This definition of bullying is broad enough to incorporate both physical and relational means of bullying others.

Harmful Effects of Bullying and Victimization

The issue of school bullying has received enormous media attention over the past few years due to school shootings in a number of areas across the country. Bullying and victimization are problems that are common in schools. For instance, recent research indicates that between 20% and 30% of elementary age children are the perpetrators or victims of ongoing hitting, pushing, or teasing by their peers (e.g., Leff, Kupersmidt, Patterson, & Power, 1999; Nansel et al., 2001).

Much research from the developmental psychology literature has demonstrated that the perpetrators and victims of aggression are at great risk for developing behavioral, emotional, and academic difficulties. For instance, students who are physically aggressive towards others often have immature social relationships and are rejected by their peers (e.g., Coie & Kupersmidt, 1983; Pope & Bierman, 1999). In addition, because overtly aggressive behavior is associated with academic problems (Kazdin, 1994), difficulty regulating emotional arousal (e.g., Cummings, Iannotti, & Zahn-Waxler, 1985; Lochman & Wells, 1996), and social problem-solving deficits (e.g., Dodge, 1986; Lochman & Dodge, 1994), it is not surprising that many of these children experience increasing psychological difficulties as they grow older (e.g., Coie, Terry, Lenox, Lochman, & Hyman, 1995; Loeber, Green, Lahey, & Kalb, 2000). Other research has documented that students who are relationally aggressive towards their peers are at high risk for externalizing and internalizing problems (e.g., Crick, 1996; Crick & Grotpeter, 1995).

Victims of peer aggression are also at risk for internalizing problems, including depression, anxiety, loneliness, and low self-esteem (e.g., Crick & Grotpeter, 1996; Kochenderfer & Ladd, 1996; Slee, 1995; Olweus, 1984). They may also experience peer relationship difficulties (Hodges & Perry, 1999; Perry, Kusel, & Perry, 1988). In addition, peer victimization is related to school maladjustment and has been associated with not liking school and wanting to avoid the school environment (Kochenderfer & Ladd, 1996).

Given that aggressors and victims both experience a host of behavioral, and social difficulties, aggression/bullying prevention programs have typically focused upon teaching these at-risk children better social, social-cognitive processing, and/or social problem-solving skills (e.g., The Anger Coping Program, Lochman, 1992; the Brain Power Program, Hudley, & Graham, 1993) or teaching all children these skills (e.g., The Bullying Prevention Program, Olweus, 1984, 1993; Promoting Alternative Thinking Strategies (PATHS), Conduct Problems Prevention Research Group, 1999a). Recently, Leff and colleagues reviewed the literature on universal and selective/indicated school-based aggression prevention programs in elementary schools across the nation (Leff, Power, Manz et al., 2001). Universal programs provide prevention services for all children in a school, while selective/indicated programs are more targeted intervention services for children at high risk for being aggressive, or who have already been identified as aggressive. Each program identified was systematically reviewed on the following criteria established by Chambless and Hollon (1998): (a) an experimental group design including random assignment procedures; (b) a well-documented treatment procedure; (c) uniform therapist training and treatment integrity monitoring procedures; (d) multi-method outcome measures demonstrating adequate reliability and validity; (e) assessment of effects at six month follow-up; and (f) replication conducted by different investigators. Programs that met all criteria were designated as "efficacious" (i.e., established), and programs that met all criteria except for an independent replication were designated as "possibly efficacious" (i.e., extremely promising). No programs were found to be "efficacious" and five programs were found to be "possibly efficacious".

Overview of Outcome Measures

The purpose of this chapter is to review the classes of outcome measures most commonly used to evaluate the effectiveness of bullying prevention programs. As such, the authors chose to examine nursing logs of injuries, discipline referrals, student self-report measures, teacher report measures, peer sociometric measures, and behavioral observation systems. In addition, the authors describe three newly designed measures that are based on ratings provided by playground and lunchroom supervisors (Leff, Power, Costigan, & Manz, in press; Leff, Power, Costigan, Manz, & Clarke, 2001). These latter measures were designed in partnership with school personnel and community members to facilitate community-responsive assessment. Parent report measures of bullying were not reviewed because there are few measures of this type available and because parents are not typically present at school to witness bullying episodes.

Each class of measures is reviewed across the following categories: (a) *brief description*, including an overview of the rationale and main uses of each class of measures; (b) *psychometric properties*, including reliability and validity information; (c) *strengths*; (d) *limitations*; and (e) *future directions* for research and practice. An overview of strengths, limitations, and recommended uses for each measure is provided in Table 14.1.

Nursing Logs of Injuries

Brief Description.   Nurses' logs of encounters with students who present with injuries represent a relatively straightforward way in which to collect school level data to assess the effectiveness of school-wide bullying prevention programs (Krug, Brener, Dahlberg, Ryan, & Powell, 1997). This methodology is related to the practice of using medical records and hospital discharge summaries as outcome variables for community-based interventions (Davidson et al., 1994). Given that the goals of bullying and violence prevention programs are often to decrease the incidence of fighting and student injuries, researchers hypothesize that, if an intervention is effective, there should be a decrease in visits to the school nurse for fighting-related injuries (Brener, Krug, Dahlberg, & Powell, 1997).

Psychometric Properties.   The psychometric properties of nursing logs have not been well-established. A review of the literature on the use of nursing logs yielded only one study, conducted by Brener and colleagues (1997). Results of this study suggested that this method has questionable reliability and validity (Brener et al., 1997). For example, it is difficult to ensure that personnel within the same school follow the same standardized procedure in collecting, coding,

TABLE 14.1
Summary of Outcome Measures

Measure	Strengths	Limitations	Recommended Uses
Nursing Logs	Easy to collect No disruption of class time Reflects a wide range of school contexts Records injuries, which are often physically aggressive actions	No systematic procedures for recording Lack of psychometric properties May not be sensitive to relational aggression Difficult to determine if necessary conditions of bullying (e.g., intentional injury, power differential) are met	As a supplement to other measures being used to identify physically aggressive children In conjunction with other measures to determine rates of injury in a school
Discipline Referrals	Feasibility and ease of use No disruption of classroom learning Reflects a wide range of school contexts Information is easily tabulated	Lack of standardization in data collection Subjectivity of measure Limited generalizability May not be sensitive to relational aggression May underestimate rates of aggression for girls while overestimating rates for boys	Guide decision making when choosing a bullying-prevention program As a supplement to other measures being used to identify physically aggressive children
Self-Report Measures	Widely accepted by researchers, educators, and students Established psychometric properties for some measures Likely sensitive to relational and physical bullying and victimization Provides unique information about bully or victim	Biases in reporting may underestimate rates of bullying and victimization Administration/data collection may interfere with class time Using anonymous self-reports makes analyzing change over time difficult	To better understand subjective experiences of bully and/or victim As an outcome measure for universal or indicated interventions (provided that the same children participate at pre- and post-testing)
Teacher Report Measures	Easy to administer, score, interpret Established psychometrics for many measures May eliminate parent concerns about children participating in peer report methods	May be too time consuming to complete on multiple students Not sensitive to playground context May not be sensitive to relational bullying	Can be used to screen out children who are not involved in bullying problems In conjunction with peer reports to identify aggressive children

(Continued)

273

TABLE 14.1
(Continued)

Measure	Strengths	Limitations	Recommended Uses
Teacher Report Measures			As an outcome measure for indicated intervention for physical aggression/bullying
Peer Sociometric Measures (Peer Nominations & Peer Rating Scales)	Widely accepted by researchers Strong psychometric properties Sensitive to relational and physical aggression and victimization Sensitive to all school contexts	Labor- and time-intensive Parents, teachers, and institutional review boards may not fully understand or appreciate the reasons for using Low participation rates may compromise generalizability	Arguably, the best method to identify bullies, aggressors, and victims (physical and relational) Peer rating scales can be used as outcome measures for indicated or universal intervention
Behavioral Observations	Can be used in playground settings Has been used to document impact of bullying programs Adequate psychometrics have been established for some systems	More complicated systems are time- and labor-intensive May require extensive training of coders Reactivity issues Has not been used for relational aggression for elementary age children Requires validation in each new school used in	Can be used as an outcome measure for universal or indicated intervention Strong method for examining children's play behaviors and physical aggression on playground
Playground Supervisor Methods	Feasibility and ease of use No disruption of classroom learning Created in partnership with school staff and community members Sensitive to playground/lunchroom context Provides school-level data Focuses upon important school climate variables	Does not provide data on individual children More validity data is needed on PEQ and LEQ More research needed related to relational aggression	Guide decision making when choosing a bullying-prevention program As a supplement to other measures in determining outcome of universal bullying-prevention programs

and analyzing this information. In addition, there are no uniform procedures for gathering this information across schools, thereby making comparisons of nursing logs from different schools almost impossible. Further, it is difficult to ensure that all visits to the nurse are recorded, which may bias the results.

Strengths. There are several strengths in using nursing logs (Brener et al., 1997). First, they are extremely easy to collect. As most schools have a mechanism already in place to collect nursing logs of injuries this type of data requires little time or financial expense. In contrast, developing questionnaires can be very time consuming and expensive. Second, as the nurse collects the data, there is no disruption of class time or school schedule. Third, as compared to peer and self-report measures, nursing reports of injuries do not require informed parental consent. Finally, this method is free from effects of time-sampling bias (e.g., collecting data just before holidays or at the end of the school year), as data are collected throughout the school year (Brener et al., 1997).

Another benefit to using this method is that the data gathered reflect behavior across a wide range of school contexts. As children may be referred to the nurse from any number of school locations (e.g., classroom, lunchroom, playground) nurses may track where a student was when they were injured. This method may also be an appropriate outcome measure for school-wide bullying prevention programs as it can easily provide aggregate school-level data (Brener et al., 1997).

Limitations. Although nursing logs are relatively easy to use, there are several limitations to consider when including them as an outcome measure. One of the main limitations is the aforementioned lack of strong psychometric properties. Nursing logs have both questionable reliability and validity. Because nursing logs typically reflect the results of a physical action (i.e., a punch or a kick), they are likely to be insensitive to relational forms of aggression (i.e., damage to a child's social standing. Further, although rates of physical actions may be recorded, it would likely be difficult for nurses to differentiate between intentional and unintentional injuries (with the former being much more relevant to determine effectiveness of a bullying intervention). Related, it would also be challenging for a nurse to determine whether or not an injury was the result of a bullying incident (e.g., due to a power differential) without extensive knowledge of all participating students. Finally, nursing logs may underestimate the extent of aggression or bullying, as they record primarily physical actions that result in injury.

Future Directions. Future directions should focus on improving the ways in which nurses gather data so that their reports may be included in research studies and may be more helpful in documenting and directing clinical services. Steps to be taken include standardizing the fields of data to be collected and training school personnel in how to maintain the logs (Brener et al., 1997). These steps should be implemented by having researchers and educators partner with school nurses and community members to ensure that nursing logs of injuries are documenting socially meaningful behaviors that occur within the school.

Discipline Referrals

Brief Description.   Typically, schools track student misbehavior through written reports to the main office generated by a teacher or by another school staff member (Wright & Dusek, 1998). Similar to the rationale for using nursing logs, it is hypothesized that, if a bullying or aggression prevention program is effective, there should be a decrease in student referrals to the office for misbehavior.

Psychometric Properties.   The psychometric properties of discipline referrals have not been well established, and are a limitation of their use. The reliability is threatened by the subjectivity of the methodology. Although the actual discipline referral may be an objective, measurable event, teachers and school personnel, both within and across schools, may vary considerably in their definition of a referable behavior. This potential difference in definition, combined with a range of teacher tolerance for behavior difficulties, impacts when, and if, a discipline referral is made. To date, there has been no systematic study of the variables moderating an educator's decision to use a discipline referral (Nelson, Benner, Reid, Epstein, & Currin, 2002). As a result, discipline referrals have limited generalizability both within and between schools.

Recent research suggests that discipline referrals are not sensitive enough to be used as the sole screening measure to identify at-risk school-age children (Nelson et al., 2002). For instance, Nelson and colleagues (2002) found that many children who were identified as scoring within the clinical or borderline clinical range on a commonly-used teacher report measure did not receive any discipline referrals. In this study, using discipline referrals alone would have resulted in not identifying many children whom the teachers rated as having considerable difficulties.

Other aspects of discipline referrals create confounds to data analyses, making their meaning as an outcome measure complicated to understand. For example, a minority of students typically account for a disproportionate number of discipline referrals. Thus, for a bullying prevention program to have a measurable impact on rates of discipline referrals, there would need to be a significant decrease in discipline referrals for students who are likely to be the most troubled. This problem may be averted by not only looking at the number of referrals for a school, overall, but also for individual students. Second, a recent study found that discipline referrals increase over the course of the school year (Tobin, Sugai, & Colvin, 2000). As a result, these potential seasonal effects, as well as possible changes in teachers' tolerance levels for various behaviors, must be accounted for when using this variable as an outcome measure.

Strengths.   Similar to nursing logs of injuries, feasibility and ease of use are strengths of discipline referrals. The information is easily accessible, can be compiled into frequency counts for different classes of behaviors, and the procedures do not disrupt classroom learning (Wright & Dusek, 1998). And, as was noted with respect to nursing logs of injuries, discipline referrals are advantageous as the referral may originate from any area of the school and reflects behaviors across a wide variety of school contexts. Discipline referrals may supplement other measures used to identify students who are frequently getting into trouble for physically bullying others.

Limitations. Overall, discipline referrals appear to have limited utility as an outcome measure for bullying programs. Although this type of data is readily available and reflects variable school contexts, many schools may not collect or record the data in an accurate and consistent manner. The lack of standardization limits the data's generalizability. Using this type of measure may also underestimate rates of aggression among girls. Due to the fact that boys are more likely than girls to engage in physical aggression (e.g., Crick & Grotpeter, 1995), discipline referrals may underidentify girls, who tend to engage in relational forms of aggression that may not result in a disciplinary problem.

Future Directions. Nelson and colleagues (2002) recommended that the reliability and validity of discipline referrals be improved before this measure is used in program development, as an outcome measure, or for early screening. In addition, similar to nursing reports of injuries, partnerships between researchers, school administrators, and community members are needed to ensure that the behaviors for which students are given discipline referrals are behaviors that the school and community are concerned about and believe should be targets for intervention. An alternative strategy is to use discipline referrals as needs assessment data for determining what type of prevention program may be most appropriate for a particular school (Sprague, Sugai, Horner, & Walker, 1999).

Self-Report Measures

Brief Description. Self-report methods may be the most commonly used method for examining the prevalence of bullying and victimization (Rigby, 2002). Typically children are provided definitions for bullying or victimization, and then asked to rate how often these behaviors occur at school. The most widely known and used self-report measure of bullying is based on Dan Olweus' self report of bullying questionnaire (e.g., Olweus, 1993). This questionnaire asks children to report how frequently they bully and/or are the victim of bullying across varied school contexts. The original questionnaire has been translated, disseminated, and adapted for use in many countries across the world, including the United States, The Netherlands, Norway, England, and Japan (Smith, Cowie, Olafsson, & Liefooghe, 2002).

Psychometric Properties. Although Olweus' self-report measure has been used by numerous researchers, nationally and internationally, the psychometric properties of this and related measures are difficult to determine. This is primarily due to the fact that, when the measure is translated into a new language, its psychometric properties need to be re-established in that language and with the new population to which the measure is administered. Oftentimes, information about the psychometric properties of the measures within specific populations is lacking in the published literature.

Results of psychometric analyses have been reported on several newer self-report measures. For example, Ladd and Kochenderfer-Ladd (2002) provided data suggesting that a brief, four-item, self-report measure of victimization had moderate internal consistency (i.e., the items appear to measure the same dimension), was relatively stable across grade, and correlated in the expected directions with indices of relational adjustment (i.e., loneliness and peer rejection). In addition, factor analyses, internal consistency analyses, and correlations with related measures have been reported for a self-report measure of physical and relational aggression (Children's Peer Relations Scale; Crick & Grotpeter, 1995) and for a self-report measure of physical and relational victimization (Social Experience Questionnaire; Crick & Grotpeter, 1996).

There are other methodological issues to consider with respect to self-reports that influence both their psychometric properties and use. For example, the accuracy and sophistication of children's responses on these measures are, in part, related to children's age and cognitive maturity. Research suggests that younger children may define bullying more broadly than older children (Madsen, 1996; Smith & Levan, 1995). As a result, younger children completing self-report measures may be less discriminating as to what constitutes bullying behavior than older children (Smith & Levan, 1995). It is also possible that children may confuse "bullying" with "aggression" when responding to questionnaires (Rigby, 2002). Both of these issues may independently influence the construct validity of the measure; the respondents (children) may apply a definition of bullying that is different from the one intended by the researchers.

Strengths.   Much of what we know about bullying and victimization has come from self-report measures, and they are widely accepted by researchers, teachers, and students. These measures appear to be sensitive to relational and physical forms of aggression and victimization (e.g., Crick & Grotpeter, 1995; 1996) and are particularly helpful for better understanding the child's private experience of victimization (Ladd & Kochenderfer-Ladd, 2002). In addition, self-reports of victimization can provide unique information that may not overlap with other informants' assessments of victimization. Specifically, self-reports of victimization may relate to more "intrapersonal indicators of maladjustment," such as loneliness and depression (Ladd & Kochenderfer-Ladd, 2002, p. 76).

Limitations.   There are several broad limitations to using self-report measures. First, although the psychometric properties have been established for some of the measures, they are still questionable, and limit the way in which the data may be used. Although Olweus' measure has been widely disseminated, the fact that different countries and societies apply somewhat different terminology when describing bullying makes cross-national comparisons difficult (Smith et al., 2002). In addition, in many of the larger scale bullying intervention programs (e.g., Menesini et al., 1997; Olweus, 1984), the self-report measures used as primary outcome measures are completed anonymously. This method protects the confidentiality of the respondent, but it makes it difficult, if not impossible, to compare an individual student's responses before and after an intervention. As a result, self-report measures completed anonymously may not be helpful if one is interested in the effects of a targeted intervention on a given student's behavior. They may, however, have value in determining the effectiveness of a universal intervention, assuming the same group of children completes the measure at pre- and post-testing.

Relying on children to be primary informants introduces another limitation of self-report measures. These measures may lack objectivity, as they depend upon children's ability to selectively remember details of specific encounters. This methodology may result in an underestimation of bullying problems in an environment. Bullies may minimize their involvement in bullying episodes (e.g., Craig & Pepler, 1997; Smith & Sharp, 1994), and victims may not wish to recall an incident of victimization if it was embarrassing or upsetting for them (Ladd & Kochenderfer-Ladd, 2002). In addition, there may be social pressures against children reporting instances of victimization, especially when these measures are group administered in classroom settings, where a victim can see the bully as they are completing the measure (Austin & Joseph, 1996).

Future Directions.   Although self-report measures are arguably the most commonly used outcome measures, there are still many ways in which this methodology can be strengthened and improved. First, it is recommended that researchers partner with students to design, adapt, and modify existing self-report measures (e.g., Leff, Power, Grossman, Gill, & Blom-Hoffman, 2002), so that these measures reflect the concerns of children and are worded in a manner that is developmentally appropriate. Second, it is suggested that practitioners train children on how to complete self-report surveys, to ensure that the measures employed are well understood by children.

Some researchers have developed innovative ways in which to address limitations of self-report measures. One example is the use of field diaries as a way of gathering students' perspectives on bullying and victimization episodes immediately after a recess period, or in places where direct observations are not feasible, such as in bathrooms and locker rooms (e.g., Pellegrini, 1996). This method may provide more objective reporting that is not impaired by selective memory, and may help researchers to better understand contextual factors related to bullying and victimization. Finally, innovative research by Smith and colleagues (2002) examined the meaning of different terms related to bullying by designing a set of

25 stick-figure cartoons to depict a wide range of physical, relational, and verbal bullying episodes. This measure was administered to over 1200 children from 14 different countries, in an effort to compare how children from different countries viewed various subtypes of bullying without the limitations of language translation. Results suggested that a cartoon-based methodology was successful in better understanding children's perceptions of bullying in an international sample.

Teacher Report Measures

Brief Description. Teacher report measures of behavior problems are often used in both school- and clinic-based settings to help with educational planning and intervention monitoring. Teacher report measures vary considerably in their length and comprehensiveness. For instance, several studies have utilized broad-band measures such as the Child Behavior Checklist – Teacher Report Form (TRF; Achenbach, 1991) and the Behavior Assessment System for Children (BASC; Reynolds and Kamphaus, 1991), to assess children's behavioral functioning across multiple domains (e.g., Kamphaus, Huberty, DiStefano, & Petoskey, 1997; McConaughy & Achenbach, 1996). In addition, several researchers have designed narrow-band teacher measures focused more specifically on aggression or bullying (e.g., Coie & Dodge, 1988; Crick, 1996; Huesmann, Eron, Guerra, & Crawshaw, 1994). An example of a narrow-band measure is the Children's Social Behavior Questionnaire (CSB; Crick, 1996), which requests teachers to rate a given student's levels of overt aggression, relational aggression, and prosocial behaviors.

Psychometric Properties. Some of the most commonly used broad-band, teacher report measures (e.g., BASC and TRF) have demonstrated strong psychometric properties (i.e., reliability and validity) across many studies (e.g., Kamphaus et al., 1997; McConaughy & Achenbach, 1996). In addition, brief teacher report measures, such as the CSB, have demonstrated adequate psychometric properties in several studies (i.e., factor analyses and internal consistency analyses; Crick, 1996; Rys & Bear, 1997). Teacher report measures have been found to correlate moderately with peer nominations and behavioral observation systems (e.g., Achenbach, McConaughy, & Howell, 1987; Rys & Bear, 1997).

Strengths. Teacher report measures are generally easy to administer, score, and interpret. Using teacher report measures of aggression and bullying is consistent with school practice as teachers regularly rate children's academic performance and competence. Teacher report measures may also eliminate parents' concerns about children participating in peer sociometric procedures (Leff et al., 1999).

Brief teacher report measures may have their greatest use as an initial step in a multiple gating procedure to screen out children who are not the perpetrator or victim of bullying (Leff et al., 1999). The more in-depth measures (i.e., peer sociometrics, behavioral observations, or more comprehensive teacher report measures) can then be used with the remaining children to identify those at highest risk for being a bully or victim. Several studies have used teacher report measures in conjunction with peer sociometrics to identify at-risk children in need of interventions (e.g., Conduct Problems Prevention Research Group, 1999a, 1999b; Prinz, Blechman, & Dumas, 1994).

Limitations. Teacher report measures have some limitations that may make their use somewhat problematic as a sole outcome measure for a bullying or aggression prevention program. Generally, they are not particularly sensitive to behaviors in the playground setting or to more subtle forms of aggression, which limits both their contexts of use and the type of information they provide. In general, it is unclear how well teachers understand and are concerned by the more subtle forms of aggression and bullying (e.g., relational bullying).

Teacher ratings scales are also limited by their impracticality. The most commonly used teacher report measures are quite lengthy, making it difficult for busy teachers to find time to rate multiple students' behaviors. Even brief teacher-report measures (e.g., 17-item CSB) may be too time-consuming for teachers to complete on multiple students.

Future Directions. Several innovative techniques can be used to improve the accuracy of teacher reports in identifying bullies and victims. Huesmann and colleagues (1994) developed a procedure whereby they ask teachers to estimate peer ratings of aggression (as opposed to asking teachers for their own opinions). Having teachers take the perspective of peers may be a feasible alternative to using the more labor- and time-intensive peer sociometric procedures in some situations for identifying peer aggressors and victims. Second, Leff and colleagues have found that including reports from multiple teachers (e.g., homeroom teacher plus related arts teachers) greatly increases the correspondence between peer and teacher reports (Leff et al., 1999). In the future, it is important to focus research on gaining a better understanding of teachers' perceptions of relational bullying. Knowing how teachers view relational bullying will help researchers and professionals to determine the utility of teacher reports for assessing relational aggression.

Peer Sociometric Measures

Brief Description. Peer sociometric measures for assessing children's social and behavioral status are widely used in research and have been employed in hundreds of studies over the past 25 years. The two most common peer sociometric measures are peer rating scales and peer nominations (Terry & Coie, 1991). Peer rating scales require students to rate each classmate on a likert-type scale related to a behavioral construct of interest (e.g., "rate the following children on how often they start fights"). Peer nomination methods ask students to identify a small number of classmates who exhibit specific behaviors (e.g., "circle the names of three students who start fights").

Psychometric Properties. Peer sociometric measures (both rating and nomination methods) have been found to have strong psychometric properties across many studies. Peer sociometric procedures utilize multiple observations of the same behaviors by all participating children in the classroom or grade, resulting in multiple informants (Terry & Coie, 1991). Peer sociometric measures have demonstrated high test-retest reliability (e.g., Hymel, Wagner, & Butler, 1990; Pekarik, Prinz, Liebert, Weintraub, & Neal, 1976), and are stable over time (e.g., Coie & Dodge, 1983; Terry & Coie, 1991) and across context (Coie & Kupersmidt, 1983). In addition, Terry (2000) has found that brief peer nomination procedures have extremely high inter-rater consensus reliability—an index of agreement between all peer raters in their rating of each particular classmate.

The concurrent and predictive validity of peer sociometric measures of aggression and social competence have also been well-established (Terry & Coie, 1991). For example, being nominated as aggressive has been associated with a number of negative outcomes in childhood, adolescence and adulthood (e.g., Cowen, Pederson, Babigian, Izzo, & Trost, 1973; Kupersmidt & Coie, 1990). Factor analytic studies of peer sociometric procedures have also demonstrated that they can reliably discriminate between different subgroups of aggressive children (e.g., Crick & Grotpeter, 1995).

As peer nomination methods are relative rating measures, they always categorize some children as exhibiting problematic social behaviors. This fact may limit the use of peer nomination methods for determining the effectiveness of school-level bullying or aggression prevention programs. For example, a child's social behavior may improve dramatically following an intervention. But, if the child is still viewed as having more of a problem than his or her peers, the child's sociometric standing on this relative rating measure may not change. In addition, because peer sociometric measures are relatively stable over time, they may not be sensitive to intervention effects (Pepler & Craig, 1998).

Strengths. Peer sociometric measures have extremely strong psychometric properties across many studies. This, combined with the fact that peers have more frequent contact with classmates across all school settings, may make peer sociometric measures the methodology of choice for identifying perpetrators and victims of relational aggression. Peer sociometric measures have also often been used in conjunction with teacher report measures for identifying at-risk children for research and intervention efforts (e.g., Conduct Problems Prevention Research Group, 1999a, 1999b; Prinz et al., 1994). When comparing peer ratings and peer nominations, the former likely would be more suitable for use as an outcome measure; this type of index provides a rating of each child on a behavioral construct of interest that is not dependent upon others' ratings.

Limitations.   Although many researchers have used peer sociometric measures for identifying high-risk children in the schools, this method can be extremely labor-intensive and time-consuming. As opposed to using a teacher- or self-report method for a handful of at-risk children, this method necessitates involving all children in a class (and/or grade) in the procedure. This typically requires that time be set aside by the classroom teacher for the peer sociometric procedure to be group-administered to all participating students. Finally, the data entry and analyses associated with peer sociometric measures are more complex and time-consuming than evaluating teacher or self-report questionnaires.

A second limitation to using this methodology is the perceived negative effects. To successfully implement a peer sociometric method in a school, the researcher is encouraged to explain, thoroughly and clearly, the procedure to children, parents, teachers, and institutional review boards. It is important that all of the parties involved understand the strengths of this methodology, and the research demonstrating no deleterious effects of using these procedures (Bell-Dolan, Foster, & Sikora, 1989; Hayvren & Hymel, 1984). Each participating student must have active parental permission to complete the measures, but, at times, parents and teachers may still be resistant to using this methodology, as children are asked to rate each other on negative characteristics. This may translate into relatively low participation rates (i.e., 50%–60%), which may affect the generalizability of the procedure (Hamilton, Fuchs, Fuchs, & Roberts, 2000). Recent research indicates that when participation rates are lower than 75%, standard peer nomination procedures may not be able to provide accurate estimates of children's social standing within the classroom or grade (Hamilton et al., 2000).

Future Directions.   In future research, gaining a better understanding of parents' and teachers' concerns with this methodology would be useful. Given the numerous strengths of peer sociometric methods, it will be extremely important to continue to educate parents and teachers on the strategies for employing these methods in a collaborative fashion in the schools. In addition, each time a peer sociometric measure is used, it is important that the researcher or practitioner first talk with students to ensure that they understand what information is being requested. This is especially true for relational aggression items, which may be more difficult for children to understand. Finally, it is important that researchers and educators fully debrief children after using these procedures (e.g., explain why students are being requested to rate others in their class) and talk with children about the importance of keeping their responses private (i.e., it could hurt others feelings to discuss responses).

Behavioral Observations

Brief Description.   Observational systems provide a relatively objective way of examining social behavior in a manner that is not influenced by prior relationships or pre-existing reputations. Behavioral observation systems range

considerably in breadth and complexity. For example, some observation procedures have been developed for identifying the frequency of different behaviors,
whereas other coding systems have been designed to characterize and better understand the interactional sequences children engage in, and the antecedents and
consequences of different peer-directed behaviors.

Psychometric Properties. Some observation systems have demonstrated
adequate reliability and precision in examining children's playground behaviors
(e.g., McNeilly-Choque, Hart, Robinson, Nelson, & Olsen, 1996; Pellegrini,
1989; Pellegrini & Bartini, 2000; Pepler & Craig, 1995). However, each observational system needs to be examined for reliability and cultural-relevance
within a specific population of interest (i.e., are the behavioral codes meaningful
and can coders use the system to categorize behaviors consistently within each
context?). Prior research has demonstrated that, with appropriate training, observers are able to use observation rating systems to make important distinctions
between behaviors, such as rough, vigorous play versus aggressive behaviors
(e.g., Boulton, 1993; Smith & Hunter, 1992). Further, this methodology can be
used to examine children's play and aggressive behaviors in various contexts, including: laboratory situations, in which researchers retain much experimental control (e.g., Johnston, DeLuca, Murtaugh, & Diener, 1977); contrived play group
situations with familiar or unfamiliar peers (e.g., Coie, Dodge, Terry, & Wright,
1991); and in naturalistic settings, that can be recorded live (e.g., Pellegrini, 1989;
McNeilly-Choque et al., 1996) or videotaped using sophisticated audio- and
video-recording systems (Pepler & Craig, 1995).

The challenge of accurately coding low-base rate behaviors (e.g., relational
aggression) can make an observational system difficult to validate. For instance,
it is necessary to conduct a number of observations in order to see a child exhibit
a full range of behaviors, especially those of low frequency.

Strengths. A number of researchers have used behavioral observation systems as a means to identify and/or better understand children who engage in aggression, bullying, and victimization (e.g., Pellegrini, 1989; Pepler & Craig,
1995). In particular, several researchers have focused their observational research
on developing systems to examine these behaviors on the school playground (e.g.,
McNeilly-Choque et al., 1996; Pellegrini, 1989; Pepler & Craig, 1995). Further,
research has successfully employed behavioral observation methodologies to determine whether children's behavior improves following an intervention (e.g.,
Conduct Problems Prevention Research Group, 1999a, 1999b).

Limitations. Although behavioral systems designed to record discrete
child behaviors are relatively easy to use and evaluate, the more complicated observation systems investigating interactional patterns are usually time- and labor-
intensive to design, adapt, and implement. In addition, these more complicated

systems typically require extensive training of coders in order to ensure adequate inter-rater reliability (Pepler & Craig, 1998). Further, observational systems often require a considerable baseline period during which data is not analyzed, as children become comfortable with the system and reactivity is minimized. Finally, time needs to be spent to ensure that the behaviors targeted are viewed as meaningful by school staff, community members, and/or students.

It is unclear how well any of the methodologies can be used to identify the more subtle forms of aggression, such as relational aggression. For example, to accurately code relationally aggressive behaviors, it is necessary to see each child's facial and body expressions, hear their ongoing conversation, and understand the particular social context in which the behavior occurs. McNeilly-Choque and colleagues (1996) have developed an observational system to examine preschoolers' relationally aggressive actions, but similar systems have not yet been fully developed for elementary and middle school age children.

Future Directions. Future research is needed in establishing systems that can reliably code elementary school children's relationally aggressive behaviors. This will be especially important in better understanding girls' bullying and victimization episodes. Pepler and Craig (1995) have developed a technique for examining children's playground behaviors by attaching microphones to individual children and then videorecording their behaviors from a remote and unobtrusive location on the playground. This method helps to lessen reactivity, while utilizing technology to improve coding systems. Further, it will be interesting to see if, in the future, this type of system will be able to reliably code relationally aggressive actions.

Playground and Lunchroom Supervisor Measures

Brief Description. In many schools, teachers do not supervise children in the unstructured school settings (i.e., during lunch and recess periods). Rather, lunchtime supervisors, who are often paraprofessionals, parents, and/or community members, oversee children's lunchroom and playground behavior (Leff, Costigan, & Power, in press). Surprisingly, few, if any, measures have been designed to assess these individuals' perspective, despite the important roles they serve related to children's peer relationships. Leff and colleagues have recently partnered with lunchtime supervisors to combine theory and prior empirical research with extensive feedback from key stakeholders to design and provisionally validate a series of questionnaires (Leff, Power, Costigan et al., 2001; Leff, Power, et al., in press). The Playground and Lunchroom Climate Questionnaire (PLCQ) is a 23 item questionnaire that assesses playground and lunchroom supervisors' perceived communication skills, the availability and appropriateness of play activities during recess, the use of clear and consistent rules in the lunchroom and on the playground, and the frequency and appropriateness of adult supervision across these settings. The Playground Experience

Questionnaire (PEQ) and the Lunchroom Experience Questionnaire (LEQ) are 15-item questionnaires that were designed to assess playground and lunchroom supervisors' perception of the frequency of children's overall level of aggression and prosocial actions that occur on the playground and in the lunchroom, respectively.

Psychometric Properties.   Playground and lunchroom personnel from seven urban elementary schools and two community members worked with our research team to make sure that each proposed item on the three questionnaires measured an important aspect of playground and lunchroom climate and/or children's behavior, and that items and response scales were worded in a developmentally appropriate and culturally sensitive manner (Leff, Power et al., in press). Then, over one hundred and ten playground and lunchroom personnel from 17 urban schools (12 elementary schools, 3 kindergarten–8th-grade schools, and 2 middle schools) completed the finalized versions of the PLCQ, PEQ, and LEQ as part of a series of bullying prevention workshops. Results of factor analyses of the PLCQ revealed that there are two main dimensions measured by the questionnaire: (a) Playground structure for activities and monitoring (10 items including: "There are many games for children to play on the playground"; "There are enough staff to monitor children on the playground") and (b) Staff collaboration (9 items including: "Staff members work well together and as a team"). These dimensions were internally consistent and stable over a three-week interval (see Leff, Power et al., 2003 for details). Finally, initial results suggest that these two dimensions are sensitive to treatment effects (Leff, Costigan, Manz, & Power, 2000).

Factor analyses of the PEQ revealed two main dimensions: (a) aggressive behavior (9 items that relate to relational, physical, and/or verbal aggression), and (b) prosocial actions (6 items that relate to prosocial behavior and following rules). Both factors were internally consistent (Leff, Power, Costigan et al., 2001). Initial analyses suggest that similar dimensions characterize the LEQ.

Strengths.   A strength of these measures is that they are sensitive to the dynamics that occur in playground and lunchroom settings. In addition, these measures were designed through partnerships with diverse school staff and community members. These collaborations helped to ensure that these measures are able to provide valuable information about students' behaviors across the playground and lunchroom settings (PEQ and LEQ, respectively), and about often neglected school climate and contextual variables that may contribute to bullying behaviors (PLCQ).

Another strength of these measures is that they are brief, can be administered together in approximately 20 minutes, and do not disrupt class time. These measures have the potential for helping schools to conduct a thorough needs assessment that can be used to guide intervention planning. In addition, the measures can be used to provide school-level data at multiple time periods during the implementation of bullying programs.

Limitations. These measures are not designed to provide information about specific at-risk children. Thus, they would not be recommended to track student outcomes for a selective/indicated intervention program (e.g., with high-risk youth). Further, more research is needed to validate the PEQ and LEQ. For instance, it will be important to see whether these new measures demonstrate adequate test-retest reliability and are sensitive to treatment change over time. Similar to teacher report measures, more research is also needed to determine playground assistants' perceptions of relational aggression.

Future Directions. In general, the development of playground supervisor measures that are constructed through active partnership with school and community members is a fruitful area for research (Leff, Power et al., in press). In the future, it will be extremely important to better understand how playground and lunchroom supervisors view different types of bullying behaviors (i.e., physical versus relational) and which strategies they believe are most successful across the unstructured school contexts.

Translating Research Into Practice: Implications for Bullying-Prevention and Intervention Programs

Using Community Partnership-Based Methods

Establishing partnerships among educators, community members, and researchers are an important way to enhance a school's ability to design, adapt, and use outcome measures in a sensitive manner to determine program effectiveness (Ho, 2002; Nastasi et al., 1998, 2000). A partnership-based model is distinguished from other scientific models by several key features. First, a strong emphasis is placed upon how the researcher may best meet, understand, and partner with key stakeholders to foster collective ownership of the process (Nastasi et al., 2000). Second, in the formative stage of the research, the researcher combines psychological theory and empirical research with ideas generated by key stakeholders to fine-tune outcome measures (e.g., Ho, 2002; Nastasi et al., 1998, 2000). The methodology employed in PAR is not only rigorous, but it is also responsive to the needs of the school and community (Leff, Costigan et al., in press; Leff, Power et al., in press; Dowrick et al., 2001). As a result, PAR often leads to higher levels of sustainability and institutionalization than research employing more traditional research frameworks (Nastasi et al., 2000). In sum, the researcher contributes expertise in research conceptualization while stakeholders help to ensure that the project is responsive to and useful for the local culture and community. This framework is particularly well-suited to develop and evaluate assessment measures and school-based prevention and intervention programs (Leff, Costigan et al., in press).

Using MultiMethod, Multi-Informant Outcome Measures

Although each set of outcome measures reviewed has its potential strengths and limitations, it is apparent that no single method is sufficient for determining the effects of bullying prevention programs (Leff, Power, Manz et al., 2001). Instead, researchers and interventionists must work with school administrators to determine which combination of methods will provide the most comprehensive and yet feasible outcome assessment. In addition, it is extremely important for researchers and practitioners to provide a strong rationale for how the measures they are using to assess treatment impact are relevant and appropriate for cultural groups served by the school (Soriano, Soriano, & Jimenez, 1994).

Selecting Measures and Partnering with School Staff

In order to determine which sets of measures might be most appropriate for use within a particular school, it is suggested that practitioners consider the following questions:

1. What particular behaviors are being targeted by the bullying intervention (e.g., rough, physical play on the playground, relational bullying in the lunchroom, etc.)?
2. Is the program designed as a universal or selective/indicated intervention program?
3. How feasible are the different sets of measures to employ?
4. Who are important school and community stakeholders that can work with the practitioner to ensure that measures are feasible and community responsive?
5. Are there opportunities to talk with school staff (i.e., at a faculty meeting) to explain to them the reasons why certain measures are valuable to collect information on?

Conclusion

The research base regarding bullying has grown exponentially since Dan Olweus' pioneering intervention research in the late 1970s and early 1980s. However, the field is still in a relatively early phase of development. Several types of measures have been developed to assist school professionals in monitoring the progress of bullying interventions. It is recommended that practitioners and educators work together to identify a set of measures for determining the effectiveness of school-based bully prevention programs. It is also important that the field moves beyond trying to select the "best method" for assessing intervention outcomes. Instead, the development and validation of integrated multi-method protocols that assess social behavior across multiple contexts and are responsive to the needs of children, families, and schools are critical goals for future research.

ACKNOWLEDGMENTS

We would like to extend our appreciation to the Pew Charitable Trusts for funding our research efforts. Correspondence should be mailed to Stephen S. Leff at Children's Seashore House of The Children's Hospital of Philadelphia, Dept. of Pediatric Psychology, 3405 Civic Center Blvd., Philadelphia, PA 19104. Electronic mail may be sent to leff@email.chop.edu.

REFERENCES

Achenbach, T. M. (1991). *Manual for the teacher's report form & 1991 profile.* Burlington, VT: University of Vermont, Department of Psychiatry.

Achenbach, T. M., McConaughy, S. H., & Howell, C. T. (1987). Child/Adolescent behavioral and emotional problems. Implications of cross-informant correlations for situational specificity. *Psychological Bulletin, 101,* 213–232.

Austin, S., & Joseph, S. (1996). Assessment of bully/victim problems in 8- to 11-year-olds. *British Journal of Educational Psychology, 66,* 447–456.

Bell-Dolan, D. J., Foster, S. L., & Sikora, D. M. (1989). Effects of sociometric testing on children's behavior and loneliness in school. *Developmental Psychology, 25,* 306–311.

Block, J. H. (1983). Differential premises arising from differential socialization of the sexes: Some conjectures. *Child Development, 54,* 1335–1354.

Boulton, M. J. (1993). Children's abilities to distinguish between playful and aggressive fighting: A developmental perspective. *British Journal of Developmental Psychology, 11,* 249–263.

Brener, N. D., Krug, E. G., Dahlberg, L. L., & Powell, K. E. (1997). Nurses' logs as an evaluation tool for school-based violence-prevention programs. *Journal of School Health, 67,* 171–174.

Chambless, D. L., & Hollon, S. D. (1998). Defining empirically supported therapies. *Journal of Consulting and Clinical Psychology, 66,* 7–18.

Coie, J. D., & Dodge, K. A. (1983). Continuities and changes in children's social status: A five-year longitudinal study. *Merrill-Palmer Quarterly, 29,* 261–282.

Coie, J. D., & Dodge, K. A. (1988). Multiple sources of data on social behavior and social status in the school: A cross-age comparison. *Child Development, 59,* 815–829.

Coie, J. D., Dodge, K. A., Terry, R., & Wright, V. (1991). The role of aggression in peer relations: An analysis of aggression episodes in boys' play groups. *Child Development, 62,* 812–826.

Coie, J. D., & Kupersmidt, J. B. (1983). A behavioral analysis of emerging social status in boys' groups. *Child Development, 54,* 1400–1416.

Coie, J. D., Terry, R., Lenox, K., Lochman, J., & Hyman, C. (1995). Childhood peer rejection and aggression as predictors of stable patterns of adolescent disorder. *Development and Psychopathology, 7,* 697–713.

Conduct Problems Prevention Research Group (1999a). Initial impact of the Fast Track Prevention Trial of Conduct Problems: II. Classroom effect. *Journal of Consulting and Clinical Psychology, 67,* 648–657.

Conduct Problems Prevention Research Group (1999b). Initial impact of the Fast Track Prevention Trial of Conduct Problems: I. The High Risk Sample. *Journal of Consulting and Clinical Psychology, 67*, 631–647.

Cowen, E. L., Pederson, A., Babigian, H., Izzo, L. D., & Trost, M. A. (1973). Long-term follow-up of early detected vulnerable children. *Journal of Consulting and Clinical Psychology, 41*, 438–446.

Craig, W. M., & Pepler, D. J. (1997). Observations of bullying and victimization in the school yard. *Canadian Journal of School Psychology, 13*, 41–59.

Crick, N. R. (1996). The role of overt aggression, relational aggression, and prosocial behavior in the prediction of children's future social adjustment. *Child Development, 67*, 2317–2327.

Crick, N. R., & Grotpeter, J. K. (1995). Relational aggression, gender, and social-psychological adjustment. *Child Development, 66*, 710–722.

Crick, N. R., & Grotpeter, J. K. (1996). Children's treatment by peers: Victims of relational and overt aggression. *Development and Psychopathology, 8*, 367–380.

Cummings, E. M., Iannotti, R. V., & Zahn-Waxler, C. (1985). Influence of conflict between adults on the emotions and aggression of young children. *Developmental Psychology, 21*, 495–507.

Davidson, L. L., Durkin, M. S., Kuhn, L., O'Connor, P., Barlow, B., & Heagarty, M. C. (1994). The impact of the Safe Kids/Healthy Neighborhoods injury prevention program in Harlem, 1988 through 1991. *American Journal of Public Health, 84*, 580–586.

Dodge, K. A. (1986). A social information processing model of social competence in children. In M. Perlmutter (Ed.), *Cognitive perspective on children's social and behavioral development.* (pp. 77–125). Hillsdale, NJ: Erlbaum.

Dowrick, P. W., Power, T. J., Manz, P. H., Ginsburg-Block, M., Leff, Stephen, S., & Kim-Rupnow, S. (2001). Community responsiveness: Examples from under-resourced urban schools. *Journal of Prevention and Intervention in the Community, 21*, 71–90.

Hamilton, C., Fuchs, D., Fuchs, L. S., & Roberts, H. (2000). Rates of classroom participation and the validity of sociometry. *School Psychology Review, 29*, 251–266.

Hayvren, M., & Hymel, S. (1984). Ethical issues in sociometric testing: Impact of sociometric measures on interactive behavior. *Developmental Psychology, 20*, 844–849.

Ho, B. S. (2002). Application of participatory action research to family-school interactions. *School Psychology Review, 31*, 106–121.

Hodges, E. V. E., & Perry, D. G. (1999). Personal and interpersonal antecedents and consequences of victimization by peers. *Journal of Personality and Social Psychology, 76*, 677–685.

Hudley, C., & Graham, S. (1993). An attributional intervention to reduce peer-directed aggression among African American boys. *Child Development, 64*, 124–138.

Huesmann, L. R., Eron, L. D., Guerra, N. G., & Crawshaw, V. B. (1994). Measuring children's aggression with teachers' predictions of peer nominations. *Psychological Assessment, 6*, 329–336.

Hymel, S., Wagner, E., & Butler, L. J. (1990). Reputational bias: View from the peer group. In S. R. Asher & J. D. Coie (Eds.), *Peer rejection in childhood* (pp. 156–186). Cambridge, Mass.: Cambridge University.

Johnston, A., DeLuca, D., Murtaugh, K., & Diener, E. (1977). Validation of a laboratory play measure of child aggression. *Child Development, 48*, 324–327.

Kamphaus, R. W., Huberty, C. J., DiStefano, C., & Petoskey, M. D. (1997). A typology of teacher-rated child behavior for a national U.S. sample. *Journal of Abnormal Child Psychology, 25*, 453–463.

Kazdin, A. E. (1994). Interventions for aggressive and antisocial children. In L. D. Eron, J. H. Gentry, & P. Schlegel (Eds.), *Reason to hope: A psychosocial perspective on violence and youth.* Washington, D.C.: American Psychological Association.

Kochenderfer, B. J., & Ladd, G. W. (1996). Peer victimization: Cause or consequence of school maladjustment. *Child Development, 67*, 1305–1317.

Krug, E. G., Brener, N. D., Dahlberg, L. L., Ryan, G. W., & Powell, K. E. (1997). The impact of an elementary school-based violence prevention program on visits to the school nurse. *American Journal of Preventative Medicine, 13*, 459–463.

Kupersmidt, J. B., & Coie, J. D. (1990). Preadolescent peer status, aggression, and school adjustment as predictors of externalizing problems in adolescence. *Child Development, 61*, 1350–1362.

Ladd, G. W., & Kochenderfer-Ladd, B. (2002). Identifying victims of peer aggression from early to middle childhood: Analysis of cross-informant data for concordance, estimation of relational adjustment, prevalence of victimization, and characteristics of identified victims. *Psychological Assessment, 14*, 74–96.

Leff, S. S., Costigan, T. E., Manz, P. H., & Power, T. J. (2000, March). *Evaluating violence prevention procedures in the lunchroom and on the playground*. Poster presented at the annual conference of the National Association of School Psychologists, New Orleans.

Leff, S. S., Costigan, T. E., & Power, T. J. (in press). Using participatory-action research to develop a playground-based prevention program. *Journal of School Psychology*.

Leff, S. S., Kupersmidt, J. B., Patterson, C., & Power, T. J. (1999). Factors influencing teacher predictions of peer bullying and victimization. *School Psychology Review, 28*, 505–517.

Leff, S. S., Power, T. J., Costigan, T. E., & Manz, P. (in press). Assessing the climate of the playground and lunchroom: Implications for bullying prevention programming. *School Psychology Review*.

Leff, S. S., Power, T. J., Costigan, T. E., Manz, P., & Clarke, A. T. (2001, April). *Developing a measure for recording aggressive and prosocial behaviors on the playground: The Playground Experience Questionnaire: PEQ*. Poster presented at the biennial meeting of the Society for Research in Child Development, Minneapolis, MN.

Leff, S. S., Power, T. J., Grossman, M., Gill, J., & Blom-Hoffman (2002, August). Designing a cartoon-based attributional measure for use with urban African American females. In D. Nelson & W. Craig (Chairs), *Innovative approaches to understanding forms of aggression*. Symposium conducted at the International Society for the Study of Behavioral Development, Ottawa, Canada.

Leff, S. S., Power, T. J., Manz, P. H., Costigan, T. E., & Nabors, L. A. (2001). School-based aggression-prevention programs for young children: Current status and implications for violence prevention. *School Psychology Review, 30*, 343–360.

Lochman, J. E. (1992). Cognitive-behavioral intervention with aggressive boys: Three-year follow-up and preventive effects. *Journal of Consulting and Clinical Psychology, 60*, 426–432.

Lochman, J. E., & Dodge, K. A. (1994). Social-cognitive processes of severely violent, moderately aggressive, and nonaggressive boys. *Journal of Consulting and Clinical Psychology, 62*, 366–374.

Lochman, J. E., & Wells, K. (1996). A social-cognitive intervention with aggressive children: Prevention effects and contextual implementation issues. In R. Dev. Peters & R. J. McMahon, (Eds.) *Prevention and early intervention: Childhood disorders, substance use, and delinquency*. Newbury Park, CA: Sage.

Loeber, R., Green, S. M., Lahey, B. B., & Kalb, L. (2000). Physical fighting in childhood as a risk factor for later mental health problems. *Journal of the American Academy of Child and Adolescent Psychiatry, 39*, 421–428.

Madsen, K. C. (1996). Differing perceptions of bullying and their practical implications. *Educational and Child Psychology, 13*, 14–22.

McConaughy, S. H., & Achenbach, T. M. (1996). Contributions of a child interview to multimethod assessment with EBD and LD. *School Psychology Review, 25*, 24–39.

McNeilly-Choque, M. K., Hart, C. H., Robinson, C. C., Nelson, L. J., & Olsen, S. F. (1996). Overt and relational aggression on the playground: Correspondence among different informants. *Journal of Research in Childhood Education, 11*, 47–67.

Menesini, E., Eslea, M., Smith, P. K., Genta, M. L., Giannetti, E., Fonzi, A., & Costabile, A. (1997). Cross-national comparison of children's attitudes towards bully/victim problems in school. *Aggressive Behavior, 23*, 245–257.

Nansel, T. R., Overpeck, M., Pilla, R. S., Ruan, W. J., Simons-Morton, B., & Scheidt, P. (2001). Bullying behaviors among U.S. youth: Prevalence and association with psychological adjustment. *Journal of the American Medical Association, 285*, 2094–2100.

Nastasi, B. K., Schensul, J. J., De Silva, M. W. A., Varjas, K., Silva, K. T., Priyani, R., & Schensul, S. (1998). Community-based sexual risk prevention program for Sri Lankan youth: Influencing sexual-risk decision-making. *International Quarterly of Community Health Education, 18*, 139–155.

Nastasi, B. K., Varjas, K., Schensul, S. L., Silva, K. T., Schensul, J. J., & Ratnayake, P. (2000). The participatory intervention model: A framework for conceptualizing and promoting intervention acceptability. *School Psychology Quarterly, 15*, 207–232.

Nelson, J. R., Benner, G. J., Reid, R. C., Epstein, M. H., & Currin, D. (2002). The convergent validity of office discipline referrals with the CBCL-TRF. *Journal of Emotional and Behavioral Disorder, 10*, 181–188.

Olweus, D. (1984). Aggressors and their victims: Bullying at school. In N. Frude & H. Gault (Eds.), *Disruptive behavior in schools*. New York: Wiley.

Olweus, D. (1993). *Bullying at school*. Cambridge, MA: Blackwell.

Pekarik, E. G., Prinz, R. J., Liebert, D. E., Weintraub, S., & Neale, J. M. (1976). The pupil evaluation inventory: A sociometric technique for assessing children's social behavior. *Journal of Abnormal Child Psychology, 4*, 83–97.

Pellegrini, A. D. (1989). Elementary school children's rough-and-tumble play. *Early Childhood Research Quarterly, 4*, 245–260.

Pellegrini, A. D. (1996). *Observing children in their natural worlds: A methodological primer*, Mahwah, NJ: Erlbaum.

Pellegrini, A. D., & Bartini, M. (2000). An empirical comparison of methods of sampling aggression and victimization in school settings. *Journal of Educational Psychology, 92*, 360–366.

Pepler, D. J., & Craig, W. M. (1995). A peek behind the fence: Naturalistic observations of aggressive children with remote audiovisual recording. *Developmental Psychology, 31*, 548–553.

Pepler, D. J., & Craig, W. M. (1998). Assessing children's peer relationships. *Child Psychology & Psychiatry Review, 3*, 176–182.

Perry, D. G., Kusel, S. J., & Perry, L. C. (1988). Victims of peer aggression. *Developmental Psychology, 24*, 807–814.

Pope, A. W., & Bierman, K. L. (1999). Predicting adolescent peer problems and antisocial activities: The relative roles of aggression and dysregulation. *Developmental Psychology, 35*, 335–346.

Prinz, R. J., Blechman, E. A., & Dumas, J. E. (1994). An evaluation of peer-coping skills training for childhood aggression. *Journal of Clinical Child Psychology, 23*, 193–203.

Reynolds, C. R., & Kamphaus, R. W. (1991). *Behavior Assessment System for Children (BASC)*. Circle Pines, MN: American Guidance Service, Inc.

Rigby, K. (2002). *Bullying in childhood*. In P. Smith & C. Hart (Eds.), Childhood social development. Malden, Mass: Blackwell.

Rys, G. S., & Bear, G. G. (1997). Relational aggression and peer relations: Gender and developmental issues. *Merrill Palmer Quarterly, 43*, 87–106.

Slee, P. T. (1995). Peer victimization and its relationship to depression among Australian primary school students. *Personality of Individual Differences, 18*, 57–62.

Smith, P. K., Cowie, H., Olafsson, R. F., & Liefooghe, A. P. D. (2002). Definitions of bullying: A comparison of terms used, and age and gender differences, in a fourteen-country international comparison. *Child Development, 73*, 1119–1133.

Smith, P. K., & Hunter, T. (1992). Children's perceptions of playfighting, playchasing and real fighting: A cross-national interview study. *Social Development, 1*, 211–229.

Smith, P. K. & Levan, S. (1995). Perceptions and experiences of bullying in younger pupils. *British Journal of Educational Psychology, 65*, 489–500.

Smith, P. K., & Sharp, S. (1994). *School bullying: Insights and perspectives* (1–19). London: Routledge.

Soriano, M., Soriano, F. I., & Jimenez, E. (1994). School violence among culturally diverse populations: Sociocultural and institutional considerations. *School Psychology Review, 23*, 216–235.

Sprague, J. R., Sugai, G., Horner, R., & Walker, H. M. (1999). Using office discipline referral data to evaluate school-wide discipline and violence prevention interventions. *OSSC Bulletin, 42,* 3–18.

Terry, R. (2000). Recent advances in measurement theory and the use of sociometric techniques. In A. Cillessen and W. Bukowski (Eds.), *Recent advances in the measurement of acceptance and rejection in the peer system: New directions in child and adolescent development* (pp. 27–53). San Francisco: Jossey-Bass.

Terry, R., & Coie, J. D. (1991). A comparison of methods for defining sociometric status among children. *Developmental Psychology, 27,* 867–880.

Tobin, T., Sugai, G., & Colvin, G. (2000). Using discipline referrals to make decisions. *NASSP Bulletin, 84,* 106–117.

Wright, J. A., & Dusek, J. B. (1998). Compiling school base rates for disruptive behaviors from student disciplinary referral data. *School Psychology Review, 27,* 138–147.

V

Effective Prevention and Intervention Programs

15

Elementary School Bully Busters Program: Understanding Why Children Bully and What to Do About It[1]

Arthur M. Horne, Pamela Orpinas
University of Georgia

Dawn Newman-Carlson
Private Practice, Gainesville, Florida

Christi L. Bartolomucci
Private Practice, Atlanta, Georgia

Children's elementary education experience involves learning academic subjects, as well as learning appropriate social skills and behaviors. Not all students enter school having mastered the ability to get along with other children, which is part of the learning process. The ability to resolve conflict, to play fair, to treat each other with kindness, and to share are not innate characteristics of most children

---

[1] Material describing the Bully Busters Program is summarized from Horne, A. M., Bartolomucci, C. L., and Newman-Carlson, D. (2003). *Bully Busters: A Teacher's Manual for Helping Bullies, Victims, and Bystanders (Grades K-5)*. Champaign, IL: Research Press. Used with permission from the authors and the publisher.

in the early elementary school grades. Learning these skills is part of the outcome of good educational programs. Moreover, building social skills to improve interpersonal interactions is a key facet of effective school antiviolence programs (Gregg, 1998). Bullying, however, goes beyond the normal developmental shortcomings and may result in serious problems with fellow students and teachers. Thus, detecting and stopping bullying requires special training of school personnel and specific education of students. The purpose of this chapter is to describe a training process for bullying prevention for schoolteachers, the Bully Busters Program (Horne, Bartolomucci, & Newman-Carlson, 2003). This chapter is divided into four sections and a final summary. The first section defines bullying and explains how it is taught to students. The second section describes the assumptions of the Bully Busters Program. The third section describes the basic skills that teachers need for the prevention of bullying. The final section explains the implementation of each of the modules of the Bully Busters Program.

Explaining Bullying to Elementary School Children

While the definitions vary among scholars, researchers, and practitioners, there are three common components to all definitions of bullying (Olweus, 1994, p. 1173; Roland, 1989, p. 143; Smith & Sharp, 1994, p. 1; Tattum, 1989, p. 10). First, it is a purposeful aggressive behavior. Second, there is an imbalance of power between the victim and the bully. Third, it occurs more than once. It is important that teachers, students, and parents understand how bullying is different from play and recognize it for what it is—an abuse of power. Bullying behaviors are instrumental, that is, they serve to achieve a goal. Some children turn to bullying when they do not have other, more appropriate means of achieving their goals. Instead of developing positive means of interacting with and communicating their needs to others, these children learn to control others through intimidation and fear.

When teaching the concept of bullying to elementary school students, we should define it in ways that they can easily understand, such as the PIC acronym: Purposeful, Imbalanced, and Continual. Elementary school children can understand the concept of *purposeful* behavior. "He meant to do it" or "They did that on purpose" are both examples that students use regularly to show they know that the behavior was intentional. Students are generally very quick to pick up on the difference between accidental behavior and intentional or purposeful behavior. A child who accidentally bumps a desk, causing books to spill is understood by children to be different than an aggressive child who purposefully causes the spilling of the books.

Bullying behavior is also imbalanced, because the bully has more power or influence than the victim. Elementary students also understand the idea of *imbalance* and use phrases such as "That's not fair, he's bigger" or "They weren't playing even—the sides weren't even." While not all young students can grasp the imbalanced nature of some relationships, they can usually understand the notion of fairness. Even though they may not always have the words to express the term, they do have a sense of justice related to the imbalance of power.

The third part of the definition, bullying is *continual*, means it occurs more than once. While all aggression needs to be stopped, bullying is characterized by being ongoing. Students easily understand this concept. Children may say, "I'm afraid to enter the classroom because she is always picking on me."

Elementary school children easily learn the acronym PIC. Strategies used to facilitate learning include providing a poster with the definitions and examples, asking students to develop their own posters, and asking children to take turns explaining and giving examples of each element of PIC.

Assumptions of the Bully Busters Program

Bullying is an instrumental behavior. It provides a payoff for the bully either in tangible rewards, such as gaining lunch money or extra time on the playground equipment, or intangible rewards, such as prestige among peers or power over another child. Thus, bullying would be significantly reduced if the system in which it occurs did not allow the payoffs and if there were costs—punishment—for engaging in the behavior. The focus of the Bully Busters Program is on changing the social system so that bullying does not occur. This involves changing teachers' and administrators' responses to bullying and aggression and developing an elementary school student culture that encourages peer action to reduce or eliminate the problem. The basic assumptions of the program are that changing the environment is more powerful than changing individuals, that prevention is better than intervention, and that changing the environment requires support and understanding among teachers.

Changing the Environment Is More Powerful Than Changing Individuals. The problem of bullying and victimization in schools could be described as a function of an interaction between two people—one who has more power and who purposefully and continually bullies another. This description implies that programs developed to change the perpetrator, to change the response of the victim, or to modify the relationship between the perpetrator and the victim might sufficiently solve the problem. However, most individually oriented approaches have shown limited effectiveness. Mytton and colleagues, in a review of the literature, found only 16 studies that have evaluated the effect of an intervention for primary school children selected for displaying high levels of aggression. The results varied greatly among studies and, overall, showed only a modest reduction in aggression as a result of the intervention (Mytton, DiGuiseppi, Gough, Taylor, & Logan, 2002). Similarly, we have found that individual and small group counseling programs for bullies, for victims, or for both bullies and victims are not successful at reducing the prevalence of aggression (Horne et al., 2003; Newman et al., 2000; Turpeau, 1998). However, studies oriented at changing the school environment have been more promising (e.g., Orpinas, Horne, & Staniszewski, in press). These studies place a strong emphasis on increasing the awareness and skills of teachers and of all students, regardless of whether they have been bullied.

Another reason for working with the whole school is because all children are affected by bullying experiences. The bullies and victims are affected directly, but numerous other students—whom we call bystanders or observers—observe bullying interactions and are impacted by the experience. Our experience with children and adolescents is that they all experience the pain of bullying. The observers of bullying may fear for their own safety, for they worry that bullies may target them next or may harass them if they intervene on the side of the victim. Another negative outcome for observers or bystanders is that they may experience guilt because they were unable or failed to stand up for their classmates, the victims of bullying.

Elementary school is an ideal time to instill antiviolence values and peaceful conflict strategies within all students so that these characteristics may be called upon continuously throughout their school years. Based on our experience, it is crucially important to change the school culture of violence by working with the largest group impacted by the aggression, the observers and bystanders. Impacting the larger group of students, not just the bullies and victims, facilitates class-wide and school-wide change.

Prevention Is Better Than Intervention.   Prevention of a problem is always preferable to fixing the problem. Violence usually occurs as a chain of events. In order to prevent it, we must understand where that chain starts. To accomplish this prevention goal, all teachers participate in the Bully Busters Program training so that they may institute the program for all students within their classroom. Thus, all the teachers within the school engage in the same learning and application process, so that the impact will extend beyond a single class. A comprehensive program, in which the teacher works with all of the students in the classroom, is generally more powerful in reducing bullying and increasing school safety than concentrating on individual students. It is better to prevent problems by having teachers and students develop more effective skills than it is to treat the problems after they are full-blown.

Changing the Environment Requires Support and Understanding Among Teachers.   Managing classrooms, establishing classroom rules, and developing solutions to problematic behaviors while attempting to achieve excellence in teaching is a taxing job. Teachers have shared that they benefit greatly by having resources available to facilitate problem solving and to provide support and encouragement during difficult times. Thus, creating a teacher support team is essential to the development of a successful program. The Bully Buster Teacher Support Teams are devised for a small group of teachers organized by grade level, by subject, or by teams. They meet at least once a month to review new interventions, to solve current conflicts with students, and to share ideas on effective classroom management. Teachers have enormous resources to share with one another, but frequently sharing does not happen unless a formalized structure is established.

Skills for Bullying Prevention

To establish the Bully Busters Program, it is essential that teachers review or learn basic skills that will enable them to set up their classrooms for success and prevent aggression before it starts. To accomplish this goal, teachers need to review and learn basic setting up for success procedures and skills, which are described below.

Understand the ABC's.   Basic behavioral principles are reviewed with teachers, including the ABC's of behavior: understanding the Antecedents, Behaviors, and Consequences of bullying. When bullying occurs and a child is hurt, is embarrassed, or loses something like lunch money, the consequences are unacceptable and need to be changed. We can change the consequences by changing the antecedent or the behavior. Helping teachers understand how the antecedent—what led up to the bullying—influences the outcome is powerful for preventing problems from occurring. Small group exercises are designed to help teachers practice the skill of predicting and preventing problems before they happen. For example, when students are told to line up to go to lunch and are left on their own as they begin to form a line (antecedent), a bully may take this opportunity to push and shove his way to the front (behavior). As a result, some children may get hurt or begin to push back; thus, causing an aggressive situation (consequence). If, instead, the teacher assigned the class to line up by rows or by seating arrangement and then monitors the process, the likelihood of aggression taking place is reduced. In this case, the antecedent may be clear instructions for lining up, the behavior is that the students follow specific instructions, and the consequence is an orderly line-up for lunch.

Understand the Sphere of Influence.   Teachers are very sensitive to the fact that bullying behavior has a number of contributing factors, often represented by the concentric ellipses presented in Fig. 15.1. This figure represents the

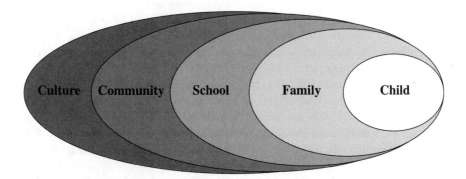

FIG. 15.1.   Ecological model of influences on bullying behavior.

ecological, systemic influences on a child's behavior. The first ellipse represents the characteristics of the child, including temperament, gender, intellectual ability, and other factors that influence how the child will behave. The second ellipse indicates the influence of the family, such as family structure and size, parenting styles, family support of schooling, parental criminality, and socio-economic status. The third ellipse represents the school influences and includes the adequacy of the school facilities, the characteristics of the teaching staff and of the students, the supervision of hallways and lunch area, and the size of the classrooms. The fourth ellipse represents the community, including the socio-economic level, the emphasis on safety and health, the level of crime, and whether it is urban or rural. The fifth ellipse is indicative of cultural influences on children's development and includes popular entertainment such as television, films, and music, and the political nature of the cultural group.

Teachers understand the levels of influence and recognize the power of the family, the community, and the popular culture to influence behavior. What they often do not understand is the extent or limit of their sphere of influence. When teachers are asked to identify risk factors for the development of bullying, they generally rank the family and cultural factors such as television, films, and pop music as having the strongest impact on children's development of bullying behaviors. When teachers are asked to indicate which factors they can influence, they recognize that their influence, for the most part, is limited to the classroom and school environment. Teachers are encouraged to focus their energy and resources on changing the areas within their sphere of influence, that is, the classroom and school. While this is a difficult position for some teachers to take, because they would prefer to assign all the responsibility to families and culture, they do agree that they should work with the children in the areas in which they can impact bullying. The family and cultural factors are usually beyond their ability to change.

Rearrange the Environment.   One way to prevent bullying is to arrange the classroom in a manner that provides the least opportunity for bullying to occur. Exercises to help teachers identify classroom arrangements and situations that may result in aggression are implemented in Bully Buster Support Team Groups. In these groups, teachers serve as "consultants" to each other to help review classroom structure and procedures and identify potential ways of improving them. For example, a frequent opportunity for aggressive behaviors to occur is during classroom transitions. To address the rowdiness of classroom transitions, one teacher brought wind chimes to her class. As each transition began, she brushed her hand across the chimes and told students they had time until the chimes were quiet to be ready for the next activity. The students lowered their voices as they listened to the chimes, becoming quieter and quieter in the process.

Establish Clear Classroom Guidelines and Be Consistent.   We encourage teachers to clearly identify their classroom rules and then share those rules with the Bully Buster Support Team Group. The teachers then work as consultants to one another on the establishment of effective classroom rules. When teachers ask students to report what rules they think exist and how consistently the teachers enforce them, teachers are often surprised how differently students perceive the rules. In addition to students not knowing the rules, common complaints that students have is that the rules "just aren't fair" or are applied in an unfair manner because some students are exempt from the rules while others are expected to obey them. Thus, teachers are often reminded of the importance of consistency within their classroom.

Use Respectful, Polite, Clear, Specific Language.   At the beginning of our Bully Busters Program, we explain that there are three values or beliefs that we hold to, and that we expect all members of the group to endorse these values as well. These values have also been used in other teacher training programs (Orpinas, Horne, & Multisite Violence Prevention Project, in press). They include the following:

1. All children can learn.
2. All people in school deserve to be treated with respect and dignity.
3. There is no place for violence, aggression, or bullying in our schools.

In the Bully Buster Support Team Group teachers review effective and less effective means of talking with students about aggression and bullying. The language expected from teachers is polite and respectful. If we expect students to demonstrate respect for one another, we must model this respect with our language. It is important that language used by teachers with students be clear and specific, not sarcastic, critical, or punitive. We have reports from students and at times from fellow teachers that some teachers may use inappropriate language or methods of speaking with the children. While we understand the frustrations that teachers may have and we understand how difficult it is to get some students' attention, we emphasize the value of the teachers' positive modeling.

Avoid Public Confrontations.   We often observe the bullying behavior in public settings such as the classroom, playground, lunchroom, or hallway. While teachers should attempt to stop the bullying behavior at once, they should try to solve the problem in a private setting. Attempting to change bullying behavior in the public forum puts the student on the spot in terms of having to defend or explain. The student may respond negatively, so as to avoid "losing face" or being "dissed" by the teacher in front of peers. Public confrontations by teachers can lead to an escalation of emotions and aggression, neither of which is conducive to positive change. Rather, it is better to stop an altercation and establish a later time for remediation. For example, a teacher might say, "Tracy, stop that now. Our rule is we do not name call and tease. I'll talk with you when we return to the classroom about how we are going to handle this. Now continue with your lunch." Helping teachers learn to avoid public confrontations also means helping them learn to avoid power struggles with students. It is almost never a good idea for a teacher to get into a public power struggle with a bully. Engaging in a power struggle is likely to escalate the conflict, and the student may resort to increased aggression and to refuse to back down or yield. This is not a good spot to be in, and all children need a way out of this kind of situation. In a public forum, it is difficult, but important, for the teacher to help the student find a graceful way out of a conflict situation.

Teach New Skills.   Many of the students in our classes lack the skills necessary to engage in positive peer relationships. If students do not have the skills, or have inappropriate ones, then it becomes the responsibility of teachers to incorporate the appropriate skill development into their work with them. As teachers and researchers, we truly believe that students need to develop emotional intelligence, and they need to develop the necessary assets to lead an effective life. An effective life involves being able to live and work with one another harmoniously. Effective people skills, problem solving skills, and personal responsibility are equally important as the content of the subject matter we teach our students. To assist students in developing their social and problem solving skills, teachers need to know how to evaluate what level of skills students have and what additional skills they need to learn. With this information, teachers can provide opportunities for students to learn such skills.

We have found that all teachers agree that skill development is an essential element of education, but most focus their skill development activities on academic subjects, such as reading or math. Very few teachers have identified and initiated the use of specific development activities for social skills such as conflict resolution, problem solving, anger management, and empathy development. The importance of the development of these skills is emphasized throughout the teacher training workshop and the support groups.

Use a Solution-Focused Approach to Problems.   Problem-focused approaches to dealing with children's behavior problems lead us to focus on the root causes of the problem, the background that has led to the current situation, and the reason for the behavior. While it is helpful for teachers to understand why a problem exists, the understanding does not always lead to answers about what to do about solving the problem. A solution-focused model intends to help teachers find solutions when a problem is encountered.

Even though there are definite drawbacks to the problem-focused approach, much of our school culture is focused on the problems that teachers encounter. We have spent considerable time in schools hearing extensive discussions about the problems encountered and the diagnosis of problems, but the discussions often end there without developing effective strategies that lead to solutions. When teachers use a problem-focused approach they put the emphasis on what is wrong, on what students can't do. This emphasis on the problem generally leads to a sense of frustration and exasperation, and students may be left with teachers who want to "give up." Helping teachers learn to focus on solutions, rather than problems, helps them to change the beliefs and expectations they have about their students. It allows them to be more oriented toward solving the problem than just describing the problem; to spending time seeking a solution to the problem rather than spending time investigating its cause. Being solution-focused leads teachers to become more proactive rather than reactive, and to look for and identify solutions to the problems. One aspect of the solution-focused approach is for teachers to review their sphere of influence. Energy should be spent on what can be influenced instead of what can't.

Our goal of assisting teachers to work from a solution-focused approach is to help challenge the labels given to both bullies and victims. To achieve this goal, we provide opportunities for teachers and the students to see bullies and victims differently. Are bullies always bullying? Not typically. Are victims continuously victimized? Not usually. These students have numerous other characteristics that may be overlooked due to some of their more troublesome behaviors. A problem-focused approach leaves everyone frustrated because the teachers and the students feel stuck and there is little room to grow and change. Having teachers use a solution-focused approach helps to create change because it allows teachers and students to create new options and opportunities for behaviors. We are chronically optimistic about the potential for positive change.

Use the Big Questions. The Big Questions provide a solution-focused technique that can help teachers become more efficient and effective problem-solvers and, thus, have a stronger impact with solving bullying problems. Teachers may also use the big questions with students to help them learn more effective means of managing conflict. The Big Questions are as follows (examples are shown in italics):

Question 1: What is the problem and what is my goal? [Identify the problem and what you are attempting to achieve]
Randy and Roy are being disruptive again, calling each other names. My goal is to help teach my students conflict resolution skills.
Question 2: What am I doing? [Identify how you are reacting to the situation]
I am standing in front of the class, but I don't have the attention of the students. I am feeling upset, tired, and frustrated. I feel like quitting for the day.
Question 3: Is what I am doing helping me achieve my goal? [Evaluate the effectiveness of my behaviors]
No, I am getting upset and frustrated. I am not teaching the conflict resolution skills effectively.

Question 4: (If not) What can I do differently that will help me to achieve my goal? [Generate alternative solutions]

I am going to take a minute and think about what is happening in my class-room. What usually gets the students' attention and allows them to have a good time while learning something new? Sometimes, it is better if we sit on the floor together in a circle or if I ask for several volunteers to help teach. Let me think of what other ideas I can come up with and try one out.

Question 5: Is my new strategy working? [Look back and evaluate how the new strategy is working.]

These five questions are very powerful for helping teachers examine their methods of working with disruptive and conflictual students. In the process, teachers can incorporate the ABC's of examining situations, behaviors, and consequences, as well as the core components of setting up for success. The use of the Big Questions takes practice and support to use, but when teachers incorporate the process into their thinking and practice, it is very powerful for creating change and reducing bullying behaviors.

Implementation of the Bully Busters Program

The Bully Busters Program is implemented through a teacher training workshop followed by teacher support groups. The teacher workshop is offered to as many teachers as are interested, ideally to all the teachers in the school. The teacher workshop includes the basic theoretical material presented in the prior section, as well as the specific classroom materials described in this section. The workshop is designed to provide the opportunity for small group experiences supervised by the trainer. Two days are required to complete the workshop. In addition to the workshop, a powerful component of the Bully Buster Program is the use of Bully Buster Teacher Support Teams. The Support Teams are scheduled to meet approximately eight times during the school year, about once a month. Teams are usually composed of six to eight teachers. Teachers determine the composition of the teams, and they can be organized by grade level or by specialty areas such as reading. The support team fulfills several roles: it serves as a reminder to teachers to continue addressing the problem of bullying, it provides an opportunity to discuss situations in the classroom or with specific students that continue to be problematic, and it offers the chance to review what works and what is not effective in the prevention of bullying. Most important of all, the group should be a place where teachers feel supported and understood.

The workshop consists of eight modules. Each module addresses a particular element of the bully/victim problem. The goals for each module are described in Table 15.1. Each module is composed of an overview, a rationale for the

TABLE 15.1

Goals by Module of the Bully Busters Program

Module	Goal
Module 1: Increasing Awareness of Bullying	To differentiate between bullying and aggression, identify the types of bullying problems in the classroom and school, examine the role teachers can play in creating a safe, bully-free school, explain how to nourish the developmental assets of students in order to prevent bullying interactions.
Module 2: Preventing Bullying in Your Classroom	To understand the role of prevention in eliminating school bullying, become familiar with teacher characteristics that maintain bullying, identify school characteristics that affect bullying, and develop methods to prevent bullying and victimization in your classroom.
Module 3: Building Personal Power	To understand the importance of attending to social, as well as to academic development in students; create an atmosphere of respect and kindness in the classroom and school; learn to teach basic social skills needed to handle and prevent bullying interactions in the classroom; gain awareness of the need to increase students' abilities to engage in more positive and effective interactions; and increase the personal resources of teachers and students.
Module 4: Recognizing the Bully	To understand theories of how bullying behaviors develop and recognize the purposefulness of bullying behaviors; differentiate between the many forms of childhood bullying; differentiate between male and female bullying; examine the essential role teachers play in helping the child that bullies; and analyze the positive, social assets of children who bully.
Module 5: Recognizing the Victim	To increase our understanding of victims and their needs; challenge common myths about victims and victimization; recognize characteristics of victims and the signs of victimization; and identify four types of victims: passive, provocative, relational, and bystander.
Module 6: Recommendations and Interventions for Bullying Behavior	To identify specific ways to create an invitational approach in initiating contact and establishing rapport with bullies; review basic behavior change principles as they relate to bullying; recognize examples of bullies, victims, and bystander and how each child can actively prevent and intervene in bullying interactions; identify specific skills that can be developed in bullies to help them change their behaviors; and examine the "Four R's" of bully control.
Module 7: Recommendations and Interventions for Helping Victims	To recognize the importance of teacher's ability to offer victim support; identify strategies to directly help children who are in the victim role; help children learn to avoid the victim role through skills training, encouragement, and empowerment; and implement intervention strategies specifically targeted at each type of victim.
Module 8: Relaxation and Coping Skills	To become familiar with the role of stress and its effects; examine the role of thoughts, beliefs, and behavior in maintaining or eliminating stress; become aware of general stress management skills; and develop specific relaxation techniques to reduce stress on a daily basis.

importance of the topic, objectives to be accomplished, discussions about the topic, and activities that teachers may use with students in the classroom that are related to the topic. The eight modules are taught in the workshop and then modules are reviewed in the ongoing Bully Busters Teacher Support Groups.

Module 1: Increasing Awareness of Bullying

Module 1 is designed to help teachers and students increase their awareness of the extent of the problem of bullying, develop a common definition of bullying, understand the myths related to bullying, and develop classroom exercises to help students understand the problem. We often hear from teachers that bullying is not a problem at their school. In some cases, this statement is accurate, but generally the situation is not as positive as teachers portray it. An exercise designed to increase awareness is to ask teachers and students to complete a survey evaluating the extent to which a number of topics related to bullying and violence are problematic at school. Examples of topics are vandalism, teasing, name-calling, fighting, weapon-carrying, unsafe areas at school, threats, and level of teacher help to stop bullying. Most frequently, compared to teachers' responses, students report a much higher level of bullying and a much lower level of teacher help with bullying problems. This information usually surprises teachers, and many of them discount the accuracy of the students' reports. However, even if students' views are inaccurate, it is important—even essential—to address their perceptions.

The second part of Module 1 is to develop definitions of bullying that are acceptable and usable by teachers and students, including physical, emotional and relational bullying. Teachers are requested to track bullying behavior. We differentiate among rough-and-tumble play (normal), bullying (requiring action from teachers and peers), and conduct disorders/delinquency (legal or police action, or perhaps requiring consultation from counselors, school psychologists, or special education staff). In rough-and-tumble play, children often choose their roles and engage in role reversals (e.g., good guy/bad guy), while the roles almost always remain stable in bullying situations (e.g., victim and bully). Another difference between bullying and play is the voluntary nature of the process. Victims of bullying do not voluntarily participate in activities in which there is an imbalance of power. Teachers are asked to share the PIC definition with students. Teachers are also assisted in identifying and locating the more common places where bullying occurs. This is also a time when teachers are asked to review the school's public statement, if any, about aggression and bullying, and to review the school crisis or emergency plan, sometimes a new experience for teachers.

In the third part of Module 1, common myths or misconceptions about bullying are discussed. It is important that the myths be discussed with teachers, and that teachers review these myths with their students. Many teachers hold erroneous beliefs and until their beliefs change, teachers' behavior will not change.

TABLE 15.2
Challenges to Teachers' Erroneous Beliefs About Bullying

Erroneous Teacher Beliefs About Bullying	Challenges to the Beliefs
Bullying is just a normal part of childhood.	Bullying is not a normal part of growing up. Children can and should be socialized to respect and treat others kindly, and to know that hurting others is inappropriate.
Children will outgrow bullying.	While some aggression and bullying will decrease as children mature, unless action is taken by adults or influential peers, bullying is likely to continue and, in some cases, escalate to violence, delinquency, or criminal behavior.
Some children are just born rough.	Bullying behavior is learned and maintained in a social situation (school, classroom, neighborhood) and can be stopped there as well.
Teachers "can't" intervene in bullying situations because they lack adequate training and skills.	Many teachers believe they do not have the knowledge and skills to intervene in bullying situations. However, students trust teachers and rely on them to help them when they are in need. Teachers can become experts at managing bully problems and supporting students on a daily basis. Programs such as Bully Busters can help teachers develop their skills.
Intervening will only add "fuel to the fire" and result in continued or increased bullying.	In fact, the opposite is more accurate. The more we ignore bullying, the stronger the likelihood that its frequency will escalate. If bullies learn that they can usually get away with their behavior, their behavior will tend to continue or even increase.
It is best to ignore bullying incidents.	This sends the message to bullies that they can continue to act as they have, and a message to victims that they are on their own and vulnerable to the bullying; thus, confirming students' beliefs that teachers are unaware of or insensitive to the problem.

Some of the common beliefs that teachers have endorsed and the challenges to those beliefs are presented in Table 15.2.

Module 1 concludes with several activities for teachers to use with students. One of these activities is *Framing the Bully*. Each child receives a sheet of paper with the outline of a picture frame. The teacher asks the students to draw a picture of a bully inside the picture frame without using names and to focus on what a bully is like. When students finish, they share their pictures with the class and discuss the meaning of their drawing. This powerful activity begins to establish a class awareness of what is an acceptable and an unacceptable behavior. It helps bullies, victims, and bystanders understand what the majority of students think about bullies.

Module 2: Preventing Bullying in Your Classroom

The primary focus of Module 2 is on prevention. In this section, we apply the Setting Up For Success information presented in the prior section, and we discuss the personal characteristics of teachers and administrators that hinder or enhance a violence-free school. The module starts by discussing how to initiate administrative support from the principal and other administrators in the building, which is a crucial element for the success of the program. Strategies discussed include sharing with administrators the importance of prevention, the data collected about student and teacher perceptions of the problem, the cost (time, resources) of fixing the problem after it has developed, and the importance of having an administrator who can garner community and family support. Goldstein (1999) reported that schools characterized by low aggression generally have administrators who exhibit the following qualities:

- They are highly visible and available to students and teachers.
- They know the "pulse" of the school—they know what is occurring in their school.
- They recognize problems in the school and rapidly take steps to address them.
- They have created fair and consistent responses to the needs and complaints of students and teachers and are quick to respond to grievances.
- They support and empower teachers and school personnel to meet the needs of their students.

Also, according to Goldstein (1999), schools characterized by high aggression generally have administrators who exhibit the following characteristics:

- They provide too strict/rigid or too lax guidelines for teachers and students.
- Their interactions are impersonal and they separate themselves from the needs of their teachers and students.
- They provide inconsistent means of addressing school problems and implementing responses to problems.
- They overuse punishment and harsh discipline with teachers and students.
- They provide weak or inconsistent support to faculty.

We have developed the term FAMOUS teacher to help identify some of the core characteristics of meeting the emotional and behavioral needs of students, particularly students who may be involved in the bully/victim interaction. What are FAMOUS teachers? FAMOUS teachers work with their students in a positive manner that can build meaningful relationships and help to create a peaceful classroom environment ideal for learning. A FAMOUS teacher is

Fair and Firm
Arranges reasonable rules and consequences
Models positive and respectful behaviors

Open and trustworthy
Understands the diverse needs and experiences of students
Shows genuine interest in students

Module 2 concludes with a series of activities to help the students become more sensitized to the extent of bullying and seek help to stop the problem. For example, one activity includes the development of a drop box, which gives students permission to report bullying. Twice a week, students turn in note cards describing what is working and what is not working for reducing bullying in the classroom. All students are asked to drop in cards so that the children who need help are not singled out by being the only ones submitting cards to the box. This activity is very empowering for it gives the students an outlet to ask for help and to provide feedback on what is working to help them with the problem of aggression. Teachers discuss the concerns students have raised with the whole class and act on the information as appropriate.

Module 3: Building Personal Power

Module 3 was developed to help teachers assist all students in developing personal power. Power is defined as confidence in their ability to manage bullying and aggression problems in the classroom and school by enhancing their social skills. Teachers develop increased self-efficacy for managing bullying in their classrooms by rehearsing practical strategies that they can use with their students. The strategies are designed to help students overcome adversarial social situations by enhancing their strengths and by learning how to manage conflict and anger. In addition, a drop-box is installed as a practical mechanism to report bullying and ask for help.

Bullies victimize children because they are perceived, sometimes accurately, as lacking power. One strategy to help children develop a sense of power is by helping them develop a narrative—a story to themselves—about their strengths and abilities. By using animal stories or by telling stories about children, the teacher shares information about how the animals or the children were able to overcome adversarial conditions by building upon their strengths.

Teachers are taught specific exercises and activities to teach the seven skills for positive conflict resolution to the class. These skills will help students to be more effective in their interactions with peers. The seven skills are:

1. A belief that non-violence and respect are essential for managing conflict.
2. The development of emotional intelligence so that children who are able to look at their own feelings in a situation become able to consider how others involved may feel (Goleman, 1995).
3. An ability of children to control emotions and behaviors (Bodine & Crawford, 1999).
4. A capability to communicate feelings and thoughts to others.

5. An ability to listen to others.
6. An ability to brainstorm numerous options in handling a conflict.
7. The ability to ask the Big Questions: What is my goal? What am I doing? Is what I'm doing working? In not, what can I do differently? Is what I am doing now working?

Another component of developing personal power is learning to recognize and manage anger. Animal stories identifying different ways that anger may be managed are shared with the students. "Feeling charts" are used to help describe their level of emotions, and role-plays are used to practice different emotions. Students are also taught how to do team work and how to value supporting one another. Stories are shared that help students recognize the importance of group support for reducing aggression.

Activities to help demonstrate ways of managing conflict in the classroom are discussed with teachers. The activities include helping students learn how to request help and support from peers and teachers, how to take risks to address problems they are experiencing, and how to use their own story to provide themselves with encouragement and positive directions for interactions with others. They are also taught the use of humor and laughter, and how social skills often include learning to laugh at problems, deflect criticism, and avoid confrontations.

There are a number of activities that teachers can use with students to help them gain greater personal power. One such activity is "Name that Feeling." This activity promotes personal power by helping students identify common feelings others may have in various challenging situations. Knowing what others are experiencing can empower students to manage their own feelings and behavior more effectively. To accomplish this activity, students are given worksheets with various emotion faces (smiling, frowning, angry, etc.) and situations that students may encounter (being left out of a play group, being pushed by another child, getting a present from a friend). Students then match the face to the situation and explain why they thought the particular situation would evoke the emotion they selected on the face.

Module 4: Recognizing the Bully

The goal of Module 4 is to help teachers recognize the characteristics of the different types of bullies, as well as the risk and developmental factors that contribute to the development of bullying and aggression in children. It helps teachers identify risk factors that may be operating in the classroom and school environment, as well as the external factors that influence bullying behaviors. Teachers are taught the differing types of bullies and what behavioral and emotional components characterize bullies: the aggressive bully, the passive bully, and the relational bully.

The aggressive bully is the most common type of bully, one who initiates aggression towards peers and is characterized as fearless, coercive, tough, and impulsive.

The aggressive bully has an inclination towards violence and a desire to dominate others (Olweus, 1996; Ross, 1996), shows little expression of empathy towards victims (Olweus, 1994), openly attacks victims, enjoys having control over others, often sees the victim's behavior as provocative regardless of the victim's intentions, and often views the world through a paranoid lens (Ross, 1996). Common behaviors of the aggressive bully include pushing or hitting; threatening physical harm; stealing money, lunches, or materials; and trapping the victim in hallways or bathrooms.

The passive bully is less common than the aggressive bully and tends to be dependent on the more aggressive bully. He or she can be insecure and anxious and seeks the attention and acceptance of the aggressive bully, may value the norm of aggression and violence, is likely to join in the bullying if he or she sees that bullying is rewarded, and lacks a defined social status among peers without the bully. The passive bully is referred to as a "follower" (Olweus, 1996; Ross, 1996). Commonly, the passive bully supports the aggressive bully's actions, copies the actions of the aggressive bully, uses indirect methods to bully others (such as social exclusion and name-calling), and typically does not initiate aggressive behaviors without the aggressive bully.

The relational bully is the most common type of bully among girls, but is not limited to females. The relational bully often attempts to gain social status and power through the exclusion and manipulation of others. They intentionally isolate peers from social activities and events, and when upset with peers, they "get even" through excluding them from the peer group. Common behaviors of the relational bully include spreading rumors or lies about a peer, attempting to get others not to like a peer through storytelling, excluding others from social activities (on the playground, at the lunch table, or during after-school events), and threatening to not be friends with a peer unless the peer does what the bully wants (Crick, 1996).

In Module 4, teachers review differences between male and female bullies. Boys often exhibit direct, aggressive forms of bullying, which teachers and students alike can usually recognize. They tend to engage in verbal and physical bullying, and bully both male and female classmates. Boys who are rough are often called bullies, even if their behaviors do not meet the bullying criteria. Conversely, girls' negative behavior is more often classified as "mean."

Bullying by girls is more difficult to detect because they frequently use less visible and more indirect means of harassment. Whereas males bully both sexes, females are more likely to bully other females. Many teachers, school personnel, students, and even female bullies themselves have difficulty recognizing the behaviors of the female bully (Eslea & Smith, 1998). Female bullies are frequently not aware that their behavior would be considered bullying and, consequently, do not see the need for change. Although physical bullying is not as common, girls also engage in it.

Because female bullying is more difficult to detect, developing successful interventions is more challenging. Several anti-bullying programs have found decreases in male bullying but either found no change or an increase in the amount of female bullying. These results may have been found for two reasons: (1) the bullying interventions did not effectively target the behaviors of the female bully; (2) the increased awareness of female bullying lead to a needed increased awareness of female bullying, which may have led then to increased reporting of it.

In some ways, children who become bullies are attempting to gain the recognition and attention that they crave and have not experienced in healthy relationships. These children do the best they can, use what they know, and learn that bullying others can get them what they want and need. Although we cannot change the family factors influencing aggression, we can work together to understand what factors lead to bullying and help children who bully have a more positive experience while at school, find new ways of interacting with their peers, and learn more appropriate behaviors. The great news is that teachers have a powerful influence to reduce bullying behaviors, by facilitating the development of more adaptive skills, of more effective means of problem solving, and of more positive peer relationships.

Just as teachers may believe unfounded myths about bullying, as described in Table 15.2, there are often also mistaken beliefs about the development of bullying. These mistaken beliefs can influence teachers' perception of whether or not bullying is occurring and can interfere with their ability to intervene successfully. Table 15.3 includes several of these beliefs and the challenges to them.

Teachers use a number of activities with the students to help them become more attuned to bullying. An example of these activities is "Bullies at Work." In this activity, students receive a handout describing three types of bullies: aggressive, passive, and relational. Working in pairs or small groups, the students then consider a number of scenarios and identify the type of bullying in each. One scenario is:

> Julia thinks people will like Shari better than they like her. So Julie decides she will ruin Shari's reputation by spreading lies about her. What type of bully is Julia?

Module 5: Recognizing the Victim

The goal of Module 5 is to assist teachers in understanding the victim and the victim's role in the bully/victim interaction. This Module prepares teachers to conduct skills training activities to help all students, but especially those who have been the targets of the bully's attention, learn more effective methods for managing the bully problem.

The old cliché "sticks and stones may break my bones but names will never hurt me" is commonly used but it is erroneous. Name-calling, excluding peers from social activities and relationships, and threatening to hurt are all examples of how bullies inflict harm on a daily basis and create life-long psychological

TABLE 15.3

Challenges to Teachers' Beliefs That Maintain Bullying

Teacher Beliefs that Maintain Bullying	Challenges to the Beliefs
Only male children bully.	Direct male bullying is the most obvious form of bullying and the most common among school children. Female bullying often is relational and may not be as obvious to detect as direct male bullying.
Bullying is child's play.	Bullying has long-term consequences, is not outgrown, and is likely to get worse in middle school. Further, the number of bullies in school may decrease with each grade level, but those who continue are likely to engage in more serious and aggressive behaviors. Children who engage in bullying at a young age are more likely to continue with these behaviors and have an increased risk of adolescent and adult criminal activity.
I can't change the way children are treated at home.	Children may learn to react aggressively at home or in their neighborhood but they can learn to be non-aggressive in school. When a child forms meaningful bonds within the school community and perceives the school environment as encouraging and supportive, it is less likely that the child will respond with aggression.
Aggressive behaviors of bullies are related to school frustrations.	School is one of the many contexts that can influence the development of bullying behaviors. Children may experience difficulty with their schoolwork for a variety of reasons but typically, signs of behavior problems occur before the onset of academic problems.
Bullies only bully because they are frustrated with their school experience.	Bullies frequently experience school difficulties and frustrations but academic difficulties typically follow aggressiveness, not precede it. School problems are common in students who are aggressive or who bully, because they are less likely to attend to school matters, pay attention in class, and spend time on their schoolwork.
Bullies only pick on kids that are different in some way.	Bullies target their peers who appear less powerful than themselves. Some of the bullies' targets do have unique features, but the primary characteristic that bullies target in a victim is a sense of helplessness or powerlessness.
I won't see bullying because it happens to and from school and not during the school day.	A great deal of bullying does occur to and from school, especially on the school bus. However, even more bullying occurs during the school day, for example in the bathrooms and on the school playground. Bullying is most likely to occur when there is a lack of adult supervision and structured activity.
If I don't see it happen, there's nothing I can do about bullying behavior because I'm not sure it happened.	Bullies are particularly adept at being aggressive in sneaky or private ways, but that does not mean the behavior is not happening. It is our responsibility to provide a classroom environment that is safe and supportive and in which students may seek help.

struggles. Name-calling, a form of emotional abuse that is commonly overlooked or not perceived as particularly harmful, appears to be the most prevalent and devastating (Besag, 1989). Name-calling often precipitates physical attacks and can be a cause for a student to be embarrassed, isolated from others, or excluded from a peer group. In addition, victims of verbal bullying, such as teasing and ridiculing, often report having their property stolen or vandalized. The effects of victimization are far reaching and expand into adulthood, severely traumatizing both boys and girls. This trauma has been linked to depression, feelings of helplessness, and suicide. In recent years, we have witnessed the link between long-term victimization and retaliation through mass school shootings, the most extreme form of victim retaliation. The children who are victimized often go unnoticed, forgotten, or ignored, which often perpetuates the problem. Most frequently it is the bully who receives the attention, while the victims go unnoticed or are blamed for being the victim.

Modules 1 and 4 have already presented examples of erroneous thinking or faulty beliefs that teachers at times have which maintain bullying and aggressive behaviors. A primary focus of Module 5 is recognizing and attending to teacher beliefs related to victims of bullying. The erroneous thinking patterns may hinder the victims' healthy growth. Examples of commonly held teacher beliefs and their associated facts about victimization of students are described on Table 15.4.

Module 5 is also designed to help teachers recognize the signs of possible victimization, such as looking fearful, avoiding the bathroom or parts of the classroom, not eating lunch, developing physical ailments, becoming tearful, and missing school.

Teachers rehearse several activities that facilitate helping all students become sensitized to the problems that children who are the target of bullying experience. These sensitive activities are designed to help students develop more positive beliefs about children who have been victimized, to make certain that they do not inadvertently blame the victim, and to increase all children's level of empathic responding to their peers. One activity used with Module 5 is called "Bye, Bye, Bully." In this activity, children discuss the different kinds of things bullies do when they victimize other children. To help them consider the perspective and feelings of children who have been victimized, students draw a picture to show what someone being bullied might look like to them. Then, they discuss how the victim might feel if students worked together to eliminate bullying.

Module 6: Recommendations and Interventions for Bullying Behavior

Module 6 provides a number of specific activities and classroom structuring strategies for the prevention of bullying and aggression, as well as interventions if bullying does occur. Much of the material presented in Module 6 has been implied from earlier discussions.

TABLE 15.4
Challenges to Teachers' Beliefs That Maintain Victimization

Teacher Beliefs That Maintain Victimization	Challenges to the Beliefs
Some kids ask to be bullied. They do things in unusual ways that attract the bully.	Each child is doing the best he or she can, and no child deserves to be victimized. The teacher's job is not to blame the victim, but to solve the problem. Teachers can teach the victims skills to handle bullying more effectively.
Bullying is just child's play; all kids will outgrow bullying and victimization.	Bullying is done intentionally and repeatedly to harm someone. It is not normal child's play for children to intentionally hurt one another. The effects of the trauma caused by bullying may be long lasting.
Bullies help kids that seem weaker by pushing them to learn to stand up for themselves.	Bullies typically have much more power in the form of strength, intellectual abilities, or social clout than victims. Children can learn assertiveness skills to stand up to bullies, but those skills are best learned in an encouraging and supportive setting, not in an interaction founded on fear and intimidation.
Name-calling, spreading rumors, or purposefully embarrassing a student is simply kids being kids.	Name-calling, rumor spreading, and causing embarrassment are all forms of serious bullying. Relational bullying often lead victims to be isolated or rejected by their peers. The feelings of rejection from peers at school can have serious, long-term consequences, such as school dropout, severe adult psychological problems, and even suicide.
Only boys bully, and they only bully other boys; I don't have to worry about girls bullying or being victimized.	Both boys and girls can bully and be victimized. Female bullies typically bully other females and use indirect tactics, such as excluding peers from social situations, spreading rumors. Male bullies more commonly engage in overt, direct, and physical bullying, and bully both males and females.
There isn't enough time during the school day to address bullying incidents or to introduce issues related to bullying into my classroom's curriculum.	Bullying and victimization interferes with children's ability to succeed academically. Children who bully or are victimized are not likely to be in an emotional state to succeed academically. Introducing the topic of bullying creates a forum to discuss issues related to bullying. Teaching problem-solving skills may help to prevent the problem.
I want to help my students and hope that they will talk to me, but I really don't want to create a situation where everyone is tattle-telling on each other.	Initially, teachers may experience an increase in the number of students reporting problems. This is a good sign; it means that the students trust that teachers will do something about bullying. As students learn new skills to problem-solve and intervene in bullying, they will feel more confident to handle situations independently. Both teachers and students should learn to differentiate between tattling and reporting.
Bullying is not a problem in my class or in my school.	For some teachers and classrooms this may be the case. However there is a "code of silence" that students of all ages adhere to out of fear that they will be targeted by the bully. Discussing issues related to bullying may help students to feel more comfortable in breaking the "code of silence."

A key focus of Module 6 is helping teachers establish a working relationship with bullies. This includes teachers' understanding that bullies actions often indicate a need for attention, revenge, or power, and how each of those goals of misbehavior requires different ways of approaching the bully. For example, when a bully is acting out because of a desire to demonstrate that he or she can be seen as powerful rather than impotent, instead of a "put the bully in his place" attitude, the teacher should identify ways of helping the bully feel more powerful among peers by developing more socially appropriate skills.

Another aspect of responding to bullying in the classroom is to use what we call the "Four R's of Bully Control." The Four R's are practiced in the Bully Busters Support Group so that all teachers are comfortable following this process.

Recognize that a problem exists and remember to stay calm. (When a problem exists, it must be recognized and defined.)

Remove yourself or step back from the situation, if you do not feel you can effectively intervene. (Examining what you are doing reflects how important it is to step back, to remove oneself from the conflict in order to understand the situation better.)

Review the situation (Review the situation to figure out whether what you are doing is working to solve the problem.)

Respond to the situation (If you feel competent to intervene, then do so. If you are uncertain how to intervene, assist students in finding help elsewhere.)

The next component of helping teachers address the problem of bullying in the classroom is to review the basic behavioral change strategies. Most teachers are very familiar with the strategies but they have not had the opportunity or encouragement to think of ways of applying the specific strategies to problems of bullying. Several of the more common behavioral interventions to review with teachers include the following:

Modeling
Positive reinforcement
Removal of positive reinforcement
Praise and encouragement
Impulse control activities
Empathy training
Help students change their reputations
Social skills training
Problem solving skills

In reviewing these strategies with teachers, the facilitator should be familiar with each method and have thought about specific age-appropriate applications.

For example, in helping teachers to learn the effective use of praise versus encouragement, it is important to explain the differences and provide examples:

Initially, verbal reinforcement may not bring behavior change. As we have said, children are most likely to respond positively when teachers combine social and tangible reinforcements. For example, when the class behaved well for a substitute teacher, the teacher might say, "I am so proud of your good behavior while I was out yesterday. Hearing about how well you all did made me feel so happy. Therefore, today I am allowing the class 15 minutes extra at lunch today." Eventually, students will come to desire the praise and the words of praise will be sufficient.

The terms *praise* and *encouragement* are often used together and viewed as interchangeable. However, the two terms are quite different. Praise generally comes from the teacher and describes a characteristic that the teacher has noticed and one in which the teacher feels good. Praise is very powerful to get the students' attention, to help them to identify and recognize appropriate behavior, and to continually encourage positive behavior. Examples of praise are as follows:

"Peter, I really liked how you helped Ryan with moving that desk. Thank you for your help."

"Robin, thank you for including Melissa—I like that a lot."

"Lonny, you really paid attention all during math today. Great job!"

The potential problem with praise is that it is external to the student. The student is inclined to behave in a particular way just to get the teacher to notice and give praise, not because the student wants to behave that way. Our goal is to help children learn to be responsible for their own behavior. While praise helps them initially in recognizing their good behavior and in realizing that other people do notice their good behavior, it does not influence them to take ownership of their behavior.

An alternative to praise is encouragement. With encouragement, the goal of the reinforcement switches from the external (the teacher) to the internal (the student). When the teacher encourages, he or she is helping the student internalize the reinforcing message. When students internalize the importance of behaving well and associate it with feeling good about themselves, they are likely to take ownership of their behavior. Examples of encouragement are:

"Jeff, you seemed really happy with how well you did on your school work today. I'll bet that makes you feel good."

"Laura, you were so eager to help Mia get her papers together. It must make you feel happy to know you are helping someone else."

"Jonas, you really are trying hard on that tough problem. You really seem to be motivated to work through even the hardest problems. Good job!"

"Karin and Eric, I know it can be hard to work as partners on this activity, but I know you two can find a way to work well together, and achieve both of your goals. I'm sure you can do it."

There are many activities that may be used by teachers to help students learn more effective ways of managing the bully problems they encounter. One such activity is the "Turtle Club," where students learn an anger management strategy for controlling impulsive behavior. Students have the opportunity of practicing this technique, and they are encouraged to use it in their daily classroom routine. The Turtle Club involves telling the students a story about Timmy the Turtle who got in trouble a lot, but who learned to pull into his shell, calm himself down, identify the problem and the feelings he was having, decide on several things he could do to fix the problem, then come out of the shell and carry out his decision. This behavior change activity can be effective to help all students in the classroom learn better self control skills.

Module 7: Recommendations and Interventions for Helping Victims

We often hear teachers say that helping the victim will only make matters worse for the victim. As described previously, this is the number one myth of victim intervention. Victims are desperately in need of their teacher's help. Teachers can help victims in many ways: by implementing this program, by addressing the problem of bullying, and by actively taking steps to prevent bullying in classes. By helping bullies, victims are also being helped indirectly. However, victims also need direct intervention. Direct help to the victim openly communicates to the victim that they are believed and that they are worth the teachers' time and energy. Our society has made a commitment to protect children. For example, we value reporting child abuse and neglect. Bullying is another form of childhood trauma that cannot be ignored or overlooked. Learning how to help victims, in their varying forms, is the purpose of this module.

If children could defend themselves against bullying, they would. Many children who are not victimized have learned skills or have characteristics that buffer them from victimization. Children need training, skills, and support to stop the bullying. If children are being victimized at school and teachers do not have the resources to teach victims how to better fend for themselves, then the school counselor, school psychologist, or an administrator with skills in this area should be called in to help.

Just as we adults do not want to be left to our own resources on the streets of our communities when muggers and vandals want to relieve us of our wallets or purses, similarly the students in our schools do not want to be left to their own resources to figure out how to manage the bullies. They need support and skills training. Instead of children having to defend themselves, teachers can support victims through the following:

- Conducting the activities of each module with students in classes.
- Reviewing materials on social skills building that may be relevant to children who are victimized.

- Creating an environment in the classroom in which each child is treated with respect and dignity and that provides a process for mediating and solving conflicts.
- Developing a culture of support so that if the teacher is not available to assist children who are picked on, other classmates will move from the bystander/observer role into an intervener or facilitator role.

Bullying is an interaction between a bully and a victim. The bully selects the victim because he or she believes that the victim will be an easy target who will not defend himself or herself. The bully wants to feel powerful and does so by selecting victims that are perceived as less powerful. Therefore, just as we teach the bully new skills to substitute their aggression towards others, we also need to teach victims skills to protect themselves from the bullying interaction. Victims can feel empowered when they learn to use their own skills to make changes in the bullying interaction. Rather than feeling like a helpless recipient of undue attention from the bully, victims will learn how to take an active role in changing the bully/victim interaction. As victims take this role, they can begin to see themselves differently. They may no longer see themselves as victims; they will be able to gain confidence in their abilities to change interactions in their lives.

No child is to blame for being the victim. However, we do believe that victims can also take an active role in changing the bullying interaction. Victims should not have to change their identity to avoid being bullied. However, victims can learn skills so that they feel better about who they are and feel more confident in their abilities to protect themselves. One way to reduce school aggression is to help victims learn skills and behaviors that will reduce the likelihood that they will be targets of aggressive acts time and time again. Similarly, we do not want to strip bullies of their identity and experiences; but we do want to teach them new skills so they have more positive interactions and feel better about themselves and their relationships.

By teaching the victims skills to reduce their victimization, we are by no means placing the responsibility for change solely on the victims. What we are doing is exploring with the victims possible changes that they may be interested in and willing to make. While some victims have characteristics that attract bullies to them, such as bodily characteristics or appearance—over which they have no control—others do at times engage in behaviors and activities that elicit the attention of bullies. No student should live in fear and anxiety, so we need to work to change the environment to be more accepting and supportive. At the same time, we offer victims the opportunity of developing skills that may help reduce the bullying and that do not compromise their integrity. There is a difficult balance between not blaming the victim and allowing him or her to be their genuine selves, and talking with the victim about developing new social skills to handle the bullying situation more effectively.

Module 8: Relaxation and Coping Skills

The goal of Module 8, the last module of the workshop, is to help teachers cope with stress, as well as to discuss strategies that teacher can use to help students manage their own stress. Stress is an inevitable part of life and an unavoidable component of teaching. How teachers deal with stress may have a profound effect on their ability to teach students, as well as on the likelihood of job burnout. In Module 8, teachers discuss a variety of activities to help themselves and students learn coping and relaxation skills. The more efficiently teachers manage their own stress, the more effective they will be in their professional and personal lives. Teachers often tell us they have too much to do to be able to take some time for themselves. All day, they devote themselves to their students. Teachers will deplete their energy and enthusiasm if they do not take time to replenish themselves.

Similarly, students need to learn effective stress management skills. We are often asked, "What do kids have to worry about?" Many adults believe children do not experience stress, "It is so nice to be young and carefree with no worries in the world." However, youth today are experiencing an increase of stress and pressure, and it is important to provide them with the skills to manage stress. Each child brings to the classroom unique situations that they use, attempting to cope. Teachers may serve as a positive role model to demonstrate the best means of coping with stress and give students encouragement to relax and do something they love. As part of this module, activities have been developed to use with students, both as classroom exercises and as personal skills development that students may practice beyond the classroom. Examples of strategies discussed with teachers are explained below.

Relax and Meditate.   There are numerous resources to learn about relaxation and meditation, and some techniques are discussed in the Bully Busters workshop. In one school, the Bully Busters Support Team members purchased books designed to enhance their learning about relaxation and stress management, and they used the group to provide ongoing encouragement to take the time to incorporate daily meditation.

Use Humor.   When we are stressed, we lose our sense of humor and our ability to laugh. Laughter is an excellent way to release stress. It can change the level of internal tension, as well as the tension in the school environment. If the students are able to laugh together in a classroom, they may be less likely to release their stress through aggression outside of the classroom. Teachers are encouraged to invite students to share their sense of humor, and to tell appropriate funny stories. Teachers help students appreciate that laughing can be a great experience that reduces stress, as long as it is not at some one else's expense. Laughing at ourselves or laughing with others is appropriate, but laughing at others is not. Teachers identify examples of both types of humor and provide examples for students to learn to differentiate and practice.

Exercise.   Incorporating moderate exercise activities into the daily routine is an effective way to reduce stress. Additionally, it serves as an emotional outlet for the release of anger and frustration. Exercise also prevents stressors from becoming overwhelming. It provides an ideal time to "blow off some steam" or a private time to make sense of difficult situations. Students also can benefit by incorporating exercise into their daily routine. In becoming active, students are able to release negative energy or "blow of their own steam." This release can prevent a child from using this energy against another child and reduce their level of stress.

Work at School, Not at Home.   Teachers share with us that leaving work at school sounds great, but in reality there are just not enough hours in the school day to accomplish all their work. We can relate to this. Teachers need a reminder that they not only deserve a break, but also probably need a break. If teachers do need to work at home, they need to set limits. Students will also benefit by helping them schedule time for homework. Homework is inevitable; however, students may perform better if they have a consistent time period to complete their work. The student should be involved in choosing what time they feel they can best complete their work. Some parents prefer their children to complete their homework immediately after school; others after their chores are complete.

Use a Support Team.   Consider two words: Illness. Wellness. There are numerous differences in what the two words imply, but let's examine a simpler difference. Illness starts with "I" and Wellness starts with "We." We often hear teachers who say, "I have so much work to do; I have to do so many things with students; I feel so alone in the work I'm doing, I just don't know what to do." We encourage teachers to move toward a "we-ness" and use a support group to help find solutions to problems, understand the difficulties of teaching, and encourage them to take care of themselves and their students. The Support Team serves as an ongoing resource to dispel fears, help teachers feel supported, and solve problems collaboratively. Sharing and communication are central to the team's purpose and can be very effective in reducing stress. Students are encouraged to create their own support teams to deal with bullying and other stressful situations.

Translating Research Into Practice: Implications for Bullying-Prevention and Intervention Programs

The Bully Busters Program is a comprehensive, theory-based program designed to empower teachers to prevent and reduce aggression in their classrooms and to work as a team to develop a school culture that supports positive relationships among all members of the school community. The Bully Busters program described in this chapter was designed to be used in elementary schools. The teacher training consists of a two-day workshop that is followed with at least eight support group sessions. The workshop is composed of eight modules that address awareness of the problem, bullying prevention skills, recognition of bullies and victims, strategies for intervening with bullies and with victims, and strategies for relaxation and coping. Each module is designed to provide a rationale for the importance of the topic, objectives to be accomplished, discussions about the topic, and activities that teachers may use with students in the classroom. The purpose of the support groups is to share ideas of best classroom management and bullying prevention practices, to develop creative solutions to problems that individual teachers may face or that they face as a group, and to provide support and encouragement to solve problems.

REFERENCES

Besag, B. (1989). *Bullies and victims in schools: A guide to understanding and management*. United Kingdom: Open University Press.

Bodine, R. J., & Crawford, D. K. (1999). *Developing emotional intelligence: A guide to behavior management and conflict resolution in schools*. Champaign, Illinois: Research Press.

Crick, N. R. (1996). The role of overt, relational aggression, and prosocial behavior in the prediction of children's future social adjustment. *Child Development, 67*, 2317–2327.

Eslea, M., & Smith, P. K. (1998). The long-term effectiveness of antibullying work in primary schools. *Educational Research, 40*, 203–218.

Goldstein, A. (1999). *The prepare curriculum: Teaching prosocial competencies*. Champaign, IL: Research Press.

Goleman, D. (1995). *Emotional intelligence*. New York: Bantam Books.

Gregg, S. (1998). *School-based programs to promote safety and civility. AEL Policy Briefs*. Charleston, WV: Appalachia Educational Labortatory. (ED 419-180)

Horne, A. M., Bartolomucci, C. L., & Newman-Carlson, D. (2003). *Bully busters: A teacher's manual for helping bullies, victims, and bystanders (grades K-5)*. Champaign, IL: Research Press.

Mytton, J. A., DiGuiseppi, C., Gough, D. A., Taylor, R. S., & Logan, S. (2002). School-based violence prevention programs: Systematic review of secondary prevention trials. *Archives of Pediatrics & Adolescent Medicine, 156*, 752–762.

Newman, D., Horne, A., & Bartolomucci, C. (2003). *Bully Busters*: A teachers manual for helping bullies, victims, and bystanders. Champaign, IL: Research Press.

Olweus, D. (1994). Annotation – Bullying at school: Basic facts and effects of a school-based intervention program. *Journal of Child Psychology and Psychiatry, 35*, 1171–1190.

Olweus, D. (1996). Bully/victim problems at school: Facts and effective interventions – reclaiming children and youth. *Journal of Emotional and Behavioral Problems, 5*, 15–22.

Orpinas, P., Horne, A. M., & Multisite Violence Prevention Project. (in press). The GREAT teacher program. *American Journal of Preventive Medicine*.

Orpinas, P., Horne, A. M., & Staniszewski, D. (in press). School bullying: Changing the problem by changing the school. *School Psychology Review*.

Roland, E. (1989). A system-oriented strategy against bullying. In E. Roland & E. Munthe (Eds.), *Bullying: An international perspective*. London: Professional Development Foundation.

Ross, D. M. (1996). *Childhood bullying and teasing: What school personnel, other professionals, and parents can do*. Alexandria, VA: American Counseling Association.

Smith, P. K., & Sharp, S. (1994). *School bullying: Insights and perspectives*. London: Routledge and Kegan Paul.

Tattum, D. P. (1989). Violence and aggression in schools. In D. P. Tattum & D. A. Lane (Eds.), *Bullying in schools*. Stoke-on-Trent, England: Trentham.

Turpeau, A. M. (1998). Effectiveness of an antibullying classroom curriculum intervention on an American middle school (Doctoral Dissertation, University of Georgia). *Dissertation Abstracts International, 60*, 351.

16

Expect Respect: A School-based Intervention to Promote Awareness and Effective Responses to Bullying and Sexual Harassment

Daniel J. Whitaker
Centers for Disease Control and Prevention

Barri Rosenbluth
SafePlace, Austin, Texas

Linda Anne Valle
Centers for Disease Control and Prevention

Ellen Sanchez
SafePlace, Austin, Texas

Injury and violence prevention are important concerns for researchers and practitioners who are interested in promoting children's and adolescents' health. Homicide and suicide are among the leading causes of death for children and adolescents (Anderson, 2002). Schools are one potential site for youth violence to occur. More than 30% of high school seniors reported having committed a violent act in the past year, with half of those acts resulting in injuries (Johnston,

2000, as cited in U.S. Department of Health and Human Services, 2001). Although violence at schools is tragic and highly publicized, deadly violence on school grounds is actually quite rare (Anderson et al., 2001). Extreme violence is also rare in that only 10% of schools report one or more serious violent crimes (National Center for Education Statistics, 1998).

Less severe forms of violence such as physical and verbal bullying (e.g., teasing, name-calling) and sexual harassment are more common and are perceived by students to be a greater problem than more severe forms of violence (Galinsky & Salmond, 2002). Bullying is a common occurrence in schools. Almost 30% of students reported moderate or frequent involvement in bullying (either as perpetrator or victim) between 6th and 8th grades. The impact of bullying is well documented, with victims of bullying reporting more physical and psychological problems than nonvictims (Olweus, 1993). Bullies are also at risk for poor outcomes, including antisocial activities such as fighting, truancy, theft, and arrests (Olweus, 1993).

Sexual harassment and dating violence also are problems related to bullying. Although sexual harassment is commonly believed to occur between adults, 83% of female and 79% of male students in grades 8–11 reported experiencing sexual harassment at some point in their life, with more than 25% experiencing harassment "often" (American Association of University Women, 2001). Experiences of sexual harassment have been linked to negative outcomes including poor academic or work performance, poor physical and mental health, and problematic interpersonal relationships (see review by Lenhart, 1996).

Dating violence is also common. A survey of eighth- and ninth-grade students indicated 25% and 9% had been victims of nonsexual and sexual dating violence, respectively (Foshee et al., 1996). National estimates indicate similar overall prevalence rates, with women more likely than men to have been victimized (Sugarman & Hotalling, 1989). Dating violence has been associated with many negative consequences, including eating disorders (Ackard & Neumark-Sztainer, 2002; Thompson, Wonderlich, Crosby, & Mitchell, 2001), low self-esteem, emotional problems (Ackard & Neumanrk-Sztainer, 2002), and suicidal ideation (Coker et al., 2000; Silverman, Raj, Mucci, & Hathaway, 2001).

It has been argued that teasing and bullying are precursors to gendered violence such as sexual harassment, adolescent dating violence, and later intimate partner violence (e.g., Stein, 1995). Recent studies have linked perpetration of bullying with perpetration of sexual harassment (Pellegrini, 2001) and with the use or receipt of aggression in dating relationships (e.g., Connolly, Pepler, Craig, & Taradash, 2000). Given this connection and the prevalence and negative impact of bullying and sexual harassment in schools, there is a clear need for school-based prevention programs to address bullying and sexual harassment. The Expect Respect Elementary School Project was designed to address this need.

Background on SafePlace and the Inception of the Expect Respect Program

SafePlace is the primary provider of sexual and domestic violence prevention and intervention services in Austin, Texas. SafePlace offers a continuum of services including emergency shelter, counseling, legal and hospital advocacy, transitional housing, and community education. In 1990 SafePlace initiated a school-based program entitled Expect Respect to provide counseling, support groups, and educational programs in local schools. Expect Respect initially served adolescents involved in abusive dating relationships and provided classroom presentations for middle and high school students on healthy relationships and dating violence prevention.

Through their clinical work, SafePlace staff observed that many young girls in the program, some as young as 12 years of age, had already experienced repeated acts of physical and sexual abuse from boyfriends. SafePlace counselors also observed that a large number of teenagers believed that abusive and controlling behaviors in relationships were normal and even expected. Conversations with elementary school teachers and counselors revealed that children as young as 11 years old were already engaging in dating behaviors and that these dating relationships frequently involved physically, sexually, and emotionally aggressive behaviors such as hitting, pushing, unwanted touching, name-calling, and put-downs. In light of these experiences, SafePlace became interested in promoting safe and respectful relationships among younger children to increase their knowledge, skills, and expectations for respectful behavior in future dating relationships. Given the relations among bullying, sexual harassment, and dating violence—each referring to a relationship in which aggressive acts are intended to hurt or control another person, are often repeated over time, occur in the context of a relationship in which the perpetrator has more power than the victim, and can lead to a hostile school environment—SafePlace expanded the focus of the Expect Respect Program to address the problems of bullying and sexual harassment in elementary school. SafePlace collaborated with the Austin Independent School District (AISD) and researchers from the University of Texas (UT) to develop, implement, and evaluate a program for the prevention of bullying and sexual harassment, which became known as the Expect Respect Elementary School Project.

The previous decade of collaboration between SafePlace and AISD provided a strong foundation for an effective partnership for conducting the project. The long-term goal of the project was to prevent violence and abuse in intimate relationships, whereas the immediate goals of the project were to make schools safer by raising awareness of bullying and sexual harassment as problems and promoting effective responses in students and staff members who witness these behaviors, thereby reducing the social acceptability of peer-to-peer mistreatment. The evaluation project matched pairs of schools on demographic characteristics, with random assignment of one school in each pair either to the intervention activities or to serve as a comparison school. Twelve AISD schools participated. The project was supported with funding from the Centers for Disease Control and Prevention.

The theoretical foundation of the Expect Respect Project was based on the multilevel, multicomponent, school-based prevention program developed by Olweus and colleagues (Olweus, Limber, & Mihalic, 1999). The Olweus Bullying Prevention Program was developed and refined in Norway in the 1980s and is currently being implemented throughout Norway. The Bullying Prevention Program includes a schoolwide intervention comprised of staff training, formation of a bullying-prevention committee, development of school rules and polices, a classroom level intervention, parent interventions, and an individual-level intervention that includes meetings with bullies, meetings with victims, and meetings with parents of bullies or victims. There is strong empirical support for this program with successful implementation. For example, the Bullying-Prevention Program reduced bullying behaviors by up to 50%; reduced general antisocial behaviors such as vandalism, fighting, and truancy; and improved the overall school climate (Olweus, 1993).

Like Olweus' program, the Expect Respect Project attempted to take a whole-school approach to preventing bullying and sexual harassment by preparing all members of the school community to recognize and respond effectively to bullying and sexual harassment. The Expect Respect Project utilized five program components: a 12-week classroom curriculum for students, trainings for staff, education and support for parents, encouragement and guidance to administrators for policy development, and support services for students who had been affected by bullying, sexual harassment, or sexual or domestic violence.

Classroom Curriculum

Twelve weekly sessions adapted from *Bullyproof: A Teachers Guide on Teasing and Bullying for Use with Fourth- and Fifth-Grade Students* (Stein & Sjostrom, 1996) were provided to all 5th-grade students in the intervention schools. *Bullyproof*, a joint publication of the Wellesley College Center for Research on Women and the National Education Association Professional Library, had been developed and piloted in classrooms by teachers and was designed to be taught in conjunction with literature typically read by students in the 4th and 5th grades. Although no program evaluation had been completed, *Bullyproof* was chosen by project staff because it appeared to best fit the project's goals and was designed to integrate easily into existing classroom lessons.

The *Bullyproof* curriculum focused on increasing the ability and willingness of bystanders to intervene and thus reducing the social acceptance of bullying and sexual harassment. *Bullyproof* lessons were designed to help students distinguish playful teasing and joking from hurtful teasing and bullying, enhance students' knowledge about bullying and sexual harassment, and develop students' skills for responding as a target or bystander of bullying or sexual harassment. Students were encouraged to become "courageous bystanders" by speaking up or getting help from an adult when they witnessed someone being mistreated. The lessons included writing assignments, role-plays of how to intervene upon witnessing bullying, class discussions, and opportunities for students to practice intervention skills in the classroom.

Although the *Bullyproof* curriculum was designed to be implemented by teachers, the curriculum was co-led by SafePlace staff and teachers or school counselors. The intent in having SafePlace staff co-teach the curriculum was for SafePlace staff to serve as models for the teachers, allowing them to observe the first year and take on responsibility for teaching the lessons in subsequent years. Teacher participation varied, with some teachers preferring to remain uninvolved while others took leadership roles in presenting the curriculum.

Two SafePlace educators presented the curriculum. Although the educators received training in using the curriculum, managing classroom behavior, and engaging all students in the curriculum activities and discussion, no formal behavioral criteria indicating mastery of skills prior to implementation were utilized. Supervision of the educators was ongoing and consisted of weekly meetings and classroom observations by the Program Coordinator to attempt to ensure fidelity to program goals and effective teaching methods, albeit no formal data of fidelity were collected.

Staff Training

At the beginning of the project, the author of *Bullyproof* provided a six-hour training to project staff, administrators, counselors, and 5th-grade teachers. In addition, a three-hour session was provided once each semester at each campus for all personnel, including bus drivers, cafeteria workers, hall monitors, and office staff. A combination of lecture, discussion, and experiential activities from the curriculum was used. These sessions were designed to raise awareness of bullying and sexual harassment and to prepare school personnel to respond effectively to witnessed or reported incidents. The training presentation thus included research on bullying and sexual harassment; strategies for building a consistent response at the individual, classroom, and school-wide levels; strategies to enhance mutual respect among students; practice in using lessons from the curriculum; and methods for integrating the lessons into other subject content areas including social studies, language arts, and health.

Policy Development

The project staff encouraged administrators to develop a campus policy to ensure consistent responses by all staff members to incidents and reports of bullying and sexual harassment. To facilitate this process, project staff developed a policy template that was provided to campus administrators. The template included a statement of philosophy, working definitions of bullying and sexual harassment, expectations for actions in response to incidents and reports, and a statement of commitment to maintaining the confidentiality of targets, witnesses who report incidents, and students accused of bullying or harassing others. Principals were urged to solicit input from school staff and create a policy document that would be approved by the Campus Advisory Council (comprised of staff and parent representatives) at each school. Principals were expected to present the policy to school staff, students, and parents and provide training as needed for implementation. The extent to which this happened varied between schools.

Parent Education

Project staff attempted to build parental support for the project and its objectives through educational presentations and newsletters. Educational presentations were offered twice each year in the evening at each school, with parent attendance varying by site. The presentations provided information about the project; the vocabulary being used to discuss bullying and sexual harassment at school; strategies for helping children who are bullied, bully others, and witness bullying; tips for responding to and preventing bullying among siblings; and school and community resources for children and families experiencing bullying, sexual harassment, and dating, sexual, or domestic violence. Parent newsletters were sent home each semester with students in participating schools. The newsletters contained updates on the project activities, samples of students' *Bullyproof* classwork, strategies for helping children with bullying problems and for responding to bullying behavior among siblings, summer reading lists of children's books dealing with the subject of bullying, and information about relevant school and community resources.

Support Services

SafePlace counselors were available to assist school counselors by providing school-based counseling and advocacy for victims of sexual and domestic violence. A specialized session was provided to school counselors to help them respond effectively to students who repeatedly were targets or perpetrators of bullying or harassment. This session provided alternative approaches such as interviewing the victim and bully separately to ensure victim safety and reduce vulnerability to further incidents or retaliation, to the widely used conflict resolution approach for dealing with bullying. Finally, staff were informed of their legal responsibility to document and respond to sexual harassment.

At the beginning of the project, all school counselors received a comprehensive resource manual containing reading and resource materials on bullying, sexual harassment, and dating, sexual, and domestic violence. The manual was intended to help school counselors in their efforts to link children and families with community resources. The extent to which counselors used the manual was not formally assessed, albeit anecdotal evidence obtained through requests to SafePlace for additional training and support suggests that some counselors used the materials.

Method

Selection of Schools

The Expect Respect Project was implemented in elementary schools because it was believed that changing behaviors and beliefs about bullying and sexual harassment would be facilitated through working with younger children for whom normative behaviors and beliefs were still developing. Because resources were not sufficient to provide the curriculum to all grade levels, 5th-grade students were selected. Fifth-graders were believed to be most likely to benefit from the project because they would soon be exposed to more serious forms of bullying and sexual harassment in middle school and to new roles as boyfriend or girlfriend. Fifth-grade students could also serve as role models for the younger students in the school.

With the support of the AISD Director of Guidance and Counseling, six pairs of schools representing a cross-section of the AISD were selected. The pairs of schools were located in four distinct geographic areas of Austin that served ethnically and economically distinct communities. The school pairs were matched to be similar in ethnicity, limited-English proficiency, the socioeconomic status of students, the school's passing rates on the statewide academic skills test (TAAS), total school population, and 5th-grade population. Through random assignment, one school in each pair was placed in the intervention group and one school was placed in the comparison group.

Study Sample

Minimal demographic information was collected on students and staff that participated in the project. At the beginning of the intervention, there were 929 and 834 students in the intervention and comparison schools, respectively. The sample was evenly split between boys (50.3%) and girls (48.3%). Fifty-five percent self-identified as White, 27.6% as Hispanic, and 15.4% as African American. Ethnic distribution was similar across the intervention (54.9% White, 27.1% Hispanic, 15.9% African American) and comparison schools (55.1% White, 28.0% Hispanic, 15.0% African American).

Time 1 assessments were completed by 1175 staff members, 666 (56.7%) at intervention schools and 509 (43.3%) at comparison schools. At both the intervention and comparison schools, staff members were primarily female (89.6% at intervention schools and 89.2% at comparison schools, $p = .91$). At the intervention schools, 57.6% of staff identified as White, 25.1% identified as Hispanic, and 14.3% identified as African American. At the comparison schools, 63.3% identified as White, 20.0% identified as Hispanic, and 12.6% identified as African American. The ethnic distribution of staff at intervention and control schools did not differ ($p = .10$). A large majority of staff at both the intervention (70.1%) and comparison schools (77.2%) identified themselves as teachers; comparison schools had a greater percentage of teachers than intervention schools ($p < .01$).

Evaluation Design

Questionnaires were used to assess the impact of the Expect Respect Project. Fifth-grade students completed questionnaires at three time points, the beginning of the Fall semester, the end of the Fall semester, and the end of the Spring semester. Staff completed questionnaires at the beginning of the Fall and end of the Spring semester. Because SafePlace staff implemented the curriculum, it was not possible to deliver the intervention to all schools in a single semester. As a result, the intervention was delivered in the Fall semester in three of the intervention schools and in the Spring semester in the other three. For purposes of statistical analyses, the post-intervention datum point was considered to be the student assessment that followed the delivery of the intervention—that is, the end of the Fall semester at schools in which the intervention was delivered in the Fall semester, and the end of the Spring semester at schools in which the intervention was delivered in the Spring semester. Because staff completed only the assessments at the beginning of the Fall semester and at the end of the Spring semester, the baseline and post-intervention data points are the same for all staff regardless or when the intervention was delivered.

Measures

The results of the analyses reported here focused on variables congruent with the goals of the curriculum, including students' and staff reports of bullying behaviors, staff and students' self-reported reactions to verbal and physical bullying, students' perceptions of staff reactions to verbal and physical bullying, and students' and staff awareness of specific behaviors as bullying or sexual harassment, attitudes toward bullying and sexual harassment, and perceptions of the safety of the school. As subsequently described, response indexes for the analyses were constructed through separate factor analyses of students' or staff responses to the baseline questionnaires. One particular response, telling the victim of bullying to ignore the bullying, alternately loaded on different factors (i.e., with responses consistent with either no intervention or mild intervention) depending on the particular scenario described in the questionnaire. Conceptually, this response was not indicative of the desired staff response to intervene to stop the bullying, but it did not consistently load with items indicating no intervention or response to a bullying scenario. It is possible that in less severe instances of bullying (e.g., name-calling), this response was perceived as a mild intervention.

Bullying Behaviors.   Students were asked at baseline if they had ever bullied another student and if they had ever been bullied. At post-intervention, students were asked if they had bullied another student in the past three months and been bullied in the past three months. Students who indicated they had been bullied were asked what the bully did (i.e., name calling, threatening, hit/kick/shove) and what the student did when it happened. These responses were categorized into physical bullying (i.e., hit/kick/shove) and verbal bullying (i.e., name-calling, threats). Students' self-reported responses to being bullied were factor analyzed, with three factors being derived: told an adult (two items: told a parent, told an adult at school), made a verbal response (three items: told the bully to stop, asked friends for help, said something to make the bully stop), or ignored/did not respond to the bullying (two items: ignored the behavior or a lack of physical response such as hit, kicked, or shoved the bully). In addition, students and staff reported how often they had witnessed bullying in the past week (never, once or twice, almost every day). This measure was dichotomized into witnessed or did not witness bullying.

Actions Upon Witnessing Bullying Behaviors.   Students and staff were asked about the probable responses made by themselves and by other staff and students upon witnessing physical bullying (i.e., a student beating up on another student) and verbal bullying (i.e., a student calling another student names). For each question, a number of responses were provided and the respondent was asked to check all that applied.

For students' responses about their own intended actions upon witnessing another student being bullied, two factors each were derived for witnessing physical bullying and witnessing verbal bullying: telling someone (two items: telling a parent, telling an adult at school) and directly intervening (two items: telling the bully to stop, helping the student get away). For students' perceptions about school adults' actions upon witnessing physical bullying, two factors were derived: adult intervention (five items: calling the parent, sending the bully to the office, punishing the bully, telling the bully to stop, sending the bully to an alternative school) and no adult intervention (three items: tell the student to ignore the bullying, do nothing, don't know). For students' perception of adults' responses to verbal bullying, three factors were derived: strong intervention (three items: calling the parents, sending the bully to the office, sending the bully to an alternative school), mild intervention (three items: telling the bully to stop, punishing the bully, telling the victim to ignore the bully), and no intervention (two items: do nothing, don't know).

Staff's self-reports of their typical actions upon witnessing physical and verbal bullying were each grouped into three measures based on separate factor analyses: strong intervention (call the bully's parents, send the bully to office, send the bully to a school for troubled kids), mild intervention (punish the bully, tell the victim to ignore the bullying), and no intervention (do nothing, a response indicating not telling the bully to stop). For staff's perceptions of their coworkers' reactions upon witnessing physical bullying, two factors were derived: intervention (tell the bully to stop, call the bully's parents, send the bully to the office, send the bully to a school for troubled kids, punish the bully) and no intervention (tell the victim to ignore it, do nothing). For staff's perception of coworkers' reactions upon witnessing verbal bullying, three factors emerged: strong intervention, mild intervention, and do nothing (these items were identical to staff's self-report of their typical responses). Finally, staff reported what they thought most students do when they witnessed another student being physically bullied. Three factors were derived: active response (tell an adult at school, tell a parent, tell the bully to stop, help the victim get away), do nothing (1 item), and fight the bully (1 item).

Bullying and Sexual Harassment Awareness.   For each of 14 behaviors, students and staff indicated if they believed the behavior constituted bullying. Nine items consisted of bullying behaviors (e.g., pushing, taking things, threatening), and five items did not (e.g., telling someone to leave you alone, not sharing). The measure of bullying awareness was the number of behaviors correctly identified as a bullying or non-bullying item (range 0–14). Similarly, students and staff indicated if they believed each of nine behaviors constituted sexual harassment. Six items consisted of sexual harassment behaviors (e.g., making fun of someone's private body parts), and three did not (e.g., telling someone you like him or her). The measure of sexual-harassment awareness was the number of behaviors students correctly identified (range 0–9).

Awareness of Rules on Sexual Harassment.   Both students and staff were asked, "Are there rules at your school to protect students from sexual harassment by other students?" Responses were categorized as either *knew there were rules* (responded "yes"), or *did not* (responded "no" or "don't know").

Attitudes.   The items comprising the attitude scales differed for students and staff. Students responded to 21 attitude items using a 3-point agree-disagree scale. (Students in Year 2 used a 5-point scale, but responses were recoded to a 3-point scale to combine the data.) Items were factor analyzed, and five factors were derived: 1) positive attitudes about bullying (6 items; e.g., "I would be friends with someone who bullies others," "A boy is weak if he doesn't fight a bully"); 2) feeling safe at school (3 items; e.g., "I feel safe at school," "The adults at my school do a good job of stopping bullying"); 3) bullying is OK in relationships (6 items; e.g., "It's okay for a boyfriend to hit his girlfriend if she calls him mean names," "Someone who hits his or her girlfriend or boyfriend is [not] a bully"); 4) beliefs that sexual harassment happens only to adults and girls (2 items); and 5) positive attitudes about asking for help if bullied (3 items; e.g., "A boy is brave if he asks an adult for help with a bully").

Staff responded to 24 attitude items using a 5-point scale, and factor analyses revealed two factors. The first contained five items and dealt with beliefs about school safety (e.g., "The staff at my school do a good job at stopping bullying,"

"Bullying is [not] a serious problem at my school," "Students feel safe at my school"). The second factor included many items that dealt with domestic violence that was not part of the intervention focus and is not discussed further.

Statistical Analyses

All dependent measures were analyzed with hierarchical modeling using the SAS Proc Mixed for normally distributed dependent variables and the SAS macro GLIMMIX for non-normally distributed dependent variables. School was used as a clustering variable to account for the relationship among responses within a school. For analysis of each dependent measure, the statistical model crossed Group (intervention vs. comparison) and Time (baseline vs. post or baseline vs. follow-up) to examine changes by intervention group from baseline to post-intervention (reflected by the Group × Time interaction). Year (1 vs. 2) was included as a control variable in all analyses (differences in group effects over time were examined by Year but were negligible). For analyses of student data, Sex was also included in the model and fully crossed with the other variables of interest to examine differential effects of the program on boys vs. girls. Semester of intervention (fall vs. spring) was also included because students at different schools received the intervention in different semesters. For analyses of staff data, it was impossible to match many of the staff surveys from baseline to post-intervention due to difficulties with staff ID numbers. The analyses of staff data were therefore conducted with Time as a between-subjects variable rather than a within-subject variable. This results in more conservative analyses for staff data because error variance is likely to be greater when conducting between-subjects' analyses as compared to within-subjects' analyses so a larger difference between means would be required for a statistically significant result (Keppel, 1982).

Results

Tables 16.1–4 show the means and standard deviations (in parentheses) or percentages and significant effects for all dependent measures. Means or percentages for each dependent variable are shown by Group (intervention vs. comparison) and Time (baseline vs. post), with the final column indicating significant effects for Group (G), Time (T), and for the student variable Gender (S). For analyses of student data, where Gender moderated the Group × Time interaction, follow-up analyses were conducted separately for boys and girls, and results are shown by Gender. In describing the results, the focus is on those variables for which there were Group × Time interactions, which indicated significant differences in how the intervention and comparison schools changed from baseline to post-intervention.

Bullying Behaviors and Reactions to Being Bullied. Table 16.1 shows the means, standard deviations (in parentheses), or percentages for bully perpetration, victimization, and witnessing, as well as students' self-reported reactions to being bullied. For students' bullying perpetration, the Group × Time

TABLE 16.1.
Perpetration, Victimization, and Witnessing of Bullying Behaviors, and Students'
Self-reported Responses to Being Bullied

	Intervention		Comparison		
Variable	Baseline	Post	Baseline	Post	Significant Effects
Bullying behaviors					
Student: Bullied another student	10.6%	17.0%	11.2%	17.8%	T, G
Student: Been bullied	40.8%	36.7%	47.5%	34.7%	T, G × T
Student: Been physically bullied	15.2%	11.1%	19.5%	13.4%	G, T
Student: Been verbally bullied	31.2%	29.8%	36.8%	26.8%	T, G × T
Student: Witnessed bullying	38.4%	60.6%	47.3%	53.0%	T, G × T
Staff: Witnessed bullying	71.0%	83.7%	73.7%	79.4%	T
Student responses to being physically bullied					
Told an adult	0.77	0.87	0.83	0.55	G × T
	(.82)	(.71)	(.80)	(.79)	
Verbal response	0.84	1.04	0.90	0.77	S × G × T
	(.87)	(.80)	(.83)	(.79)	
Boys	0.87	1.04	0.90	0.54	G × T
	(.93)	(.86)	(.84)	(.65)	
Girls	0.81	1.03	0.90	1.08	None
	(.81)	(.72)	(.82)	(.87)	
Ignored/did not respond	1.06	1.14	0.93	1.00	S × G × T
	(.61)	(.60)	(.65)	(.74)	
Boys	1.01	1.06	0.83	1.10	T
	(.59)	(.62)	(.67)	(.79)	
Girls	1.11	1.26	1.07	0.86	G × T
	(.63)	(.57)	(.60)	(.64)	
Student responses to being verbally bullied					
Told an adult	0.59	0.44	0.64	0.48	S, T
	(.69)	(.66)	(.75)	(.72)	
Made verbal response	0.59	0.60	0.70	0.58	S
	(.76)	(.68)	(.75)	(.72)	
Ignored/did not respond	1.34	1.33	1.34	1.39	None
	(.60)	(.59)	(.59)	(.64)	

interaction was not significant. For having been bullied, there was a Group × Time interaction. Students in the intervention group reported equal amounts of being bullied at baseline and post intervention ($p > .05$), whereas students in the comparison schools reported having been bullied less at post intervention than baseline ($p < .001$). There was no significant Group × Time interaction for students' reports of having been physically bullied, but there was a significant interaction for verbal bullying. The pattern was identical to the findings for overall bullying; students in the intervention schools reported no change ($p > .05$), whereas students in the comparison schools reported a decrease in verbal bullying ($p < .001$). Thus, the decrease in overall bullying in the comparison schools appears to be due to the decrease in verbal bullying from baseline to post-intervention. Finally, for witnessing bullying there was a Group × Time interaction for student reports, but not staff reports. Students in the intervention schools reported an increase from baseline to post-intervention in witnessing bullying ($p < .001$), whereas students in the comparison schools did not ($p > .05$).

Because students' reactions to physical and verbal bullying are likely to differ, students' self-reports of what they did when they were physically or verbally bullied were analyzed separately (displayed in the lower half of Table 16.1). For physical bullying, the Group × Time interaction for the response of telling an adult was significant ($p < .001$). Students in the intervention group did not change from baseline to post intervention in their self-reports of telling an adult ($p > .05$), whereas students in the comparison schools were less likely to tell an adult ($p < .05$). There was a significant Sex = Group × Time interaction for making a verbal response after being physically bullied. Separate analyses for boys and girls indicated the effect was limited to boys. In the intervention schools, boys' verbal responses to being physically bullied did not change from baseline to post intervention ($p > .05$), whereas boys in the comparison schools reported a decrease in verbal responses ($p < .01$). For the response of ignoring physical bullying, there was also a Sex × Group × Time interaction ($p < .05$), and here the Group × Time effect was limited to girls. In the intervention schools, girls' reports of ignoring physical bullying did not change from baseline to post intervention ($p > .05$), whereas girls in the comparison schools reported a decrease in ignoring bullying ($p < .05$). For all students' responses to verbal bullying, the Group × Time interactions were not significant.

Student and Staff Intended Responses Upon Witnessing Bullying. Table 16.2 shows the means, standard deviations (in parentheses), and significant effects from the analyses of students' and staff's responses to what they would do if they witnessed physical bullying (i.e., a student beating up on another student) and what they would do if they witnessed verbal bullying (i.e., name calling). Students' intentions to tell an adult if they witnessed physical bullying resulted in only Sex and Time main effects, but students' intentions to directly intervene if they witnessed physical bullying revealed a Group × Time interaction. Students in both the intervention ($p < .001$) and comparison schools ($p < .01$) reported an increase in intentions to directly intervene from baseline to post-intervention, but the pre- to post-intervention mean difference was larger for students in the intervention schools. Analyses of students' intentions to tell an adult upon witnessing verbal bullying resulted in a Gender × Group × Time interaction. The Group × Time interaction was limited to boys, with boys in the

TABLE 16.2.
Intended Actions by Students and Staff Upon Witnessing
Physical or Verbal Bullying

	Intervention		Control		
Variable	Baseline	Post	Baseline	Post	Significant Effects
Students' intended actions upon witnessing physical bullying					
Tell an adult	1.06	1.21	1.02	1.14	T, S
	(.75)	(.78)	(.75)	(.80)	
Directly intervene	0.90	1.26	0.94	1.06	T, G × T
	(.81)	(.81)	(.81)	(.83)	
Students' intended actions upon witnessing verbal bullying					
Tell an adult	0.85	0.88	0.80	0.88	T, S × T × G
	(.78)	(.86)	(.78)	(.83)	
Boys	0.70	0.67	0.67	0.79	G × T
	(.76)	(.83)	(.76)	(.82)	
Girls	1.00	1.09	0.93	0.96	T
	(.76)	(.84)	(.78)	(.83)	
Directly intervene	0.86	1.08	0.93	0.92	T, G × T
	(.75)	(.76)	(.76)	(.80)	
Staff's typical actions upon witnessing physical bullying					
Strong intervention	1.40	1.52	1.44	1.56	T
	(.86)	(.89)	(.86)	(.86)	
Mild intervention	.28	.28	.27	.30	None
	(.48)	(.49)	(.46)	(.50)	
No intervention	.43	.38	.40	.46	None
	(.68)	(.65)	(.68)	(.71)	
Staff's typical actions upon witnessing verbal bullying					
Strong intervention	.35	.50	.34	.34	T
	(.65)	(.81)	(.66)	(.68)	
Mild intervention	.63	.81	.72	.78	T
	(.70)	(.70)	(.72)	(.73)	
No intervention	.09	.07	.11	.04	T
	(.30)	(.26)	(.33)	(.22)	

intervention schools reporting no change over time ($p > .05$), whereas boys in
the comparison schools reported an increase from baseline to post-intervention
in their intent to tell someone upon witnessing verbal bullying ($p < .01$). Students' intentions to intervene directly upon witnessing name calling also revealed a Group × Time interaction, with significant increases in intentions to tell

an adult from baseline to post-intervention found for students in the intervention group ($p < .001$), but not in the comparison group ($p > .05$). Among the six dependent measures analyzed to examine staff's self-reports of their typical reactions upon witnessing physical or verbal bullying (bottom half of Table 2), none of the Group $\times$ Time interactions were significant.

Perceptions of Others Reactions Upon Witnessing Bullying. Of the five dependent variables analyzed to examine students' perceptions of staff's reactions to physical and verbal bullying (top half of Table 16.3), the only Group $\times$ Time interaction found was for adults' mild intervention upon witnessing verbal bullying. Although the intervention and comparison groups were each more likely to believe adults would respond with a mild intervention at post-intervention than baseline ($ps < .001$), the baseline to post-intervention mean difference was greater for students in the intervention schools than the comparison schools.

Staff's perceptions of other staff members' responses to witnessing verbal and physical bullying and staff's perceptions of students' responses to witnessing physical bullying are displayed in the bottom half of Table 16.3. There were no significant Group $\times$ Time interactions found for any of these dependent measures.

Awareness and Attitudes. The top half of Table 16.4 shows the means, standard deviations (in parentheses), and percentages for students and staff's awareness of bullying behaviors, sexual harassment behaviors, and of sexual harassment rules in their school. The Group $\times$ Time interaction for bullying awareness was not significant for either students or staff. There was a significant Group $\times$ Time interaction for students' awareness of sexual harassment behaviors, but not staff's awareness of sexual harassment behaviors. Sexual harassment awareness increased from baseline to post-intervention for students in both the intervention and comparison schools ($ps < .001$), but the baseline to post-intervention mean difference was greater for students in the intervention schools. With respect to awareness of sexual harassment rules, there was a Group $\times$ Time interaction for staff, but not students. The percentage of staff in the intervention schools who knew there was a sexual harassment rule increased from 54.7% at baseline to 67% at post-intervention ($p < .01$), whereas the percentage of staff who reported awareness of sexual harassment rules in the comparison schools did not change ($p > .05$).

The bottom half of Table 16.4 shows means and standard deviations (in parentheses) of the student and staff attitude variables. As mentioned previously, students' responses to the attitude scale factored into five different subscales, two of which showed a significant Group $\times$ Time interaction from baseline to post intervention. For positive attitudes toward bullying, there was a Sex $\times$ Group $\times$ Time interaction from baseline to post-intervention. Analyses

TABLE 16.3
Students' and Staff's Perceptions of Others' Reactions Upon Witnessing Bullying

Variable	Intervention		Control		Significant Effects
	Baseline	Post	Baseline	Post	
Students' perceptions of staff's actions upon witnessing physical bullying					
Intervention	2.50	2.91	2.59	2.88	T
	(1.46)	(1.51)	(1.49)	(1.53)	
No intervention	0.19	0.26	0.17	0.20	G, T
	(.44)	(.49)	(.41)	(.44)	
Students' perceptions of staff's actions upon witnessing verbal bullying					
Strong intervention	0.94	0.85	0.97	0.97	None
	(1.00)	(1.04)	(1.02)	(1.06)	
Mild intervention	0.95	1.20	1.04	1.17	T, G × T
	(.74)	(.75)	(.78)	(.78)	
No intervention	0.11	0.14	0.07	0.13	G, T
	(.34)	(.37)	(.27)	(.35)	
Staff's perceptions of others staff's reactions to physical bullying					
Intervention	2.33	2.55	2.44	2.52	T
	(1.37)	(1.40)	(1.38)	(1.38)	
No intervention	.05	.08	.04	.05	None
	(.22)	(.34)	(.22)	(.24)	
Staff's perceptions of others staff's reactions to verbal bullying					
Strong intervention	.49	.63	.47	.54	T
	(.77)	(.88)	(.78)	(.77)	
Mild intervention	1.50	1.68	1.52	1.61	T
	(.90)	(.88)	(.91)	(.80)	
No intervention	.05	.08	.06	.09	T
	(.23)	(.28)	(.24)	(.27)	
Staff's perceptions of student reactions to physical bullying					
Active response	1.68	1.90	1.66	1.77	T
	(1.13)	(1.21)	(1.11)	(1.08)	
No intervention	.20	.17	.20	.18	None
	(.41)	(.37)	(.40)	(.16)	
Fight the bully	12.9%	16.7%	12.8%	13.8%	None

TABLE 16.4
Student and Staff Awareness of Bullying and Sexual Harassment
Behaviors and Attitudes

Variable	Intervention		Control		Significant Effects
	Baseline	Post	Baseline	Post	
Student awareness					
Bullying behavior	11.16	11.66	11.19	11.46	T, S
awareness	(2.77)	(2.27)	(2.74)	(2.45)	
Sexual harassment	7.11	8.09	7.13	7.85	T, G × T
behavior awareness	(1.53)	(1.18)	(1.52)	(1.30)	
Awareness of sexual	35.2%	44.9%	33.8%	40.9%	T
harassment rule					
Staff awareness					
Bullying behavior	12.47	12.54	12.37	12.64	None
awareness	(1.92)	(2.00)	(2.10)	(1.89)	
Sexual harassment	7.13	7.14	7.22	7.32	None
behavior awareness	(1.21)	(1.34)	(1.24)	(1.11)	
Awareness of sexual	54.7%	67.0%	58.3%	62.0%	T, G × T
harassment rule					
Student attitudes					
Positive attitudes toward	2.97	3.23	3.05	3.50	T, S, S × G × T
bullying	(2.12)	(2.36)	(2.17)	(2.47)	
Boys	3.27	3.80	3.34	3.75	None
	(2.32)	(2.71)	(2.36)	(2.68)	
Girls	2.63	2.63	2.72	3.19	T, T × G
	(1.79)	(1.76)	(1.95)	(2.26)	
Feeling safe at school	5.64	5.26	5.82	5.49	T
	(1.43)	(1.83)	(1.41)	(1.66)	
OK to bully in	11.09	11.28	11.27	11.36	T, S
relationship	(1.91)	(1.74)	(1.88)	(1.76)	
Only girls/adults are	2.49	1.82	2.28	1.89	T, S, T × G
sexually harassed	(1.43)	(1.04)	(1.32)	(1.12)	
OK to ask for help	5.30	4.99	5.28	5.01	T, S
if bullied	(0.45)	(0.43)	(0.46)	(0.46)	
Staff attitudes					
School is safe	19.03	18.34	19.02	18.87	T
	(3.05)	(3.38)	(2.93)	(3.10)	

for boys and girls indicated the Group × Time interaction was limited to girls. Attitudes of girls in the intervention schools did not change from baseline to post-intervention ($p > .05$), whereas attitudes of girls in the control schools became more positive toward bullying ($p < .001$). The second significant

Group × Time interaction occurred for beliefs about the targets of sexual harassment. Although the intervention and comparison students both showed decreases from baseline to post-intervention in the belief that only girls or adults are targets of sexual harassment ($ps < .001$), the baseline to post-intervention mean difference was larger for students in the intervention schools.

Staff's Beliefs About the Safety of Their School. There were no significant Group × Time interactions for student's feelings that their schools were safe, attitudes about the acceptability of bullying in relationships, or attitudes about the acceptability of asking for help when bullied. The Group × Time interaction for staff's attitudes about the safety of their school was not significant.

Discussion

Summary of Results

The Expect Respect Project sought to increase student safety and improve the overall school climate by reducing the social acceptance of bullying and harassment among all members of the school community. The project was designed to promote awareness of bullying and sexual harassment, increase students' ability and willingness to intervene on behalf of targets by directly intervening or getting help from an adult, and increase staff willingness and ability to intervene effectively. The implementation of the program and support for school-wide activities varied depending upon the level of commitment of the principals and school personnel.

With respect to awareness of bullying, sexual harassment, and the school's sexual-harassment rules, the only statistically significant change among the students occurred in students' awareness of behaviors constituting sexual harassment. Although students in the intervention and comparison schools each demonstrated greater accuracy over time in identifying behaviors that constitute sexual harassment, the increase in accuracy was greater for students in the intervention schools. No significant differences in students' bullying awareness, as demonstrated through students' accurate identification of behaviors that constituted bullying, or in students' awareness of their school's sexual harassment rules were observed. The absence of significant results in bullying awareness may be associated, in part, with a mismatch between the design of the student questionnaire and the curriculum. The questionnaire asked students to identify behaviors that constituted bullying and sexual harassment from a simple listing of behaviors, whereas the curriculum focused on discriminating bullying and sexual harassment behaviors within specific contexts that were absent in the survey.

With respect to responses to actual situations of having been bullied and self-reported intentions to respond to hypothetical bullying scenarios in certain ways, the intervention appeared to be related to student group differences. For actual responses to being physically bullied, students in the comparison schools were less likely from baseline to post-intervention to tell an adult, verbally respond to the bully (boys only), or ignore the bullying (girls only). Intervention students did not demonstrate decreases in these types of responses over time. It may be that as students get older, there is a greater stigma associated with behaviors such as telling the teacher or ignoring the bully when physically bullied. The intervention curriculum may have buffered students from that stigma by making these responses more socially appropriate. However, a similar pattern was not observed in students' responses to having been verbally bullied.

With respect to students' intent to respond to witnessing hypothetical bullying scenarios, the intervention was associated with increases in students' intentions to directly intervene upon witnessing physical and verbal bullying. The intervention appeared to have minimal impact on intervention students' intentions to tell an adult, whereas boys in the comparison schools indicated they were more likely to tell an adult about verbal bullying at post-intervention than baseline. Although the curriculum emphasized that students should be courageous bystanders by intervening directly or getting help from an adult when someone is being mistreated, increases in intervention students' expressed intent to directly intervene for a victim may indicate that students in the intervention schools may believe themselves to be capable of intervening on their own without needing to tell an adult.

The project also appeared to have minimal impact on staff awareness of bullying and sexual harassment. Changes were observed only for staff awareness of their school's sexual harassment rule, with a greater percentage of staff in the intervention schools than in the comparison schools reporting awareness of the rule from baseline to post-intervention. This may have been due in part to ceiling effects, as staff in both schools appeared to be relatively accurate in identifying behaviors constituting bullying and sexual harassment prior to the intervention. Similarly, no differences were observed from baseline to post-intervention in staff self-reports of their own typical responses to physical or verbal bullying.

The impact of the intervention on student and staff perceptions of others' intended reactions to witnessing bullying appeared minimal. Students in the intervention schools, relative to those in comparison schools, showed an increase in their belief that school staff would be more likely to mildly intervene (i.e., tell the bully to stop, punish the bully, tell the victim to ignore the bullying) in a situation involving verbal bullying.

With regard to attitudes, the effects also were minimal. However, the intervention may have influenced girls' attitudes about bullies. The attitudes of girls at comparison schools became more positive about bullying from baseline to post-intervention, whereas the attitudes of girls at the intervention schools did not change. This finding may represent a step in the desired direction toward reducing tolerance for abusive behavior in future dating relationships. However, it is important to note that no significant differences in students' attitudes toward the appropriateness of bullying in the context of relationships was observed. In addition, the project did not appear to impact either students' or staff's perceptions of the safety of the school, with both feeling less safe at school over time.

The results on reports of actual bullying behavior are difficult to interpret. Although both groups of students were more likely to report having bullied another student at post-intervention, students in the intervention schools reported no significant change from baseline to post-intervention in being bullied, whereas students in the comparison schools reported a decrease. Students in the intervention schools reported an increase from baseline to post-intervention in witnessing bullying, whereas in the comparison schools did not. It is unclear whether the observed changes reflect an actual increase in bullying in the intervention schools relative to the comparison schools or whether the changes reflect an increase in intervention students' awareness of, attendance to, and willingness to report bullying behaviors. Neither explanation is supported by the analyses of staff's reports of bullying. If the increase in student reports of bullying behavior reflected an actual increase in bullying or greater awareness of bullying, an intervention effect on staff reports of bullying may also have been observed, but was not. Thus, the explanation for the effect of the intervention on bullying behavior remains unclear.

Limitations

There are several limitations to the current findings. First, because many analyses were conducted with relatively few significant effects and there was no correction for multiple analyses, some of the observed group differences may have been due to chance. Moreover, the mean differences, standard deviations, and percentages suggest that the effect sizes of the statistically significant findings were relatively small. Thus the practical significance of the observed changes appears to be limited. Second, there were strong effects associated with the passage of time for many of the variables. It is unclear whether these time effects were due to repeated administrations of the survey, experimental demand, or some naturally occurring event external to the intervention. For example, the April 1998 shootings at Columbine High School would have been likely to have similar effects in increasing awareness of bullying and aggression in the intervention and comparison schools.

The lack of clarity in the findings may result from assessment and implementation issues. The measurement of outcomes for this study relied solely on self-report questionnaires completed by students and staff. Most of the items used in the questionnaires were constructed for the purpose of this project, and evidence for the validity and reliability of the questionnaires is lacking. For example, the degree to which the items actually assessed perceptions of school climate and tolerance for bullying behaviors is not known. In addition, there were no independent behavioral measures of bullying. As a result, the interpretation of the students' reports of the increased level of bullying in the intervention schools relative to comparison schools is impossible to interpret. Independent observers that are blind to group assignment would be ideal for observing bullying behaviors. Several forms of qualitative data were collected through focus groups, in-depth interviews with students following the intervention, and class assignments requiring students to write a letter describing what they learned from the program. Unfortunately, the preliminary analyses of the qualitative data do not shed light on the reasons for the relatively larger increase in bullying behavior reported in the intervention schools. As noted, there was a lack of consistency between aspects of the intervention and constructs assessed during the evaluation. For example, although the Expect Respect Project took a whole-school approach in trying to change school climate, the impact, if any, of such aspects of the program as the parent education and policy components were not evaluated.

With respect to implementation, few data were collected regarding implementation of the Expect Respect Project components. Such data often assist with understanding equivocal outcome results. For example, there appeared to be considerable variability in the extent to which school administrators implemented policy change or parents were involved. It is possible that these components are necessary and operate in conjunction with the curriculum to effect change. Similarly, fidelity in implementing the classroom curriculum was monitored periodically, but comprehensive or formal measures of fidelity were not collected. Information about implementation fidelity can assist in differentiating an ineffective curriculum from a curriculum that was not fully implemented.

Many of the limitations pertain to the way in which the evaluation was implemented and the practicalities and logistics of conducting applied research in school settings (e.g., difficulties evaluating the impact of multiple levels of intervention, logistics of employing independent observers of behavior in school setting). Despite the difficulties in correcting these limitations, it is critical to do so given the substantial need for and interest in school-based programs that attempt to prevent bullying, sexual harassment, and other types of violence.

Impact of Expect Respect

There has been substantial interest in the Expect Respect Project from the media and other schools in the AISD. During the two years of implementation (1998–2000), local media covered the project's activities on six occasions (i.e., three television, one radio, two print), and six state and national pieces were produced (i.e., one television, four satellite broadcasts, one print). By the end of the first year of implementation (1999), 10 nonparticipating schools had requested staff and parent training and classroom presentations for students. In response, project staff provided an abbreviated version of the services consisting of one staff training session, one parent session, and two classroom presentations per 5th-grade class. By the end of the second year of implementation (2000), project staff had presented at 17 local, state, and national conferences. SafePlace also provided training for all of the district's school bus drivers and school guidance counselors and numerous Parent Teacher Associations throughout the Austin area. In June 2001 and June 2002, SafePlace hosted three training sessions serving a total of 130 school and agency personnel from across the United States. These sessions, titled "From Bullying to Battering: School-based Strategies for Preventing Bullying, Sexual Harassment, and Dating Violence," focused on building partnerships between school and agency personnel. The broad interest speaks to the community's desire for comprehensive programs that include interventions for students and staff that address school climate. This interest coupled with the equivocal nature of the evaluation data speaks to the need for more careful evaluations of promising approaches such as the Expect Respect Project.

Future of the Expect Respect Program

The Expect Respect Program (referring to all of SafePlace's school-based services) was selected in 2002 as a "Promising Practice" by the National Resource Center on Domestic Violence. A report entitled "Expect Respect: A School-Based Program Promoting Safe and Healthy Relationships for Youth," which describes the program's development, implementation, evaluation, and replication guidelines, can be obtained by contacting the National Resource Center on Domestic Violence at (800) 537-2238 or on the Web site www.vawnet.org.

Although the original Expect Respect Elementary School Project ended in 2000, the lessons learned have been helpful in further developing a school-based model for intervening and preventing bullying and sexual harassment. The collaborative relationship between AISD and SafePlace continues to grow, benefiting students and families experiencing abuse and increasing access to specialized training for school staff on these issues. In 2002, SafePlace was awarded a grant from the Criminal Justice Division of the Governor's Office under the Safe and Drug-Free Schools and Communities Act Fund to establish school-wide bullying-prevention programs in Austin elementary schools. The current project and its evaluation plan have been designed to build on the lessons learned from the original project and to overcome some of the limitations identified. SafePlace continues to develop and provide school-based services to schools with the financial support of individuals, schools, private and government grants, and corporate donations.

Translating Research Into Practice: Implications for Bullying-Prevention and Intervention Programs

The substantial interest in and adoption of the Expect Respect program demonstrates the broad recognition of bullying and sexual harassment as problems requiring intervention early in childhood. It also demonstrates the need for comprehensive programs with demonstrated efficacy to address bullying and sexual harassment. The Expect Respect project received attention because school officials need programs to combat bullying and sexual harassment for elementary school children, despite the fact that no evaluation data had been published.

Although the program positively impacted children's awareness of sexual harassment and intentions to intercede upon witnessing bullying, observed changes were often small and appeared to diminish over time (Rosenbluth, Whitaker, Sanchez, & Valle, in press). The impact of the program on other outcomes, such as school climate, staff responses to bullying and sexual harassment, and actual incidence rates of bullying and sexual harassment could not be determined with the existing data. In addition, the cultural relevancy of the program has not yet been demonstrated.

The current evaluation provides lessons in conducting future evaluations of school-based and other prevention programs, particularly the selection of well-designed and valid assessment tools that adequately measure program goals and objectives and the need to obtain accurate assessments of behaviors targeted for change. Follow-up assessments need to be conducted to determine the long-term efficacy of interventions. In addition, evaluations of comprehensive school-based approaches to preventing bullying and sexual harassment should consider methods to evaluate the full range of activities that may be important agents of change.

REFERENCES

Ackard, D. M., & Neumark-Sztainer, D. (2002). Date violence and date rape among adolescents: Associations with disordered eating behaviors and psychological health. *Child Abuse & Neglect, 26,* 455–473.

American Association of University Women (2001). Hostile hallways: Bullying, teasing, and sexual harassment in school. Washington, DC.: AAUW Educational Foundation.

Anderson, M., Kaufman, J., Simon, T. R., Barrios, L., Paulozzi, L., Ryan, G., Hammond, R., Modzeleski W., Feucht, T., & Potter, L. (2002) School-associated violent deaths in the United States, 1994–1999. *Journal of the American Medical Association, 286,* 2695–2702.

Anderson, R. N. (2002). Deaths: Leading causes for 2000. *National Vital Statistics Report, 50,* 1–86.

Coker, A. L., McKeown, R. E., Sanderson, M., Davis, K. E., Valois, R. F., & Huebner, E. S. (2000). Severe dating violence and quality of life among South Carolina high school students. *American Journal of Preventive Medicine, 19,* 220–227.

Connolly, J., Pepler, D., Craig, W., & Taradash, A. (2000). Dating experiences of bullies in early adolescence. *Child Maltreatment, 5,* 299–310.

Foshee, V. A., Linder, G. F., Bauman, K. E., Langwick, S. A., Arriaga, X. B., Heath, J. L., McMahon, P. M.; Bangdiwala, S. (1996). The Safe Dates Project: Theoretical basis, evaluation design, and selected baseline findings. *American Journal of Preventive Medicine, 12*(Suppl. 5), 39–47.

Galinsky, E., & Salmond, K. (2002). *Youth and violence: Students speak out for a more civil society.* Family and Work Institute, New York.

Johnston, L. (2000). Personal Communication.

Keppel, G. (1982). *Design and Analysis: A researchers handbook.* Englewood Cliffs, NJ: Prentice Hall.

Lenhart, S. (1996). Physical and mental health aspects of sexual harassment. In D. K. Shrier (Ed.), *Sexual harassment in the workplace and academia: Psychiatric issues. Clinical practice series*, No. 38 (pp. 21–38). Washington, DC.: American Psychiatric Press.

National Center for Education Statistics. (1998). *Violence and discipline problems in U.S. public schools: 1996–7*. Washington, DC.: U.S. Department of Education.

Olweus, D. (1993) *Bullying at school: What we know and what we can do*. Willinslon, VT: Blackwell.

Olweus, D., Limber, S., & Mihalic, S. F. (1999). *Blueprints for violence prevention: Book nine, bullying prevention program*. Boulder, CO: Center for the Study and Prevention of Violence.

Pellegrini, A. D. (2001). A longitudinal study of heterosexual relationships, aggression, and sexual harassment during the transition from primary school through middle school. *Applied Developmental Psychology, 22*, 119–133.

Rosenbluth, B., Whitaker, D. J., Sanchez, E., & Valle, L. A. (in press). The Expect Respect Project: Preventing bullying and sexual harassment in U.S. elementary schools. In Smith P. (Ed.), *Bullying in school: Global perspectives on intervention*. Cambridge: Cambridge University Press.

Silverman, J. G., Raj, A., Mucci, L. A., & Hathaway, J. E. (2001). Dating violence against adolescent girls and associated substance use, unhealthy weight control, sexual risk behavior, pregnancy, and suicidality. *Journal of the American Medical Association, 286*, 572–579.

Stein, N. (1995). Sexual harassment in school: The public performance of gendered violence. *Harvard Educational Review, 65*, 145–162.

Stein, N., & Sjostrom, L. (1996). *Bullyproof: A teacher's guide on teasing and bullying for use with fourth and fifth grade students*. Wellesley, MA: Wellesley College Center for Research on Women and the NEA Professional Library.

Sugarman, D. B., & Hotaling, G. T. (1989). Dating violence: Prevalence, context and risk markers. In M. A. Pirog-Good & J. E. Stets (Eds.), *Violence in dating relationships* (pp. 3–32). New York: Praeger.

Thompson, K. M., Wonderlich, S. A., Crosby, R. D., & Mitchell, J. E. (2001). Sexual violence and weight control techniques among adolescent girls. *International Journal of Eating Disorders, 29*, 166–176.

U.S. Department of Health and Human Services. (2001). *Youth violence: A report of the Surgeon General*. Rockville, MD: U.S. Department of Health and Human Services, Centers for Disease Control and Prevention, National Center for Injury Prevention and Control; Substance Abuse and Mental Health Services Administration, Center for Mental Health Services; and National Institutes of Health, National Institute of Mental Health.

17

Implementation of the Olweus Bullying Prevention Program in American Schools: Lessons Learned From the Field

Susan P. Limber
Clemson University

Attention to bullying problems among children and youth has increased dramatically in recent years among American educators, the press, and the general public. Whereas bullying had been the focus of wide public concern in Scandinavia since the early 1980s (Olweus, 1993), and although school-based interventions were being tested in England in the early 1990s, bullying was not on the radar screens of most Americans until several years later. In the mid-1990s, stories of bullying experiences began to appear in the national news media (ABC News, 1995) and school-based bullying prevention programs first emerged in American schools (e.g., Garrity, Jens, Porter, Sager, & Short-Camilli, 1994; South Carolina Educational Television, 1995; Sjostrom & Stein, 1996). Today, a conservative count yields more than one dozen different school-based programs (including both curricula and comprehensive approaches) that focus

351

significantly on bullying and that are in use in elementary, middle, and high schools in the U.S.[1]

The dramatic increase in bullying prevention programs in American Schools may be attributed to several factors. First, the research base upon which programs may be built has become significantly stronger in recent years as research on the nature and prevalence of bullying has mushroomed in the U.S. and abroad. Second, interest in preventing aggressive and violent behavior among children has naturally led us to look for early indices of such behavior in children. Educators have correctly recognized that behaviors entrenched in middle or high school may be significantly more malleable in early elementary grades. As bullying may be viewed as an early sign of trouble among some children, attention has rightly turned to its prevention in early grades.

Third, media attention to research findings on bullying and to tragic events linked to bullying (such as suicides and the shootings at Columbine High School and several other schools) have kept bullying on the minds of Americans. As Smith and Morita (1999) noted,

> It appears to be a combination of sound research and media interest . . . which leads to governmental response and opportunities for funding and intervention work. Research on its own may just gather dust on library shelves; media interest on its own may just generate temporary concerns lacking a knowledge base for action. But an encouraging phenomenon . . . has been how at times this combination of research and concerned publicity . . . can lead to resources being devoted to tackle the problem seriously. (p. 3)

School-based bullying prevention interventions vary significantly in their approach. Some are purely curricular programs, while others provide tips and strategies for teachers to address and prevent bullying within their classrooms. Still others are more comprehensive in approach and focus on changing the school climate and norms with regard to bullying.

To date, the best-researched and one of the most widely used intervention is the Olweus Bullying Prevention Program. This chapter provides a brief overview of this comprehensive program, including its history, its use in other countries, and findings from research on its effectiveness. The chapter discusses in some detail the use of this Norwegian program in U.S. schools and will conclude by highlighting some of the major challenges and benefits that I perceive in the implementation of comprehensive bullying prevention programs in elementary and middle schools in the U.S.

---

[1]It should be noted that scores of violence prevention programs are available to U.S. educators. This rough count includes only those programs that focus to a significant extent on bullying and involve more than a minimal time commitment from school staff (i.e., videos or other materials intended for use in one or two class periods were not counted).

Overview of the Olweus Bullying Prevention Program

The Olweus Bullying Prevention Program was developed by Professor Dan Olweus, a psychologist at the University of Bergen in Bergen, Norway. The program that was launched by the Ministry of Education in 1983, was first implemented and evaluated in 42 schools in Bergen, Norway, as part of a nationwide campaign against bully/victim problems in Norwegian primary and junior high school (Olweus, 1993; Olweus, Limber, & Mihalic, 1999). The primary impetus for the national campaign was a widely-read newspaper account in 1982, of three boys who had apparently committed suicide as a result of severe bullying by their peers (Olweus, 1993).

Goals and Principles of the Olweus Program

The stated goals of the program are to (a) reduce existing bully/victim problems among elementary, middle, and junior high school students within and outside of the school setting; (b) prevent the development of new bully/victim problems; and (c) improve peer relations at the school (Olweus, et al., 1999). The program is designed to counteract known risk factors for bullying behaviors, which include a lack of parental warmth and involvement, a lack of supervision, a lack of clear and consistent rules to govern children's behavior, and harsh/corporal punishment (Olweus, 1993; Olweus, et al., 1999). Thus, the program is built upon the following principals: it is critical to develop a school environment characterized by warmth, positive interest, and involvement on the part of adults; where there are clear, firm limits to unacceptable behavior; and where there are nonhostile, noncorporal sanctions that are consistently applied when rules are violated and/or behaviors are unacceptable.

Distinguishing Characteristics of the Program

There are several important characteristics of the program that distinguish it from many other bullying-prevention programs (Olweus, et al., 2003). First, it is universal. The program represents a school-wide effort that involves all adults within the school environment (i.e., administrators, teachers, parents, and nonteaching staff) as well as students. Second, the program is both systems-oriented and individual-oriented. The program is focused on altering the school environment as a whole, as well as addressing issues with individual students. Third, as will be discussed in some detail, the Olweus program is research-based. Finally, the program is not time-limited. There are no end dates for the program. Rather, the program requires systematic efforts over time and is intended to become woven into the fabric of the school.

Program Interventions

In order to address the complex problem of bullying, interventions are implemented at three levels: the school-wide level, the classroom level, and the individual level (Olweus, 1993; Olweus, et al., 1999).

School-wide interventions include

- formation of a bullying prevention coordinating committee (a representative team from the school) to plan and coordinate the Olweus Bullying Prevention Program and other violence prevention activities
- administration of an anonymous bully/victim questionnaire (Olweus, 1996) to assess the nature and extent of bully/victim problems at the school
- intensive training ($1\frac{1}{2}$ to 2 days) for members of the bullying prevention coordinating committee, and training for all school staff
- development of school-wide rules against bullying
- use of appropriate positive and negative consequences for students who follow/don't follow the school rules
- fortification of adult supervision of children at "hot-spots" for bullying at the school, and development of systematic reporting mechanisms
- formation of staff discussion groups to provide opportunities for school staff to learn more about bullying issues and to share program successes and concerns
- a school-wide "kick-off" event to introduce the program to students
- engagement of parents around the school's bullying prevention efforts

A primary focus of classroom-level interventions involves regular (weekly) classroom meetings to discuss issues related to bullying and peer relations. The meetings are intended to improve social relations within the class and the school in general and to give the teacher an opportunity to stay abreast of social issues of concern to students. Required program materials (e.g., a teacher handbook, a video on bullying) and appropriate supplemental materials may be used by teachers to help facilitate discussions among students.

Finally, at the individual level, staff members meet with children who have been bullied to investigate bullying reports and incidents, develop safety plans, and provide emotional support. Staff meet with those who bully their peers to reinforce school rules against bullying, administer appropriate consequences for bullying behaviors, and to make children aware that their future behaviors will be closely monitored. Staff also regularly meet with the parents of involved children (both those who are victimized and those who bully). Where appropriate, referrals are made to mental health professionals for more intensive work with students and/or their families.

Research Findings and Program Dissemination

The initial evaluation of the Olweus Bullying Prevention Program in Bergen, Norway, targeting 2,500 5th–8th graders, found significant reductions in self-reported bullying and victimization (by approximately 50%), reductions in teachers' and students' ratings of bullying behavior among children in the classroom, reductions in self-reported antisocial behavior (such as vandalism, fighting, theft, alcohol use, and truancy), and increases in students' perceptions of positive school climate (Olweus, 1991; 1993; 1994).

Due to the remarkable success of the initial evaluation of the Olweus Bullying Prevention Program in Bergen schools, researchers and educators from several countries sought to replicate and evaluate the program in different cultures and schools settings around the world. Programs subsequently have been implemented and evaluated in Canada, Germany, Great Britain, Norway, and the United States, with largely positive findings.

Subsequent evaluations of the program targeting 8 to 16-year-olds in Sheffield, England (Whitney, Rivers, Smith, & Sharp, 1994), targeting 8 to 16-year-olds in Schleswig-Holstein, Germany (Hanewinkel & Knaack, 1997, as reported in Olweus, et al., 1999), and focused on students in grades 5, 6, 7, and 9 in Bergen, Norway (Olweus, 1999, as reported in Olweus, et al., 1999) also have shown significant decreases in self-reported bully/victim problems.

Use of the Olweus Bullying Prevention Program in the United States

Initial Implementation

The first wide-scale implementation and evaluation of the Olweus Bullying Prevention Program in the United States involved 6,388 4th-6th grade students in six predominantly rural schools in South Carolina (Melton et al., 1998). Compared with students in control schools, students in intervention schools reported significant decreases in reports of bullying other students and relative reductions in self-reported delinquency, vandalism, school misbehavior, and punishment for school misbehavior (Melton et al., 1998) after one year of the program. Promising findings from studies in the U.S. and abroad have led to the program's designation as one of eleven Blueprints for Violence Prevention by the Center for the Study and Prevention of Violence and an Exemplary Program by the Center for Substance Abuse Prevention. With the development of a train-the-trainer model, the program is being widely disseminated in the United States. The most intensive efforts to date have been made in the states of Massachusetts and Pennsylvania, although sites are active in more than a dozen states.

American Experiences and Adaptations

The goals and general approach of the Olweus program in the United States (as reflected in training and in program materials) have remained true to those of the original Norwegian model. From the collective experiences of American trainers and staff in U.S. schools, several themes are emerging regarding experiences and adaptations that may be somewhat unique to American schools, however.

Importance of a Committee to Coordinate School-wide Policies and Activities. Although Olweus (Olweus, et al., 1999) included the Bullying Prevention Coordinating Committee as a core component of the program, this committee appears to serve particularly important coordinating functions within

American schools and to be critical to the success of most programs. As mentioned, the Bullying Prevention Coordinating Committee is a representative team from the school whose job is to plan and coordinate all aspects of the school's bullying prevention and violence prevention activities. Membership typically includes an administrator, a teacher from each grade, a school counselor and/or other school-based mental health professional, a member of the nonteaching staff (e.g., a bus driver, cafeteria worker, custodian), and a parent. Together, this team receives intensive training in the program, develops a plan for implementing the program in their school, introduces the program to other members of the school staff, and meets regularly throughout the school year to ensure effective implementation of the program and coordination with other school activities.

There are several possible reasons why the work of this committee is so critical in American schools. First, the structure and size of American schools is somewhat different from that of their Norwegian counterparts. Students in most American middle schools change classes throughout the day and typically have 4 or 5 teachers, whereas Norwegian school children in similar grades generally have a single teacher with whom they spend the entire school day. Moreover, most American schools are significantly larger than those in Norway, where the program was first implemented, and frequently have multiple prevention/intervention initiatives in place at any given time. The size and complexity of most American middle schools and the volume of prevention and intervention initiatives demand particularly tight coordination. From experience, the Bullying Prevention Coordinating Committee serves these coordination purposes well.

A second reason why the Bullying Prevention Coordinating Committee may have taken on particular importance in American schools is that it assumes some of the coordinating functions that our Norwegian counterparts have granted to another program component—staff discussion groups. Olweus encourages schools to set aside at least one hour every several weeks for teachers to participate in staff discussion groups in order to learn about the program in detail, discuss implementation challenges that may arise, and maintain enthusiasm for the program (Olweus, et al., 1999). Administrators in most American schools have found it difficult to arrange for all staff to meet with such frequency. Instead, staff discussion groups typically meet approximately once per month. Between these meetings, members of the Bullying Prevention Coordinating Committee keep staff abreast of interim developments with the program.

Classroom Meetings with Students.   Teachers in American schools also have experienced some challenges in holding classroom meetings, a critical component of the Olweus Bullying Prevention Program. One difficulty experienced by many middle or junior high school teachers has been reserving a consistent time during the school week to focus on issues of bullying and peer relations. In most areas of this country, teachers are under mounting pressure to prepare students for standardized tests and cover required academic material. As a result, some middle school (and even elementary school) teachers report that they do not have time during the week to hold a classroom meeting in which student can discuss issues of bullying and peer relations, role play possible resolutions to bullying situations, or share their thoughts about ways to make the school safer or more humane.

Experience in implementing the Olweus program suggests that consistent use of classroom meetings tends to be more challenging in a middle school or junior high school environment, where children change classes and have multiple teachers, than in an elementary school setting, where students spend the vast majority of the school day with one teacher. Whereas elementary school teachers frequently have a good bit of flexibility to arrange their own weekly schedules to accommodate classroom meetings, staff in middle or junior high schools typically must confer with fellow grade-level teachers and administrators to designate an appropriate day and time each week to hold such meetings.

Administrator support appears to be important to the success of classroom meetings as a technique for bullying prevention, particularly in middle school and junior high school environments. Classroom meetings are more likely to be held (and used effectively) in schools where administrators champion the use of classroom meetings, actively work to schedule time in the weekly calendar for meetings, and support teachers in developing skills to facilitate meetings.

To conduct effective classroom meetings, teachers must be skilled in facilitating discussion about social issues and relationships. Without training and practice, some teachers are understandably uncomfortable stepping outside their traditional academic roles to explore such difficult issues with their students. Implementation of the Olweus program in American schools frequently has involved extra training for teachers in the use of classroom meetings. School counselors and teachers more experienced in conducting classroom meetings also have been enlisted to mentor less experienced teachers in using classroom meetings effectively.

Community Involvement.   Many American schools that are implementing the Olweus Bullying Prevention Program have recognized the importance of involving community members in their bullying prevention efforts. Although efforts vary among communities, they typically have involved attempts to (a) inform residents in the local community about the program (e.g., convening meetings with leaders of the community in order to discuss the school's program, encouraging local media coverage of the school's efforts); (b) engage community members in the school's bullying prevention activities (e.g., involving community members as playground, bus, or cafeteria aids to watch for bullying behavior; soliciting material assistance from local businesses to support aspects of the program); and (c) engage community members, students, and school staff in antibullying efforts within the broader community (e.g., introducing core components of the program into after-school activities, camp experiences, or youth gatherings within faith-based organizations). Such efforts may not only strengthen the school's program but also may influence attitudes and norms of the broader community of children, youth, and adults regarding the acceptance of bullying.

Translating Research Into Practice: Challenges in Implementing Comprehensive Bullying Prevention Programs

Comprehensive bullying prevention programs, such as the Olweus model, hold the most promise for reducing bullying within a school environment and sustaining effects over time (Limber, 2002; see also Mulvey & Cauffman, 2001, for a discussion of the importance of comprehensive approaches in violence prevention programs). As noted above, the adoption of such models has increased significantly in U.S. schools in recent years. However, perhaps not surprisingly, educators, parents, and others seeking to introduce comprehensive bullying prevention programs into American schools have faced (and likely will continue to face) some common challenges.

Resistance on the Part of Staff and Parents

One of the biggest barriers to the successful adoption of comprehensive bullying prevention efforts is resistance on the part of some school staff and parents. Although the increased national attention to bullying likely has reduced the numbers of skeptics, it still is not uncommon to find at least a handful of staff or parents at any given school who believe that bullying is not a concern. Some adults seriously underestimate its frequency. As one administrator reported to me recently, "We don't have bullying at this school. We simply don't allow it."

Others acknowledge the presence of bullying in all schools but view the experience of bullying as a rite of passage or even a positive learning experience for children (e.g., "Kids will be kids," "It's a normal part of growing up," or "Kids need to learn to deal with bullying on their own.") These adults misjudge the significant social, emotional, and academic costs of bullying for victimized children (Chase, 2001) and overestimate the ability of victimized children to stop bullying without the assistance of adults. As a young child explained to a colleague, "If I thought I could deal with bullying on my own, why would I have told an adult?"

Some adult attitudes may be changed (or at least softened) with education. Indeed, appropriate education of staff and parents is a critical component of any bullying prevention effort. Findings should be shared with school staff and parents regarding the prevalence of bullying among children and its harmful effects on victims, bystanders, and the entire school community. Data from surveys of students within a given school may be particularly compelling and may help to persuade skeptical adults that bullying is not only present in their school but also is an issue of concern for many students.

Although it is not uncommon to find a handful of naysayers at any given school (and although the attitudes of some of these adults may be swayed with time and education), efforts to introduce and sustain a comprehensive bullying prevention program may be doomed if a majority of the school staff do not believe that bullying is a serious issue. Indeed, Olweus (Olweus, 1993; Olweus, et al., 1999) argues that two important prerequisites to the successful implementation of the Olweus Bullying Prevention Program are (1) awareness of a majority of school staff regarding problems of bullying, and (2) commitment of a majority of the staff to its prevention.

The attitudes of the school principal towards bullying prevention efforts are particularly important to the success of a school-wide program. Without the active support of the principal, a program may founder. Staff may not feel supported in efforts to discipline children for bullying behavior or develop safety plans for victimized children; teachers may be reluctant to spend class time focusing on bullying prevention; and students, parents, and staff may accurately perceive that bullying prevention is not a priority at the school. In sum, it is difficult to change the climate of a school without the support of the school's natural leader.

Desires for Simple, Short-term Solutions to Bullying

As educators and members of the public are increasingly recognizing the need to focus on prevention of bullying, many are, understandably, seeking simple, short-term interventions to address bullying problems in their schools (Limber, 2002). Not uncommonly, school administrators and their staff adopt a piecemeal approach to bullying prevention. Bullying may be the topic of a staff in-service training, a PTA meeting, a school-wide assembly, or lessons taught by individual teachers. Although such individual efforts may represent important initial steps in raising awareness about the problem or in the adoption of a comprehensive bullying prevention strategy, they cannot be expected to significantly reduce bullying problems on their own. As Bob Chase, President of the National Education Association noted, "A single school assembly won't solve the problem" (2001). Nor will a curriculum that is taught for 6 weeks by the 6th grade health teacher. What is required to reduce the prevalence of bullying is nothing less than a change in the school climate and in the norms for behavior (Limber, 2002). Research on the effectiveness of school-based violence-prevention and intervention programs lends support to this conclusion (Mulvey & Cauffman, 2001). A study of elementary school-based violence interventions found that those schools that focused on the broader school environment, as opposed to more narrow curricular strategies, appeared more successful in altering students' violent behavior (Howard, Flora, & Griffin, 1999). As noted already, to effect changes in the climate of a school requires a comprehensive, school-wide effort involving the entire school community. Unfortunately, many schools elect less time-consuming, and ultimately less effective, strategies.

Limited Classroom Time to Focus on Bullying Prevention

As noted, a critical element of the Olweus Bullying-Prevention Program involves holding regular classroom meetings with students to discuss bullying and peer relations. Olweus recommends holding class meetings weekly throughout the course of the school year (Olweus, 2001; Olweus, et al., 1999) and found that those classrooms that held regular classroom meetings had significantly greater reductions in reports of bullying than those that did not (Olweus, 1993; Olweus, et al., 1999).

With increasing pressures on educators to cover required academic material and to adequately prepare students for yearly standardized tests, many administrators and teachers are understandably reluctant to set aside even 20 to 30 minutes per week for class meetings. Some opt, instead, to integrate anti-bullying themes into language arts, social studies, and other academic subjects. Lessons about bullying can and should be effectively woven throughout the elementary, middle school, and even high school curriculum. However, such opportunities do not replace the need for a regularly-scheduled classroom meeting, during which students may freely express ideas and concerns that they may have about bullying and peer relations, teachers can better keep their fingers on the pulse of students' concerns, and teachers and students together can work to build a sense of caring and community within the classroom setting.

Anecdotal evidence suggests that schools that have successfully implemented classroom meetings have been able to show that such activities are a good investment of teachers' time. By setting aside 20–30 minutes once or twice per week to discuss issues related to bullying and peer relations within a classroom, teachers may actually spend less time in dealing with such issues as they crop up throughout the school week. Additional research is needed to document possible benefits of classroom meetings for bullying prevention.

Use of Mediation and/or Conflict Resolution Techniques to Address Bullying Incidents

Other challenges to the implementation of comprehensive bullying-prevention programs relate to schools' use of competing or contradictory strategies, including conflict resolution or peer mediation. Both peer mediation and conflict resolution strategies are commonly used in American schools. Although these techniques may be effective in cases of conflict between students of relatively equal power, they may be detrimental in bullying situations and should be discouraged (Cohen, 2002; Limber, 2002; Limber, in press). Bullying is a form of victimization and should be considered no more a "conflict" than domestic violence or child abuse would be. Consequently, the messages that mediation likely sends to both parties are inappropriate. ("You both are partly right and partly wrong. We need to work out this conflict between you.") The appropriate message to a child who bullies should be that his or her behavior is wrong and that it will not be tolerated. The appropriate message to children who are victimized should be that they do not deserve to be bullied and that the adults at the school will do everything they can to see that it comes to an end. Not only may mediation send inappropriate messages to bullies and their victims, but it also may further victimize a child who has been bullied. Because of the imbalance that exists in bullying situations, children who are bullied may find it extremely distressing to face their tormenters. Mediation should be considered in bullying incidents only if a victimized child asks to confront his or her tormentor, if he or she is adequately prepared to do so, and if a qualified adult supervises the interaction.

Given the pervasiveness of conflict-resolution and peer mediation strategies in many school systems, staff must be trained to better recognize the differences between bullying and conflict among students, and efforts must be made to triage suspected cases of bullying so that they are not dealt with inappropriately.

Group Treatment for Children Who Bully

Another strategy that some schools utilize to address bullying behavior involves group therapeutic treatment for children who bully. Such treatment may focus on anger management, skill-building, empathy-building, or the enhancement of the self-esteem of children who bully (Limber, 2002). Although well-intentioned, such strategies may be counterproductive, even with skillful adult facilitators (Limber, in press). In some instances, students' behavior may further deteriorate, as group members tend to serve as role models and reinforcers for each other's antisocial and bullying behavior. Moreover, therapeutic efforts designed to boost the self-esteem of children who bully (whether done in group or in individual sessions) likely will be ineffective in reducing children's bullying behavior (Limber, 2002). Such efforts are premised on the assumption that low self-esteem is at the root of bullying behavior. Most evidence suggests that children who bully have average or above-average self-esteem (Olweus, 1993). Thus, such interventions may help to create more confident bullies but may have no effect on their bullying behavior (Limber, 2002).

Zero Tolerance (Student Exclusion) for Bullying

Other approaches to bullying prevention and intervention have focused on removing bullies from the school setting. In recent years, increasing numbers of schools and school districts have adopted zero-tolerance policies for aggressive, violent, or potentially violent behavior, including bullying. Specific policies vary widely with regard to those behaviors that trigger zero tolerance policies and the consequences for violating such policies. A number of schools and districts require suspension or expulsion for children who physically bully their peers. The state of Georgia requires by law that students in each local board of education detail a procedure by which any student in grades 6–12 who has committed an offense of physical bullying for the third time in a school year be assigned to an alternative school (Ga. Code Ann, 2001).

Such policies raise several concerns and may actually be detrimental to a community's bullying prevention efforts (Limber, 2002). First, they cast a wide net. As noted above, approximately one in five students report that they have bullied their peers at least "several times" within a school term. Even if zero tolerance policies focus only on physical bullying, there is a potential for numerous students to be affected. Second, such policies run counter to the goal of most bullying prevention programs to encourage students to report known or suspected bullying (Limber, 2002). Severe punishments for bullying, such as school exclusion, may have a chilling effect on students' (and staff members') willingness to come forward with concerns about the behaviors of their peers (Mulvey & Cauffman, 2001). Finally, children who bully their peers with some frequency are at higher risk for engaging in other antisocial behaviors such as truancy, fighting, theft, and vandalism (Olweus, 1993). If unchecked, these behaviors may escalate. Children who bully are in need of positive, prosocial role models, including adults and students in their regular school. Removal of children from such positive influences may be detrimental (see also Conolly, Hindmand, Jacobs, & Gagnon, 1997). In rare cases, public safety may demand that a child be removed from his or her public school environment. However, student exclusion as a broad-based bullying prevention/intervention policy is ill-advised and may seriously undermine other positive bullying prevention efforts.

Reasons for Cautious Optimism

Recent heightened public attention to bullying among children and youth and the increase in relevant research present an important opportunity for the implementation of sound, research-based prevention programs in schools. Unfortunately, the proliferation of neatly packaged (but unresearched) curricula and "simple solutions" to bullying prevention have the potential to overwhelm educators and distract them from strategies that are more likely to reap results. Key to the success of bullying prevention efforts will be (a) commitment to changing the school environment and norms with regard to bullying; (b) support from administrators, teachers, and parents for adopting comprehensive approaches to bullying prevention, as opposed to simpler solutions; and (c) recognition that bullying prevention efforts must not be time limited, but rather sustained over time and woven into the fabric of the school environment.

REFERENCES

ABC News (1995). *Teased, taunted, and bullied.*

Chase, B. (2001). *Bullyproofing our schools: To eliminate bullying, first we must agree to not tolerate it.* Newspaper Editorial. From www.neea.org/publiced/chase/bc010325.html.

Cohen, R. (2002, February). Stop mediating these conflicts now! *The school mediator: Peer mediation insights from the desk of Richard Cohen.*

Conolly, J. C., Hindmand, R., Jacobs, Y., & Gagnon, W. (1997). How schools promote violence. *Family Futures, 1*(1), 8–11.

Garrity, C., Jens, K., Porter, W., Sager, N., & Short-Camilli, C. (1994). *Bully-proofing your school: A comprehensive approach.* Longmont, CO: Sopris West.

Ga. Code Ann. sec. 20-2-145 (2001).

Howard, K. A., Flora, J., & Griffin, M. (1999). Violence-prevention programs in schools: State of the science and implications for future research. *Applied & Preventive Psychology, 8*, 197–215.

Limber, S. P. (2002). *Addressing youth bullying behaviors.* Proceedings from the American Medical Association Educational Forum on Adolescent Health: Youth bullying. Chicago: American Medical Association.

Limber, S. P. (in press). Efforts to address bullying in U.S. schools. *Journal of Health Education, 34.*

Melton, G. B., Limber, S. P., Cunningham, P., Osgood, D. W., Chambers, J., Flerx, V., et al. (1998). *Violence among rural youth.* Office of Juvenile Justice and Delinquency Prevention.

Mulvey, E. P., & Cauffman, E. (2001). The inherent limits of predicting school violence. *American Psychologist, 56*, 797–802.

Olweus, D. (1991). Bully/victim problems among schoolchildren: Basic facts and effects of a school-based intervention program. In D. J. Pepler & K. H. Rubin (Eds.), *The development and treatment of childhood aggression* (pp. 411–448). Hillsdale, NJ: Erlbaum.

Olweus, D. (1993). *Bullying at school: what we know and what we can do.* NY: Blackwell.

Olweus, D. (1994). Annotation: Bullying at school: Basic facts and effects of a school-based intervention program. *Journal of Children Psychology and Psychiatry, 7*, 1171–1190.

Olweus, D. (1996). *Olweus bully/victim questionnaire.* Available from the author.

Olweus, D. (2001). *Olweus' core program against bullying and antisocial behavior: A teacher handbook.* Available from the author.

Olweus, D., Limber, S., & Mihalic, S. (1999). *The Bullying-Prevention Program: Blueprints for violence prevention.* Boulder, CO: Center for the Study and Prevention of Violence.

Olweus, D., Limber, S. P., Mullin-Rindler, N., Riese, J., Flerx, V., & Snyder, M. (2003). *Training manual for the Olweus Bullying Prevention Program.* Clemson University: Authors.

Sjostrom, L., & Stein, N. (1996). *Bullyproof: A teacher's guide on teasing and bullying.* Wellesley, MA: Wellesley College Center for Research on Women.

Smith, P. K., & Morita, Y. (1999). Introduction. In P. K. Smith, Y. Morita, J. Junger-Tas, D. Olweus, R. Catalano, & P. Slee (Eds.), *The nature of school bullying* (pp. 1–4). New York: Routledge.

South Carolina Educational Television (1995). *Bullying.* Columbia, SC: Author.

Whitney, I., Rivers, I., Smith, P. K., & Sharp, S. (1994). The Sheffield Project: Methodology and findings. In P. K. Smith & S. Sharp (Eds.), *School bullying: Insights and perspectives* (pp. 20–56). New York: Routledge.

Author Index

Numbers in italics indicate entries with complete bibliographic information. Page numbers followed by "n" indicate footnotes.

Subject Index